W9-CHS-229

Drinking
Water
and
Health

Volume 4

SAFE DRINKING WATER COMMITTEE

Board on Toxicology and
    Environmental Health Hazards
Assembly of Life Sciences
National Research Council

NATIONAL ACADEMY PRESS
Washington, D.C.   1982

NOTICE: The project that is the subject of this report was approved by the Governing Board of the National Research Council, whose members are drawn from the Councils of the National Academy of Sciences, the National Academy of Engineering, and the Institute of Medicine. The members of the Committee responsible for the report were chosen for their competences and with regard for appropriate balance.

This report has been reviewed by a group other than the authors according to procedures approved by a Report Review Committee consisting of members of the National Academy of Sciences, the National Academy of Engineering, and the Institute of Medicine.

The National Research Council was established by the National Academy of Sciences in 1916 to associate the broad community of science and technology with the Academy's purposes of furthering knowledge and of advising the federal government. The Council operates in accordance with general policies determined by the Academy under the authority of its congressional charter of 1863, which establishes the Academy as a private, nonprofit, self-governing membership corporation. The Council has become the principal operating agency of both the National Academy of Sciences and the National Academy of Engineering in the conduct of their services to the government, the public, and the scientific and engineering communities. It is administered jointly by both Academies and the Institute of Medicine. The National Academy of Engineering and the Institute of Medicine were established in 1964 and 1970, respectively, under the charter of the National Academy of Sciences.

At the request of and funded by the U.S. Environmental Protection Agency, Contract No. 68-01-3169

Library of Congress Catalog Card Number 77-089284

International Standard Book Number 0-309-03198-2

Available from

NATIONAL ACADEMY PRESS
2101 Constitution Ave., N.W.
Washington, D.C. 20418

Printed in the United States of America

First Printing, April 1982
Second Printing, October 1985
Third Printing, December 1988

List of
Participants

SAFE DRINKING WATER COMMITTEE

JOHN DOULL, University of Kansas Medical Center, Kansas City, Kansas, *Chairman*

JULIAN B. ANDELMAN, University of Pittsburgh, Pittsburgh, Pennsylvania

DONALD R. BUHLER, Oregon State University, Corvallis, Oregon

WILLIAM G. CHARACKLIS, Montana State University, Bozeman, Montana

RUSSELL F. CHRISTMAN, University of North Carolina, Chapel Hill, North Carolina

STEVEN D. COHEN, University of Connecticut, Storrs, Connecticut

RICHARD S. ENGELBRECHT, University of Illinois, Urbana, Illinois

A. WALLACE HAYES, Rohm & Haas Company, Spring House, Pennsylvania

JAMES M. HUGHES, Centers for Disease Control, Atlanta, Georgia

VINCENT P. OLIVIERI, The Johns Hopkins University, Baltimore, Maryland

MALCOLM C. PIKE, University of Southern California Medical School, Los Angeles, California

R. CRAIG SCHNELL, University of Nebraska Medical Center, Omaha, Nebraska

JOSEPH C. STREET, Utah State University, Logan, Utah

CAROL H. TATE, James M. Montgomery Consulting Engineers, Inc., Pasadena, California

National Research Council Staff

RILEY D. HOUSEWRIGHT, *Project Director*
ROBERT J. GOLDEN, *Staff Officer*
FRANCES M. PETER, *Editor*
BARBARA JAFFE, *Information Specialist*

EPA Project Officer

KRISHAN KHANNA, Office of Water Supply, U.S. Environmental Protection Agency, Washington, D.C.

BOARD ON TOXICOLOGY AND ENVIRONMENTAL HEALTH HAZARDS

RONALD W. ESTABROOK, University of Texas Medical School (Southwestern), Dallas, Texas, *Chairman*

THEODORE CAIRNS, DuPont Chemical Co. (retired), Greenville, Delaware

VICTOR COHN, George Washington University Medical Center, Washington, D.C.

JOHN W. DRAKE, National Institute of Environmental Health Sciences, Research Triangle Park, North Carolina

ALBERT M. FREEMAN, Bowdoin College, Brunswick, Maine

RICHARD HALL, McCormick & Company, Hunt Valley, Maryland

RONALD W. HART, National Center for Toxicological Research, Jefferson, Arkansas

PHILIP LANDRIGAN, National Institute for Occupational Safety and Health, Cincinnati, Ohio

MICHAEL LIEBERMAN, Washington University School of Medicine, St. Louis, Missouri

BRIAN MACMAHON, Harvard School of Public Health, Boston, Massachusetts

RICHARD MERRILL, University of Virginia, Charlottesville, Virginia

ROBERT A. NEAL, Chemical Industry Institute of Toxicology, Research Triangle Park, North Carolina

IAN NISBET, Massachusetts Audubon Society, Lincoln, Massachusetts

CHARLES R. SCHUSTER, JR., University of Chicago, Chicago, Illinois

GERALD WOGAN, Massachusetts Institute of Technology, Cambridge, Massachusetts

ROBERT G. TARDIFF, National Research Council, Washington, D.C. *Executive Director*

... The man they called Ed said the muddy Mississippi water was whole-somer to drink than the clear water of the Ohio; he said if you let a pint of this yaller Mississippi water settle, you would have about half to three-quarters of an inch of mud in the bottom, according to the stage of the river, and then it warn't no better than Ohio water—what you wanted to do was to keep it stirred up—and when the river was low, keep mud on hand to put in and thicken the water up the way it ought to be.

The Child of Calamity said that was so; he said there was nutritiousness in the mud, and a man that drunk Mississippi water could grow corn in his stomach if he wanted to. He says:

'You look at the graveyards; that tells a tale. Trees won't grow worth shucks in a Cincinnati graveyard, but in a Sent Louis graveyard they grow upwards of eight hundred foot high. It's all on account of the water the people drunk before they laid up. A Cincinnati corpse don't richen a soil any.'

MARK TWAIN
Life on the Mississippi

Preface

The Safe Drinking Water Act of 1974 (PL 93-523) authorized the U.S. Environmental Protection Agency (EPA) to establish federal standards to protect humans from harmful contaminants in drinking water and to establish a joint federal-state system for assuring compliance with these standards and for protecting underground sources of drinking water. One section of the law [1412(e)] and its amendments (42 USC Subpart 300f *et seq.*, 1977) mandated that the National Academy of Sciences conduct studies on the health effects associated with contaminants found in drinking water. It stipulated that these studies evaluate the available data for use in developing primary drinking water regulations, identify areas of insufficient knowledge, and make recommendations for future research. Amendments to the act in 1977 called for revisions of the studies "reflecting new information which has become available since the most recent previous report [and which] shall be reported to the Congress each two years thereafter."

The first study in this series was published in 1977 under the title of *Drinking Water and Health*. That volume examines the health effects associated with microbiological, radioactive, particulate, inorganic, and organic chemical contaminants found in drinking water. Volumes 2 and 3 of *Drinking Water and Health* were published in 1980. Volume 2 compares the efficacy and practicability of chlorination and 11 alternative disinfection methods for inactivating microorganisms, identifies the by-products likely to be formed by the use of each major method, and evaluates the use of granular activated carbon for the reduction or removal of organic and other contaminants from drinking water. Volume 3 reviews 12 epidemiological studies concerning health effects associated with drinking water containing trihalomethanes. It also summarizes the current state of knowledge on the relationship between cardiovascular disease and water hardness. It adds to the 1977 publication's information on estimation of risk to human health by extrapolating data from experimental animals to humans and also evaluates six models for the estimation of carcinogenic risk at low doses. Furthermore, it evaluates the acute and chronic health effects associated with the products of water disinfection and other selected contaminants. One section examines the contribution of selected inorganic elements in drinking water to the optimal nutrition of humans.

The current study (Volume 4) identifies chemical and biological contaminants associated with drinking water distribution systems and the health implications of deficiencies in those systems. It also contains an evaluation of information on the toxicity of selected inorganic and organic contaminants. Some of them are reviewed for the first time in this report; others were reviewed in earlier volumes of this series. For the latter, discussions include only information that has become available since the earlier reports.

A reevaluation of the most recent information on the relationship between water hardness and cardiovascular disease was postponed pending publication of results from several important studies that were presented in an EPA-sponsored symposium at the University of Massachusetts at Amherst in 1979.

On behalf of the members of the present committee and all of the members of the previous Safe Drinking Water Committees, I would like to express our gratitude and appreciation for the special efforts of Dr. Riley Housewright, who has served as the Project Officer for the safe drinking water studies since their inception in 1975. We wish him the very best in his new position as Executive Director of the American Society for Microbiology.

We also thank Dr. Robert Golden, who completed this project after Dr. Housewright's departure, and Ms. Frances Peter, who served as Editor of the present book. We recognize Ms. Virginia White, Edna Paulson, and Barbara Jaffe, who assisted in the search of the scientific literature and reference verification.

We also acknowledge the assistance of members of the EPA staff, especially Drs. Krishan Khanna and Joseph Cotruvo.

JOHN DOULL, *Chairman*
Safe Drinking Water Committee

Contents

DRINKING
WATER
AND
HEALTH

I

Executive
Summary

The quality of a public water supply, although quite acceptable when it leaves the treatment plant, may deteriorate before it reaches the user. This may occur as a result of either chemical or biological transformations or by loss of integrity of the system. Serious sources of potential contamination arise when nonpotable water enters the system as a result of cross-connections, backflow, back-siphonage, or during repairs.

Although it is not the purpose of this report to review the optimum engineering design, construction, and operation of distribution systems, it is important to recognize that adverse health effects may result from inadequate attention to any of these areas.

Chapters II, III, IV, and V of this report contain reviews of the factors and conditions associated with retention of water quality in the distribution system and the committee's recommendations for control procedures and future research.

In Volume 1 of *Drinking Water and Health*, the Safe Drinking Water Committee examined the health effects associated with microbiological, radioactive, particulate, inorganic, and organic chemical contaminants found in drinking water. In Volume 3, it considered another selected group of chemical contaminants. Chapters VI and VII of this volume contain evaluations of the health effects of additional organic and inorganic contaminants.

1

DISTRIBUTION SYSTEMS

Chemical Effects and Water Quality

Changes in the chemical quality of water in the distribution system can result from corrosion, deposition, leaching, and reactions involving water treatment chemicals in the system. The solubility and kinetic factors that determine whether constituents in water will deposit on pipe walls or whether the materials used in the conveyance system will partially dissolve or corrode into the water are examined in this volume.

Corrosion

A number of water quality indexes have been used to predict whether water will produce corrosion of materials used in the distribution system. These indexes are used not only as criteria for treatment control, but also as a guide to selection of materials. The committee's review and evaluation of these indexes can be found in Chapter III.

. The nature and control of the corrosion process is also described in Chapter III. The chemical and electrochemical reactions involved in corrosion cause deterioration of water quality, particularly with respect to such metals as zinc, cadmium, and lead. The economic impacts of corrosion in water distribution systems are not a part of this study. Nonetheless, they are an important consideration since they provide an incentive for reducing corrosion, which ultimately affects the water to which the consumer is exposed. The economic incentive for the use of corrosion inhibitors may be counterproductive in terms of human health unless the inhibitors are selected with a full awareness of their possible toxicity.

A variety of microorganisms are known to be involved in the corrosion process. They may be heterotrophic or autotrophic and grow under aerobic or anaerobic conditions. The nature of the biologically mediated corrosion process and the organisms involved are described in Chapter IV. Considerable further attention must be directed toward this subject in order to elucidate the nature and consequences of microbial action on the pipes *in situ*.

Leaching

In contrast to corrosion, which is an electrochemical phenomenon, leaching is a process of dissolution governed by solubility and kinetics. The quality of the water influences the leaching of some materials, such as asbestos/cement (A/C) pipe.

Deposits

Following water treatment, chemicals can deposit in distribution systems and affect the quality of water distributed to the consumer. Among the elements manifesting this behavior, iron and manganese are receiving most attention, primarily because of esthetic and economic considerations. Their effects on human health are not of major importance; however, iron and manganese suspensions are associated with the growth of microorganisms in the distribution system. Furthermore, humans may be exposed to other elements that may be associated with iron and maganese deposits and their resuspension as well as to chemicals added for their control.

The control of manganese and iron in water supply systems has been widespread. Three principal methods have been used: oxidation (followed by precipitation and filtration), ion exchange, and stabilization by dispersing agents. These control measures may alter the concentration of other chemicals that coprecipitate or sorb with them, including organic chemicals, and influence the concentration of bacteria in the system.

Of special interest are the effects of stabilizing agents such as silicates and polyphosphates. Polyphosphates have the potential for adversely affecting human health, especially when complexed with manganese. Just as iron and magnesium can be maintained in solution by the addition of these dispersing agents, so can other heavy metals. The extent to which their use increases human exposure and adverse health effects is not known.

Water Treatment Chemicals

The data suggest that concentrations of trihalomethanes continue to increase in the distribution system when both chlorine and organic precursors are present. It is probable that the nonvolatile reaction products of humic material with chlorine also increases in distribution systems, although no data have been obtained from systems in operation.

Pipes and Linings

A/C pipe was originally believed to be resistant to deterioration. Recent findings, both in the laboratory and in field tests, have shown that A/C pipe, like other pipe materials, can be vulnerable to the corrosive action of water. Under certain circumstances, asbestos fibers can be released from the pipe into water supplies. Control measures for limiting the release of these fibers are discussed in Chapter III. The data do not provide an adequate basis from which to estimate health consequences from ingesting asbestos fibers. Extensive epidemiological studies and laboratory tests now under way at several locations are expected to yield useful information on this subject.

Plastic pipes used for conveying potable water are made of polyethylene (PE), polyvinyl chloride (PVC), including chlorinated polyvinyl chloride (CPVC), and acrylonitrile-butadiene-styrene (ABS). Although plastic pipe is composed principally of polymerized organic compounds, there can also be residual unpolymerized monomer present in low concentrations. This factor is especially important in PVC pipe, since vinyl chloride monomer is carcinogenic. In general, water quality is not a major factor in plastic pipe leaching, in contrast to the definite effect of water quality on the corrosion of metal or A/C pipe.

Nonmetallic linings are commonly used in potable water distribution systems to prevent corrosion of underlying metal or other components. The most common lining materials are coal tar, petroleum asphalt, vinyl, epoxy, or some combination thereof. Laboratory and field studies have shown that some of these materials, especially coal tar compounds, can be released into the water. Of concern is the content of polynuclear aromatic hydrocarbons (PAH's), several of which are known carcinogens. Some lining materials can reach the drinking water through leaching processes or through physical deterioration, which results in the release of small particles from the linings. Higher concentrations appear to leach from coal tar than from asphalt; however, the tests leading to this conclusion were not definitive.

PAH's have been found in nanogram and microgram per liter concentrations in field studies of water exposed to linings in the distribution system. The compounds most commonly found in these studies have been phenanthrene and/or anthracene. Tetrachloroethylene has recently been found in vinyl-lined A/C pipe. Studies are under way to determine concentrations of this chemical in pipes of different ages receiving varying amounts of usage.

There is a need for more research into the effect of linings on water quality.

Biological Effects and Water Quality

Living organisms may enter the distribution system through raw water receiving insufficient treatment, from in-line reservoirs, or from imperfections or breaks in the pipeline network. The microorganisms found in the distribution system and their effect on water quality are described in Chapter IV.

Microbial processes within the distribution system can significantly increase hydraulic roughness and corrosion of pipes.

Products of microbial activity include undesirable tastes and odors, e.g., "black" water, which contains sulfide, and "red" water, which contains iron. Detachment of biofilms from the pipes provides a continuing inoculum into other locations within the distribution system.

Microorganisms may proliferate in portions of the distribution system if the disinfectant residual is low or absent. A disinfectant residual (usually chlorine) provides a relatively effective barrier to growth of microorganisms in the distribution system.

Distribution networks are dynamic systems. The quality of the water in them can be affected by the quality of the raw water, treatment processes, pipe materials, and the reactions that occur within the pipes.

Implications For Human Health

Outbreaks of acute diseases associated with contaminated drinking water are reported voluntarily to the Centers for Disease Control (CDC) by state health departments or to the Health Effects Research Laboratory of the Environmental Protection Agency (EPA) by state agencies having responsibility over water supply. In the majority of these reports, the etiologic agent is not identified. However, the clinical and epidemiological evidence suggests that most of the outbreaks are caused by infectious agents.

Sources of contamination responsible for outbreaks include untreated surface water or deficient treatment of groundwater, e.g., malfunction of a chlorinator, and deficiencies in the distribution system. Examples include a large outbreak of amebiasis among guests at two Chicago hotels in 1933 and one of infectious hepatitis among members of a football team in 1972. In both outbreaks, potable water was contaminated by wastewater as a result of a defect in the distribution system.

Deficiencies in distribution systems were responsible for 15% of waterborne outbreaks reported in the United States from 1971 through 1978. The most common defects were indirect cross-connections, which permitted wastewater or toxic chemicals to gain access to the potable water system by back-siphonage through hoses or defects in water pipes during periods of low pressure. Less frequent defects include direct cross-connections, contamination of the system during construction, leaching of copper from the pipes, and contamination of open reservoirs. Health effects associated with specific constituents of drinking water and the distribution system are provided in tabular form in Chapter V, with references to discussions in this volume and the first three volumes of *Drinking Water and Health*.

The committee recommends intensifying surveillance, investigation, and reporting of outbreaks of waterborne diseases at the local, state, and federal levels. An evaluation of the health effects associated with drinking water depends, both quantitatively and qualitatively, on the completeness and accuracy of the reporting system. The committee also recommends the development of an education program focusing on the preservation of the integrity of the distribution system and emphasizing the necessity of maintaining an adequate chlorine residual throughout the system.

TOXICITY OF SELECTED CHEMICAL CONTAMINANTS IN DRINKING WATER

The contaminants reviewed in Chapters VI and VII were selected for one or more of the following reasons:

- They are contaminants that have been identified in drinking water since the first three volumes of *Drinking Water and Health* were published.
- Sufficient new data have become available to justify further examination of contaminants evaluated in the earlier studies.
- Several compounds were judged to be a concern because of potential spill situations.
- They are contaminants that have been associated with drinking water distribution systems.
- They are structurally related to known toxic chemicals.

Thus, the descriptions of some of the contaminants are limited to data generated since the first three volumes of *Drinking Water and Health* were published, whereas other contaminants and their health effects are evaluated in full for the first time. Several metallic ions were selected for evaluation because of their association with drinking water distribution systems, although contaminants such as lead and strontium pose problems only in certain local areas. The chlorine derivatives are evaluated because of their possible use as alternatives to chlorine in the disinfection of drinking water. A review of asbestos was deferred pending the outcome of ongoing feeding studies in animals.

The contaminants reviewed in this volume were selected from a list recommended for evaluation by the U.S. Environmental Protection Agency (EPA). The inclusion of each one was discussed with representatives of the EPA before a final decision was reached. Several were rejected either because the data were insufficient for a new evaluation or because there was not enough new information for a reevaluation.

The committee evaluated the data concerning both acute and chronic exposures to selected chemicals. Information derived from studies of acute exposure provides a basis for judging health effects resulting from accidental spills of chemicals into drinking water supplies. A suggested-no-adverse-response level (SNARL) for acute exposures of 24 hours or 7 days has been calculated for compounds on which sufficient data were available. The acute exposure SNARL's are based on the assumption that 100% of the exposure to the chemical was supplied in drinking water during either the 24-hour or 7-day period. When the chemical was a known or suspected carcinogen, the potential for carcinogenicity after acute exposure was ignored. The calculated acute SNARL's should not be used to estimate hazards from exposures exceeding 7 days. They are not a guarantee of absolute safety. Furthermore, SNARL's are based on exposure to a single agent and do not take into account possible interactions with other contaminants. The safety or uncertainty factors used in the calculations of the SNARL's reflect the degree of confidence in the data as well as the combined judgment of the committee members.

SNARL's for chronic exposure were calculated for chemicals that were not known or suspected carcinogens on the basis of data obtained during a major portion of the lifetime of laboratory animals. An arbitrary assumption was made that 20% of the intake of the chemical of concern was derived from drinking water. Therefore, it would be inappropriate to use these values as though they were maximum contaminant levels.

At the time of the writing of the first and third volumes of *Drinking Water and Health*, the use of statistical methods and model systems to extrapolate data from studies of animals at high doses in order to estimate risk in humans exposed to low doses was a novel and largely untested approach. When considering various approaches to this problem, the committee agreed on four principles to be used as a basis for estimating risk for nonthreshold effects:

- Effects in animals, properly qualified, are applicable to humans.
- Methods do not now exist to establish a threshold for long-term effects of toxic agents.
- The exposure of laboratory animals to high doses of toxic agents is a necessary and valid method of discovering possible carcinogenic hazards in humans.
- Data should be assessed in terms of human risk, rather than as "safe" or "unsafe."

The methodology used by the previous Safe Drinking Water Committees in projecting risk estimates have been described in Volumes 1 and 3.

That approach stimulated considerable developmental activity in this area that in succeeding years has resulted in the appearance of a variety of statistical models for making such calculations. The regulatory agencies were quick to recognize the utility of the risk estimate approach for dealing with carcinogenisis data, and the concept, if not the specific models, has achieved international recognition.

When preparing the third volume of *Drinking Water and Health*, the Subcommittee on Risk Assessment reevaluated six high-dose to low-dose extrapolation models (i.e., the dichotomous response model, the linear no-threshold model, the tolerance distribution model, the logistic model, the "hitness" model, and the time-to-tumor-occurrence model). Because of uncertainties involved in the true shapes of the dose-response curves that must be used for the extrapolation, the committee judged that a multistage model would be most useful for making the risk estimate extrapolations for the chemicals reviewed in these volumes. It pointed out that more confidence could be placed in mathematical models for extrapolation if they incorporated biological characteristics of the animal studies such as kinetics and time-to-occurrence of tumors. Although these and other concerns have tended to limit somewhat the acceptance of the various extrapolation models by the scientific community, they have led to the development of new and revised protocols for the animal studies that provide the desired information.

The current Safe Drinking Water Committee has again evaluated several of the major extrapolation models in use by the regulatory agencies or by others and has made some effort to anticipate new thrusts in what could be designated as research in applied toxicology. It concluded that since the users of this volume will be likely to favor different varieties of the conventional extrapolation models or will have access to some of the newer developmental methodologies, it is premature at this stage to recommend any single approach by selecting it for calculations in this volume. Since the committee has provided the data from animal toxicity studies for each of the agents discussed in this volume or references to documents containing the data, it should be possible for readers to apply whichever extrapolation model they wish to the data to estimate risk.

II

Elements of
Public Water Supplies

Fundamentally, a water supply system may be described as consisting of three basic components: the source of supply, the processing or treatment of the water, and the distribution of water to the users. Water from the source is conveyed to the treatment plant by conduits or aqueducts, either by pressure or open-channel flow. Following treatment, the water enters the distribution system directly or is transported to it via supply conduits.

SOURCE

For a public water supply, the raw water source must provide a quantity sufficient to meet all municipal, institutional, and industrial uses as well as the fire-fighting demand. Either surface water or groundwater may be used. Although most water systems are supplied from only one source, there are instances when both surface water and groundwater sources are utilized.

Surface water is drawn from large rivers or lakes. Even a small stream may be suitable if it is impounded by a dam. Groundwater is normally obtained by sinking wells into the saturated zone located beneath the water table.

RAW WATER QUALITY AND TREATMENT

The quality of surface waters varies. Characteristically, such waters contain microorganisms as well as inorganic and organic particulate matter and dissolved solids. They may also have an undesirable color, taste, and odor. Surface waters are subject to contamination by sewage from cities, industrial wastes, agricultural runoff, and waste from animals and birds. The temperature of surface waters fluctuates with climatic variations.

Although groundwaters are also subject to contamination as a result of human activities, they are often clear, colorless, and possess lower concentrations of organic matter and microorganisms than does surface water because of the natural filtration effected by the percolation of water through soil, sand, or gravel. Conversely, the mineral content, including calcium and magnesium ions—the main contributors to "water hardness"—may be higher in groundwater than in the nearby surface waters. In general, the mineral content of groundwaters reflects the mineral characteristics of the soil in the area. Over time, the quality of groundwaters is usually more constant than that of surface waters. The temperatures of groundwaters are also more constant, normally approaching the average annual temperature of the region instead of the constant fluctuations reflected in the temperatures of surface waters.

To be made acceptable for a public water supply, groundwater may require only disinfection to ensure adequate health protection. On the other hand, it may be necessary to remove certain objectionable constituents in the water and/or to reduce others to tolerable limits, depending upon the type of contamination, applicable criteria or standards, and/or the desire of the users. Surface waters normally require more extensive treatment than do groundwaters. Treatment of raw water might include coagulation, sedimentation, filtration, softening, and iron removal in addition to disinfection.

The corrosiveness of surface waters and groundwaters varies widely, depending on their pH, hardness, and other characteristics. Some waters may also contain dissolved minerals, which deposit on the inside of pipelines, resulting in scale formation. Highly corrosive raw waters may be treated to reduce this property in conjunction with other types of treatment required. The temperature of treated water is generally the same as that of raw water. Slight changes may be produced by ambient air temperature during the detention time in the treatment plant. High water temperatures accelerate corrosive action and decrease the viscosity of water.

DISTRIBUTION OF WATER

That portion of a public water system transporting water from the treatment plant to the users is called the distribution system. Physical aspects such as the design, construction, and operation of such systems can have important impacts on water quality. The complexity of and demands on these systems make them the most costly single element in the water supply system.

To avoid possible contamination and because it is delivered to the consumers under pressure, treated or finished water is transported in conduits or pipes rather than by open channels. In addition to a network of interconnecting mains or pipes, water distribution systems normally include storage facilities, valves, fire hydrants, service connections to user facilities, and perhaps pumping facilities. The ability of a distribution system to deliver an adequate quantity of water to meet the present and projected demands of the domestic, commercial, and industrial users and to provide the necessary flow for fire protection depends upon the carrying capacity of the system's network of pipes. In all but the largest systems, the flow that is necessary to combat a major fire is usually the major factor determining requirements for the amount of water to be stored, the size of mains in the system, and the pressure to be maintained. Fire flow standards require a minimum residual water pressure of 20 pounds per square inch gauge (psig) during flow. It is common practice to maintain pressures of 60 to 75 psig in industrial and commercial areas and 30 to 50 psig in residential areas. Distribution system mains and pipes must be designed to withstand these pressures.

The flow of water distribution systems may be controlled either by gravity or by pressure (pumping). Often, public water supply systems use some combination of both. In *gravity systems*, water is impounded at strategic locations sufficiently elevated to create the working pressure required to move the water to the points of demand. When elevated impoundment or storage is impractical, the required working pressure is provided by pumps within the system. In these *pressure systems*, the pumps are normally located at the treatment plant and perhaps within the distribution system. In *combined systems*, facilities for water storage are often provided along with provision for pumping. This type of system provides for the storage of water during times of least demand while assuring that a sufficient quantity is available to meet the peak demand. Typically, water is pumped directly into the distribution system. The quantity of water exceeding the demand automatically feeds into a storage facility or reservoir. A system may also be designed so that pumps supply the water storage facility directly; the water, in turn, might flow into the distribution system by gravity.

Reservoirs may be located at the beginning of a distribution system, i.e., immediately following water treatment, or at an intermediate point in the system. The stored water may be used to meet fluctuating demands or to equalize rates of flow or operating pressures on the system. The reservoirs may be classified as underground, ground level, elevated, or standpipe. An underground reservoir or basin, either open or covered, may be at or below grade level and formed either by excavation or embankment. It is customary to line such reservoirs with concrete, Gunite, asphalt or an asphalt membrane, or butyl rubber. A standpipe consists of a cylindrical shell with a flat bottom resting on a foundation at ground level. An elevated reservoir is a tank supported above ground by a structural framework. Steel and wood have been used in the construction of standpipes and elevated tanks, which are normally covered. It is preferable to use covered reservoirs for treated water because water in open reservoirs is subject to falling dust, dust-borne microorganisms, and soot; to contamination by animals, including birds and human beings; and to algal growth. It may be necessary to control algae and microbial slime growths in open distribution reservoirs by adding copper sulfate and/or chlorine to the water. Furthermore, to ensure adequate disinfection, it is generally believed that there should be a sufficient chlorine residual throughout the distribution system. In a large distribution system, rechlorination of the water may be required. This is often accomplished at the distribution reservoirs.

The detailed layout of a distribution system and its flow characteristics depend upon the area to be served and its topography, the street plan, the location of the source of supply, and other variables. Regardless of the type of system, there is usually at least one primary feeder line or transmission main that transports a large quantity of finished water from the treatment plant and/or pumping facility to a specific location within the system. If the distribution system is large, there may be more than one transmission main, each serving a specific geographical area within the overall system. This flow is then distributed locally to the users through a series of progressively smaller pipes or mains. The buildings being served are connected to the mains by small pipes called service lines or connections.

This network of various sizes of interconnecting pipes is normally designed as a grid with a series of loops to avoid dead ends. The result is a circulating system capable of supplying water to all points within the system, sustaining service even if a section must be removed for maintenance and repair or if a portion of the system must be taken out of service because of contamination. To accomplish this, all distribution systems should have sufficient numbers, types, and sizes of valves so that different sections can be isolated.

Mains are usually made of cast iron, ductile iron, steel, reinforced concrete, plastic, or asbestos-cement. The type of pipe used is dictated by cost considerations, local conditions, and the size pipe required. The piping material for service lines, i.e., household connections, may be galvanized wrought iron, lead, galvanized steel, copper, plastic, cast iron, or ductile iron. Of these, copper appears to be the most widely used. Lead, copper, zinc, aluminum, and such alloys as brass, bronze, and stainless steel may also be used in addition to ferrous metals in pumps, small pipes, valves, and other appurtenances. Linings may be used to prevent corrosion and/or to reduce the roughness of pipes. For example, iron and steel pipes and fittings are often lined with cement mortar and/or with bituminous material. Plastic piping may also be used in water distribution systems, especially in household connections. Thermoplastic material used in plastic pipe include polyvinyl chloride (PVC), polyethylene (PE), acrylonitrile-butadiene-styrene (ABS), polybutylene (PB) plastic, and fiberglass-reinforced plastic (FRP).

Piping used in the distribution system is manufactured in different lengths, depending upon the material and size, and must be joined. Several types of joints are used with pipes of a given material. The joints for cast-iron or ductile-iron pipes may be either bell-and-spigot, mechanical, flanged, threaded, or push-on (rubber gasket). With many joints, such as the bell-and-spigot, it is necessary to fill the space created in the joining of two ends of pipe. With cast-iron pipe, for example, the space may be packed or caulked with hemp or jute, and then lead poured into the joint to complete the seal. Thus, materials used for joints include lead and lead substitutes, sulfur compounds, cement mortar mixtures, and rubber together with asbestos, hemp, jute, and other substances applied as packing. Sections of steel pipe may be joined by welding, rubber gasket seals, threading, or mechanical coupling. Sections of asbestos-cement pipe are usually coupled with a push-on joint and a rubber ring. Plastic mains usually have push-on or roll-on joints, while flared, compression, clamp, or solvent joints are used with service lines.

The carrying capacity of mains and smaller pipes is a function of their size and length, the pressure, and the resistance to flow, i.e., internal friction, bends, or turns in the pipe, joints, control valves, and other devices. The internal surface of pipe, regardless of the material from which it is made, offers resistance to water flow. For example, new steel and unlined cast-iron or ductile-iron pipe have approximately equal resistance, while that associated with cement-lined cast-iron or ductile-iron, asbestos-cement, and plastic pipe is somewhat less. Encrustation caused by tuberculation, rust, and sedimentary deposits of various salts, such as iron and manganese precipitates, will also increase the resistance of water flow.

Tuberculation is believed to result from the corrosive action of water on metal pipes. The tubercles formed by the accumulation of corrosion products often resemble barnacles. Microorganisms, through their biochemical reactions, are also involved in corrosion and the formation of tubercles. Sulfate-reducing bacteria may be involved in the latter process. The growth of other microorganisms, including the iron bacteria, causes the build-up of biological slimes, which also contributes to frictional resistance. In a distribution system, these events may lead to a deterioration in the quality of water delivered to the users.

It is beyond the scope of this report to review established engineering practice as it relates to the proper design, construction, and operation of distribution systems. It should be recognized, however, that random or accidental events, such as pipe breakage, or situations leading to cross-connections or back-siphonage, may severely affect the chemical or bacteriological quality of water in distribution systems and, thus, the water delivered to the users. Table II-1 lists several recent incidents of this type and their consequences.

The quality of water in distribution systems may also be affected by cross-connections, which can be any direct or indirect physical connection

TABLE II-1 Some Recent Incidents Caused by Hydraulic Problems Within Distribution Systems and Resulting Effects[a]

Incident	Result
Extermination contractor caused 3 gallons (11.4 liters) of chlordane to be back-siphoned into the distribution system.	Contamination of drinking water. No immediate effects reported.
Wastewater from a meat processing plant contaminated plant's potable water.	U.S. Department of Agriculture destroyed approximately 2.9 million pounds (1.3 million kg) of pork.
Water from fire-protection system in a steam electricity-generating plant contaminated plant's potable water.	Gastroenteritis suffered by 31 of 160 employees. No hospitalizations.
Ethylene glycol from fire-protection system contaminated potable water supply at two Air Force bases.	"Temporary" illnesses reported.
Boiler in a school was receiving a heavy dose of chemical at the same time the water supply to the school was shut off. Loss of pressure resulted in back-siphonage of treated boiler water into drinking water.	Two students were hospitalized, and 11 were treated and released.

[a] From Springer, 1980.

or structural arrangement that permits nonpotable water or water of questionable or known poor quality to enter or back-flow into a potable water supply (Angele, 1974). An arrangement whereby a safe water system is physically joined to a system containing unsafe water or wastewater is considered a direct connection. If the arrangement is such that unsafe water may be blown, sucked, or otherwise diverted into a safe system, the connection is considered indirect. Contaminated water may enter a potable supply either through the distribution system or through a defect in the user's plumbing system. Cross-connections, together with back-flow or back-siphonage, are the most critical factors in protecting a distribution system from contamination. Back-siphonage occurs when a potable or safe system is at a pressure less than atmospheric; in this situation, the atmospheric pressure on the unsafe system will force the flow toward the partial vacuum associated with the safe system. Prevention of back-flow may be accomplished by using vacuum breakers designed to admit air to break any vacuum in a water main or pipe, swing connections that permit a connection either to a potable water supply or to another source of water but not to both simultaneously, air gaps, and reduced pressure back-flow preventers, i.e., a device with at least two independently acting check valves separated by an automatic pressure differential relief valve.

APPROACH TO THE STUDY

Although the quality of water in a public water supply may be acceptable immediately after treatment, it may deteriorate before it reaches the users. This may result from either chemical or biological transformations.

Public water supplies are disinfected to inactivate infectious agents, to protect the users against possible recontamination, and to control subsequent microbial growths that might alter the quality of the water. For these reasons, it is normal practice to add chlorine to a water supply to provide a residual concentration that will persist until the water reaches the user. However, small quantities of chlorine or the loss of chlorine residual in a distribution system may lead to microbial regrowths and/or the development of slime growth, which may in turn affect the turbidity of the water or cause taste and odor problems. For example, the depletion of dissolved oxygen resulting from microbial activity may promote the production of hydrogen sulfide by sulfate-reducing bacteria. Furthermore, the microbial production or release of metabolic products, e.g., endotoxins or extracellular products of algae, may affect the health of the users directly. There is evidence that the corrosion of unlined steel, cast-iron, and ductile-iron mains may be significantly influenced by microbial activity. Thus, it is possible for microorganisms to alter the quality of water in distribution systems before it reaches the users.

The corrosion of metals may not only change the surface properties of pipe but also produce soluble corrosion products, which in turn may affect the quality of the water. There is also the possibility that certain constituents in cast-iron, asbestos-cement, concrete, plastic, and other pipe materials may be leached into the water. The formation of scale and deposits on the wall of pipes during periods of low-velocity flow may lead to the release or resuspension of associated materials when the velocity of the water is increased.

This report reviews the factors or potential conditions associated with water distribution systems and their effects on water quality, with particular attention to their possible impact on the health of users of public water supplies. The discussions focus on finished water, i.e., quality changes occurring between the time the water leaves a treatment plant and the time it reaches the users. Chemical control at the treatment plant is considered only as it affects changes of quality in the finished water in the distribution system. Having reviewed and evaluated those conditions or factors influencing the deterioration of water quality in distribution systems and, in a sense, determined what is known and unknown, the committee was able to make recommendations regarding control procedures and to identify existing research needs.

It is beyond the scope of this report to consider in depth the physical reliability or integrity of a public water supply system. However, it is important to recognize that the quality of water in distribution systems can be adversely affected if the system is not designed, constructed, and maintained according to accepted engineering practice. For example, a cross-connection in the system, together with back-flow or back-siphoning, which permits an unsafe water or even wastewater to enter the system, represents a most serious source of potential contamination. This alteration in water quality can impose a direct health risk upon the users or make the water aesthetically unacceptable. Leaks or mechanical breaks in the piping of the distribution system can have the same effect. In this sense, attention must be given to proper repair procedures or, for that matter, to the installation of piping, e.g., the need to adequately disinfect new or repaired distributional pipe before placing it in service. Further, pumping equipment must be adequate to meet the demands of the system, and reserve units, ready to be placed in service immediately when needed, must be available. Low-velocity flow, whereby the water has extended contact with pipes, can also cause a deterioration in water quality. Dead ends in the distribution system or the oversizing of pipes or mains can contribute to this stagnation. Finally, it should be pointed out that open distribution or service reservoirs in the system can also lead to contamination of the water before it reaches the users. Again, the importance of having a properly engineered and operated distribution system as it relates to reliability cannot be overemphasized. Water supply personnel must be constantly vigilant of defects and problems associated with distribution systems as they might impact water quality. For example, each public water system needs a continuous cross-connection control program. In considering the reliability of a distribution system, it would seem appropriate to point out that water purveyors are legally responsible if any illness or death results from a system defect.

REFERENCES

Angele, G. J., Sr. 1974. Cross Connections and Backflow Prevention, 2nd Ed. American Water Works Association, Denver, Colorado.

Springer, E. R. 1980. A sip could be fatal. Pp. 81-88 in Proceedings, American Water Works Association Distribution System Symposium. American Water Works Association, Denver, Colorado.

III

Chemical Quality of Water in the Distribution System

Even if one could eliminate the causes of contamination associated with pipe breakages, cross-connections, back-siphonages, and other factors inherent in water distribution systems, there would still be changes in the physical, chemical, and biological properties of the water as the result of either chemical or biological activity.

Chemical activity producing changes in water quality within the distribution system is associated with corrosion, leaching, deposition, and reactions involving water treatment chemicals and their residuals. Each of these topics is discussed separately in this section.

The materials comprising pipes, pumps, storage reservoirs, and other system components can corrode through contact with water or may leach constituents in water over time. Solubility and kinetic factors will determine whether these constituents will deposit (precipitate) onto pipe walls or whether the materials used in the conveyance system will partially dissolve or corrode into the water. Chlorine and other treatment chemicals added at the water treatment plant or in the distribution system itself can continue to react with organic compounds in the water. Thus, the chemical content of water at the consumer's tap may be different from that of water leaving the treatment plant or other source as a result of its contact with materials in the distribution system and the time available for reactions to progress.

18

CHEMICAL WATER QUALITY INDEXES

A number of water quality indexes have been used to predict whether water will corrode materials used in distribution systems or home plumbing units. In most cases, these indexes are used as a criteria for water treatment control, but they can also be used as guide to the selection of materials. Their principal advantage is simplicity, but they are not always perfect predictors. Long-term tests of materials are more costly to conduct, but provide more direct evidence of water quality and its potential to corrode given materials.

The oldest and most widely used index is the Langelier Index, which is based on the solubility of calcium carbonate and the potential of the water to deposit a scale that would protect the pipe. This index has been applied to both metal and asbestos-cement pipe. A simplified version of the Langelier Index, called the Aggressiveness Index, was developed especially for asbestos-cement pipe to predict whether the water will either deposit a protective scale or seek calcium carbonate saturation by dissolving the pipe's cement. A third index, the Saturation Index, is based on solubility characteristics of a number of compounds, not just calcium carbonate. Its potential application for asbestos-cement pipe is discussed below.

Langelier Index

The Langelier Index was developed in 1936 in order to investigate systematically the chemical relationships involved in the corrosion of iron or galvanized pipe (Langelier, 1936). It is sometimes referred to as the calcium carbonate saturation index or simply as the Saturation Index. (To avoid later confusion with the term Saturation Index, which is used for a number of constituents in addition to calcium carbonate, the term Langelier Index is used herein).

The Langelier Index (LI) can be defined as follows:

$$LI = pH = pH_s, \qquad (1)$$

where

pH_s = saturation pH, the pH at which water of the measured calcium and alkalinity concentration is in equilibrium with solid calcium carbonate and

pH = actual or measured pH of the water.

In its simplest form, which is applicable between pH 7.0 and pH 9.5, the equation for calculating pH_s is as follows:

$$pH_s = (pK_2' - pK_s') + pCa^{2+} + pAlk, \qquad (2)$$

where

pK_2' = negative logarithm of second dissociation constant for carbonic acid (H_2CO_3),

$K_2' = \dfrac{[H^+][CO_3{}^{2-}]}{[HCO_3{}^-]}$,

pK_s' = negative logarithm of the solubility product of calcium carbonate ($CaCO_3$),

$K_s' = [Ca^{2+}][CO_3{}^{2-}]$,

pCa^{2+} = negative logarithm of the molar concentration of calcium, and

$pAlk$ = negative logarithm of the equivalents of alkalinity (titrable base), assuming that $[Alk] = [HCO_3{}^-]$.

The terms K_2' and K_s' are dependent upon temperature and ionic strength, which is a measure of ionic composition of the water. Corrections for temperature and ionic strength are made for each calculation.

The utility of the Langelier Index is that it predicts whether calcium carbonate will precipitate, dissolve, or be in equilibrium with solid calcium carbonate. If it precipitates, calcium carbonate can form a protective scale on pipes including asbestos-cement (A/C) or metal pipe. If calcium carbonate dissolves in water of a given quality, calcium carbonate scale, previously deposited at the water-pipe interface, will be removed, thus exposing the pipe surface to the corrosive effects of the water.

The Langelier Index is interpreted as follows:

When LI > 0, water is supersaturated with respect to solid calcium carbonate and will tend to precipitate and form a scale.

When LI = 0, water is at equilibrium.

When LI < 0, water is undersaturated with respect to solid calcium carbonate and protective calcium carbonate scales on the pipe may dissolve.

Aggressiveness Index

The A/C pipe industry developed the concept of an Aggressiveness Index for use as a guide in determining whether A/C pipe would be appropriate in a given situation. The original purpose of the index was to ensure the structural integrity of the pipe. More recently, it has been used to predict whether water quality degradation would occur from pipe dissolution. The Aggressiveness Index is a simplified form of the Langelier Index and has some shortcomings, which are noted below.

The Aggressiveness Index (AI) is defined as follows:

$$AI = pH + \log (AH), \tag{3}$$

where

AI = Aggressiveness Index,
A = total alkalinity, mg/liter as calcium carbonate, and
H = calcium hardness, mg/liter as calcium carbonate.

The Aggressiveness Index does not incorporate the corrections for temperature and ionic strength. At a selected temperature (14°C) and ionic strength (0.01) and by converting to alkalinity and calcium concentrations in mg/liter, it can be shown that:

$$AI = LI + 12.0 \text{ (Schock and Buelow, 1980).} \tag{4}$$

Application of the Aggressiveness Index to determine when A/C pipe should be used has been incorporated into standards published by the American Society for Testing and Materials (1976) and the American Water Works Association (1975b, 1980). The need for water quality guidelines is also acknowledged by the A/C Pipe Producers Association (1980). The most recent standards apply the Aggressiveness and Langelier Indexes to relate water quality and the use of A/C pipe (Table III-1). These standards recommend that nonaggressive water (AI $\geq$ 12.0) be used with Type I (nonautoclaved) or Type II (autoclaved) A/C pipe. Type II pipe is recommended for moderately aggressive water (AI between 10 and 12). For highly aggressive water, "the serviceability of pipe for such applications should be established by the purchaser in conjunction with the manufacturer" (American Water Works Association, 1980). Recognizing the relationship between water quality and the use of A/C pipe, the U.S. Environmental Protection Agency (1979a) recently proposed that the Aggressiveness Index should be ≥ 12 for water transported through A/C pipe in order to prevent adverse effects.

Data published by Millette et al. (1979) provide a perspective on the typical quality of water in the United States as it pertains to the use of A/C pipe. Through a sampling of representative utilities throughout the

TABLE III-1 The Relationship of Water Quality (Expressed as Aggressiveness and Langelier Indexes) to Asbestos-Cement (A/C) Pipe[a]

Aggressiveness to A/C Pipe	Aggressiveness Index	Langelier Index
Highly aggressive water	< 10.0	< −2.0
Moderately aggressive water	10.0 to 11.9	−2.0 to −0.1
Nonaggressive water	≥ 12.0	≥ 0

[a]From American Water Works Association, 1980.

United States, they determined that 52% of the water supplies had water that was at least moderately aggressive (Aggressiveness Index between 10 and 12). Furthermore, 16.5% of the water supplies could be classified as very aggressive. They concluded that these data suggest that as many as 68.5% of the U.S. water systems carry water that is potentially capable of corroding A/C Type I pipe and that water supplies with very aggressive waters (< 10) may be significantly corrosive to any type of pipe, including cast iron, galvanized, and other types of pipes.

When using the Aggressiveness Index, one could assume that the mechanism for A/C pipe deterioration by aggressive waters is related to release of calcium from the cement portion of the pipe. If the water is in fact attacking the pipe, the cement could be dissolving into the water. This would leave the asbestos fibers unprotected or not encapsulated within the cement matrix. This would leave the fibers free to be released into the water. These fibers could be released individually or in bundles. Hallenbeck et al. (1978) theorized that once fibers are released into the water, they can be further broken down so that counts of asbestos fiber from the breakdown products are even higher. Thus, if A/C pipe is used, there is a potential for consumers to be exposed to significant concentrations of asbestos in some drinking water supplies.

The use of the Aggressiveness Index represents an advance over the original preconception that A/C pipe is not subject to the effects of water quality. As recently as a decade ago, Bean (1970) stated that A/C pipe does not require lining, even with soft water, which could be classified as aggressive water. Since that time, both manufacturers and pipe producers have acknowledged that it is not judicious to use A/C pipe with aggressive water. Thus, the Aggressiveness Index has been a means for alerting suppliers and users that A/C pipe cannot be used under all situations and that it is not resistant to corrosion in all cases. It is also simpler to calculate than the Langelier Index.

Since the Aggressiveness Index (as well as the Langelier Index) is based on calcium carbonate saturation, it should yield a fairly accurate prediction of "nonaggressiveness" provided by a protective calcium carbonate coating if water is oversaturated (Schock and Buelow, 1980). However, if the water is undersaturated with calcium carbonate, there is no reason to expect the Aggressiveness Index to predict with accuracy the dissolution of A/C pipe since calcium carbonate is only a minor constituent of the cement and calcium silicate is the predominant pipe component. Furthermore, the Aggressiveness Index does not account for temperature and ionic strength as does the Langelier Index. Finally, the Aggressiveness Index fails to account for protective chemical reactions in drinking water.

The Aggressiveness Index has been used for several years by pipe manufacturers and the water supply industry. Therefore, the majority of the data on water quality and A/C pipe deterioration contains information on the Aggressiveness Index, calcium, and alkalinity of the water.

In the absence of a better predictor of pipe performance, this index has been used extensively and is still a simple first approximation for predicting pipe performance.

Saturation Index

The Saturation Index has been proposed by Schock and Buelow (1980) for use in predicting performance of A/C pipe under given water quality conditions. In this approach, both the solubility of pipe components and the possible protective coating of constituents in the water are considered.

The cement matrix of A/C pipe is a complicated combination of more than 100 compounds and phases. Since electrochemical corrosion is not an issue, the corrosion of A/C pipe is governed by solubility considerations. Possible dissolution reactions in A/C pipe include:

$$Ca(OH)_2 \text{ (s)} \quad \rightarrow \quad Ca^{+2} + 2OH^-, \tag{5}$$
$$Ca_3SiO_5(s) + 5H_2O \quad \rightarrow \quad 3Ca^{+2} + H_4SiO_4^0 + 6OH^-, \tag{6}$$
$$Ca_2SiO_4(s) + 4H_2O \quad \rightarrow \quad 2Ca^{+2} + H_4SiO_4^0 + 4OH^-, \tag{7}$$
$$Ca_3Al_2O_6(s) + 6H_2O \quad \rightarrow \quad 3Ca^{+2} + 2Al^{+3} + 12OH^-, \tag{8}$$

where s indicates the solid phase.

The first constituent, $Ca(OH)_2$, is lime, and the others are tricalcium silicate, dicalcium silicate, and tricalcium aluminate. Solubility constants for pure solids in Reactions 5, 6, and 7 are $10^{-5.20}$, $10^{-8.6}$, and 10^{-16}. For

Reaction 8, it is not known. The actual solubility constants in pipe are difficult to estimate, since solids in pipe are highly substituted. Schock and Buelow (1980) concluded that these materials are soluble under typical water quality conditions, but that they dissolve slowly. Pipe dissolution by Reactions 5 through 8 would increase pH, calcium, and alkalinity of water in contact with the pipe. The Langelier Index or Aggressiveness Index would also increase. These phenomena have been observed in several studies that are described below.

Schock and Buelow (1980) have also used chemical equilibrium calculations to estimate whether calcium carbonate film would form to protect pipe. Protection by metal precipitation has also been modeled for iron, zinc, manganese, and silica since they could form dense solids.

Models were estimated using the aqueous chemical equilibrium computer program called REDEQL.EPAK (Schock and Buelow, 1980). The thermodynamic state of saturation was quantified by the Saturation Index (SI), defined as the logarithm of the ratio of the ion activity product (IAP) to the solubility product constant (K_{so}). For example, for hydroxyapatite, the equilibrium reaction is:

$$Ca_5(PO_4)_3OH_{(s)} \rightleftharpoons 5Ca^{2+} + 3PO_4^{3-} + OH^-. \qquad (9)$$

Assuming activity coefficients equal to unity, the Saturation Index (SI) would be:

$$SI = \log \frac{[Ca^{2+}]^5[PO_4^{3-}]^3[OH^-]}{K_{so}}. \qquad (10)$$

If the solid and solution are in equilibrium, $IAP = K_{so}$ and $SI = 0$. If the solution is supersaturated, the SI is > 0, and undersaturation occurs if $SI < 0$.

The results of SI calculations are shown in Figure III-1. Initial water quality is 1.0 mg/liter calcium, 24 mg/liter total carbonate, 0.24 mg/liter magnesium, 0.5 mg/liter zinc, 0 mg/liter iron, 0 mg/liter phosphate, 20 mg/liter sodium, and 11-33 mg/liter chlorine. Based on this model, zinc hydroxycarbonate $[Zn_5(CO_3)_2(OH)_6]$ would precipitate if the pH was higher than 8. None of the other species would precipitate. Schock and Buelow (1980) suggested that zinc hydroxycarbonate, once precipitated, could be converted by reactions with silicates in the A/C pipe to a zinc silicate coating, which is hard and should provide good protection.

This approach to predicting pipe performance by modeling equilibrium characteristics of a number of protective solids in addition to calcium carbonate appears to contribute to the understanding of A/C pipe. Schock

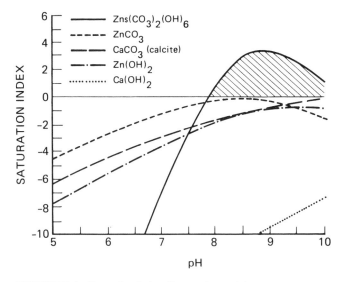

FIGURE III-1   Saturation Index diagram for model system.

and Buelow (1980) have demonstrated the applicability of the Saturation Index to several model systems. Although it is more difficult to use than the Langelier Index, it is expected to produce more accurate predictions.

CORROSION

Uhlig (1971) defined corrosion as "the destructive attack of a metal by chemical or electrochemical reaction with its environment." He also noted that the term "rusting" applies to the corrosion of iron or iron-base alloys to form corrosion products consisting mostly of hydrous ferric oxides. Therefore, other metals can corrode, but not rust.

A principal concern about corrosion in water distribution systems is the possibility that its products will have an adverse impact on the health of consumers exposed to them. Moreover, materials introduced into this system to mitigate corrosion might themselves provide a source of potentially hazardous chemicals. For example, protective coatings on pipes could leach such hazardous constituents into the water, or chemicals added to the water to inhibit corrosion could be toxic. Before discussing all of these concerns, it is necessary to consider some of the mechanisms of corrosion, its inhibition, and measurement.

Although the economic impact of corrosion in water distribution systems is not of direct concern in this report, it is of some importance because it provides an incentive for reducing corrosion. Ultimately, this may have either a positive or negative effect on the generation of corrosion products to which the consumer is exposed. The reduction of metallic corrosion resulting from economic incentives is likely to benefit human health; however, corrosion-inhibiting additives or coatings selected without full awareness of their possibly toxic nature may be counterproductive.

The Corrosion Process

Corrosion is most often considered to be an electrochemical process. That is, electrons move through the corroding metal, and separate (but not necessarily distant) locations at the metal-water interface act as anodes and cathodes for the oxidation and reduction half cell reactions that occur. For example, as described by Larson (1971), the corrosion of an iron surface in contact with water can involve the following reactions:

$$\text{Anode:} \quad \text{Fe} \rightarrow \text{Fe}^{++} + 2e^-,$$
$$\text{Cathode:} \quad 2e^- + 2H_2O \rightarrow H_2 + 2OH^-.$$

This cathodic reaction will generally occur slowly, but a faster alternative one will occur in the presence of oxygen:

$$\text{Cathode:} \quad 2e^- + H_2O + \tfrac{1}{2}O_2 \rightarrow 2OH^-.$$

For both cathodic reactions, two hydroxide ions will be produced and an alkaline condition will result near the cathode. However, the ferrous ion can be further oxidized by oxygen and precipitate ferric hydroxide:

$$2Fe^{++} + 5H_2O + \tfrac{1}{2}O_2 \rightarrow 2Fe(OH)_3 + 4H^+.$$

This clearly generates acid.

In neutral or near-neutral water, dissolved oxygen is necessary for appreciable corrosion of iron (Uhlig, 1971). The initial high rate of corrosion will diminish over a period of days as the rust film is formed and acts as a barrier to oxygen diffusion. The steady-state corrosion rate will be higher as the relative motion of the water increases with respect to the iron surface. Increased temperatures can also increase iron corrosion when it is controlled by diffusion of oxygen to the metal surface.

Because the rates of electrochemical processes are related to the electrochemical potential at the metal-solution interface, processes affecting potential can hasten or reduce the rate of corrosion. This applies particularly to "cathodic protection," which is an important approach to corrosion control. This process involves the external application of electric current, modifying the electrochemical potential at the metal-solution interface, thereby arresting the tendency for metal ions to enter solution. In some portions of the water systems, such as water tanks, a more easily corroded metal such as magnesium or zinc can be used as a sacrificial anode, and cathodic protection is achieved without the use of an impressed source of current.

Two principal types of electrochemical corrosion cells are of concern in water distribution systems (Larson, 1971; Uhlig, 1971). The first results from a *galvanic cell*, which is due to the contact of two different metals. The rate of the resultant corrosion is increased by greater differences in electrochemical potential between the two metals, as well as by increased mineralization of the water. For such a cell, the anodic metal corrodes, and the cathodic metal is, in effect, protected. Thus, when zinc-coated (galvanized) steel corrodes, the zinc will generally do so at the expense of the iron. Galvanic corrosion can be a problem when, for example, copper is in contact with iron, which will tend to corrode by galvanic action.

The other and often more important corrosion cell is the *concentration cell*. This cell involves a single metal, but different portions of the metal are exposed to different aqueous environments. Such a cell could be generated by one region of an iron surface exposed to oxygen and another one nearly protected from oxygen by rust or other surface coatings. Similarly, differences in pH, metal, or anion concentrations could generate such a concentration cell. As noted above for the corroding iron system, the anodic and cathodic reactions generate different corrosion products, which can enhance the ability of the concentration cell to cause corrosion.

Corrosion can also be classified with respect to the resulting outward appearance or altered physical properties of the piping (Uhlig, 1971). *Uniform corrosion* takes place at a generally equal rate over the surface. *Pitting* refers to a localized attack resulting, in some cases, in marked depressions. In water containing dissolved oxygen, oxide corrosion products can deposit at the pitting site and form tubercles. *Dezincification* is a corrosive reaction on zinc alloys (e.g., brass, which contains copper) in which the zinc corrodes preferentially and leaves behind a porous residue of copper and corrosion products. Soft waters high in carbon dioxide content may be particularly aggressive to brass. *Erosion corrosion* can result when the protective (often oxide) film is removed, such as by abrasion occurring in fast-moving waters. Normally, many metals in contact with water will form such a protective oxide coating. One example of erosion corrosion occurs near joints and elbows of copper pipes when water flows at high velocities.

It is apparent from the above discussion that the corrosion process is highly complex and is influenced by a large number of factors, including the nature of the corrodible materials, the physicochemical quality of the water, and the physical structure and hydrodynamics of the distribution system.

Biologically Mediated Corrosion

The role of microorganisms in the corrosion of metal pipe in the water distribution system has been recognized for some time (Hadley, 1948). Microorganisms may influence corrosion by affecting the rate of cathodic or anodic activity, producing corrosive end products and metabolites, creating electrolytic concentration cells on the metal surface, and disrupting or breaking down the protective film (natural or otherwise) at the metal surface. The microorganisms may be heterotrophic or autotrophic and may grow under aerobic or anaerobic conditions.

The pipe surface, joints, valves, and gates provide a wide variety of niches for the growth of many different microorganisms that can alter the chemical and physical habitat and produce conditions very different from those observed in the water passing through the pipe. Although water in the distribution network is generally well aerated, containing several milligrams of oxygen per liter, microenvironments without oxygen may occur in the pipe. Concentrations of organic matter promote the growth of aerobic microorganisms that deplete the oxygen and create anaerobic conditions. Tuberculation, sediments, and pipe joints can yield protected environments in which neither dissolved oxygen nor disinfectant residuals can penetrate.

Under anaerobic conditions, low oxidation-reduction potentials occur, and, in the presence of sulfate, sulfate-reducing bacteria may proliferate. *Desulfovibrio desulfuricans* can grow autotrophically under the above conditions, reduce the sulfate to sulfite, and oxidize the hydrogen. Uhlig (1971) suggested that an iron surface aids the process by which sulfate-reducing bacteria function. These anaerobic bacteria generally possess hydrogenase enzymes that act on hydrogen and require ferrous iron (Booth and Tiller, 1960). Since the possible corrosion products of iron pipe are ferrous iron and hydrogen, the sulfate reducers may provide a mechanism for the continual removal of corrosion products, thereby influencing the equilibrium of the corrosion reaction (Lee and O'Connor,

1975). Tuovinen *et al.* (1980) conducted a series of experiments in which iron coupons (thin plates) were immersed under various aqueous conditions. He observed that the corrosive effects were less pronounced in sterile solutions than in solutions that contained ground tubercles or cultures of *D. desulfuricans.* These same microorganisms were isolated from cast-iron coupons in polyvinyl chloride and steel pipe loops. Other anaerobic microorganisms may also play a role in the corrosion in water distribution systems. More detailed discussions of microbiologically mediated corrosion can be found in reviews by Davis (1967), Iverson (1974), Miller and Tiller (1978), and Uhlig (1971).

Aerobic microorganisms have also been reported to contribute to corrosion. *Gallionella*, *Sphaerotilus*, and *Leptothrix* are the predominant members of the "iron bacteria" commonly found in water distribution systems. These microorganisms convert soluble ferrous iron to insoluble ferric iron, which often accumulates on their stalks and sheaths. Olsen and Sybalski (1949) suggested that the "iron bacteria" initiated tubercle formation on pipe walls and that this process was the critical factor for the corrosion of iron pipes. Other microorganisms can remove iron from solutions indirectly. Strains of *Pseudomonas*, *Aerobacter* (*Enterobacter*), and *Mycobacterium* strains can form precipitates containing iron (Macrae and Edwards, 1972). Sulfur-oxidizing bacteria (*Thiobacillus*, *Beggiatoa*) may also contribute to corrosion under aerobic conditions.

Although the activity of microorganisms in water distribution systems has been well documented, the extent and nature of the microbial activity in the internal corrosion of the pipe network require considerable elucidation. Following microbial populations on the pipe *in situ* has been difficult.

The Effect of Water Quality on Corrosion

Because of the electrochemical nature of the corrosion reaction, the quality of the water in contact with the corrodible surface has a substantial impact on the rate at which the reaction occurs. Constituents in the water are also important because they can form products that coat the surface, and these can similarly affect the corrosion process. Some combinations of water quality factors may lead to high rates of corrosion that may expose consumers to potentially dangerous levels of corrosion products. In such circumstances, alteration of water quality prior to its entry into the distribution system may reduce some risks.

Camp (1963) reported observations of some aspects of water quality that can effect the corrosion of iron. He noted that an increase in oxygen concentration initially resulted in an increased corrosion rate. Subsequently, it reduced corrosion by the formation of oxide films. Waters of low alkalinity and hardness are more corrosive than waters of high alkalinity and hardness, primarily due to their actions in the formation of calcium carbonate precipitate coatings. Other electrolytes that often promote corrosion include sulfates and chlorides. Corrosion is more rapid in acid solution, principally because potentially passivating layers are more soluble in such solutions.

Larson (1971) noted that chloride and sulfate salts increase the corrosion rate of mild steel at a pH below the range where pitting occurs in the presence of oxygen and in the absence of carbonates. Pitting can occur at local unprotected points of corrosion, under deposits of debris, or at the water line of surfaces exposed partly to air and partly to water. In the presence of oxygen, but no calcium, carbonate minerals inhibit corrosion by countering the acceleration effect of such salts as chlorides and sulfates. This inhibiting effect reaches a maximum when the alkalinity is more than 5 to 10 times the sum of the chloride and sulfate and the pH is 6.5 to 7.0. It is at a minimum at pH 8 to 9. When the alkalinity ratio to these other ions is less than 5, corrosion rates increase.

Finally, Larson (1971) noted that from the standpoint of corrosivity the most widely accepted criterion of water quality is the stability of its saturation by calcium carbonate. As discussed above, the Langelier Index can be used to measure this.

A water with a positive Langelier Index is oversaturated with calcium carbonate, which would tend to form a protective coating on the pipe, thereby reducing corrosion. A water with a negative Langelier Index would be undersaturated with calcium carbonate. Thus, a protective coating would not be formed, and corrosion would be more likely to occur. If a water had such a negative index, due to low calcium, pH, and/or carbonate-bicarbonate species, its Langelier Index could be increased by the addition of lime or soda ash. Uhlig (1971) noted that a Langelier Index of +0.5 is often considered to be satisfactory, and that higher values may cause scaling (excessive deposition of calcium carbonate), especially at elevated temperatures. The attainment of values less positive than +0.5 is a common goal in water treatment. However, Larson (1971) indicated that the Langelier Index may have to be as great as +1.0 to +1.3 to maintain protection in lime-softened waters with low alkalinity and calcium concentrations approaching 50 mg/liter. In these waters softened by high pH, complexes of calcium and magnesium can form with carbonate and bicarbonate, thereby decreasing the effective concentration of both. As noted by Millette et al. (1980), a substantial fraction of surveyed U.S. water supplies have chemical water quality indices and pH values that could lead to corrosion in the distribution systems. Clearly, this should be evaluated on a continuous basis to ascertain whether such corrosion does indeed occur and result in concentrations of corrosion products that could adversely affect human health.

Corrosion Inhibitors

As discussed by Uhlig (1971), corrosion may be reduced effectively by the addition of small concentrations of chemicals, called inhibitors. Of these, the passivators (usually inorganic oxidizing agents) act by shifting the electrochemical corrosion potential several tenths of a volt in the noble (corrosion-resistant) direction. They are often successful in reducing the corrosion rates to very low values. The nonpassivating inhibitors, usually organic substances, have only a slight effect on the corrosion potential and are, therefore, usually less efficient than the passivators.

Many substances used to inhibit corrosion in water supply systems are nonoxidizing alkaline inorganic chemicals that indirectly cause passivation of iron. Apparently, they facilitate the sorption of dissolved oxygen, which acts as the oxidizer and, hence, is the actual passivating agent. The excess oxygen may form a passive film at the surface of the iron, although other films, such as those of iron silicate or phosphate, could also form. Sodium silicate and sodium polyphosphate are examples of such indirect inhibitors. Uhlig (1971) noted that the addition of 2 mg/liter sodium polyphosphate to water supplies reduces the corrosion rate to a modest extent if the water is fully aerated and is not stagnant, but there is probably no practical benefit in stagnant parts of a distribution system. Larson (1971) reported that there are some data indicating that at low velocities polyphosphates may even cause a slight increase in corrosion. He noted that the effectiveness of sodium silicate appears to depend on its absorption in the hydroxide corrosion products of iron and zinc, that treatment must be relatively continuous, and that its effectiveness is favored by high velocity and generally low pH. Zinc-glassy phosphates have also been used to control corrosion in water distribution systems, presumably by forming a protective film at the pipe surfaces (Schweitzer, 1970).

Although most of the corrosion inhibitors that may be added to public water supplies are relatively innocuous inorganic chemicals that are unlikely to cause adverse human health effects at the concentrations used, there should be a continuing evaluation of any possible effects, especially taking into account the results of animal and other toxicity tests. Bull and Craun (1977) considered possible health effects from polyphosphates used in water treatment. They concluded that, although they are generally safe at the low concentrations applied in water treatment, they should be used with care because of their possible adverse effects on human health.

Studies of animals showed that manganese and stoichiometric equivalent amounts of sodium hexametaphosphate fed at high concentrations in water interfere with trace metal metabolism, as judged by their effect on growth. They concluded that the biological effects of the entire range of polyphosphate compounds used in water treatment and their various metal complexes should be studied further. Nevertheless, although they did express concern about the use of these polyphosphates, they did indicate that at least for sodium hexametaphosphate it could continue to be used with care at dosage rates in water resulting in concentrations not to exceed that required to complex manganese by more than 10%, i.e., no more than 1 mg/liter.

Pipes and Linings

A variety of materials are available for use in both large and small pipes (Table III-2). Improper selection of piping materials may have an adverse influence on the quality of the distributed water.

Among the metals that can be introduced into the water from the corrosion of these materials are zinc, cadmium, copper, iron, and lead. The latter is probably of the greatest concern because of its known toxicity and the results of numerous studies indicating that it can be corroded readily and accumulate in concentrations higher than generally accepted health-related maximum contaminant levels, e.g., 0.05 mg/liter, which was specified in the Interim Primary Drinking Water Regulations (U.S. Environmental Protection Agency, 1979a, 1980).

Although the use of plastic piping and linings of bituminous coal tar may be effective in reducing or eliminating the adverse impacts of metallic

TABLE III-2 Lined and Unlined Piping Used in Water Distribution Systems[a]

Main System Piping		
Used Without Lining	Used With or Without Lining[b]	Small Piping
Concrete (on steel)	Steel	Plastics (polyvinyl chloride)
Cement-asbestos	Cast iron	Galvanized iron
Plastics (e.g., polyvinyl chloride)	Ductile iron	Lead

[a]From Bean, 1970.
[b]Linings may be cement, factory-applied bituminous seal coat, or coal-tar enamel.

corrosion of pipes, such materials need to be continuously evaluated with regard to the possible leachings of their constituents into the water distribution system. (See section entitled "Leaching" later in this chapter.)

Lane and Neff (1969) have discussed the need to select proper materials to reduce corrosion in hot and cold water distribution systems. Indeed, they regard this step as the first line of defense and believe that chemical treatment should serve only a supplementary role. Although they focused primarily on distribution systems in institutions, their experience is germane to this report because it provides an insight into practical corrosion problems, it is consistent with general principles for reducing corrosion, and it would be applicable to homes as well as to institutions. They noted that compatible materials should be installed in the same system; for example, copper-lined heaters should be used with copper tubing, and the same type of piping used throughout the system. The widespread practice of softening water in homes and institutions to very low hardness values can cause serious corrosion of galvanized steel and other metal piping. Lane and Neff (1969) pointed out that blending to a final hardness of 60 to 90 mg/liter (calcium carbonate hardness) has often reduced corrosion in domestic hot water piping, but at temperatures above 60°C, corrosion is more severe. They suggested that more corrosion-resistant material such as stainless steel should be used when higher temperatures may be required.

The role of water quality and its impact on the corrosion of various materials were also evaluated by Lane and Neff (1969). They categorized midwestern U.S. water supplies into five types, primarily related to their hardness and to their chloride and sulfate content. For example, they suggested that copper piping was preferable to galvanized piping for hard waters with high chloride and sulfate content. In addition, the water should be softened, the pH adjusted to levels between 8.0 and 8.4, and sodium silicate treatment might be required. In contrast, they noted that hard waters that are not aerated and contain low to moderate chloride and sulfate are compatible with galvanized steel piping, although softening may be important in domestic hot water systems. This study by Lane and Neff emphasizes the principles that should be used to reduce corrosion in water systems in homes and institutions, particularly when it they may lead to excessive trace metal concentrations at the tap.

Monitoring and Evaluating Corrosion and Its Control

A variety of methods can and have been used to monitor and evaluate corrosion in water distribution systems. To control such corrosion effectively, these methods must be used to evaluate the success of specific steps that are undertaken.

Wagner (1970) has summarized the methods that have been used. These methods can be divided into three groups. In the first, the mass of material formed is measured visually, by weight determination, or by measurement of thickness. In the second, the production of specific corrosion products, such as the evolution of hydrogen, is measured. The third involves the measurement of electrical and electrochemical parameters, including electrical resistance, corrosion current, pH, and electrical potential. Many of these tests are standardized by such organizations as the American Society for Testing and Materials (ASTM) and the National Association of Corrosion Engineers (NACE).

A recent example in which such tests were used to monitor corrosion-reducing measures was reported by Mullen and Ritter (1980). The corrosion problem they encountered arose in a public water supply system in New Jersey after a hard well-water supply (260 mg/liter calcium carbonate hardness) used for many years was replaced by a much softer surface water source (68 mg/liter hardness). When the new supply was in use, many consumer complaints of discolored water were reported. Various chemical control measures were then undertaken. Primarily, they examined the rate of corrosion by measuring the weight loss of a mild steel coupon. This was determined both by laboratory tests in which specific chemical controls and additives in the water were introduced and by the periodic measurement of coupons placed in the distribution system. They evaluated pH adjustment by caustic addition, temperature, and the addition of two corrosion inhibitors, sodium zinc-glassy phosphate and zinc orthophosphate, each added in amounts to produce zinc concentrations of 0.5 mg/liter in the water. Initially, the laboratory bench studies showed that the sodium zinc phosphate offered little corrosion protection compared to that of pH adjustment alone to 7.8 or 8.1, while the zinc phosphate caused an average of 55% reduction. Over a temperature range of 4°C to 25°C, adjustment of pH and the use of zinc phosphate were more effective than pH adjustment alone. However, below approximately 13°C, the inhibitor was more effective without pH adjustment. They then used the coupon tests over a 5-year period to measure the effectiveness of their corrosion-reduction steps in the actual distribution system, using pH control and the addition of zinc phosphate. In the warm months, their zinc dosages were 0.43 to 0.49 mg/liter, and the corrosion rates ranged from 0.8 to 1.4 μm per year.

The example discussed above indicates how steps can be taken systematically to mitigate corrosion by the adjustment of water quality and the use of corrosion inhibitors and that the effects of such steps can be measured. Although the principal interest here is reduction of the possible adverse health effects from the corrosion products, it is highly likely that this will be achieved simultaneously, even though the evaluative process focuses on the integrity of the pipe material, rather than on the potentially harmful corrosion products.

Field Studies of Metallic Corrosion in Distribution Systems

In this discussion of metallic corrosion in distribution systems, the metals of particular interest are cadmium, copper, iron, lead, and zinc. To the extent that they may be present in lower concentrations in pipe or distribution fixtures, other metals such as nickel and chromium might also contribute to corrosion products in water. Corrosion is not the only source of these products in treatment and distribution systems. They could also be introduced as contaminants in chemical additives, such as lime.

In the first volume of *Drinking Water and Health* (National Academy of Sciences, 1977), it was reported that the high concentrations of several heavy metals in household tap water samples from Dallas, Texas, could be attributed to corrosion at various points in the distribution system. Among these metals were iron from the steel water mains, copper and zinc from household plumbing, and lead and nickel due to "local influences." In the Denver, Colorado, municipal system, there were both increases and decreases in heavy metal content between the finished water at the treatment plants and samples taken at the domestic taps, although frequently there were no significant changes (Andelman, 1974). Typically, the maximum decrease at the tap for most metals was approximately 50%, but in some cases they were larger. Iron increased by a factor as large as 25, zinc and copper by approximately 5, and manganese by 4. Corrosion did not necessarily account for all of the increases, but was probably playing a role.

McCabe (1970) reported increases in the trace metal content of the Chicago water treatment system. In this study, 550 samples taken at various points in the distribution system were compared to 2-week composite samples at the treatment plants. McCabe used the criterion that a distributed water sample had "picked up" metal if its concentration was higher than that of any of the composite samples at a treatment plant. On this basis, it can be seen in Table III-3 that a substantial proportion of the distributed samples increased their trace metal content.

Dangel (1975) reported the results of a U.S. Environmental Protection Agency (EPA) study of corrosion products in the Tolt River portion of the public water supply system of Seattle, Washington. That portion was

TABLE III-3   Percent of Distributed Water
Samples with Increased Metal Content
in Chicago System[a]

Trace Metal	Percent with Increase
Cadmium	15
Chromium	17
Copper	9
Iron	39
Lead	20
Manganese	32
Silver	15
Zinc	67
Cobalt	10
Nickel	34

[a]From McCabe, 1970.

studied because its relatively low pH (approximately 6), alkalinity, and hardness and the many complaints of "red water" indicate that it is a corrosive system. The hypothesis of the study was that increases in metal concentrations in the distribution system could arise from unprotected metal service connections and residential plumbing, since the water mains were predominantly lined with cement and bituminous coatings. A comparison was made for several constituents in running (30 seconds) and standing water samples in residences. The standing samples had been collected from the water that had been in contact with household piping for at least one night. The results, for constituents that appeared to differ substantially, and a comparison of raw water concentrations of those constituents, are shown in Table III-4. Conductivity and the inorganic ions normally present at higher concentrations than those of the trace metals did not vary significantly. These include chloride, fluoride, calcium, and magnesium. However, the concentrations of the six metals shown in Table III-4 all were higher in the standing water samples. Copper, iron, zinc, and lead concentrations were clearly higher in the running water samples than in the raw water. Dangel concluded that most of the increases in metal concentration occurred in the service lines and plumbing inside the buildings.

Subsequent to the EPA study of the Seattle Tolt River system, the Seattle Water Department in 1976 and 1977 conducted a similar but larger study, which included both its Tolt River and Cedar River supplies (Hoyt *et al.*, 1979). Samples were taken by both the Seattle Water Metals Survey Committee (SWMS) and the National Heart and Lung Institute (NHLI). In both the EPA Tolt River study and the SWMS study, almost all of the distribution sample sites selected were likely to have corrosion problems. That is, they had either visible water quality deterioration or copper plumbing less than 3 years old. In contrast, the NHLI selected a larger number of samples to represent a statistically valid cross-section of Seattle families in order to evaluate typical tissue uptake of waterborne metals. A comparison of the preliminary results of the three surveys for standing water samples in the distribution system is shown in Table III-5. This table indicates the percentage of those samples exceeding maximum contaminant levels (MCL's) of the EPA Interim Primary or Secondary Drinking Water Regulations (U.S. Environmental Protection Agency, 1979a,b, 1980).

It is apparent that there are substantial differences in the percentage of samples exceeding the MCL's. The larger percentage for the Tolt River system may be attributed to its water being more aggressive. Hoyt *et al.* (1979) indicated that after the very soft water of the Tolt River was brought into the system, a large increase in the complaints of "red water" occurred. Except for copper, the relatively smaller fraction of samples exceeding the MCL's in the larger NHLI survey can probably be attributed to the fact the study did not focus on homes with known or likely water quality problems. Although the aggressive waters in the Seattle system are not typical of most U.S. public supplies, they do demonstrate the kinds of

TABLE III-4 Concentrations of Trace Metals in Raw and Distributed Water in the Seattle Tolt River System[a]

| | Concentrations in Distributed Water, mg/liter | | | | |
| | Running | | Standing | | Raw Water |
Trace Metal	Mean	Maximum	Mean	Maximum	
Cadmium	<0.0004	0.0008	0.002	0.025	<0.0004
Copper	0.12	1.7	0.45	2.1	0.002
Iron	0.28	1.2	1.4	5.4	0.17
Lead	0.005	0.022	0.039	0.170	0.001
Manganese	0.014	0.045	0.024	0.079	0.018
Zinc	0.15	1.7	1.7	5.5	<0.015

[a] From Dangel, 1975.

TABLE III-5 Distribution of Standing Water Samples Exceeding Maximum Contaminant Levels in Three Seattle Studies[a]

Study	Number of Samples	Percentage of Samples Exceeding Limit					
		Lead	Cadmium	Copper[b]	Zinc[b]	Iron[b]
Tolt River (EPA)	22	23	9	23	9	73
Tolt River and Cedar River (SWMS)	149	13	1	10	2	68
Tolt River and Cedar River (NHLI)	1,000	2.6	0.2	11	0.3	—[c]

[a]From Hoyt et al., 1979.
[b]Secondary Standards.
[c]No data reported.

corrosion problems that can cause increased exposures of the public to heavy metals.

The corrosion of lead pipe resulting in high lead concentrations in the water in distribution systems is a well-known phenomenon in which the characteristics of water quality play a substantial role. Large concentrations of lead in distributed water have been found in Bennington, Vermont. McFarren *et al.* (1977) reported that the pH of raw water was 5.5 and that the alkalinity was 1.0 mg/liter, both unusually low. The lead concentration in the raw water was less than 0.005 mg/liter. In contrast, high lead concentrations were found in water in the street mains and the service lines and in water in contact with interior plumbing. The latter was defined as the "first water" collected in the morning. Table III-6 shows the results of the three types of samples collected from 10 homes in Bennington. It is clear that the water from the street main was high in lead content in that every sample was approximately equal to or greater than the 0.05 mg/liter EPA MCL. Moreover, in almost every instance there was a higher lead concentration in the service line water compared to that in the street main. In contrast, most of the water in the interior plumbing had either comparable or somewhat lower lead concentrations than the water in the service lines. Although there was limited discussion of these results by McFarren *et al.* (1977), it appears that both the water mains and service lines are the likely sources of the lead and that the water quality may be playing an important role in the corrosion.

Karalekas *et al.* (1976) reported a 1974 study of lead and other trace

TABLE III-6   Lead Concentrations (mg/liter) in Various Water Samples Servicing Several Residences in Bennington, Vermont[a]

Interior Plumbing	Service Line	Street Main
0.17	0.44	0.10
0.11	0.10	0.05
0.16	0.18	0.11
0.12	0.14	0.06
0.17	0.54	0.07
0.15	0.45	0.20
0.15	0.13	0.45
0.19	0.86	0.16
0.33	0.60	0.59
0.17	0.46	0.15

[a] From McFarren *et al.*, 1977.

metals in drinking water in the Boston, Massachusetts, metropolitan area. They compared the trace metal concentrations, with emphasis on lead, in distribution samples from Cambridge with those from Boston and Somerville. The Cambridge water had a higher pH, hardness, chloride, sulfate, and total dissolved solid content than did the other two, which had a common reservoir source. Typical hardness of the Cambridge supply before distribution was 56 mg/liter, while that of the others was 14 mg/liter. Thus, the finished waters in the Boston metropolitan area can be considered quite soft. There was also a widespread existence of lead in water service lines in the three cities. Of the 383 households studied, approximately 60% had lead pipe.

A total of 936 standing, running, composite (three equal portions taken during the day), and early morning samples were taken. Samples of finished water were also taken prior to distribution. Of the 10 trace metals analyzed, 5 were found in a substantial portion of the samples (Table III-7). It is apparent that many (15.4%) of the water samples exceeded the EPA interim primary standard for lead.

Table III-8 compares the results of lead analyses of the samples from the three Boston-area cities. Boston and Somerville had a higher percentage of households with lead exceeding the drinking water standard. This may be attributable to the differences in water quality described above. The authors suggested that when the lead content was high in the absence of an indication that lead pipe was used, either the record may have been faulty or the source could have been brass or bronze pipe, which contain substantial amounts of lead.

TABLE III-7   Trace Metal Concentrations in Water Distribution Samples in Boston Area Study[a]

Trace Metal	Concentration in Sample, mg/liter		EPA Standard, mg/liter	Percent Exceeding Standard
	Mean	High		
Copper	0.18	2.3	1.0[b]	0.8
Iron	0.18	10.2	0.3[b]	12.0
Lead	0.03	1.5	0.05[c]	15.4
Manganese	0.02	0.32	0.05[b]	5.0
Zinc	0.11	3.8	5.0[b]	0

[a]From Karalekas et al., 1976.
[b]EPA Secondary Drinking Water Regulations (U.S. Environmental Protection Agency, 1979b).
[c]EPA Interim Primary Drinking Water Regulations (U.S. Environmental Protection Agency, 1979a).

TABLE III-8   A Comparison of Lead in the Distributed Water of
Three Cities in the Boston Area[a]

Characteristic of Sample	Percentage by Household		
	Cambridge	Boston	Somerville
Exceeding lead standard in one or more samples	14.5	25.5	30.1
Having lead pipe	59.1	51.8	68.4
Exceeding lead standard with no record of lead piping	1.8	5.1	4.4

[a]From Karalekas et al., 1976.

The early morning and the daily composite samples were much higher
in lead content than were the running and standing samples taken during
the day. The highest contrast existed between the early morning samples
(a mean lead concentration of 0.104 mg/liter, and 47% of the samples exceeded the standard) and the running samples (0.031 mg/liter, and
5.5%). The authors concluded that additional water treatment, such as
raising the pH to 8.5, was needed to prevent corrosion of lead in these
systems.

In 1976 and 1977, an attempt was made to reduce this lead corrosion in
the Boston area. As reported by Karalekas et al. (1978), the application of
zinc orthophosphate, a corrosion inhibitor, was not particularly successful
in that the average lead concentration in 18 to 23 homes was not reduced
below 0.05 mg/liter. However, it was found subsequently that raising the
pH from 7.5 to 7.7 was somewhat effective in that the average lead concentration was substantially reduced. Nevertheless, approximately one-
third of the samples in this high-lead group of homes still exceeded the
0.05 mg/liter standard.

Summary and Conclusions

It is apparent from the case studies discussed above that metallic corrosion products in tap water distributed to the consumer can originate from
water mains, service lines, and interior plumbing. Of these products, lead
is of particular concern because of its known effects on health. The quality
of the water also clearly affects the corrosion process. Thus, the choice of
the system materials and the treatment regime undertaken at the treatment plant are both possible points of attack in the mitigation of corrosion
that may arise in distribution systems.

The chemical quality of the finished water at the treatment plant can affect the rates of corrosion, which can be mitigated by chemical additions, including corrosion inhibitors. Bacteria in the distribution system are also known to affect corrosion.

Although corrosion can be reduced by pipe linings and chemical additives, the latter must be used judiciously to minimize human exposures. Also, there is evidence that potentially hazardous chemicals can leach from some, but not all, materials used to line the pipes. The adverse effects of the chemicals need further evaluations.

LEACHING

In contrast to corrosion, which is an electrochemical phenomenon, leaching is a process of dissolution governed by solubility and kinetic proporties of the materials involved. Materials that were initially part of the water distribution system pipes, storage reservoirs, and other components may slowly dissolve into the water. For some of them, such as the components of A/C pipe, leaching is strongly influenced by water quality. For other materials, such as those in linings and plastic pipe, water quality does not appear to govern leaching. In this section, A/C pipe, lining materials, and plastic pipe are discussed.

Asbestos-Cement Pipe

A/C pipe was originally introduced to the water supply industry as a material that was believed to be resistant to deterioration. However, recent findings have shown that A/C pipe is similar to other pipe materials commonly used in water distribution systems in that it can be subject to corrosive action of water in certain situations.

The potential release of asbestos fibers from A/C pipe in the water distribution system is but one potential source of asbestos contamination in potable water supplies. Other sources include natural erosion of asbestos-containing minerals and dumping of asbestos-containing materials from industrial projects, such as those contributing asbestos fibers to the drinking water of Duluth, Minnesota, and other nearby communities using Lake Superior water supplies (Cook *et al.*, 1974). These other sources of asbestos in drinking water are beyond the scope of this study, which emphasizes presence of asbestos fibers in potable water distribution systems resulting from deterioration of the A/C pipe itself.

The concern about asbestos in drinking water from all sources, including pipes, is relatively recent. The first report of asbestos fibers in drinking water was published by Canadian investigators in 1971 (Cunningham and Pontefract, 1971). In the United States, the first major concern arose in 1974 when asbestiform fibers were found in the drinking water of Duluth, Minnesota, as a result of discharges from an iron ore processing plant (Cook *et al.*, 1974). The same year, the American Water Works Association (AWWA) Research Foundation (1974) began its own investigation of the asbestos in drinking water, including a review of the possible effects of A/C pipe. At that time, there was very little information regarding the release of asbestos fibers from A/C pipe. The AWWA concluded:

> At present there are not adequate data for a description of the quantitative or qualitative role of asbestos-cement pipe as a contributor to asbestos fibers found in potable water distribution systems. However, the available data do indicate that additional studies need to be made and also afford a first approximation of the magnitude of the possible health hazard.

The AWWA also concluded that further research was necessary to answer the question, "Does the use of asbestos-cement pipe in potable water systems constitute a health hazard?" Among the recommended research priorities were determinations of the increment of asbestos fibers added to the water as it traverses asbestos-cement, metal, and plastic pipe systems under varying conditions. A more complete understanding of the health effects of ingested asbestos fibers was also suggested as a research need.

Since 1974, a considerable amount of work on health effects of asbestos, water quality impacts of A/C pipe, and control measures has been sponsored by the EPA's Health Effects Research Laboratory and Municipal Environmental Research Laboratory.

At the time of the publication of the first volume of *Drinking Water and Health* (National Academy of Sciences, 1977), the concern about the release of fibers from A/C pipe was noted, and the relationship between soft water and dissolution of the calcium carbonate in the pipe was mentioned. The report noted that EPA studies under way had produced tentative results suggesting that some fibers are emitted from A/C pipe in corrosive waters.

Since that time, there has been a considerable amount of new evidence regarding the release of asbestos fibers from A/C pipe under various conditions. Both laboratory tests and field investigations have shown that, under certain circumstances, asbestos fibers can be released from A/C pipe into water supplies.

The data concerning the health effects of asbestos ingested in drinking water are indecisive, but it is known to be a carcinogen when inhaled (National Academy of Sciences, 1977). Thus, there has been some concern over the use of A/C pipe and possible release of asbestos fibers into drinking water. The concern over the addition of asbestos fibers and potential health effects in drinking water supplies led to a proposal by the EPA that corrosion control be required for systems using A/C pipe. The Aggressiveness Index (discussed above under "Corrosion Indexes") was proposed as a criterion to determine suitability of water quality for A/C pipe use (U.S. Environmental Protection Agency, 1979a).

The principal issue regarding the use of A/C pipe and its possible deterioration within a distribution system is the quality of water transported in the pipe. A considerable body of evidence collected to date suggests that there is a link between aggressive water and degradation of the pipe. Many investigators have linked a low Aggressiveness Index with release of fibers. However, the Aggressiveness Index does not always predict where the fibers will be released.

Current understanding of the factors influencing behavior of A/C pipe under various conditions is discussed below. Data from laboratory studies and field investigations regarding the release of fibers from A/C pipe are also summarized. Finally, control measures for limiting the exposure of the population to asbestos fibers derived from A/C pipe are presented.

USE OF ASBESTOS-CEMENT PIPE

Originally introduced in Italy during the early 1900's, A/C pipe is now widely used in potable water distribution systems throughout the world. The formulation of A/C pipe from Portland cement and asbestos fibers was originally developed in an effort to provide a corrosion-resistant material of sufficient strength to be used for transmission of water. From 1906 to 1913, a company (Societa Anonima Eternit Pietra Artificiale) in Genoa, Italy, combined asbestos fibers with cement to produce a reinforced pipe that would withstand the high pressure necessary to pump salt water up to the City of Genoa for its street-flushing system (Olsen, 1974). Subsequently, A/C pipe began to be used more widely in Europe and was in limited use 20 years later in the United States. Today, A/C pipe is used throughout North America and Europe as well as in other parts of the world (Craun and Millette, 1977).

A/C pipe was first introduced in the United States around 1930 (American Water Works Association Research Foundation, 1974, 1975b; Hallenbeck *et al.*, 1978). By 1974, there were an estimated 2.4 million km of A/C pipe in service worldwide and approximately 320,000 km in use in the United States (Olsen, 1974). According to a recent survey by the A/C pipe industry, approximately 38% of U.S. cities with a population of 1,000 or more specify, purchase, or have in service A/C pipe (Craun and

Millette, 1977). Thus, approximately 65 million people in the United States may be receiving water that has passed through an A/C pipe distribution system. As of 1978, approximately one-third of all water distribution pipe currently being sold in the United States was made from an asbestos-cement combination (Hallenbeck et al., 1978). In addition to A/C pipe, gaskets and insulation used in treatment and pumps also contain asbestos (Levine, 1978). Advantages of using A/C pipe have been noted by pipe manufacturers and others. Some of them have been listed by Olsen (1974):

- resistance to corrosion, both internal and external;
- strength sufficient to withstand internal forces imposed by water hammer and shock earthloads from earthquakes;
- benefits to water quality, since A/C pipe does not rust, cause discolored water, or contain jute and other types of joints that serve as focal points for bacterial growth;
- light in weight and easy for contractors to install, resulting in lower installation costs; and
- a permanently smooth interior wall, leading to low pumping costs.

Levine (1978) cites advantages of A/C products over nonasbestos counterparts as follows: better tensile strength, strength to weight ratio, strength under heat stress, resistance to acid, and smoothness of finished surface (critical to ensure laminar flow in pipe used for transport of liquids).

As shown later, the purported advantage of corrosion resistance of A/C pipe has not always been found to be true, especially in aggressive waters.

COMPOSITION OF A/C PIPE

A/C pipe is composed of a mixture of asbestos fibers, Portland cement, and inorganic hydrated silicates. In the manufacture of A/C pipe, asbestos fibers are mixed, either wet or dry, with Portland cement and silica in proportions ranging from 10% to 70% of the total material. Typically, the asbestos fibers comprise less than 20% of the A/C pipe (A-C Pipe Producers Association, 1980; American Water Works Association, 1978a,b).

For dry mixtures, the mixture is generally distributed in a flat layer onto an open surface, where the water is then applied by an overhead spray. The thin layer can then be wound onto mandrels in a spiral mat to produce pipe until the required thickness is built up. For wet mix products, a similar winding process can be used for the slurry or the mixture can be cast (Levine, 1978). After pipes are made, the water content is reduced by autoclaving and air drying.

The AWWA specifications for A/C pipe also include physical and chemical requirements for the pipe itself. For the pipe composition, it requires:

Asbestos-cement pipe shall be composed of an intimate mixture of either:

(1) Portland cement or Portland blast furnace slag cement and asbestos fiber with or without silica; (2) or Portland pozzolana cement in asbestos fibers. Both (1) and (2) can be with or without the addition of curing agents. The pipe shall be formed under pressure and cured. The finished pipe shall be free from organic materials (American Water Works Association, 1980).

The same specifications limit the amount of uncombined calcium hydroxide, presumably to curtail pipe dissolution: for Type I, there is no limit, and for Type II, 1.0% or less uncombined calcium hydroxide is permitted. Type I, which is not autoclaved, is no longer manufactured in the United States.

The asbestos portion of A/C pipe is composed of naturally occurring hydrated mineral silicates that possess a crystalline structure. There are four main types of asbestos, as described by Michaels and Chissick (1979):

1. chrysotile ($3MgO \cdot 2SiO_2 \cdot 2H_2O$) or white asbestos, which occurs as fine silky flexible white fibers and is mined mainly in Canada, Russia, and Rhodesia;

2. amosite [$(FeMg)SiO_3$], a straight brittle fiber, light grey to pale brown in colour and found in South Africa;

3. crocidolite [$NaFe(SiO_3)_2 \cdot FeSiO_3 \cdot H_2O$] or blue asbestos, which is found as a straight blue fibre in South Africa, Western Australia, and Bolivia; and

4. anthophyllite [$(MgFe)_7 \cdot Si_8O_{22} \cdot (OH)_2$], a brittle white fibre mined in Finland and Africa.

Other types of asbestos include tremolite [$Ca_2Mg_5Si_8O_{22} \cdot (OH)_2$] and actinolite [$CaO \cdot 3(MgFe)O \cdot 4SiO_2$].

The principal type of asbestos found in A/C pipe is chrysotile. According to the A-C Pipe Producers Association (1980), the chrysotile is added for reinforcement purposes. Another type of asbestos, crocidolite (or blue asbestos), is also used for reinforcement of the pipe manufacturing process.

EFFECT OF WATER QUALITY ON PIPE PERFORMANCE

In contrast to the original expectations that A/C pipe would not be attacked by corrosive water, it is now recognized that under certain circumstances A/C pipe can be attacked by aggressive water. If the pipe is exposed to aggressive water, the cement matrix constituents will dissolve, thereby exposing asbestos fibers and releasing some of them into the water. Concepts developed to predict pipe performance are described above under "Chemical Water Quality Indexes."

LABORATORY TESTS

Only a few laboratory studies have been conducted to investigate the influence of water quality on deterioration of A/C pipe. One A/C pipe manufacturer, Johns-Manville, developed a semiclosed recirculating system with 9.1 meters of A/C pipe (Transite) (American Water Works Association Research Foundation, 1974). Water ahead of the pipe was filtered in an attempt to remove all asbestos fibers prior to contact with the pipe. A series of runs at various levels of pH (4.9-7.4) and total hardness (12 to 105 mg/liter) were made from 1969 to 1971. The data do not supply sufficient information to calculate either the Langelier Index or the Aggressiveness Index. Fiber analyses were performed using particle and fiber counts from magnified electron microscope photographs combined with a radioactive tracer technique. They showed that asbestos fibers were present in the water leaving the pipe in average concentrations ranging from 0.37 to 4.44 $\times$ 10^{-5} μm/liter.

In a pilot study conducted in Seattle, Kennedy Engineers (1978) evaluated the aggressiveness of two water supplies, the Tolt River and Cedar River, and the effectiveness of various inhibitors in reducing the aggressiveness of water to A/C pipe. Corrosivity measures were weight loss, electron microscopy spectrum analysis, asbestos fiber pickup, and water quality analysis. The results confirmed the aggressiveness of both water supplies, which were low in pH, alkalinity, calcium, and total dissolved solids (TDS), to A/C pipe. For the Cedar River, a treatment with lime and soda ash appeared to be the inhibitor strategy most likely to provide protection to A/C pipe. For the Tolt River, lime plus zinc orthophosphate gave the best protection.

Since 1973, the EPA has been conducting a series of laboratory tests using A/C coupons in an experimental pipe loop system (Buelow et al., 1980). In one experiment, the EPA noted two important findings: (1) iron dissolved in water precipitates to provide a protective coating to A/C pipe, even under highly aggressive water quality conditions, and (2) waters indexed as moderately aggressive attacked Type II A/C pipe, even though this result was not predicted. Another important finding of this early work was that pipe drilling and tapping operations can greatly influence asbestos fiber counts in water.

Following the pilot-scale A/C pipe loop experiments, the EPA proceeded

TABLE III-9 Summary of Individual EPA Bench Scale Tests of A/C Pipe[a]

pH	Calcium as Calcium Carbonate, mg/liter	Total Alkalinity as Calcium Carbonate, mg/liter	Aggressiveness Index	Corrosion Control Method	Findings
8.2	6	20	10.28	None	Inner pipe surface softened.
8.2	6	20	10.28	Zinc orthophosphate	Gray coating on pipe surface; pipe remained hard and smooth.
7.0	10	10	9.3	None	Pipe softened.
7.0	10	20	9.3	Zinc orthophosphate	Pipe somewhat softened; increase in alkalinity and calcium.
8.2	6	20	10.28	Zinc chloride	Protective film formed; clean and hard surface on A/C coupon.
7.5	145	125	11.76	None	Pipe softened; light coating present; pipe attacked despite high Aggressiveness Index.
7.9	145	125	12.16	Slightly positive Langelier Index	Pipe hard and clean.
9.0	25	40	12.00	Calcium carbonate saturation	Pipe very slightly softened.

[a]From Buelow, 1980.

to conduct more rigorous tests with bench scale equipment that could be more carefully controlled. Water was recirculated through 6-in. coupons cut from 4-in. Type II A/C pipe. Findings of these experiments are summarized in Table III-9 (Buelow *et al.*, 1980).

Schock and Buelow (1980) reported that results of several of these EPA experiments and other tests were compared with Saturation Indexes and precipitation diagrams calculated for model systems with equivalent water quality and treatment. A good correlation of experimental and predicted results was found in all cases.

The results of these investigations provided several pieces of information elucidating mechanisms of deterioration of A/C pipe. The principal findings are as follows:

• Zinc can provide a protective coating, which prevents the surface from deteriorating even when Aggressiveness Indexes predict that the water will be moderately aggressive to A/C pipe. This protective action of zinc appears to be dependent on pH, higher pH's providing more effective protection.

• Zinc orthophosphate and zinc chloride appear to provide equivalent protection. This suggests that the protective mechanism is related to zinc rather than to the anion or to the compound as a whole.

• The Aggressiveness Index alone cannot be used as a single means of predicting performance of pipe under a given water quality condition. This observation is based on the fact that water with a high Aggressiveness Index, but not saturated with calcium carbonate, has attacked A/C pipe.

• Control of calcium carbonate saturation may, under certain situations, prevent deterioration of A/C pipe.

Some of the more promising findings are being tested by the EPA in field applications for controlling pipe deterioration.

FIELD TESTS

In recent years, concern that A/C pipe can deteriorate under certain water quality conditions has led to numerous studies, including field observation of water quality, pipe conditions, and/or other factors. These studies are summarized below chronologically.

Effects of A/C pipe on water quality were first observed in 1945 in Vermont. Tracy (1950) reported increases in pH, hardness, and alkalinity in water after exposure to A/C pipe. The tendency for water quality changes diminished after several years of exposure to the pipe. Another problem with A/C pipe was reported in 1971 (American Water Works Association,

1971). The investigators reported that the pH of water exposed to new A/C pipe would rise as high as 11.5, if the pipe was not used continuously.

Kay (1974) published a summary of asbestos concentrations found in distribution system samples from 22 cities in Ontario, Canada. Fiber counts by electron microscopy ranged from 136,000 to 3.87 million fibers per liter. The calculated mass concentrations ranged from a low of 0.93 to a high of 35.4×10^{-4} μg/liter. Although there was evidence that the distribution samples contained asbestos, it was not clear whether the fibers originated in the raw water supply or whether they were contributed by action of the water on A/C pipe.

Johns-Manville researchers studied the waters from nine cities using A/C pipe from 8 to 17 years (Olsen, 1974). The asbestos content of the water at the source and at a point in the distribution system following exposure to A/C pipe was tested with an electron microscope technique. Source concentrations varied between 0.26 and 1.32 μg/liter. Fiber content after exposure to A/C pipe ranged from 0.26 to 1.58 μg/liter. The differences do not appear to be significant.

Two municipalities using A/C pipe in their distribution systems were sampled from 1969 through 1970 (American Water Works Association Research Foundation, 1974). In Malvern, Pennsylvania, the content of fibers in well water prior to exposure to A/C pipe was 0.04 μg/liter. After exposure to water having an Aggressiveness Index of 11.3, the water in the distribution system had an average fiber level of 0.12 μg/liter. The water in Glendale, Arizona, had an Aggressiveness Index of 11.8 and an average initial fiber level of 0.006 μg/liter. After exposure to A/C pipe, the average fiber level was 0.01 μg/liter. Thus, both of these early field studies of water in the distribution system indicated an increase in asbestos fiber content.

In 1975, the EPA conducted a study in the Seattle area to determine if water quality changes were occurring as a result of exposure of aggressive water to A/C pipe (Dangel, 1975). Prior to entrance into the distribution system, the pH of the raw water was low (5.4), as was its alkalinity (approximately 4 mg of calcium carbonate per liter) and calcium content (2 mg/liter), and its Aggressiveness Index was 6.7. After exposure to approximately 3.2 km of A/C pipe mains, the water exhibited changes in pH, alkalinity, calcium content, and conductivity, all of which increased with longer exposure to the pipe. Dangel concluded that as the cement binders dissolved, asbestos fibers may have been leaching from the pipe walls. This study was conducted by the EPA to determine if asbestos pipe was degrading. Later studies found that the concentration of asbestos in the raw water was approximately the same as in some parts of the distribution system that were not exposed to A/C pipe. Therefore, subsequent studies were conducted on removal of asbestos from the raw water itself (Kirmeyer *et al.*, 1979).

Another aspect of the A/C pipe deterioration—potential economic losses—was addressed by Hudson and Gilcreas (1976). In a water utility described by the authors, alkalinity of water leaving the treatment works increased by 6 mg of calcium carbonate per liter by the end of the distribution system, which consisted of reinforced concrete, asbestos-cement, and cement-lined cast-iron pipe. The plant was not able to provide sufficient lime-feeding capacity to produce an effluent stable in calcium carbonate content. Based on alkalinity increases in the distribution system, the authors concluded that the water system was losing approximately 455 metric tons of transmission and distribution piping annually as calcium carbonate. No comment was made about the potential introduction of asbestos fibers from the A/C pipe.

McFarren *et al.* (1977) reported an EPA survey of six public water supply systems that used A/C pipe for distribution. These systems had various combinations of pH, alkalinity, and calcium hardness with Aggressiveness Indexes ranging from 5.34 to 12.85. The results of this yearlong survey are summarized in Table III-10. Asbestos fiber counts, measured by transmission electron microscope, were consistently quantified only in the two systems with very aggressive waters. The authors stated that the pH, alkalinity, and calcium hardness increased as the water passed through the pipe, presumably as a result of the water's reaction with the cement in the pipe, which caused the water to become less aggressive to pipe downstream. In a sample of pipe taken from the King County water district system in Seattle, pipe exposed to the water was shown by scanning electron micrographs to have been changed substantially as compared to new pipe.

Craun and Millette (1977) studied the use of A/C pipe in Connecticut public water supplies and the incidence of gastrointestinal cancer. A total of 149 public water supplies in 82 towns were evaluated. Preliminary electron microscopy measurements indicated that 19 water samples exposed to A/C pipe contained chrysotile fiber ranging from below detectable limits (10,000 fibers/liter) to 700,000 fibers/liter. Some amphibole fibers were detected, but concentrations were less than 50,000 fibers/liter. The majority of towns had an Aggressiveness Index under 9.8. The observation of relatively low fiber counts leads to the conclusion that the Aggressiveness Index alone is not a sufficient predictor of the release of fibers from A/C pipe.

Information on exposure of A/C pipe to other types of water quality has been presented by Webster (1974). Photographs of A/C pipe that had

TABLE III-10 EPA Survey of Systems Using A/C Pipe[a]

Location	pH	Alkalinity as Calcium Carbonate, mg/liter	Calcium Hardness, mg/liter	Aggressiveness Index	Average Chrysotile Fiber Count, fibers/liter
Pensacola, Fla.	5.2	1.0	1.4	5.34	5.52×10^6
King County Water District #58, Seattle, Wash.	7.2	14	14.5	9.51	0.66×10^6
Grant Hill Association, Bloomfield, Conn.	7.5	88	82	11.56	NSS[b]
Clark Counties Utilities, Northridge, Ohio	7.8	220	250	11.54	BDL[c]
Lockhart, Tex.	9.4	50	44	12.74	BDL
Cleburne, Tex.	9.7	36	39	12.85	BDL

[a]From McFarren et al., 1977.
[b]NSS = Not Statistically Significant.
[c]BDL = Below Detection Limit.

been carrying brine (water with a high Saturation Index) for several years showed a well-marked deposition of calcium salts in the interior of the pipe, which should protect the pipe from corrosion. A/C pipe subject to acid conditions while carrying sewage developed rough interior surfaces, which presumably could release fibers through erosion. The sewage probably contained hydrogen sulfide, which can attack A/C pipe (McCabe and Millette, 1979). High levels of hydrogen sulfide in a Florida well water source were apparently responsible for attacking A/C pipe. The Aggressiveness Index calculated for this water would not lead to such a conclusion, but it does not take into account the corrosive effects of water quality characteristics other than pH, calcium, and alkalinity. Removal of hydrogen sulfide from the Florida well water supply is being studied.

Hallenbeck *et al.* (1978) reported the results of a study of water samples from 15 public water supply systems in Illinois before and after exposure to A/C pipe of various ages, length, and diameter. Five were groundwater systems, and 10 were surface water systems from Lake Michigan. Aggressiveness Indexes ranged from 11.2 to 12.8; Langelier Saturation Indexes were calculated at -0.8 to 0.5. Pipe ages ranged from 0.5 to 50 years. Measurements by transmission electron microscope indicated that there was no statistically significant difference in the fiber content of water samples collected before and after exposure to the A/C pipe. Thus, there was no statistically significant release of chrysotile fibers from the A/C pipe into these moderately aggressive to nonaggressive water supplies.

In an investigation of domestic water supplies in the San Francisco Bay Area, Cooper *et al.* (1978) reported on asbestos concentrations within distribution systems that contained an A/C pipe. The authors concluded that there was no substantial increase in fiber counts, measured by transmission electron microscopy, after the water passed through A/C pipe. Some increases were observed, but they were not significant compared to the error of measurement.

Millette *et al.* (1979) compiled a summary of more than 1,500 analyses of asbestos in the water supplies of 43 states, Puerto Rico, and the District of Columbia to assess the overall exposure of the U.S. population to asbestos in drinking water. Some of the highest concentrations of asbestos fibers were attributed to A/C pipe (Table III-11). This report also contains tabulations of the miles of A/C pipe, concentrations of fibers, and other information for the 1,500 water samples, which had been collected by the EPA.

Millette *et al.* concluded as follows:

The majority of persons receiving water from asbestos cement pipe distribution systems are not exposed to significant numbers of fibers from the pipe. Many

TABLE III-11 Selected Locations in Which Asbestos Concentrations Have Been Attributed to A/C Pipe[a]

City	Reported Concentration, million fibers/liter	Probable Source	Remarks
Bishopville, S.C.	Up to 547	A/C pipe	Aggressive water
Kentucky Dam Village, Ky.	Up to 45	A/C pipe	Aggressive water
Pensacola, Fla.	Up to 32	A/C pipe	Current levels below 2 million fibers/liter
Lakeland, Fla.	Up to 16	A/C pipe	Hydrogen sulfide attack on pipe; corrective studies under way
Paint, Pa.	Up to 19	A/C pipe	Aggressive water
Amherst, Mass.	Up to 190	A/C pipe tapping	Low concentrations in the system, but high in hydrant
Farmington, Conn.	Up to 10.2	A/C pipe tapping	Resampling showed much lower concentration
Greenwood, S.C.	Up to 3.1	A/C pipe	Aggressive water
San Francisco, Calif., and cities within the Bay Area	Up to 9	Erosion of natural serpentine and some A/C pipe	

[a]Adapted from Millette et al., 1979.

residents using asbestos cement pipe may be exposed to intermittent amounts of asbestos fibers in their water if pipe tapping work is done improperly. In areas of very aggressive water (estimated to be 16 percent of the U.S. water utilities) consumers using asbestos cement mains may be exposed to high concentrations of fibers, over 10 million fibers/liter.

Tarter (1979) has conducted a statistical study of the size of asbestos fibers in the San Francisco Bay Area water systems. A slight but not necessarily statistically significant shift to longer fibers was observed in water after it flowed through A/C pipe in the East Bay Municipal Utility District distribution system. Examination of samples obtained before and after passing through A/C pipe in the East Bay system and in the San Francisco Water Department Hetch-Hetchy system led to the conclusion that water exposed to A/C pipe contained a significantly larger portion of long fibers than did raw water. Craun and Millette (1977) also reported that samples obtained after passing through A/C pipe in a Connecticut system had a higher percentage of fibers exceeding 1 μm in length than a sample with a natural source of fibers obtained from the San Francisco raw water reservoir. The respective median values for the asbestos fiber length were 2.0 μm from the A/C pipe distribution system and 0.7 μm from the natural fiber source.

McCabe and Millette (1979) have summarized a number of EPA-sponsored studies pertaining to deterioration of A/C pipe under varying water quality conditions. In an update on the Connecticut study, they indicated that source waters in 45 Connecticut A/C pipe systems were thought to be very aggressive because the Aggressiveness Indexes were less than 10. However, an epidemiological evaluation of the exposures revealed that there were no high concentrations of asbestos in the distributed water sampled after passing through A/C pipe in any of the systems. Furthermore, none of the pipe that had been dug up over the years had been reported to be significantly deteriorated. With one exception, all samples collected from the Connecticut A/C pipe system contained asbestos concentrations below 1 million fibers per liter, measured by electron microscopy. Distribution system maintenance work and tapping were believed to be the sources of asbestos in one Connecticut sample, which contained 10 million fibers per liter on one occasion and less than 1 million fibers per liter on another. The higher concentration was believed to be the result of pipe tapping. If devices are not used to flush the cutting debris from the pipe or if samples are collected from dead-end areas or from fire hydrants that have not been completely flushed, samples may contain high concentrations of asbestos fiber that are not an accurate representation of the system as a whole. Thus, what may be attributed to pipe deterioration

TABLE III-12 Summary of EPA Field Studies[a]

Initial Aggressiveness Index	pH	Alkalinity as Calcium Carbonate, mg/liter	Calcium Hardness as Calcium Carbonate, mg/liter	Consistently Quantifiable Fibers	Pipe Wall Deteriorated, as Determined by Inspection
5.34	5.2	1.0	1.4	Yes	Yes
5.67	4.8	3.0	2.5	Yes	Yes
7.46	6.0	4.0	7.5	No	No
8.74	7.1	89	0.5	Yes	Yes
9.51	7.2	14	14.5	Yes	Yes
10.48	8.3	20	7.5	No	[b]
11.56	7.5	88	82	No	[b]
12.54	7.8	220	250	No	[b]
12.74	9.4	50	44	No	[b]

[a] Adapted from Buelow et al., 1980.
[b] Not inspected.

in some cases may actually be a result of accumulation of sediments from previous pipe tapping.

In a summary of EPA field work, Buelow *et al.* (1980) discussed evaluation studies at nine water utilities using A/C pipe with various water qualities (Table III-12). Asbestos fiber counts, made by transmission electron microscopy, were consistent in four of the five systems where the Aggressiveness Index was less than 10.0. Inspection of one system with an Aggressiveness Index below 10 (third line in the table) revealed that the pipe had a protective coating resembling iron rust. Fibers were also found in one system with an Aggressive Index greater than 10.0. In the systems with an Aggressiveness Index exceeding 11.56, there were either no asbestos fibers or their occurrence was very inconsistent, regardless of the combinations of pH, alkalinity, and calcium hardness. Unfortunately, water quality data from field studies were insufficient to calculate Saturation Indexes.

Results from this field study also indicated that the longer the water was exposed to the A/C pipe, the greater were the increases in pH and calcium. This should cause the water to become less aggressive. Therefore, the investigators concluded that major pipe deterioration will usually occur in the sections of the pipe located just after the water enters the A/C pipe distribution system. However, a section of pipe farther from the source will not always be attacked less than the pipe closer to the source due to different flow patterns through different distribution lines.

Buelow *et al.* (1980) reported the major conclusions from this study as follows:

1. Calculation of the Aggressiveness Index alone is not always sufficient to predict actual behavior of A/C pipe.

2. Collecting a single sample for an asbestos fiber count is often insufficient to judge the actual behavior of A/C pipe in a given situation.

3. Wet drilling and tapping of A/C pipe, if not performed with a flushing device on a tapping machine, can cause a major release of fibers.

4. Metals such as zinc, iron, or manganese in the water can change A/C pipe behavior.

5. Water is not expected to be attacking A/C pipe when the initial Aggressiveness Index is above about 11, the pH or the concentration of calcium do not change significantly as the water flows through the pipe, and no asbestos fibers are found consistently in representative water samples....

6. Water is likely to be attacking A/C pipe when the initial Aggressiveness Index is below 11, and the pH and the concentration of calcium as the water flows through the pipe increase significantly, and the water does not contain iron, manganese, or similar metals....

In summary, this study has demonstrated that asbestos cement pipe behaves much like other piping materials, except PVC, that are commonly used for distribution of drinking water. If aggressive water conditions exist, the pipe will corrode and deteriorate; if aggressive water conditions do not exist, the pipe will not corrode and deteriorate.

CONTROL OF A/C PIPE DETERIORATION

Various methods have been suggested for curtailing or preventing the corrosion of A/C pipe within water distribution systems. These methods fall into the following basic categories:

• adjustment of water quality to control Langelier Index;
• adjustment of water quality to control Aggressiveness Index;
• addition of materials expected to form protective films or coatings such as zinc, iron, and manganese;
• elimination of hydrogen sulfide;
• rehabilitation of distribution system;
• institution of proper maintenance procedures;
• limitation of the use of A/C pipe; and
• judicious selection of new locations for A/C pipe use.

Adjustment of water quality by controlling Langelier Index is also used to prevent corrosion of metal pipe. Therefore, it is a method with which many utilities are already familiar. The EPA listed adjustment of water quality to a positive Langelier Index as a method for corrosion control and mentioned it specifically for A/C pipe (U.S. Environmental Protection Agency, 1979b). McFarren *et al.* (1977) suggested that A/C pipe corrosion might be controlled by adjusting the pH upward and adding calcium (in effect adjusting either the Langelier Index or the Aggressiveness Index upward). He added, however, that some people might object to an increase in hardness of their water. Buelow *et al.* (1980) agreed that calcium carbonate saturation can be used to prevent attack on A/C pipe. However, it is acknowledged that the greatest weakness in the use of the Saturation Index occurs with water of relatively low alkalinity and calcium. Nevertheless, corrective lime treatment is an option.

Adjusting the Aggressiveness Index is another alternative for controlling the corrosion of A/C pipe. Methods for accomplishing this would include adjustment of pH upward or the addition of calcium or alkalinity to the water. Adding lime, caustic, or soda ash might be considered, but pilot tests should be conducted for an exact selection of chemicals.

In certain cases, the addition of small amounts of metal salts such as those of iron, zinc, and manganese may contribute to the formation of a protective film. The EPA is in the process of evaluating natural inhibitory factors in a Massachusetts drinking water supply to determine why water that would otherwise be classified as very aggressive is not extremely corrosive to A/C pipe and other materials (U.S. Environmental Protection Agency, 1979c). The potential protective effect of these metal compounds is being investigated. Since coatings resembling iron rust have been observed in laboratory experiments on existing systems, the addition of iron may be able to protect A/C pipe. Zinc and manganese have also been shown to have protective effects. However, applicable drinking water standards and potential effects on industrial users would have to be considered before control measures using either compound could be implemented. In addition, the anion of choice needs to be carefully considered. For example, a study in Seattle showed that although zinc phosphate was effective in reducing corrosion, the phosphate demonstrated a potential to stimulate algal growth in open distribution reservoirs (Courchene and Kirmeyer, 1978). This finding suggests the need for study of other forms of zinc, such as zinc chloride. The costs for adding zinc orthophosphate and zinc chloride have been estimated by the EPA (1979b). Coating of pipe with zinc orthophosphate and pH adjustment are being evaluated as control measures to prevent deterioration of A/C pipe in Greenwood, South Carolina (McFarren et al., 1977).

In a few cases, deterioration of A/C pipe may be curtailed by removing hydrogen sulfide, which may attack the pipe under low pH conditions. A Florida town is currently studying the hydrogen sulfide problem and is planning to implement treatment to eliminate it from water prior to exposure to A/C pipe (McCabe and Millette, 1979). In an EPA-sponsored research project, a utility is adding zinc to the water to determine if it can reduce the amount of asbestos fibers released from A/C pipe that is slightly attacked.

The institution of proper maintenance practices is another approach to controlling occasional additions of asbestos from the distribution system itself. This may be applicable in situations where the water itself is not attacking the pipe, but where occasional high asbestos fiber concentrations have been attributed to residues remaining from improper maintenance procedures. Some tapping devices on the market today force debris from cutting operations to be flushed from the pipe, preventing contamination of drinking water with those fibers. The A-C Pipe Producers Association (1980) recommends that equipment with a positive purge should be used to tap A/C pipe under pressure. This equipment is reported to eject 99% of the asbestos cement chips. Another alternative is the use of heavy walled tapped couplings supplied directly from the factory. According to Buelow *et al.* (1980) many regular pressure tapping machines can be modified by adding a flushing valve from a commercially available kit. New tapping machines can be purchased with a flushing valve.

The American Water Works Association (1978a,b) has published detailed procedures for the use of A/C pipe in water utilities. For "dry" tapping of pipe not under pressure, it recommends that dust and cuttings should be removed from the pipe's interior by flushing with water, wet mopping, or vacuuming prior to placing the pipe in service. This should minimize the fouling of valves, regulators, meters, and other equipment with chips and minimize the unnecessary addition of asbestos to drinking water. For "wet" tapping of pipe in service, it recommends that provision should be made for downstream flushing or use of tapping equipment with positive purge or "blow-off" features.

Another approach to preventing the occurrence of asbestos fibers in drinking water supplies has been to restrict the use of A/C pipe by legal means. Some cities have either banned the future use of A/C pipe or are in the process of considering such bans.

The more careful selection of locations where A/C pipe should be used is a preventive measure with merit. During the past 10 years, pipe manufacturers and trade organizations have recommended caution in the use of A/C pipe with aggressive waters, but this advice has not always been heeded. By using predictors such as the Saturation Index and the laboratory coupon tests developed by the EPA, a utility should be able to determine judiciously if A/C pipe is an appropriate material for a given water quality.

Summary and Conclusions

Under certain water quality conditions, A/C pipe can deteriorate. Evidence from laboratory and field tests has shown that asbestos fibers can be released from deteriorated pipe. Other water quality changes observed after exposure to A/C pipe include increased pH, calcium, and alkalinity. Consistent with these observations, the cement portion of the pipe, consisting principally of calcium silicates plus a small amount of free lime, can dissolve if water is not saturated with a number of calcium compounds. Release of cement constituents would be followed by increased pH, calcium, and alkalinity. After cement is dissolved or otherwise weakened, asbestos fibers in the matrix are released. Since asbestos in A/C pipe is principally the chrysotile form, the majority of fibers released to the pipe are chrysotile.

A number of indexes have been developed to predict pipe performance under given water quality. The Langelier Index estimates whether water will be oversaturated, undersaturated, or at equilibrium with respect to calcium carbonate. If water is oversaturated, this index is positive and a protective calcium carbonate film can deposit on A/C or other types of pipe. The Aggressiveness Index, a simplified version of the Langelier Index, has been used extensively in the water supply field.

Since both the Langelier Index and the Aggressiveness Index are based on calcium carbonate solubility, there are shortcomings in their ability to predict the performance of A/C pipe. When the indexes indicate oversaturation, experimental and field observations have frequently (but not always) shown that pipe is not deteriorated. When exposed to water predicted to be aggressive by the Aggressiveness Index, some pipes deteriorate and others do not. In the latter instance, protective films of zinc, iron, or other material compounds have been found. Thus, it is clear that water quality factors other than pH, calcium, and alkalinity should be considered before water's aggressiveness to A/C pipe can be determined.

Schock and Buelow (1980) have proposed a chemical equilibrium model that accounts for the potential protective action of silica, iron, manganese, and zinc as well as that of pH, carbonate, calcium, temperature, and disinfectant residual in determining a Saturation Index for several compounds. This appears to be a promising method for predicting performance of A/C pipe, but it will require field tests for confirmation.

Plastic Pipe

In recent years, plastic pipe materials of various compositions have been used in transmission mains of water distribution systems and in individual home services. Plastics were brought into use to provide low-cost pipe materials that were not subject to the action of aggressive waters. Within the past few years, however, there has been some concern over possible leaching of organic compounds and other constituents of plastic pipe into the water. The limited number of tests that have been conducted on this subject have dealt primarily with polyvinyl chloride (PVC) pipe. This section contains discussions of the types of plastic pipe commonly used in the United States, their composition, their use in water distribution systems and home plumbing, the effects of water quality as measured by laboratory and field studies, control measures, and conclusions.

Use of Plastic Pipe

Thermoplastic pipe was first introduced as a commercial product in the United States about 1941, but initially its use in potable water supplies was limited. By 1968, Farish (1969) reported that approximately 234 million kg of pipe and fittings were produced from three materials used in potable water applications: polyethylene (PE); polyvinyl chloride (PVC), including chlorinated polyvinyl chloride (CPVC); and acrylonitrile-butadiene-styrene (ABS).

The most common plastic piping material, PVC, has been in use in the United States since approximately 1960 (Dressman and McFarren, 1978; McFarren *et al.*, 1977). In 1975, Rawls reported that approximately 180 million kg of PVC resin was used in the production of water pipe annually. The use of plastics in distribution systems and home services within the United States has been summarized by compiling the results of a questionnaire distributed by the American Water Works Association (1979). Based on responses received from 514 water suppliers, the approximate percentages of all types of plastic pipe used for distribution system mains were as follows: 80% PVC, 13% PE, 5% polybutylene (PB), and 2% fiberglass-reinforced plastic pipe (FRP). For home services, the percentages of various plastic materials were as follows: 43% PE, 20% PB, and 36% PVC. The relative percentage of PVC used was shown to be increasing.

In a survey of water distribution materials present in European households, Haring (1978) reported that PVC and PE (as Polythene) comprise between 1% and 12% of the total materials used in Belgium, France, the Federal Republic of Germany, Ireland, Italy, the Netherlands, and the United Kingdom.

There are several advantages and disadvantages in the use of plastic pipe for distribution systems and services. The American Water Works Association (1979) has reported the following advantages: ease of installation, low cost, external and internal noncorrodibility, better flow characteristics, ease of repair, and greater strength relative to A/C pipe. Disadvantages noted by utilities using plastic pipe include problems in cold weather, difficulty in locating nonmetallic pipe, need for careful bedding and backfilling, capping problems, problems with solvent weld joints, deterioration from storage in direct sunlight, costly and often unavailable transition fittings, nonstandardization of fittings and adaptors, weakness relative to cast or ductile iron, and problems with splitting, cracking, and scoring of the pipe. A few users were concerned about possible migration of vinyl chloride monomer from PVC pipe into potable water.

Composition of Plastic Pipe

Plastic is defined by the National Sanitation Foundation as "a material that contains as an essential ingredient an organic substance of high molecular weight, is solid in its finished state, and at some stage in its manufacture or its processing into finished articles can be shaped by flow." Thermoplastics are plastics that are "capable of being repeatedly softened by an increase of temperature and hardened by a decrease of temperature" (Farish, 1969).

The polymerized product is the principal constituent of plastic pipe. In some cases, there is a small residual of unpolymerized monomer in the finished pipe. Some monomers, such as unpolymerized vinyl chloride in PVC pipe, have toxic properties and are a potential source of concern if they leach out into potable water. Vinyl chloride is a known carcinogen in humans and animals (National Academy of Sciences, 1977).

As a result of potential health effects of unpolymerized monomers, steps have been taken in industry to curtail the use of certain materials that could be leached from the plastics. Efforts to reduce the amount of vinyl chloride monomer in PVC have been made since 1973, when the Food and Drug Administration found that vinyl chloride leached into liquor contained in PVC bottles, which were subsequently banned for liquor sales by the Department of the Treasury. New methods for manufacturing PVC are aimed principally at reducing the residual level of vinyl chloride monomer in the plastic. Rawls (1975) reported that technology for reducing the amount of vinyl chloride in vinyl chloride polymers is improving rapidly and that a goal of less than 1 ppm residual vinyl chloride in PVC is reasonable.

In addition to the organic polymer, which is the main component of plastic pipe, other materials are included in the pipe for various purposes. Therefore, any impacts on water quality related to the use of plastic pipe may derive from leaching of these components. For example, unplasticized PVC (uPVC) pipe contains pigments, lubricants, and stabilizers in addition to the polymer PVC (Packham, 1971a). Pigments, added to make the pipe opaque, commonly include carbon black or titanium dioxide. Lubricants, which reduce the adherence of pipe material to extrusion tools used in pipe manufacture, include a range of materials such as stearic acid, calcium stearate, glycerol monostearate, polyethylene wax, and montan wax. Stabilizers, incorporated to reduce the rate of decomposition of PVC at elevated temperatures used for extrusion and injection molding, include compounds of lead, cadmium, barium, tin, calcium, and zinc. In general, pigments and lubricants are physically and chemically inert, but many of the stabilizers are toxic.

Products used to join plastic pipe sections may also, under some circumstances, leach into water in contact with the pipe. Some jointing methods involve the use of solvent cement, push-on joints, mechanical joints, and heat-fused joints. Primers and cements used in solvent-welded joints contain such constituents as methyl ethyl ketone, cyclohexanone, tetrahydrofuran, and *N, N*-dimethylformamide.

Plastic Pipe and Water Quality

Although plastic pipe does not appear to be subject to major degradation by contact with the water, there has been some concern that small amounts of materials in the plastic pipe could leach into the water. Similar concerns have been expressed about materials that come into contact with food. There has been a limited amount of testing on plastic pipe in contact with potable water. Effects on water quality observed in laboratory studies and field tests are summarized below. Most of the information pertains to PVC.

The quality of water appears to be of minor importance in the release of substances from plastic pipe materials (McFarren *et al.*, 1977). This is in contrast to other types of pipe from which the release of constituents is definitely affected by water quality.

Laboratory Tests

In the United States, some of the first studies of plastic pipes were conducted by the National Sanitation Foundation in conjunction with the University of Michigan School of Public Health. The potential toxic effects of plastic pipe were studied during a 3-year research program beginning in 1952 (Farish, 1969). In these studies plastic pipes (composition not specified) were exposed to aggressive water at pH 5.0 for 72 hours at 37.78°C. Taste and odor were evaluated, and chlorine residuals were measured. Wistar white rats exposed to plastics in their drinking water were studied for 18 months. Autopsies showed no evidence of damaging effects attributable to contaminants in water resulting from continuous exposure to various plastics.

Materials other than organic chemicals can be extracted from plastic pipe. The National Sanitation Foundation (Farish, 1969) found that lead, cadmium, strontium, lithium, antimony, and other toxic elements used as stabilizers in plastic pipe could be extracted by typical potable waters in concentrations exceeding the standards established in 1962 by the U.S. Public Health Service. In laboratory tests (Farish, 1969) of lead-stabilized PVC plastic pipe produced in the United States and abroad, lead concentrations in water ranged from 0.3 to 2.0 mg/liter. The concentrations were lower at high pH's, but even at pH 9.0 they exceeded the U.S. Public Health Service drinking water standard of 0.05 mg/liter. Whether these concentrations are typical of those found in water distribution systems was not reported.

Subsequent to these laboratory tests, the National Sanitation Foundation developed a standardized testing procedure for plastic pipes. Both physical and toxicological properties of pipes, fittings, and joining compounds used to transport potable water have been tested in the prescribed manner.

A number of laboratory test procedures have been used in Europe to determine the concentration of lead extracted from unplasticized polyvinyl chloride (uPVC) pipe. Packham (1971a,c) argued for the necessity of a standardized test. With his procedures, he found lead could be extracted from uPVC at concentrations typically ranging from 0.01 to 2 mg/liter, depending on flushing time, extraction procedure and sequence, and pipe manufacturer. The amount of lead extracted depends on the concentration of lead in the pipe material, the form in which it is present, and the process used in the manufacture of the pipe. Results from other researchers supported a conclusion that extractable lead was present in the form of a thin film on the inner pipe surface.

Eklund *et al.* (1978) conducted laboratory scale tests to evaluate the influence of different pipe materials on water quality. Sections of PVC and nonplastic water pipes were thoroughly rinsed with tap water for several hours, then filled with drinking water and stored for 24 hours. Volatile organics were analyzed with closed loop stripping and gas chromatography/mass spectrometry. With homogeneous PVC pipe, there were indications of three contaminants added to the tap water; however, these were present in concentrations too low (< 1 ng/liter) for structure elucidation. Nonvolatile organic substances and inorganic compounds were not determined.

The most extensive testing of PVC pipe to date has been conducted under the auspices of the California Department of Health Services. The goal of one study was to determine the health risks, if any, posed by the use of plastic pipe systems in homes. James M. Montgomery, Consulting Engineers, Inc. (1980), conducted laboratory tests to evaluate water quality in PVC and CPVC pipe for a number of constituents: solvent cements used for joints, volatile halogenated organics, volatile aromatic organics, base/neutral extractable organics, and metals.

Both static and usage simulation tests were made with piping and joints typical of those found in a two-bedroom house. The static system was designed to simulate new plumbing, containing stagnant water prior to occupancy so that leachable organics would be similar to those encountered during the first several times the system was used by the consumer. A

2-week period of stagnation was followed by flushing, refilling, and sampling intervals. The second system, postoccupancy usage simulation, was set up to simulate normal household use for a 30-day period, alternating 12 hours of flowing water with 12 hours of stagnant water. The kinetics of the static samples were also tested. Other variables in the tests included water temperature, water source, pipe material, type of solvent cement, and cementing procedure.

Solvents used for PVC cement and primers typically include methyl ethyl ketone, tetrahydrofuran, N,N-dimethylformamide, and cyclohexanone. The diffusion of solvent in 2-week static CPVC samples described above ranged from a low of 0.11 mg/liter for dimethylformamide in conventional systems filled with cold water to 375 mg/liter for tetrahydrofuran in the cold water in a poorly constructed system in which excess cement and primer were used. The most important variable affecting solvent diffusion appeared to be the quality of workmanship in the system. Bonded surfaces with excess cement and primer leached appreciably more of each solvent than the conventional systems. In subsequent refills of the CPVC pipes, the level of each solvent dramatically decreased although their residence time in the pipe was shorter. Most of the solvents were gone after the first 2 weeks of use.

In the usage simulation described above, solvent concentrations were measured in samples taken when 360, 1,800, 3,600, and 10,800 gallons (1,368, 6,840, 13,680, and 41,040 liters) of water had flowed through the system. Solvent levels decreased rapidly between samples analyzed at the 360- and 1,800-gallon mark. The level of methyl ethyl ketone, tetrahydrofuran, and cyclohexanone measured at the 1,800-gallon mark were nearly constant throughout the remainder of the experiment. Detectable levels of methyl ethyl ketone and tetrahydrofuran (12 and 33 mg/liter, respectively) continued to be leached after 34,280 gallons (130,264 liters) had passed through the system during 98 days of operation. N,N-Dimethylformamide was not detected in any sample; cyclohexanone was present at 0.05 mg/liter in the sample taken at 360-gallons but was not detectable at 10,800 gallons.

In these tests, 32 volatile halogenated or volatile aromatic organic compounds identified as priority pollutants by the EPA were analyzed by gas chromatography/mass spectrometry (GC/MS). Several volatile halogenated organic compounds were detected at levels higher than those found in the raw water, suggesting that they had leached from the PVC pipe. Concentrations of chloroform in the 2-week CPVC samples were 5 to 11 times greater than those in the raw water. Levels of carbon tetrachloride were 52 to 125 times higher than the concentration in the raw water. The maximum concentrations (146 μg/liter for chloroform and 50 μg/liter for carbon tetrachloride) were found in the excess-cement/cold-water system. These two compounds may have been formed when residual chlorine in the raw water reacted with methyl ethyl ketone and tetrahydrofuran acting as precursors or they may have diffused from the pipe material. The total trihalomethane concentration in water residing for 2 weeks in the excess-solvent/cold-water system (152 μg/liter) exceeded the 100 μg/liter standard set by the EPA. No other system in this study exceeded the limit.

Vinyl chloride monomer was not detected in any of the samples. The detection limit was 0.1 μg/liter. In the PVC pipe tests, 30 nonvolatile organic compounds were analyzed by base neutral and acid extraction followed by GC/MS. All that were found were attributable to contamination. Heavy metals were also analyzed in the PVC pipe test since they are sometimes used as heat stabilizers. After 2 weeks in the static PVC system, concentrations of metals in the water from the pipe were below EPA maximum contaminant levels and generally at or below levels in the influent water (Table III-13).

Field Tests

The few field tests conducted on water collected from the distribution system or home services also concentrated on PVC pipe. Packham (1971b) summarized findings of studies in European systems in which uPVC with lead stabilizers was used. In a study conducted in the Netherlands, 7 of 15 distribution systems contained no detectable lead, several were at or below 0.05 mg/liter, and the highest was 0.10 mg/liter. Pipes ranged in diameter from 15 to 100 mm and in age from 2 months to 5.5 years. In Italy, water from 32 uPVC distribution pipes containing lead in the pipe varying from 0.031% to 1.619%, had less than 0.07 mg/liter lead in 31 water samples.

TABLE III-13 Metal Concentrations in Static Polyvinyl Chloride Systems[a]

Metal	Colorado Raw Water	Concentration in Colorado 2-Week Sample, mg/liter	State Project Raw Water	State Project 2-Week Sample
Cadmium	<0.005	<0.005	<0.005	<0.005
Copper	0.039	0.031	0.01	0.007
Lead	0.004	0.003	0.005	0.001
Tin	<0.01	<0.01	<0.01	<0.01
Zinc	0.017	0.043	0.034	0.025

[a] From James M. Montgomery Consulting Engineers, Inc., 1980.

TABLE III-14 Vinyl Chloride in PVC Distribution System Piping[a]

Water Utility	Year of Pipe Manufacture	Total Pipe Length, km	Total Wall Area, m^2	Vinyl Chloride Concentration, µg/liter
Coolidge. Ariz.	Approximately 1964	2.7	540	<0.03
Georgetown. Tex.	1975	20.0	7,920	1.3
Pioneer, Calif.	Approximately 1966	11.2	4,680	0.06
Roseburg. Calif.	1966–1967	5.58	1,260	0.03
Salados, Tex.	Approximately 1968	0.83	360	<0.03

[a]From Dressman and McFarren. 1978.

Packham sampled 53 points in English distribution systems with uPVC pipe, under both normal flow and night flow conditions. The pipe had been in service from 0 to 74 months and ranged in length from 9 to 4,300 meters. Most lead concentrations were less than 0.01 mg/liter; the highest was 0.05 mg/liter.

In 1975, Dressman and McFarren (1978) studied five U.S. water distribution systems using PVC pipes to determine vinyl chloride monomer concentrations in samples collected before and after exposure to PVC pipe. Very low concentrations of vinyl chloride (0.03 to 1.3 µg/liter) were detected in four of the five water samples studied. The lowest concentration was found in a 9-year-old system and the highest was found in the newest system. In the fifth system, no vinyl chloride was detected at a detection limit of 0.03 µg/liter. These findings are summarized in Table III-14.

Vinyl chloride concentrations in the samples prior to exposure to the PVC pipe were less than the detection limit (i.e., < 0.03 µg/liter). The newest and longest system appeared to have the highest vinyl chloride concentration and the next longest had the next highest concentration. Traces of vinyl chloride at the nanogram per liter level were still present in two California systems, Pioneer and Roseburg, approximately 9 years after they were installed.

Control Measures

Since plastic pipes have only recently been tested for deterioration and possible leaching of contaminants into the water of distribution systems, control measures have not been fully developed. However, some control measures have been mentioned in the literature. These include requiring tests on pipe materials to demonstrate that the materials are acceptable for use in water distribution systems, specifying desired properties of plastic pipe materials, and limiting the use of plastic pipe in individual distribution systems.

The concept of requiring tests prior to using new pipe materials for potable water supplies is not a new one. Farish (1969) described the testing procedures used by the National Sanitation Foundation to evaluate physical properties of the pipe materials and toxicological and organoleptical evaluations. In some states, plastic pipe manufacturers are being required to demonstrate the leaching characteristics of their material. In California, for example, these tests have been used to determine if the state should restrict the use of PVC pipe materials (James M. Mongomery, 1980).

Another approach is to require conformance to standards. Both the American Water Works Association (1975a, 1978b) and the American Society for Testing and Materials (1974, 1978) have developed standards for PVC and PE pipe. In the Federal Republic of Germany, recommended quality criteria for PVC pipe encompass the following factors: raw materials, catalysts and additives, residues of decomposition products from catalysts, residues from emulsifiers, protective colloids, residues of precipitating materials, and stabilizers (Anonymous, 1977). Adherence to these pipe material standards could control the amount of unpolymerized monomer, stabilizers, or other constituents that may have toxic properties. Requiring that only certain evaluated components be permitted in cements and primers is another quality control method (James M. Montgomery, 1980).

Other recommendations involve the alteration of construction procedures so that both construction workers and homeowners are protected from solvent cements and primers that could leach into water. The California Department of Health Services (James M. Montgomery, 1980) has recommended the use of warning labels on all solvent-cemented pipe outlets in new construction and a specific protocol to be used by contractors for flushing newly installed pipe systems.

A final method of control includes regulatory actions such as banning the use of specific plastic materials for certain uses. For example, the U.S. Department of the Treasury has banned the sales of liquor in PVC bottles, and the FDA at one time proposed regulations to ban the use of vinyl chloride polymers in materials coming into contact with food to preclude the migration of vinyl chloride gas into the food (Rawls, 1975). However, these proposed regulations excluded certain uses such as water pipes.

Based on the evidence collected to date, a combination of materials testing and standards specification has been the typical approach to control.

Summary and Conclusions

There has been only a limited amount of work concerning the effects of plastic pipe on water quality, and this research has concentrated on PVC. Plastic pipe was developed to provide a material that would be inert to water, but some materials can leach out in trace quantities. In general, the initial water quality is not a major factor in the leaching of materials from these pipes in contrast to the definite effect of water quality on corrosion of metal and A/C pipe.

Plastic pipe is composed principally of polymerized organic compounds, but there can be residual unpolymerized monomer present in low concentrations. This is especially important in PVC pipe, since the vinyl chloride monomer is known to be carcinogenic in humans and animals (National Academy of Sciences, 1977). Plastic pipe can also contain other components, such as pigments, lubricants, stabilizers, and plasticizers. Pipe sections may be joined with cement and primers, which contain volatile solvents. When predicting the effect of piping on water quality, all of the pipe's constituents should be considered.

Laboratory tests have shown that effects of plastic pipe on water quality are a function of the type of pipe, the manufacturer, the flow pattern and duration, the contact time, the jointing material, the residual monomer concentration, the stabilizer type and concentration, and the testing protocol. A variety of laboratory tests of lead-stabilized PVC have shown that the lead is extracted by water and can be found in concentrations ranging from less than 0.01 to 2 mg/liter, depending on test conditions and pipe composition. There is a possibility that unpolymerized vinyl chloride monomer can be leached into water, but recent tests have shown no detectable monomer. Solvents from cement and primers as well as heavy metals have been found in laboratory tests of PVC and CPVC.

Samples of water exposed to PVC pipe in distribution systems have contained low concentrations of leachates from PVC pipe, presumably because the pipe had aged and the contact times were short. Samples from uPVC pipe in Europe contained lead concentrations typically between 0.01 and 0.05 mg/liter. In the United States, an EPA survey of five PVC distribution systems found vinyl chloride monomer concentrations ranging from below detection limits (0.03 μg/liter) to 1.4 μg/liter.

Possible control measures include standards for pipe composition, laboratory tests to ensure leachate concentrations are below accepted limits, or curtailment of pipe use.

LINING MATERIALS

Nonmetallic linings are commonly used in potable water distribution systems to prevent corrosion of underlying metal components. Strictly speaking, linings are materials on the interior surfaces of pipes, tanks, or other facilites, thereby coming into direct contact with water. Coatings, on the other hand, are applied to the external surfaces of pipes or tanks and, thus, are not in contact with the water. Sometimes the terms "linings" and "coatings" are used interchangeably, but "linings" in its strict definition will be used herein for the sake of accuracy and to avoid confusion.

Frequently, steel or ductile iron pipes are lined with cement mortar, asphalt, coal tar, or compounds containing coal tar, vinyls, or epoxies. Steel water-storage tanks are lined with materials similar to those used in metallic pipe.

Although lining materials have been used successfully to help prevent deterioration of water quality by controlling corrosion and its by-products, the possibility that the materials might themselves affect water quality has recently been raised. Laboratory and field studies have shown that some of these materials, especially coal tar compounds, can leach contamintants into the water with which they come into contact. There is also some speculation that small particles of intact lining material can also be released from deteriorating linings.

The concern about linings and their potential impact on water quality is based primarily on the fact that most of these materials are organic in composition and many of them contain carcinogens. Examples include the polynuclear aromatic hydrocarbons (PAH's) found in coal tar compounds.

The amount of information on concentrations of materials released into the water from linings and coatings is limited. There have been a few laboratory studies of lined panels and several studies of water quality before and after exposure to distribution system materials; however, the extent to which the general population is exposed to materials released from linings is as yet unknown.

To obtain more in-depth information regarding the effects of linings on water quality, the EPA has formed an Additives Evaluation Branch within its Office of Drinking Water. This group is conducting further research to answer some of the questions about linings.

Many types of materials are used to line pipes, water storage tanks, and appurtenant facilities in the distribution system. For pipelines, the most commonly used materials in the United States are cast iron, ductile iron, asbestos-cement, and steel. Cast-iron and ductile-iron pipes are typically lined with cement mortar or cement mortar plus a bitumastic (asphalt combined with a filler) sealing coat. Steel pipes are usually lined with cement mortar. A/C pipe is typically unlined, although vinyl linings are used occasionally with aggressive water. Other linings for pipes include coal tar epoxy, other epoxy, coal tar emulsion, and polyamide cured expoxy.

To protect the approximately 0.5 million steel water-storage tanks in the United States from corrosion, a number of linings are used on the interior surfaces, including coal-tar-based materials, vinyl, expoxies, zinc rich, metallic rich, chlorinated rubber, and phenolic based materials. There are no statistical data on the number of tanks lined with specific materials (Goldfarb et al., 1979). We know, however, that the predominant paints are vinyl, epoxy, and coal tar. Estimates of the percentages of these various materials used vary widely.

The earliest U.S. water tanks were made of riveted wrought iron. At that time, little consideration was given to protective paint. Iron plates were usually primed with iron oxide paint, and the interior surfaces were painted with a single coat of asphalt paint or red lead. Most of the protection from corrosion resulted from the inherent resistance of the wrought iron itself. In the early 1900's, wrought iron was replaced with steel structures, which were painted the same way as the iron. However, since the steel had a lower corrosion resistance than the iron, paint failures were frequent. As a result, new linings were developed (Brotsky, 1977).

The protective mechanism of lining materials has been described by Wallington (1971). Paints protect steel principally by their high ionic resistance and low permeability to ions such as chlorides and sulfates, which accelerate corrosion. Paints do not have sufficiently low permeability to water and oxygen to stop corrosion simply by excluding them from the metal surface, although very thick linings probably retard this process.

The formulations of the different tank lining materials have been described by Goldfarb *et al.* (1979), Wallington (1971), and others. A practical guide to the selection of materials has been published by Banov and Schmidt (1978). Characteristics of typical lining materials are described below.

Coal Tar

Coal tar linings have been used in the United States since 1912 to protect the interior of steel pipelines carrying potable water (Goldfarb *et al.*, 1979). They have also been used to line steel water-storage tanks.

Coal tar linings are made by combining coal tar pitch with other material to provide the desired properties. According to definitions developed by the American Society for Testing and Materials, coal tar is "a dark brown to black cementitious material produced by the destructive distillation of bituminous coal" and pitches are "black or dark-brown solid cementitious material which gradually liquifies when heated and which is obtained as residue in the partial evaporation or fractional distillation of tar." Coal tar pitch is "composed almost entirely of polynuclear aromatic compounds and constitutes 48-65 percent of the usual grades of coal tar" (American Petroleum Institute, 1971).

In the United States, coal tar is usually produced as a by-product of the manufacture of metallurgical coke, and it is obtained by the destructive distillation of bituminous coal. The tar is recovered from coke oven gases by partial condensation. The material that escapes the initial partial condensation is "light oil" and gas. Further processing of the tar by fractional distillation produces tar acids, tar bases, naphthalene, and creosote oil. The residue that remains after distillation is commonly referred to as pitch. The pitch fraction resists penetration by water and deterioration by water action. For this reason, it is used for waterproofing and roofing and as protective coatings on buried or submerged iron and steel structures and pipelines (Goldfarb *et al.*, 1979).

The coal tar material most commonly used in the United States for lining is coal tar enamel, as described in Standard C-203 of the American Water Works Association (1978a). The enamel is manufactured by dispersing coal in a mixture of coal tar pitch or refined coal and coal tar base oil with a high boiling point. It is strengthened by the incorporation of talc at approximately 30% by weight.

The resulting coal tar enamel has a long service life (in excess of 50 years), good resistance to erosion, a smooth surface, and seems to resist the buildup of algae and other growths (Goldfarb *et al.*, 1979).

It is well established that coal tar contains polynuclear aromatic hydrocarbons (PAH's). Some of the PAH's found in coal tar and water are shown in Table III-15. The constituents of tar, summarized by Lowry (1945), include PAH's such as naphthalene, 1-methylnaphthalene, 2-methylnaphthalene, acenaphthene, fluorene, anthracene, phenanthrene, chrysene, pyrene, and fluoranthene. Other PAH's, heterocyclic nitrogen compounds, phenols, and a number of other constituents have also been found. Similarly, Wallcave (1971) has reported a number of PAH's in coal tar pitches.

Other coal tar derivatives are described below.

Asphalt

Asphalt is a "dark-brown to black cementitious material in which the predominating constituents are bitumens which occur in nature or are obtained in petroleum processing" (American Petroleum Institute, 1971). In contrast to coal tar, which is derived from coal, asphalt is derived from petroleum.

Ductile-iron pipes used in water distribution systems are typically lined with a sealing coat of petroleum asphalt, which is in direct contact with the water. This lining serves primarily to control the curing rate of an inner layer of Portland cement, which is used to retard corrosion of the pipe by aggressive waters (Miller *et al.*, 1980). The asphalt lining aids the cement curing process by retaining moisture, and it protects the cement mortar from decalcification in soft water (Goldfarb *et al.*, 1979). The asphalt lining for ductile pipe is more completely described by the American National Standard Institute (1980). According to the Ductile Iron Pipe Research Association, all U.S. manufacturers of cast- and ductile-iron pipe use an asphalt sealing material derived from the distillaton of petroleum products; this material does not contain any coal tar pitch (Stroud, 1980).

Concentrations of PAH's are much lower in asphalt linings than they are in coal tar linings. Miller *et al.* (1980) analyzed asphalt paint for several PAH's (fluoranthene, benzo(*b*)- and benzo(*k*)fluoranthene, benzo-(*a*)pyrene, perylene, ideno(1,2,3,-*cd*)pyrene, benzo(*ghi*)perylene, anthracene, and chrysene). They found these compounds in concentrations ranging from 0.1 to 10 μg/g. Concentrations of the alkyl derivatives of these PAH's were 2 to 10 times greater. Wallcave *et al.* (1971) analyzed eight asphalts. They found 17 PAH's, typically ranging from 1 to 10 μg/g. Again, alkyl derivatives were frequently found in concentrations up to an order of magnitude higher.

Other Materials

Other materials used to line water distribution piping or tanks include coal tar epoxy, other epoxy, cement mortar, coal tar emulsion, epoxy phenolic formulations, and polyamide cured expoxy formulations (Goldfarb *et al.*, 1979). When water is known to be aggressive to A/C pipe, vinyl linings have been used. Some of the other materials used to line water storage tanks include chlorinated rubber, metalized zinc, wax (applied cold or hot), phenolic, and zinc rich. As actually applied, the linings include coal tar enamel (hot), three-coat vinyl, metalized zinc, four-coat vinyl, chlorinated rubber, coal tar paint (applied cold), coal tar epoxy, two-component epoxy, asphalt, wax, one-component epoxy, phenolic compounds, and zinc (Goldfarb *et al.*, 1979).

Release of Lining Materials into Distribution System

Research on the leaching of lining components into water has been limited. Most of it has been concentrated on PAH's from coal tar and asphalt material. Due to experimental conditions, laboratory investigators have typically found higher concentrations of these materials in the test water than are actually found in water distribution systems.

The magnitude of contamination in distribution systems is determined by a number of factors. These include the age of the coating, contact time of the water, ratios of surface area to water volume, the type of coating used, manner of application, and deposits of materials such as carbonate (Sorrell *et al.*, 1980).

Many PAH's have been found in water in distribution systems (Sorrell *et al.*, 1979). Structures of some of these compounds are shown in Table III-15. PAH contamination of raw waters has also been found.

There are no drinking water regulations for PAH's or other materials released from linings of distribution systems in the United States. The *In-*

TABLE III-15   Polynuclear Aromatic Hydrocarbons Found in Water

Structure	Name	Abbreviation
	Anthracene	An
	Benzo(*a*)anthracene	B(*a*)A
	Benzo(*b*)fluoranthene	B(*b*)F
	Benzo(*j*)fluoranthene	B(*j*)F
	Benzo(*k*)fluoranthene	B(*k*)F
	Benzo(*a*)pyrene	B(*a*)P
	Benzo(*e*)pyrene	B(*e*)P

TABLE III-15   *Continued*

Structure	Name	Abbreviation
	Benzo(*ghi*)perylene	B(*ghi*)P
	Chrysene	Ch
	Fluoranthene	Fl
	Indeno(1,2,3-*cd*)pyrene	IP
	Phenanthrene	Ph
	Perylene	Per
	Pyrene	Pyr

ternational Standards for Drinking Water (World Health Organization, 1971) contains limits for PAH's since several of them are known to be carcinogenic. These standards indicate that "the concentration of six representative PAH compounds (fluoranthene, 3,4-benzfluoranthene, 11,12-benzfluoranthene, 3,4-benzpyrene, 1,12-benzperylene, and indeno[1,2,3-*cd*]-pyrene should ... not, in general, exceed 0.2 μg/liter." An update on PAH's and their significance to health is discussed in Chapter VII of this volume.

Laboratory Tests

The few laboratory tests conducted on the effect of linings on water quality have evaluated the leachings from coal tar, coal tar enamel, asphalt, and other materials. There is no standard procedure for conducting these tests. Thus, a variety of experimental conditions have prevailed. Furthermore, they have not been very representative of actual exposure conditions in the distribution systems. Therefore, the data from these tests can be used to show whether compounds do or do not leach from the coatings, but they are not valuable in predicting the concentrations of materials that would be found under actual conditions in the distribution system. A summary of the findings of those laboratory tests is contained in Table III-16.

Alben (1980a) conducted tests on steel panels coated with coal tar. After 1 week of static testing, several PAH's were found in the leachate samples. The highest concentration was phenanthrene (and possibly anthracene) at 125 μg/liter. According to Alben, phenanthrene and its isomer anthracene were not resolved by the GC/MS technique used in this study, but anthracene was considered to be the minor constituent based on the relative solubilities of the two compounds and analyses of coal tar. Concentrations of naphthalene, three methylated naphthalenes, fluorene, fluoranthene, and pyrene ranged from 13 to 56 μg/liter.

The U.S. Army Corps of Engineers (Lampo, personal communication, 1980) coated steel panels with coal tar pitch and immersed them in water. Compounds found in the leachate by liquid chromatography and GC/MS were not the typical PAH's, and no benzo(*a*)pyrene was found. Aza-arenes were detected; acridene was found in concentrations of 5 to 10 μg/liter. Although concentrations of the aza-arenes in the coal tar pitch are lower than those of the PAH's, the heterocyclic nitrogen compounds are more soluble in water, a factor that Lampo credits for the concentrations of aza-arenes in the leachate being higher than those of the PAH's. In a similar test with a 5-year-old panel, no compounds of these types were detected in the leachate; detection limits were not specified.

In an EPA laboratory, coal-tar-based coatings were tested on glass plates with flowing tap water (Sorrell *et al.*, 1980). Concentrations of PAH's in the water after 25 and 165 days were phenanthrene at 230,000 to 290,000 ng/liter; fluoranthene, pyrene, and anthracene at 14,000 to 46,000 ng/liter; chrysene and benzo(*a*)anthracene at approximately 1,000 ng/liter; and others at approximately 100 ng/liter or less.

Petroleum asphalt coatings on ductile-iron pipe have been investigated by Miller *et al.* (1980). Samples were analyzed by high-pressure liquid chromatography with fluorescence detection and GC/MS. Using a recirculation test system and sampling times ranging from 10 minutes to 293 hours, Miller found that the sum of the concentrations of the six PAH's [fluoranthene, benzo(*b*)fluoranthene, benzo(*k*)fluoranthene, benzo(*a*)-pyrene, benzo(*ghi*)perylene, indeno(1,2,3-*cd*)pyrene] listed in the standards of the World Health Organization (1971) was less than 10 ng/liter. Concentrations typically were less than 1 ng/liter. Fluoranthene was measured at 7 ng/liter, the highest concentration for any single PAH covered by the World Health Organization standards. In one sample, anthracene was detected at a maximum concentration of 41 ng/liter. This test suggests that lower concentrations of PAH's are leached from asphalt coatings than from coal tar coatings, presumably because the asphalt initially contains lower concentrations of these PAH's.

Eklund *et al.* (1978) evaluated cast-iron water pipe with cement lining and with asphalt and polyurethane linings. Analyses were conducted by closed-loop stripping enrichment and GC/MS. Leachate from polyurethane-coated pipe was contaminated with chlorobenzene at about 1 μg/liter and by aromatic substances at approximately 5 μg/liter. Naphthalene, methylnaphthalene, biphenyl, methylbiphenyl, and dibenzofuran were also detected. For the cast-iron pipes with cement and asphalt linings, no influence on water quality was observed; however, the investigators did not analyze for nonvolatile organic substances and inorganic compounds.

An epoxide-alkyl enamel and a vinyl chloride/vinyl acetate copolymer paint proposed for painting submersible well pumps were tested as coatings on iron metals (Kupyrov *et al.*, 1977). Neither the enamel nor the paint had any significant effect on the organoleptic or chemical properties of the water.

Sorrell *et al.* (1977) tested cement- and asphalt-lined cast-iron pipe. Using a number of analytical techniques, they identified phenanthrene (65 ng/liter), fluoranthene (4 to 6 ng/liter), pyrene (6 ng/liter), and 1-methylpyrene (2 ng/liter) in the water that had been in contact with the asphalt lining.

TABLE III-16 Summary of Laboratory Tests on Linings

Material	Flow Conditions	Lining Surface Area/ Water Volume, m^2/liter[a]	Contact Time	Findings	References
Coal tar on steel panels	Static	0.006	1 week	Phenanthrene/anthracene at 125 μg/liter and other PAH's at 13–56 μg/liter.	Alben, 1980a
Coal tar pitch on steel	Static	0.03	1 week	Aza-arenes from new panel; 5–10 μg/liter acridene. No PAH's from 5-year-old panel; detection limit not stated.	Lampo, personal communication
Coal tar enamel on glass	Flowing	0.08	25 and 165 days	Phenanthrene at 230,000 to 290,000 ng/liter; fluoranthene, pyrene, anthracene at 14,000 to 46,000 ng/liter; other PAH's ~1,000 ng/liter or less.	Sorrell et al., 1980

Asphalt- and cement-lined cast iron	Static	0.04	Several days	Phenanthrene at 165 ng/liter; fluoranthene at 4-6 ng/liter; pyrene at 6 ng/liter; and 1-methyl-pyrene at 2 ng/liter.	Sorrell et al., 1977
Asphalt on ductile iron	Circulating	0.02	10 min to 293 days	Sum of six PAH's from World Health Organization regulations < 10 ng/liter; fluoranthene at <1-7 ng/liter; anthracene at <2-41 ng/liter; other PAH's <1 ng/liter.	Miller et al., 1980
Cement lining on cast iron	Static	—	24 hr	No effects on water quality observed.	Eklund et al., 1978
Asphalt on cast iron	Static	—	24 hr	No effects on water quality observed.	Eklund et al., 1978
Polyurethane on cast iron	Static	—	24 hr	Chlorobenzene at 1 µg/liter; aromatic hydrocarbons at 5 µg/liter.	Eklund et al., 1978

[a]Calculated.

Field Tests

Most of the limited number of field studies conducted on this subject have focused on surveys of organic compounds, particularly PAH's, in the distribution system. This emphasis is apparently due to the fact that many pipes and reservoirs are lined with organic materials. However, there is no systematic information on leaching rates, changes in leachate composition over time, or decomposition products, nor is there complete information on constituents and their concentrations to which the public is generally exposed. Therefore, it is difficult to estimate the health effects that may result from these exposures.

Field studies often consider an inadequate number of distribution system materials that might come into contact with the water. Initial water quality data (other than PAH's) are generally not included in reports of distribution system sampling, but it is assumed that water quality is not an important factor in the leaching of these types of materials.

After surveying the data on the leaching of PAH's in U.S. water distribution systems, Sorrell *et al.* (1980) reported that only limited information is available. These data, including the presence of coal tar or asphalt lining, are summarized in Table III-17. Several interesting observations can be made from this accumulation of data. First, the concentrations of the majority of PAH's analyzed were less than 1 ng/liter. Second, phenanthrene appeared in higher concentrations than those of the other compounds, which is in agreement with the laboratory studies of leaching described above. Third, the Portland, Oregon, system, which had a coal tar lining, contained substantially higher concentrations of some of the PAH's than did the three systems with asphalt linings; however, the PAH concentrations in the water of the other two systems with coal tar linings were similar to those in systems with asphalt linings. It would be necessary to have more information on the size and age of the distribution system, the materials used in them, and the amount of water flow to make more substantive comments on the findings.

Another survey of PAH's in distribution systems has been conducted by Saxena *et al.* (1978). Treated water was collected from the treatment site as well as from various locations in the distribution system. Information from the analyses of the six PAH's included in the drinking water standards of the World Health Organization (1971) is summarized in Table III-18. Except for the samples from Wheeling, samples contained low concentrations of PAH's at ppt (ng/liter) levels. In many cases, water sampled from the distribution system contained higher concentrations of individual PAH's as well as of the total of the six PAH's in comparison to

-concentrations in undistributed treated water at the water treatment plant. At two of the sites, the major PAH's introduced by the distribution system lines were benzo(*ghi*)perylene and indeno(1,2,3,-*cd*)pyrene. At two of the sites (Elkart and Fairborn), trace quantities of some PAH's were found in the undistributed treated water, but after the water was exposed to the distribution system piping, all six PAH's were detectable. In some cases, notably in Wheeling, levels of PAH decreased after exposure to the distribution system. This suggests that PAH may have been removed by adsorption onto the surface of certain kinds of pipes. The authors could not link PAH levels to distribution system linings because definitive information on lining materials at these locations could not be obtained.

An EPA-sponsored study (Saxena, 1979) is currently in progress. Water samples from several water supplies throughout the United States are being analyzed for PAH's and mutagenic activity. Preliminary results from four cities indicate that the six PAH's contained in the World Health Organization standards range in concentration from below detection limits to 6 ng/liter. These results are only preliminary, since the work is expected to continue for some time.

Zoeteman and Haring (1976) have studied PAH concentrations in European distribution systems. They found detectable levels of PAH's in 88% of 25 tap waters tested in the United Kingdom and in the Netherlands. The mean concentration of six PAH's in ng/liter was as follows: fluoranthene, 17 ng/liter; 1,12-benzoperylene, 5 ng/liter; 11,12-benzofluoranthene, 3 ng/liter; indeno(1,2,3-*cd*)pyrene, 3 ng/liter; 3,4-benzofluoranthene, 3 ng/liter; and benzo(*a*)pyrene, 3 ng/liter. The authors also analyzed for PAH's at pumping stations and taps in 10 cities. Concentrations ranged from less than 3 ng/liter to 30 ng/liter for individual compounds at the tap. In most cases, there was no difference between the concentrations before and after exposure to the distribution system. In two cases, the concentration of total PAH's was less at the tap. The authors concluded that there was no significant PAH contamination in the tap waters resulting from exposure of the water to asphalt linings of cast-iron pipes. However, they also note that such linings are not used frequently in the Netherlands and more studies should be conducted in countries such as the United Kingdom where these materials are more commonly used.

Another approach to analyzing water in the distribution system is to measure the mutagenic activity of concentrates collected from various distribution systems. Schwartz *et al.* (1979) analzyed concentrated samples of water from three medium-sized water supplies using the Ames *Salmonella* test for mutagenicity. Thirty-liter raw water samples and 60-liter finished water samples were concentrated using polyurethane foam, solvent extracted, and evaporated to 1 ml for mutagenic testing.

TABLE III-17 Polynuclear Aromatic Hydrocarbons in Finished and Distributed Waters[a]

Concentration, ng/liter

Compound	Standish, Maine[b]		Ludlow, Mass.[b]		Columbus, Ohio[c]		Portland, Oreg.[b,c]		Seattle, Wash.[b]		Colorado Springs, Colo.[b]	
	Fin.	Dist.[d]	Fin.	Dist.[d]	Fin.	Dist.[d]	Raw	Dist.[e]	Fin.	Dist.[e]	Fin.	Dist.[e]
Phenanthrene	5	57	2	3	3	17	8	3,300	2	32	3	29
Fluoranthene	2	10	1	1	1	13	4	640	3	8	2	6
Pyrene	1	5	1	1	<1[f]	8	6	340	2	2	<1	<1
1-Methylpyrene	<1	<1	<1	<1	<1	<1	<1	<1	<1	<1	<1	<1
Anthracene	<1	<1	<1	<1	—	—	—	—	<1	<1	<1	<1
Chrysene	<1	<1	<1	<1	<1	4	<1	26	<1	<1	<1	<1
Benzo(a)-fluoranthene	<1	<1	<1	<1	<1	3	<1	2	<1	<1	<1	<1
Perylene	<1	<1	<1	<1	<1	<1	<1	<1	<1	<1	<1	<1
Benzo(e)pyrene	<1	<1	<1	<1	<1	<1	<1	<1	<1	<1	<1	<1

Benzo(a)pyrene	<1	<1	<1	<1	<1	—	<1	<1	<1	<1	<1	<1
Benzo(ghi)-perylene	<1	<1	<1	<1	<1	2	<1	<1	<1	<1	<1	<1
Benzo(b)-fluoranthene	<1	<1	<1	<1	<1	4	<1	3	<1	<1	<1	<1
Benzo(k)-fluoranthene	<1	<1	<1	<1	<1	3	<1	<1	<1	<1	<1	<1
Dibenzo(a,h)-anthracene	<1	<1	<1	<1	<1	<1	<1	<1	<1	<1	<1	<1
Indeno(1,2,3-cd)pyrene	<1	<1	1	1	<1	<4	<1	<1	<1	<1	<1	<1
TOTAL	8	72	5	6	4	54	18	4,300	7	42	5	35

[a] From Sorrell et al., 1980.
[b] Data from Zoldak, 1978.
[c] Data from Sorrell et al., 1979.
[d] Asphalt lining.
[e] Coal tar lining.
[f] < Indicates that the compound may or may not have been present at less than this concentration.

TABLE III-18 Effect of the Water Distribution Process on the Levels of Polynuclear Aromatic Hydrocarbons[a]

Water Supply System	Sampling Location	Concentrations of Six PAH's Detected, ng/liter						
		Fluor-anthene	Benzo(j)-fluor-anthene	Benzo(k)-fluor-anthene	Benzo(a)-pyrene	Indeno(1,2,3-cd)pyrene	Benzo-(ghi)-perylene	Total
Appleton, Wisc.	Treatment site	—	0.4	0.2	0.4	1.4	3.7	6.1
	1.6 miles (~2.56 km) from treatment site	—	0.4	0.3	0.3	1.4	5.4	7.8
	3.5 miles (~5.6 km) from treatment site	—	1.4	0.9	1.2	3.3	11.2	18.0
Fairborn, Ohio	Treatment site	—	—	—	0.1	0.7	2.1	2.9
	2.5 miles (~4 km) from treatment site	—	—	—	0.4	—	—	0.4
	4 miles (~6.4 km) from treatment site	6.5	0.3	0.3	0.3	0.6	0.6	8.6
Elkhart, Ind.	Treatment site	—	—	—	—	0.3	—	0.3
	1.5 miles (~2.4 km) from treatment site	8.1	0.4	0.3	0.3	0.6	1.4	11.1
Wheeling, W. Va.	Treatment site	94.5	1.4	—	2.1	7.8	32.7	138.5
	4 miles (~6.4 km) from treatment site	81.7	0.8	—	0.8	3.7	14.1	101.1
	12 miles (~19.2 km) from treatment site	—	1.4	—	1.9	4.9	21.6	29.8
Midwest location (CH)[b]	Treatment site	—	0.3	0.3	—	0.1	1.3	2.0
	5.3 miles (~8.48 km) from treatment site	—	0.6	0.5	0.5	1.1	3.5	6.2

[a]From Saxena et al. 1978.
[b]City not identified. Referred to only as CH.

Materials in the distribution systems included cast iron in one midwestern city, cement-lined ductile iron in another midwestern city, and a mixture of copper, cast iron, cement-lined ductile iron, and asbestos-cement in a southeastern city. No further details on linings were described. Assays of the samples from the first two sites showed that mutagens were being contributed by the distribution process. Samples from the third site were not mutagenic. Only nonvolatile mutagens could be measured by this technique. Volatile compounds such as trihalomethanes or vinyl chloride would be lost during the sample preparation procedures. Results suggested that the distribution systems probably introduce two different classes of mutagens: low-molecular-weight polar compounds and high-molecular-weight, nonpolar compounds.

Schwartz et al. (1979) suggested that several mechanisms may be responsible for increased mutagenic activity in the water after distribution. First, mutagenic compounds could be leached from the interior surface of tanks and pipelines, which are frequently lined with coal tar—a mixture containing proven mutagens and animal carcinogens. Second, mutagens could be synthesized in water during its travel from the treatment plant to the sampling site as a result of chemical reactions (e.g., reaction of residual chlorine with organics), oxidation, or microbial action, which converts inactive chemicals into mutagens.

In addition to the general surveys of PAH's and the mutagenic properties of distribution system samples, there have been some case studies relating changes in water quality to linings at individual sites. The most notable case studies have been conducted in Pascagoula, Mississippi, and Portland, Oregon.

In Pascagoula (McClanahan, 1978), two water storage tanks were cleaned and lined with coal tar pitch. The larger Bayou Cassotte tank held 750,000 gallons, the Beach Tank was a smaller, elevated storage tank. After the tanks were filled, there were immediate taste and odor changes in the smaller tank. The tanks were drained, refilled, and again put into service, after which the appearance of bacteria were reported. Following another draining and filling cycle, complaints were again received, and a citizen inquired about the advisability of using the coal tar pitch as a lining material. Subsequent to two more draining, inspection, and filling cycles, the EPA collected samples from the Bayou Cassotte tank. Several PAH's were detected in concentrations ranging from 1 to 10 μg/liter. A number of solvents and other organics were also found in the water. The compounds in the highest concentrations were phenanthrene/anthracene (apparently not resolved by the analytical techniques) at approximately 9 μg/liter and naphthalene at about 6 μg/liter. Approximately 4 months later, the tank was drained and filled again. Samples taken shortly thereafter again showed a number of PAH's at µg/liter concentrations: phenanthrene/anthracene was approximately 5 µg/liter and fluorene was about 2 µg/liter. Again, several solvents and other organics were detected. From a sample collected about 1 month later, there were again several PAH's ranging from 1 to 10 µg/liter, and phenanthrene/anthracene was found in a concentration of 14 µg/liter in the bottom of the tank. Results are shown in Table III-19. The samples collected at the top and the bottom of the tank were affected differently by flow rate and solar heating. The EPA Region IV used the results of these analyses to estimate the concentration of phenanthrene/anthracene in water that had been exposed to a storage tank lined with coal tar pitch for approximately 1.5 days, an average exposure time under regular operating conditions. They estimated that a phenanthrene/anthracene concentration of approximately 5 µg/liter would be produced.

Subsequent to the sampling program in Pascagoula, the EPA recommended that the tanks be placed back in service on an interim basis to meet the water needs of that city (Kimm, 1978), but that monitoring should continue for 1 year. According to McClanahan (1978), the phenanthrene/anthracene concentrations decreased over time until they were less than 1 µg/liter in water samples taken from the outlet of the Bayou Cassotte Reservoir.

Leaching of material from coal-tar-based lining materials was also studied by the EPA in Portland, Oregon (Robeck, 1978). Water samples were collected from the source and at the terminal point of a pipe lined with coal tar of an unspecified type. The pipe was 24 in. (60.96 cm) in diameter and 2.43 mi (3.89 km) in length. Samples were analyzed for a number of PAH's (Table III-20). The PAH's were undetectable or at concentrations of approximately 1 µg/liter in the water obtained at the source, while detectable quantities of five PAH's were found after exposure to the coal-tar-lined pipe. Phenanthrene was again the compound found at the highest concentration (3,225 ng/liter, while fluoranthene and pyrene were found at approximately 600-700 ng/liter). Other compounds were present at lower concentrations.

Alben (1980a) collected samples at the inlet and outlet of a 12,000-gallon (45,600-liter) storage tank, which had a 5-year old commercial coal-tar lining. Concentrations of PAH's in the effluent from the tank were 5 to 30 times higher than those in the influent. Influent and effluent concentrations in µg/liter were: naphthalene (0.004 and 0.025), fluorene (0.001 and 0.021), phenanthrene/anthracene (0.019 and 0.210), fluoranthene (0.003 and 0.081), and pyrene (0.002 to 0.071). The sum of the PAH's increased from 0.029 to 0.410 µg/liter.

In Champaign, Illinois, Lampo (personal communication, 1980) collected

TABLE III-19   Constituents Leached from Bayou Cassotte Tank, Pascagoula, Mississippi[a]

| | Concentration, μg/liter | | | | |
| | 9/6/77 | | 1/16/78 | 2/21/80 | |
Constituent	Bottom of Tank	Top of Tank	Bottom of Tank	Bottom of Tank	Top of Tank
Polynuclear Aromatic					
Hydrocarbons					
Naphthalene	5.4	6.7	—	1.3	2.7
Methylnaphthalene (two isomers)	0.75	1.4	0.63	<1	1.3
Acenaphthene	2.8	4.6	1.3	3.1	8.0
Fluorene	3.4	5.1	1.5	2.9	8.0
Phenanthrene/ anthracene	8.7	9.3	4.5	14	35
Indene	<10	<10	—	—	—
Methylenephen- anthrene	<10	<10	<10	—	—
Pyrene	<10	<10	<10	2.2	7.0
Dimethylnaphthalene	—	—	—	1.2	2.7
Fluoranthene	—	—	—	2.7	9.7
Methylenephen- anthrene/methyl- phenanthrene	—	—	—	1.2	4.0
Other Organics					
Biphenyl	0.21	0.40	—	<1	<1
Dibenzofuran	3.1	5.0	1.1	2.3	6.3
Carbazole	0.70	1.3	0.44	3.9	11
Bromoform	<10	<10	<10	—	—
C_4 alkyl chloro- benzene (two isomers)	<50	<50	<50	2.7	7.3
C_3 alkyl benzene	<10	<10	—	—	—
Anthraquinone	<10	<10	<10	2.3	8.3
Methylbenzofuran	<10	<10	—	<10	1.0
Quinoline	<10	<10	—	<1	<1
Methylstyrene/ indan	<10	<10	—	—	—
2,5-Diethyltetra- hydrofuran	—	—	11	—	—
Methylstyrene/ indan/indene	—	—	—	1.7	2.6

[a] Adopted from McClanahan, 1978.

TABLE III-20   Compounds Detected in the Water
Samples Obtained in Portland, Oregon[a]

Compound	Concentration, ng/liter	
	At the Source	At the End of 2.43 mi (~3.9 km) of Coal-Tar-Lined Pipe
Phenanthrene	3	3,225
1-Methylphenanthrene	—	NQ[b]
2-Methylphenanthrene	—	NQ
Fluoranthene	<1	572
Pyrene	<1	671
Chrysene	—	32
Benzo(b)fluoranthene	<1	4
Fluorene	—	NQ
Acenaphthene/biphenyl	—	NQ

[a] From Goldfarb et al., 1979.
[b] Not quantifiable.

water samples from a tank relined a year earlier with a coal tar pitch/epoxy coating. Using liquid chromatography and GC/MS analyses, he did not detect materials in the water after exposure to the tank.

One feature regarding water quality deterioration, evident from several studies, is that some linings can introduce taste and odors into the water if the linings are improperly cured. For example, taste and odors noticed shortly after a tank was relined with coal tar pitch/epoxy in Champaign were believed to be caused by a solvent, xylene (Lampo, personal communication, 1980). In the Pascagoula incident, taste and odors resulting from the new coal tar lining were responsible for the initial investigation of organic contaminant concentrations. The compound(s) responsible for the taste and odor were not identified by McClanahan (1978). In addition to the solvents used to formulate or apply the coatings, another possible source of taste and odors is naphthalene, which is reported to have a threshold odor concentration in water of approximately 1 µg/liter (Zoeteman and Haring, 1976).

Another type of lining material, vinyl, has recently been found to leach organic compounds into water in the distribution system. In April 1980, the EPA recommended that installation of vinyl-lined A/C water pipe be suspended in New England because concentrations of tetrachloroethylene as high as 665 µg/liter were found in drinking water carried by the pipe. Tetrachloroethylene has been used to apply the lining to the A/C pipe. EPA is currently gathering information on the problem, including concentrations of the chemical in the pipe of different ages and in pipes that receive varying degrees of use (Anonymous, 1980).

The literature contains a few general comments on the deterioration of cement linings. For example, the AWWA Committee on Control of Water Quality in Transmission and Distribution Systems (Anonymous, 1971) has noted that there can be an increase in pH in mortar-lined pipe, even with a fairly continuous flow, if there is sufficient contact time. A pH increase of 0.4-0.6 was noted in an 28.8-km mortar-lined pipe in Grand Junction, Colorado. In Seattle (Dangel, 1975), increases in pH, alkalinity, and calcium have been observed in water from freshly relined mains. Water quality changes were reported to cease after a few weeks of flow, presumably after the uncombined calcium oxide had been removed from the cement.

Summary and Conclusions

In the United States and abroad, a number of lining materials are used in drinking water distribution systems to protect pipes and tanks. The most common of these materials are coal tar, petroleum asphalt, vinyl, epoxy, or some combination thereof.

Generally, concern about the use of these lining materials is rooted in their formulations, which are based on organic compounds. Some materials, such as coal tar, are comprised primarily of polynuclear aromatic hydrocarbons (PAH's), several of which are known to be carcinogenic in animals and humans. Constituents of the linings could reach the drinking water at the tap through leaching processes or possibly through physical deterioration and release of small particles of the lining material.

There have been a few laboratory studies on leaching from linings, principally from coal tar or asphalt linings. A number of PAH's and some heterocyclic compounds have been found to be leached from these types of coatings. Higher concentrations appear to leach from coal tar than from asphalt. However, these laboratory studies have not been conducted under standardized conditions, so it is difficult to compare one study to another and to predict from these studies what the actual concentrations of constituents would be in a water distribution system.

A number of field studies have been conducted to measure organic constituents after exposure to linings in the distribution system. Some of these studies have found PAH's at nanogram to microgram per liter levels. The compound most commonly found in these studies has been phenanthrene and/or anthracene. In some cases, these compounds are not resolvable by mass spectrometric techniques, but the isomer is believed to be phenanthrene. In addition to releasing PAH's, some linings have been found to release solvent constituents and compounds that produce tastes and odors if the lining is not properly cured. Finally, a limited amount of work has been done on mutagenic activity of water in the distribution system. In two of three samples studied, water after exposure to lining materials had higher mutagenic activity than water before exposure to these materials.

There is a need for more research on the effects of linings on water quality. The recently formed Additives Evaluation Branch of the EPA should begin to answer some of these questions. In particular, there are needs for specific and systematic data collection procedures, including information on the type of material, time in service, and water flow rates. Some standard exposure factor, such as square meters of lining area per liter of flowing water, is needed to establish a basis from which results of various research can be compared. Most studies have been conducted either on coal tar or on asphalt linings. More work needs to be done on other types of lining materials to gain a complete picture of potential water quality changes upon exposure to distribution system materials.

Deposits and Their Effects

Following water treatment, chemicals can deposit in water distribution systems, thereby affecting the quality of water distributed to the consumer. The most widely studied elements exhibiting this behavior are iron and manganese, but these studies have been examined primarily for their aesthetic and economic effects instead of their effects on health. Nevertheless, one can reasonably estimate the exposures of humans to these and other elements associated with their deposition and resuspension, as well as exposures to chemicals added for their control.

Aside from the aesthetic concerns—the visual impacts of iron and manganese suspensions including their discoloration of materials—these two elements are frequently associated with the growth of microorganisms in distribution systems (O'Conner, 1971). Their deposits are often resuspended, due to changes in flow, water temperature and quality, and water hammer.

High concentrations of iron and manganese affecting water quality in distribution systems are found not only in groundwaters but also in surface water supplies from deep lakes and eutrophic lakes and in surface waters exposed to mine drainage or acid industrial wastes (O'Connor, 1971). Calcium carbonate deposition and its effect on water quality have been discussed earlier in this chapter in the sections on chemical water quality indexes and corrosion. This discussion will briefly consider the behavior and control of chemical deposits, primarily to indicate possible exposures of humans. However, such exposures will necessarily be speculative because of the paucity of available information.

APPROACHES TO IRON AND MANGANESE CONTROL

The control of manganese and iron in water supply systems has been widely practiced by one of three principal methods: oxidation (followed by precipitation and filtration), ion-exchange, and stabilization (O'Conner, 1971). The latter involves the use of dispersing agents to prevent their deposition in distribution systems. Despite these well-established techniques, however, water treatment plants are frequently unsuccessful in controlling these elements. In Nebraska, a survey of 29 water treatment plants practicing iron and manganese removal indicated only 60% were effective based on their ability to meet EPA secondary criteria of 0.3 mg/liter for iron and 0.05 mg/liter for manganese (Anderson *et al.*, 1973). Even when the concentrations of iron and manganese in the raw water were quite low in one plant, the deposits accumulated and were flushed in the distribution system following fluctuations in the water's flow pattern. Similarly, O'Conner (1971) cited a 1960 survey of Illinois plants that indicated that iron in a reduced oxidation state was often found in the effluent from the filter at the water treatment plant.

STABILIZING AGENTS

Both naturally occurring and purposefully added organic or inorganic complexing agents can prevent oxidation and settling of iron or manganese in distribution systems. O'Conner (1971) discussed organic substances that behave in this fashion, including tannic, gallic, and ascorbic acids. Two common stabilizing agents applied at water treatment plants are phosphates and silicates.

One of the early uses of silicates for the prevention of iron deposition in a distribution system was reported by Henry (1950). He found that a silica sol (activated sodium silicate) produced by the partial neutralization of sodium silicate was effective in preventing or delaying the settling out of iron and produced no turbidity. In these pilot studies, it was also observed that large amounts of polyphosphates provided some similar protection, but produced objectional amounts of turbidity.

More recent studies of addition of silica to prevent iron and manganese deposition have been reported by Dart and Foley (1970, 1972) for well water supplies in Ontario, Canada. They noted that for waters with a natural silica content of 30 to 40 mg/liter, little decrease in iron concentrations resulted either from aeration or from chlorination followed by filtration. Although the finished waters contained concentrations of iron as high as 0.3 to 1.0 mg/liter, they appeared to be acceptable to the consumers. In contrast to the study of Henry (1950), Dart and Foley (1970,

1972) found that it was not necessary to activate (partially neutralize) the silicate, which in their studies was an effective additive retaining the iron in solution when used simultaneously with chlorination.

Dart and Foley (1970, 1972) followed the efficacy of such silicate treatment for approximately 2 years. They found it to be successful with initial iron concentrations up to 1.3 mg/liter and silicate additions up to 6.2 mg/liter. They noted that the iron-staining properties of the distributed waters diminished. There had been some concern that domestic hot water tanks might accumulate iron by thermal break-up of the silicate complex, but this apparently did not happen. They judged that the likely mechanism of iron control by the addition of silicate depended on the chelation of freshly produced ferric ions by the orthosilicate anion. Considering the adsorption by anion exchange resins, they concluded that the complex species formed by the ferric and silicate ions was negatively charged, although Weber and Stumm (1965) have demonstrated the formation of a positively charged iron silicate $[FeSiO(OH)_3^{2+}]$ complex. Dart and Foley (1972) also found that silicate sequestered (complexed) manganese in a well water when chlorination and elevated pH resulted in the desired oxidation of the manganese.

Although a variety of inorganic phosphorus compounds can be used in water treatment, Aulenbach (1971) noted that polyphosphates are the most effective in controlling iron, although the dispersion of the iron may not be permanent, particularly as the polyphosphate breaks down, hydrolyzing to orthophosphate. To be most effective, the polyphosphate should be added before oxidation, e.g., by aeration or chlorination, and applied at concentrations ranging from 1 to 5 mg/liter as phosphate at a suggested weight ratio of two parts phosphate to one part iron.

Anderson *et al.* (1973) reported the frequent use of sodium hexametaphosphate, a polyphosphate, in controlling iron and manganese in water supply systems, but described one such groundwater supply in which this additive was not successful. Of special interest is their finding that copper was also precipitated into the distribution system with the iron and manganese deposits. They noted that copper ions can sorb onto ferric hydroxide colloids at pH values greater than 5.

Tuovinen *et al.* (1980) have also shown that heavy metals are associated with tubercles in distribution systems. Such metals as iron, manganese, lead, and copper can, when they are freed by hydraulic stresses and increased flow velocities, increase in concentration in the water delivered to the consumer. Table III-21 compares heavy metal concentrations in "red waters" with annual average concentrations in finished water in the Columbus, Ohio, distribution system.

TABLE III-21   Heavy Metals in Analysis of Red Water and in Finished Water in the Columbus Distribution System[a]

| | Red Water, mg/liter[b] | | | Finished Water, mg/liter | |
| | Fire Hydrant Flush | | Domestic Faucet | | |
Element	Sample 1	Sample 2		Sample 1[c]	Sample 2[d]
Aluminum	0.55	0.60	<0.10	0.080	0.084
Arsenic	<0.001	<0.001	<0.001	<0.001	<0.001
Silver	<0.0002	<0.0002	<0.0002	<0.001	<0.0001
Barium	0.078	0.074	0.033	0.03	0.03
Cadmium	0.00005	0.00005	<0.00005	<0.0001	<0.0001
Chromium	0.001	0.001	0.001	0.0003	<0.0005
Copper	0.044	0.044	0.090	0.0432	0.0104
Iron	21.0	23.1	<0.10	0.060	0.031
Manganese	0.244	0.236	0.001	0.0007	0.0005
Lead	0.0024	0.0026	<0.0010	0.0013	0.0001
Selenium	<0.001	<0.001	<0.001	<0.001	0.002
Zinc	0.040	0.044	<0.010	0.018	0.024

[a] From Tuovinen et al., 1980.
[b] Collected from sample 2 piping.
[c] 1979 annual average of Columbus water plant tap composites.
[d] 1979 average of grab samples from all pressure districts.

SUMMARY AND CONCLUSIONS

Several metals can be deposited and resuspended in water supply distribution systems. There may be fluctuations in the concentrations of other organic or inorganic chemicals that coprecipitate or sorb with the metals and may influence the bacterial concentrations.

Of special interest is the possible potential adverse health effects of silicates and polyphosphates, which are added as stabilizing agents, particularly when complexed with manganese. Other heavy metals are also maintained in solution by the addition of these dispersing agents. Whether this can cause a substantial increase in the exposures of humans to these metals is not known.

Reactions Involving Water Treatment Chemicals in the Distribution System

Reactions initiated in a water treatment plant may not achieve chemical equilibrium at the treatment site. Thus, entirely new reactions may be initiated between treatment chemicals and extraneous substances in the distribution system. The potential for systemic chemical change through homogeneous and heterogeneous chemical reaction is too large to support the sanguine notion that water quality leaving a treatment plant is identical to that flowing from individual consumer outlets (Larson, 1966).

The reactions of chlorine with organic carbon in the treatment plant (Rook, 1974; Thomason et al., 1978) and with model organic compounds (Larson and Rockwell, 1979; Norwood et al., 1980; Rook, 1974) have received increased attention in recent years. Studies have been focused on reactions in the plant itself or on reactions under simulated treatment plant conditions. Emphasis has been placed on the apparently ubiquitous trihalomethane reaction product. Unfortunately, there are only limited data on the continued reactions of chlorine in actual distribution systems. There are more limited experimental data on the effects of ozone (Sievers et al., 1977) and chlorine dioxide (Gordon et al., 1972; Stevens and Symons, 1976) on selected organic structures and treated river water. Virtually no scientific data exist on the reactions of other disinfectants, e.g., ozone, chloramines, and chlorine dioxide, in actual distribution systems.

Therefore, this section is necessarily limited to the few reports of extended chlorine-trihalomethane reactions in distribution systems and the reactions of chlorine residuals with organic substrates that may exist in distribution systems.

The rapid hydrolysis of chlorine (Reaction 1) is well documented, and the equilibrium constant (3.96×10^4 at 25°C) requires that very little molecular chlorine be present at pH values above 3 and total chlorine concentrations below 1,000 μg/liter (Morris, 1967):

$$Cl_2 + H_2O \rightarrow H^+ + Cl^- + HOCl. \qquad (1)$$

Similarly, the initial reaction of chlorine with ammonia in aqueous solutions is rapid (Weil and Morris, 1949):

$$HOCl + NH_3 \rightarrow NH_2Cl + H_2O. \qquad (2)$$

When concentrations of ammonia are low, this reaction is followed by further and slower chloramine reactions, which eventually oxidize ammonia nitrogen to N_2 with subsequent loss of oxidant (Wei and Morris, 1974). The latter reactions can occur in the distribution system along with chlorine exchange reactions with organic nitrogen (Wajon and Morris, 1980).

Most studies of chlorine interactions with nitrogen compounds have focused on reactions with ammonia. In most high-quality raw water, only a small part of the total nitrogen is present as free ammonia. Reactions with organic nitrogen compounds involve both cleavage of compounds such as protein and heterocyclic nitrogen-containing compounds and the formation of N-chloro organic species (Morris, 1967), which may be analytically mistaken as free chloramines. There are insufficient data to permit further characterization of these reactions or their effects on water quality in distribution systems. It is clear from even the earliest data on hypochlorite ion and aquatic humic reactions that the ultimate concentration of total trihalomethanes (TTHM) is a function of reaction time, temperature, and pH, given an initial total aqueous carbon value and the presence of chlorine as hypochlorite ion. The analytical methodology for TTHM recognizes these variables and distinguishes between trihalomethane values measured at any point in time (instantaneous THM) and those values for samples held in bottles for longer periods (5–7 days) (THM formation potential) (Stevens and Symons, 1976). Recent studies (Brett and Calverly, 1979; DeMarco, personal communication, 1980) have verified that THM values actually increase with residence time in distribution systems as long as both chlorine and organic precursors are available.

It cannot be ascertained whether this phenomenon is due to simple homogeneous reaction kinetics of the humic materials and hypochlorite ion or to more complex heterogeneous reactions controlled by the physical size and shape of the humic macromolecules. It is also possible that complex homogeneous reactions occur with rate-controlling steps involving the production of chloroform from several sites in the humic macromolecules, the reactivities of which are dependent on partial oxidation by hypochlorite ion. It is attractive to assume that the THM increase is not due solely to additional reaction of hypochlorite ion with extraneous organic precursors in distribution systems, since good correlations have been observed for municipal systems (Brett and Calverley, 1979) between treatment plant effluent samples aged in the laboratory and samples withdrawn from the distribution system after equivalent periods. In these cases, supported by data on real systems, samples at the consumer tap (3 days system residence) may be approximately twice the THM values leaving the plant (Brett and Calverley, 1979).

Reaction of hypochlorite ion with extraneous organic material in a distribution system is probable, although the dominant reaction products may not be THM's. Organic nitrogen compounds have already been mentioned and additional humic input from soil contact should not be disregarded.

Humic/hypochlorite ion reactions form a variety of other chlorinated and unchlorinated reaction products in laboratory experiments (Table III-22). Since the rates of these processes have not been investigated, it is

TABLE III-22 Nonvolatile Reaction Products of
Humic Materials and Hypochlorite Ion[a,b]

Chlorinated	Nonchlorinated
2-Chloropropanoic acid	Benzoic acid
Dichloroacetic acid	Hydroxytoluene
Trichloroacetic acid	Trihydroxybenzene
1-Chloroprop-2-ene-	Hydroxybenzoic acid
1,3-dicarboxylic acid	Benzene dicarboxylic acid
2,3-Dichlorosuccinic acid	Benzene tricarboxylic acid
Dichloromaleic acid	Benzene tetracarboxylic acid
Dichlorofumaric acid	Benzene pentacarboxylic acid

[a] From Christman et al., 1980.
[b] Analytical procedure involved methylation with diazomethane. Therefore, all acids were identified as their methyl esters.

not possible to state whether their concentrations might be expected to increase in distribution systems. Indeed, investigators have not even searched for them in real water distribution systems.

As discussed above, the ubiquity of PAH's in water distribution systems is well known (Blumer, 1976). They may enter drinking water via atmospheric deposition in open reservoirs or through leaching from lining materials in distribution systems.

The presence of hypochlorite ion in distribution systems may affect the qualitative distribution of the PAH's in drinking water. Alben (1980b) reported that abundant oxygenated and halogenated PAH's were found in chlorinated coal tar leachate samples, whereas parent PAH's, alkyl- and nitrogen-substituted PAH's, were predominant in unchlorinated samples. At chlorination levels of 50 mg/liter, the dominant PAH in leachate samples was fluorene, whereas phenanthrene dominated unchlorinated samples. Carlson et al. (1975, 1978) have shown that exposure of PAH's to aqueous chlorine reduces their concentration and produces material more lipophilic than the parent hydrocarbon (Table III-23). The relevance of the reactions and reaction products listed in Table III-23 to real distribution systems has not been established.

The effect of increased lipophilicity on bioaccumulation factors is unknown as is the nature of the effect of chlorine substitution on carcinogenicity of the compounds. However, it is known that the carcinogenicity of chemical compounds is enhanced by the halogen content.

The growth of algae in the reservoirs of distribution systems may result in the release of significant quantities of metabolic products into the water. The excretion of a wide variety of relatively complex organic structures is apparently common to almost all species of algae and is not confined to stressed cells (Barnes, 1978). Excretion of glycolate by *Chlorella* and *Chlamydomonas* is well documented, and green algae tend to reduce glycolate excretion in favor of higher molecular weight compounds as the cultures age. Many other types of compounds have been identified in cultures of various species (Table III-24).

Decomposition of algal biomass is another source of reactive organic material. Approximately one-half of the biomass may be converted to soluble, short-chain fatty acids in the presence of oxygen and bacteria. The remainder may be converted to refractory, humic-like substances. The reactivity of these materials with hypochlorite ion or with chloramines is virtually unexplored.

SUMMARY AND CONCLUSIONS

Although one can describe possible reactions between various organic substrates and different oxidants in distribution systems, hard scientific data on real distribution systems are extremely limited. Data suggest that THM concentrations continue to increase in the distribution system as long as both organic precursors and chlorine are present. It is probable that the nonvolatile reaction products of humic material and chlorine also increase in distribution systems, although there are no data for real systems.

It is attractive to assume that chlorine will react with trace amounts of other organic substrates in various distribution systems, e.g., PAH's from

TABLE III-23   Chlorination Products of Selected
Polynuclear Aromatic Hydrocarbons[a]

PAH	Chlorine, mg/liter	PAH, ng/liter	Product
Anthracene	2.0	552	Anthraquinone
Phenanthrene	19.3	820	9-Chlorophenanthrene
Fluoranthene	17.7	824	2-Hydroxy-3-chloro-fluoranthene
1-Methylphenanthrene	21	994	1-Methyl-9-chloro-phenanthrene
1-Methylnaphthalene	24	531	1-Chloro-4-methyl-naphthalene
Fluorene	24	1,166	2-Chlorofluorene

[a] From Carlson *et al.*, 1978.

TABLE III-24   Some Extracellular Products of Algae[a]

Compound Type	Examples
Acid salts	Malate, glycerate, lactate, citrate, oxalate, mesotartrate
Ketoacids	α-Ketoglutaric, α-ketosuccinic, pyruvic, hydroxypyruvic, α-ketobutyric, α-ketovaleric
N-Compounds	Proteins, peptides, nucleic acids, free amino acids
Carbohydrates	Arabinose, glucose, mannitol, glycerol, complex polysaccharides
Lipids	C_{16} fatty acids (from *Ochromonas damica*)
Enzymes and phosphorus compounds	Acid and alkaline phosphomonoesterase (several species), high-molecular-weight organophosphorus compounds
Vitamins	Ascorbate, pantothenate, nicotinate, thiamine, biotin
Volatiles	Formaldehyde, acetaldehyde, methyl ethyl ketone, furfuraldehyde, acetone, valeraldehyde, heptanal, geosmin
Miscellaneous compounds	2,9-Dicetyl-9-azobicyclo[4.2.1.]non-2,3-ene (very fast death factor; from *Anabaene flosaquae*)

[a] From Barnes, 1978.

pipe linings or excretion products from algae in open reservoirs. Unfortunately, no existing experimental evidence would permit testing of these assumptions.

REFERENCES

A-C Pipe Producers Association. 1980. A/C Pipe and Drinking Water. A-C Pipe Producers Association, Arlington, Va. 20 pp.

Ackerman, J. 1980. Bellotti weighs suit over water pipe hazard. The Boston Globe, June 16, 1980, pp. 17, 24.

Alben, K. 1980a. Coal tar coatings of storage tanks. A source of contamination of the potable water supply. Environ. Sci. Technol. 14:468–470.

Alben, K. 1980b. Gas chromatographic mass spectrometric analysis of chlorination effects on commercial coal tar lechate. Anal. Chem. 52:1825–1828

American National Standard Institute. 1980. American National Standard for Cement-Mortar Lining for Ductile-Iron and Gray-Iron Pipe and Fittings for Water. Standard A21.4-80. American National Standard Institute, New York.

American Petroleum Institute. 1971. Introduction. Pp. 1–2 in Petroleum Asphalt and Health. Medical Research Report No. EA 7103. American Petroleum Institute, Washington, D.C.

American Society for Testing and Materials. 1974. ASTM Standard Specification for Polyethylene (PE) Plastic Pipe (SDR-PR). ASTM D2239-74. Pp. 132-140 in Annual Book of ASTM Standards. American Society for Testing and Materials, Philadelphia, Pa.

American Society for Testing and Materials. 1976. Standard Methods of Testing Asbestos-Cement Pipe. ASTM C500. American Society for Testing and Materials, Philadelphia, Pa.

American Society for Testing and Materials. 1978. ASTM Standard Specification for Polyvinyl Chloride (PVC) Plastic Pipe (SDR-PR). ASTM D2241-78. Pp. 141-147 in Annual Books of ASTM Standards. American Society for Testing and Materials, Philadelphia, Pa.

American Water Works Association. 1971. Control of Water Quality in Transmission and Distribution Systems—Committee Report. Quality Control in Distribution Systems, AWWA Annual Conference June 17, 1971.

American Water Works Association. 1975a. Specification 4 in. Through 12 in. Polyvinyl Chloride (PVC) Pipe. AWWA C900-75. American Water Works Association, Denver, Colo.

American Water Works Association. 1975b. Standards Committee on Asbestos-Cement Pressure Pipe. AWWA standard for asbestos-cement transmission pipe, for water and other liquids. AWWA C402-75. J. Am. Water Works Assoc. 67(8):462-467.

American Water Works Association. 1978a. AWWA Standard for Coal-Tar Epoxy Coating System for the Interior and Exterior of Steel Water Pipe. ANSI/AWWA C210-78. American Water Works Association, Denver, Colo. 9 pp.

American Water Works Association. 1978b. AWWA Standard for Polybutylene (PB) Pressure Pipe, Tubing, and Fittings, 1/2 in. Through 3 in., for Water. AWWA C902-78. First Edition American Water Works Association, Denver, Colo. 11 pp.

American Water Works Association. 1979. The use of plastics in distribution systems. Committee on the Use of Plastics in Distribution Systems. J. Am. Water Works Assoc. 71:373-375.

American Water Works Association. 1980. AWWA Standard for Asbestos-Cement Distribution Pipe, 4 in. Through 16 in. (100 mm Through 16 in.) (100 mm Through 400 mm) NPS, for Water and Other Liquids. AWWA C400-80. American Water Works Association, Denver, Colo.

American Water Works Association Research Foundation. 1974. A study of the problem of asbestos in water. J. Am. Water Works Assoc. 66:1-22.

Andelman, J.B. 1974. The effect of water treatment and distribution of trace element concentrations. Pp. 423-440 in A.J. Rubin, ed. Chemistry of Water Supply, Treatment, and Distribution. Ann Arbor Science Publishers, Inc., Ann Arbor, Mich.

Anderson, D.R., D.D. Row, and G.E. Sindelar. 1973. Iron and manganese studies of Nebraska water supplies. J. Am. Water Works Assoc. 65:635-641.

Anonymous. 1971. Control of water quality in transmission and distribution systems. Committee report. Quality control in distribution. J. Am. Water Works Assoc. 63:741-742.

Anonymous. 1977. Gesundheitliche Beurteilung von Kunststoffen und anderen nichtmetallischen Werkstoffen im Rahmen des Lebensmittel und Bedarfsgegenständegestzes für den Trinkwasserbereich. Bundesgesundheitblatt 7:10-13.

Anonymous. 1980. TCE leaching prompts EPA to seek halt to installation of vinyl lined pipes. Chem. Regulation Reporter 4(3):63-64.

Aulenbach, D.B. 1971. Determining phosphate additive for iron control in water. J. Am. Water Works Assoc. 63:197-198.

Banov, A., and H.J. Schmidt, Jr. 1978. Techniques and materials for preventing corrosion. In R.L. Sanks, ed. Water Treatment Plant Design for the Practicing Engineer. Ann Arbor Science Publishers, Inc., Ann Arbor, Mich.

Barnes, D.B. 1978. Trihalomethane-Forming Potential of Algal Extracellular Products and Biomass. Master's Thesis, Virginia Polytechnic Institute and State University, Blacksburg, Va.

Bean, E.L. 1970. Water quality goals and corrosion by soft waters. Pp. 1-16 in Control of Corrosion by Soft Waters. Education Committee, American Water Works Association, and U.S. Public Health Service, Environmental Control Association, Washington, D.C.

Blumer, M. 1976. Polycyclic aromatic compounds in nature. Sci. Am. 234(3):34-45.

Booth, G.H., and A.K. Tiller. 1960. Polarization studies of mild steel in cultures of sulfate-reducing bacteria. Trans. Faraday Soc. 56:1689.

Brett, R.W., and R.A. Calverley. 1979. A one-year survey of trihalomethane concentration changes within a distribution system. J. Am. Water Works Assoc. 71:515-520.

Brotsky, B. 1977. Interior maintenance of elevated storage tanks. J. Am. Water Works Assoc. 69:506-510.

Buelow, R.W., J.R. Millette, E.F. McFarren, and J.M. Symons. 1980. The behavior of asbestos-cement pipe under various water quality conditions: A progress report. J. Am. Water Works Assoc. 72:91-102.

Bull, R.J., and G.F. Craun. 1977. Health effects associated with manganese in drinking water. J. Am. Water Works Assoc. 69:662-663.

Camp, T.R., ed. 1963. Water and Its Impurities. Reinhold Publishing Corp., New York. 355 pp.

Carlson, R.M., R.E. Carlson, H.L. Kopperman, and R. Caple. 1975. Facile incorporation of chlorine into aromatic systems during aqueous chlorination processes. Environ. Sci. Technol. 9:674-675.

Carlson, R.M., R. Cople, A. R. Oyler, K.J. Welch, D.L. Bodenner, and R. Liukkonen. 1978. Aqueous chlorination products of polynuclear aromatic hydrocarbons. Pp. 59-65 in R.L. Jolley, H. Gorchev, and D.H. Hamilton, Jr., eds. Water Chlorination: Environmental Impact and Health Effects. Vol. 2. Ann Arbor Science Publishers, Inc., Ann Arbor, Mich.

Christman, R.F., J.D. Johnson, F.K. Pfaender, D.L. Norwood, M.R. Webb, J.R. Haas, and M.J. Bobenrieth. 1980. Chemical identification of aquatic humic chlorination products. Pp. 75-83 in R.L. Jolly, W.A. Brungs, R.B. Cumming, and V.A. Jacobs, eds. Water Chlorination: Environmental Impact and Health Effects. Vol. 3. Ann Arbor Science Publishers, Inc., Ann Arbor, Mich.

Cook, P.M., G.E. Glass, and J.H. Tucker. 1974. Asbestiform amphibole minerals: Detection and measurement of high concentrations in municipal water supplies. Science 185:853-855.

Cooper, R.C., M. Kanarek, J. Murchio, P. Conforti, L. Jackson, R. Collard, and D. Lysmer. 1978. Asbestos in Domestic Water Supplies in Five California Counties. Progress Report for Period April 25, 1977 to June 30, 1978, Contract No. R804366-02. U.S. Environmental Protection Agency, EHS Publ. No. 78-2. School of Public Health, Environmental Health Sciences, University of California, Berkeley.

Courchene, J.E., and G.J. Kirmeyer. 1978. Seattle Internal Corrosion Control Plan. Phase I. Summary. Seattle Water Department, Seattle, Wash.

Craun, G.F., and J.R. Millette. 1977. Exposure to asbestos fibers in water distribution systems. Pp. 1-13 in Proceedings of the American Water Works Association 97th Annual Conference, Anaheim, Calif., May 8-13, 1977. American Water Works Association, Denver, Colo.

Cunningham, H.M., and R. Pontefract. 1971. Asbestos fibres in beverages and drinking water. Nature 232:332-333.

Dangel, R.A. 1975. Study of Corrosion Products in the Seattle Water Department Tolt

Distribution System. EPA-670/2-75-036. U.S. Environmental Protection Agency, Cincinnati, Ohio. 22 pp.

Dart, F.J., and P.D. Foley. 1970. Preventing iron deposition with sodium silicate. J. Am. Water Works Assoc. 62:663-668

Dart, F.J., and P.D. Foley. 1972. Silicate as Fe, Mn deposition preventative in distribution systems. J. Am. Water Works Assoc. 64:244-249.

Davis, J.B. 1967. Petroleum Microbiology. Elsevier Publishing Company, New York.

Dressman, R.C., and E.F. McFarren. 1978. Determination of vinyl chloride migration from polyvinyl chloride pipe into water. J. Am. Water Works Assoc. 70:29-30.

Eklund, G., B. Josefsson, and C. Roos. 1978. The leaching of volatile organic compounds from different types of water pipes. Vatten 34:207-208.

Farish, C.A. 1969. Plastic pipe and water quality. J. Am. Water Works Assoc. 61:480-482.

Goldfarb, A.S., J. Konz, and P. Walker. 1979. Interior Coatings in Potable Water Tanks and Pipelines. Coal Tar Based Materials and Their Alternatives. MTR 7803. Prepared for EPA Criteria and Standards Division, Office of Drinking Water, EPA Contract 570/9-79-001. Mitre Corp., McLean, Va. 140 pp.

Gordon, G., R.G. Kieffer, and D.H. Rosenblatt. 1972. The chemistry of chlorine dioxide. Pp. 201-286 in S.J. Lippard, ed. Progress in Inorganic Chemistry. Vol. 15. Wiley-Interscience, New York.

Hadley, R.F. 1948. Corrosion by micro-organisms in aqueous and soil environments. Pp. 466-481 in H.H. Uhlig, ed. The Corrosion Handbook. Sponsored by the Electrochemical Society, Inc., New York. John Wiley & Sons, Inc., New York.

Hallenbeck, W.H., E.H. Chen, C.S. Hesse, K. Patel-Mandlik, and A.R. Wolff. 1978. Is chrysotile asbestos released from asbestos-cement pipe into drinking water? J. Am. Water Works Assoc. 70:97-102.

Haring, B.J.A. 1978. Human exposure to metals released from water distribution systems, with particular reference to water consumption patterns. Trib. CEBEDEAU No. 4l9:349-355.

Henry, C.R. 1950. Preventioin of the settlement of iron. J. Am. Water Works Assoc. 42:887-896.

Hoyt, B.P., G.J. Kirmeyer, and J.E. Courchene. 1979. Evaluating home plumbing corrosion problems. J. Am. Water Works Assoc. 71:720-725.

Hudson, H.E., Jr., and F.W. Gilcreas. 1976. Health and economic aspects of water hardness and corrosiveness. J. Am. Water Works Assoc. 68:201-204.

Iverson, W.P. 1974. Microbial Corrosion of Iron in Microbial Iron Metabolism. Academic Press, Inc., San Francisco, Calif.

James M. Montgomery, Consulting Engineers, Inc. 1980. Solvent Leaching From Potable Water Plastic Pipes. Final Report. Prepared for the Hazard Alert System, California Department of Health Services/Department of Industrial Relations. James M. Montgomery, Consulting Engineers, Inc., Pasadena, Calif. 67 pp.

Karalekas, P.C., Jr., G.F. Craun, A.F. Hammonds, C.R. Ryan, and D. J. Worth. 1976. Lead and other trace metals in drinking water in the Boston Metropolitan area. J. N. Engl. Water Works Assoc. 90:150-172.

Karalekas, P.C., Jr., C.R. Ryan, C.D. Larson, and F.B. Taylor. 1978. Alternative methods for controlling the corrosion of lead pipe. J. N. Engl. Water Works Assoc. 92:159-178.

Kay, G.H. 1974. Asbestos in drinking water. J. Am. Water Works Assoc. 66:513-514.

Kennedy Engineers. 1978. Internal Corrosion Study. Prepared for City of Seattle Water Department, Seattle, Wash.

Kimm, V.J. 1978. Memorandum on Coal Tar Pitch Coating, Pascagoula, Miss., to Gary Hutchinson, Water Supply Representative, Region IV, Atlanta, Ga.

Kirmeyer, G.J., G.S. Logsdon, J.E. Courchene, and R.R. Jones. 1979. Removal of naturally occurring asbestos fibers from Seattle's Cascade Mountain water source. Pp. 903-927 in Proceedings of the American Water Works Association Annual Conference, Part II, June 24-29, 1979, San Francisco, Calif.

Kupyrov, V.N., V.I., Vorobets, R.K. Gakal, and S.N. Starchenko. 1977. Hygienic characteristics of some polymer coatings suggested for use in drinking water supply. Gig. Sanit. No. 3:96-97.

Lane, R.W., and C.H. Neff. 1969. Materials selection for piping in chemically treated water systems. Materials Protection 8:27-30.

Langelier, W.F. 1936. The analytical control of anti-corrosion water treatment. J. Am. Water Works Assoc. 28:1500-1521.

Larson, R.A., and A.L. Rockwell. 1979. Chloroform and chlorophenol production by decarboxylation of natural acids during aqueous chlorination. Environ. Sci. Technol. 13:325-329.

Larson, T.E. 1966. Deterioration of water quality in distribution systems. J. Am. Water Works Assoc. 58:1307-1316.

Larson, T.E. 1971. Corrosion phenomena—Causes and cures. Pp. 295-312 in Water Quality and Treatment. A Handbook of Public Water Supplies. Third Edition. Prepared by the American Water Works Assocation. McGraw-Hill Book Co., Inc., New York.

Lee, S.H., and J.T. O'Connor. 1975. Biologically mediated deterioration of water quality in distribution systems. American Water Works Association 95th Annual Conference Proceedings. Paper 22-6. American Water Works Association, Denver, Colo.

Levine, R.J. 1978. Asbestos—An Information Resource. DHEW Publ. No. (NIH) 79-1681. U.S. Department of Health, Education, and Welfare, Bethesda, Md.

Macrae, I.C., and J.F. Edwards. 1972. Adsorption of colloidal iron by bacteria. Appl. Microbiol. 24:819.

McCabe, L.J. 1970. Corrosion by soft water: Metal levels found in distribution samples. Presented at Seminar on Control of Corrosion by Soft Waters. Education Committee of American Water Works Association and U.S. Public Health Service, Washington, D.C. 6 pp.

McCabe, L.J., and J.R. Millette. 1979. Health effects and prevalence of asbestos fibers in drinking water. In Proceedings of the American Water Works Association Annual Conference, June 24-29, 1979, San Francisco, Calif.

McClanahan, M. 1978. Water Supply Branch, EPA Region IV. Memorandum on Coal Tar Pitch Coating, Pascagoula, Miss., to J.A. Cotruvo, Director, Criteria and Standards Division, Office of Drinking Water, U.S. Environmental Protection Agency, Washington, D.C.

McFarren, E.F., R.W. Buelow, R.C. Thurnau, M. Gardels, R.K. Sorrell, P. Snyder, and R.C. Dressman. 1977. Water quality deterioration in the distribution system. Pp. 1-10 in Proceedings of the 5th Annual AWWA Water Quality Technology Conference, Kansas City, Mo., Dec. 4-7, 1977. American Water Works Association, Denver, Colo.

Michaels, L., and S.S. Chissick, eds. 1979. Asbestos. Properties, Applications, and Hazards. Vol. 1. John Wiley & Sons, Inc. 568 pp

Miller, H.C., W.J. Barrett, and R.H. James. 1980. Investigation of potential water contamination by petroleum asphalt coatings in ductile-iron pipe. Pp. 561-578 in 1980 Annual Conference Proceedings; Water for the World Challenge of the 80's. Atlanta, Ga., June 15-20, 1980. American Water Works Association, Denver, Colo.

Miller, J.D.A., and A.K. Tiller. 1970. Microbial corrosion of buried and immersed metal. In J.D.A. Miller, ed. Microbial Aspects of Metallurgy. American Elsevier Publishing Co., Inc., New York.

Millette, J.R., P.J. Clark, and M.F. Pansing. 1979. Exposure to Asbestos from Drinking

Water in the United States. EPA-600/1-79-028. Health Effects Research Laboratory, U.S. Environmental Protection Agency, Cincinnati, Ohio. 87 pp.

Millette, J.R., A.F. Hammonds, M.F. Pansing, E.C. Hansen, and P.J. Clark. 1980. Aggressive water: Assessing the extent of the problem. J. Am. Water Works Assoc. 72:262-266.

Morris, J.C. 1967. Kinetics of reactions between aqueous chlorine and nitrogen compounds. Pp. 23-53 in S.D. Faust and J.V. Hunter, eds. Principles and Applications of Water Chemistry. Proceedings of the Fourth Rudolfs Research Conference, Rutgers—The State University, New Brunswick, N.J. John Wiley & Sons, New York.

Mullen, E.D., and J.A. Ritter. 1980. Monitoring and controlling corrosion by potable water. J. Am. Water Works Assoc. 72:286-291.

National Academy of Sciences. 1977. Drinking Water and Health. A Report of the Safe Drinking Water Committee, Advisory Center on Toxicology, Assembly of Life Sciences, National Research Council, National Academy of Sciences, Washington, D.C. 939 pp.

Norwood, D.L., J.D. Johnson, R.F. Christman, J.R. Hass, and M.J. Bobenrieth. 1980. Reactions of chlorine with selected aromatic models of aquatic humic material. Environ. Sci. Technol. 14:187-190.

O'Connor, J.T. 1971. Iron and manganese. Pp. 378-396 in Water Quality and Treatment. A Handbook of Public Water Supplies. Third Edition. Prepared by the American Water Works Association. McGraw-Hill Book Co., Inc., New York.

Olsen, H.L. 1974. Asbestos in potable-water supplies. J. Am. Water Works Assoc. 66:515-518.

Olsen, E., and W. Sybalski. 1949. Aerobic microbiological corrosion of water pipes, Parts I and II. Acta Chemica Scand. 3:1094.

Packham, R.F. 1971a. The leaching of toxic stabilizers from unplasticized PVC water pipe. I. A critical study of laboratory test procedures. Water Treat. Exam. 20(Pt.2):108-124.

Packham, R.F. 1971b. The leaching of toxic stabilizers from unplasticized PVC water pipe. II. A survey of lead levels in uPVC distribution systems. Water Treat. Exam. 20(3):144-151.

Packham, R. 1971c. The leaching of toxic stabilizers from unplasticized PVC water pipes. III. The measurement of extractable lead in uPVC pipes. Water Treat. Exam. 20(Pt. 3):152-161.

Radziui, J.V., S.J. Campbell, R.M. Brinkos, and E.J. Shervin. 1967. A liquid cement-calcite pipe-coating process. J. Am. Water Works Assoc. 59:1413-1426.

Rawls, R.L. 1975. PVC makers confident on food-contact uses. Chem. Eng. News 53(37):11-12.

Robeck, G.G. 1978. Health Effects of PAH's. Memorandum to J. Garner, Director, Health Effects Research Laboratory, U.S. Environmental Protection Agency, Washington, D.C.

Rook, J.J. 1974. Formation of haloforms during chlorination of natural waters. Soc. Water Treat. Exam. J. 23:234-243.

Rook, J.J. 1977. Chlorination reactions of fulvic acids in natural waters. Environ. Sci. Technol. 11:478-482.

Saxena, J. 1979. Technical Progress Report for Period February 10, 1979-October 10, 1979. Study of the Water Distribution System as a Potential Source of Mutagens/Carcinogens in Drinking Waters. EPA Grant No. R-806 413. U.S. Environmental Protection Agency, Washington, D.C.

Saxena, J., D.K. Basu, and D.J. Schwartz. 1978. Methods development and monitoring of polynuclear aromatic hydrocarbons in selected U.S. waters. Pp. 119-126 in J. Albarges, ed. Proceedings of the International Congress on Analytical Techniques in Environmental Chemistry, Barcelona, Spain, Nov. 27-30, 1978. Pergamon Press, New York.

Schock, M.R., and R.W. Buelow. 1980. The behavior of asbestos-cement pipe under various water quality conditions; A progress report: Part 2-Theoretical considerations. Unpublished.

Schwartz, D.J., J. Saxena, and F.C. Kopfler. 1979. Water distribution system, a new source of mutagens in drinking waters. Environ. Sci. Technol. 13:1138-1141.

Schweitzer, G.W. 1970. Zinc-glassy phosphate inhibitors in potable water. Pp. 1-4 in Control of Corrosion by Soft Waters. Presented by Education Committee, American Water Works Association, and U.S. Public Health Service, Washington, D.C.

Sievers, R.E., R.M. Barkley, G.A. Eiceman, R.H. Shapiro, H.F. Walton, K.J. Kolonko, and L.R. Field. 1977. Environmental trace analysis of organics in water by glass capillary column chromatography and ancillary techniques. Products of ozonolysis. J. Chromatogr. 142:745-754.

Sorrell, R.K., R.C. Dressman, and E.F. McFarren. 1977. High pressure liquid chromatography for the measurement of polynuclear aromatic hydrocarbons in water. Pp. 1-22 in Proceedings of the AWWA Water Quality Technology Conference, Kansas City, Mo., Dec. 4-7, 1977. American Water Works Association, Denver, Colo.

Sorrell, R.K., R. Reding, and H.J. Brass. 1979. Analysis of polynuclear aromatic hydrocarbons in selected water supplies. Pp. 318-320 in Papers Presented at the 177th Meeting of the American Chemical Society, Division of Environmental Chemistry: Symposium on Analysis of Polar and High Molecular Weight Compounds in Water, held in Honolulu, Hawaii, April 1-6, 1979. American Chemical Society, Washington, D.C.

Sorrell, R.K., H.J. Brass, and R. Reding. 1980. A review of occurrences and treatment of polynuclear aromatic hydrocarbons. Environ. Int. 4:245-254.

Stevens, A.A., and J.M. Symons. 1976. Measurement of Trihalomethane and Precursor Concentration Changes Occurring During Water Treatment and Distribution. Appendix 4 to Interim Treatment Guide for the Control of Chloroform and Other Trihalomethanes. U.S. Environmental Protection Agency, Washington, D.C.

Stroud, T.F. 1980. President's Message. Ductile Iron Pipe News. Ductile Iron Pipe Research Association, Oak Brook, Ill. 20 pp.

Tarter, M.E. 1979. Data Analysis of Drinking Water Asbestos Fiber Size. Final Report. Environmental Protection Agency No. 600/1-79/020. National Technical Information Service, Springfield, Va. 71 pp.

Thomason, M., M. Shoults, W. Bertsch, and G. Holzer. 1978. Study of water treatment effects on organic volatiles in drinking water. J. Chromatogr. 158:437-447.

Tracy, E.L. 1950. Observations on water samples from cement-asbestos pipe systems in Vermont. J. N. Engl. Water Works Assoc. 64:164-178.

Tuovinen, O.H., K.S. Button, A. Vuorinen, L. Carlson, D.M. Mair, and L.A. Yut. 1980. Bacterial, chemical, and mineralogical characteristics of tubercles in distribution pipelines. J. Am. Water Works Assoc. 72:626-635.

Uhlig, H.H., ed. 1971. Corrosion and Corrosion Control: An Introduction to Corrosion Science and Engineering. Second Edition. John Wiley & Sons, New York. 419 pp.

U.S. Environmental Protection Agency. 1979a. Interim Primary Drinking Water Regulations; Amendments. July 19, 1979. Fed. Reg. 44:42246-42259.

U.S. Environmental Protection Agency. 1979b. National Secondary Drinking Water Regulations. July 19, 1979. Fed. Reg. 44:42195-42202.

U.S. Environmental Protection Agency. 1979c. Quarterly Reports. Health Effects Research Laboratory, U.S. Environmental Protection Agency, Cincinnati, Ohio.

U.S. Environmental Protection Agency. 1979d. Statements of Basis and Purpose for Proposed Amendments to the National Interim Primary Drinking Water Regulations and Proposed Special Monitoring Requirements. Office of Drinking Water, Criteria and Standards Division, Municipal Environmental Research Laboratory, U.S. Environmental Protection Agency, Cincinnati, Ohio.

U.S. Environmental Protection Agency. 1980. Interim primary drinking water regulations; Amendments. August 27, 1980. Fed. Reg. 45:57332–57357.

Wagner, J., Jr. 1970. Instrumentation for evaluating corrosion and corrosion inhibitors. Pp. 1–4 in Control of Corrosion by Soft Waters. Presented by Education Committee, American Water Works Association, and U.S. Public Health Service, Washington, D.C.

Wajon, J.E., and J.C. Morris. 1980. Bromamination chemistry: Rates of formation of NH_2Br and some N-bromamino acids. Pp. 171–181 in R.L. Jolley, W.A. Brungs, R.B. Cumming, and V.A. Jacobs, eds. Water Chlorination: Environmental Impact and Health Effects. Vol. 3. Ann Arbor Science Publishers, Inc., Ann Arbor, Mich.

Wallcave, L., H. Garcia, R. Feldman, W. Lijinsky, and P. Shubrik. 1971. Skin tumorigenesis in mice by petroleum asphalts and coal-tar pitches of known polynuclear aromatic hydrocarbon content. Toxicol. Appl. Pharmacol. 18:41–52.

Wallington, R.H. 1971. Protective coatings for pipes and tanks. Water Treat. Exam. 20:209–219.

Webster, I. 1974. The ingestion of asbestos fibers. Environ. Health Perspect. 9:199–201.

Weber, W.J., Jr, and W. Stumm, 1965. Formation of silicato-iron (III) complex in aqueous solution. J. Inorg. Nuclear Chem. 27:237–239.

Wei, I.W., and J.C. Morris. 1974. Dynamics of breakpoint chlorination. Pp. 297–332 in A.J. Rubin, ed. Chemistry of Water Supply, Treatment, and Distribution. Ann Arbor Science Publishers, Inc., Ann Arbor, Mich.

Weil, I., and J.C. Morris. 1949. Equilibrium studies on N-chloro compounds. II. The base strength of N-chlorodialkylamines and of monochloramine. J. Am. Chem. Soc. 71:3123–3126.

World Health Organization. 1971. International Standards for Drinking Water. Third Edition. World Health Organization, Geneva. 70 pp.

Zoeteman, B.C., and B.J. Haring. 1976. The nature and impact of deterioration of the quality of drinking water after treatment and prior to consumption. Report prepared for the Commission of the European Communities, National Institute for Water Supply, Voorburg, The Netherlands. 123 pp.

Zoldak, J.J. 1978. Analysis of Drinking Water for Trace Level Quantities of Organic Pollutants. Thesis, Miami University, Oxford, Ohio.

IV

Biological Quality of Water in the Distribution System

One objective of the physical and chemical treatment of water intended for public consumption is to reduce the levels of total coliforms to less than 1 coliform/100 ml. Such treatment has proved to be an effective barrier against transmission of infectious disease by water. Commonly used processes such as coagulation, sedimentation, sand filtration, and disinfection yield a water essentially free of disease-causing viruses, bacteria, and protozoa.

The system of pipes, valves, and connections designed to distribute the water to the consumer is disinfected but not sterilized during construction. Thus, drinking water is not sterile and may contain living material that may influence water quality in the distribution network.

In a well-designed, -constructed, and -operated water distribution system, changes in water quality will be minimal, and water provided to the consumer will be similar to that leaving the treatment plant. In poorly designed, constructed, and operated water systems, water quality will deteriorate in the distribution system and result in consumer complaints. In the worst cases, outbreaks of disease may result.

BIOLOGICAL MATERIAL IN WATER DISTRIBUTION SYSTEMS

The nature of the biological material in water distribution systems results from a complex series of physical, chemical, and biological reactions (Figure IV-1). Living organisms and nutrients may enter the distribution system with the raw water, during the treatment processes, or from sources such as leaks, cross-connections, back-siphonages, and open reservoirs. Growth may occur at or near the pipe surface, the interface of suspended particulates, and within the water itself. The chemical and biological products leave the distribution system at the consumer's tap.

Biofilms

Fouling refers to the undesirable formation of inorganic and/or organic deposits on pipe surfaces. These deposits can induce water quality changes, increase the rate of corrosion at the surface, and increase the fluid frictional resistance at the surface.

There are several types of fouling and combinations thereof: crystalline or precipitation fouling, corrosion fouling, particulate fouling, chemical reaction fouling, and biological fouling (biofouling). Biofouling can result from development of an organic film (biofilm) consisting of microorganisms and their products and from assorted detritus.

Development of an understanding of biofouling from field observations has been limited because of the interaction of several contributing rate processes. The mechanisms of fouling biofilm accumulation may be described as the net result of the following:

- *Transport and accumulation of material from the bulk fluid to the surface*. Materials can be soluble (microbial nutrients and organic salts) or particulate matter (viable microorganisms, their detritus, or inorganic particles).
- *Microbial growth within the film*. Microbial growth in the biofilm and extracellular polymers produced by the microorganisms contribute to the biofilm deposit and promote adherence of inorganic suspended solids.
- *Fluid shear stress at the surface of the film*. Such forces can limit the overall extent of the fouling deposit by reentraining attached material. The reentrained material can result in significant water quality changes in the pipe.
- *Surface material and roughness of the pipe*. Surface properties of the pipe can influence micro-mixing near the pipe wall and corrosion processes. Some metal surfaces may release toxic components into the biofilm inhibiting growth and/or attachment. Some metals produce loosely held oxide films under the biofilms. When the oxide film sloughs, the biofilm is also removed.
- *Fouling control procedures*. Chlorine, the most commonly used disinfecting chemical, oxidizes biofilm polymers causing disruption and partial removal in the shear stress field. Inactivation of a portion of the microbial

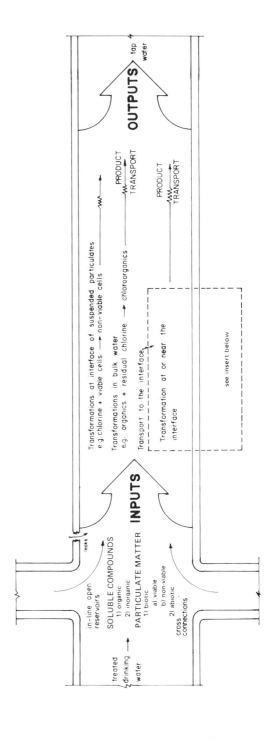

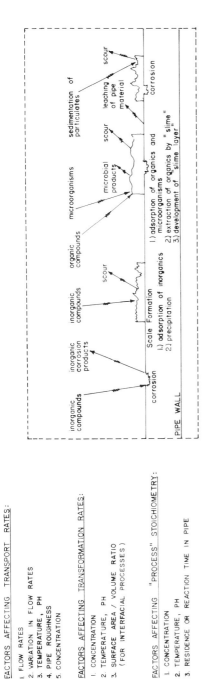

FIGURE IV-1   Schematic of water distribution pipe.

population also occurs. Altered biofilm "roughness" and decreased viable cell numbers will influence "regrowth" rates of the biofilm. Chlorine is also capable of accelerating corrosion processes.

There can be no doubt that biofilms in water supply distribution systems alter water quality. The following changes, or their combination, can occur in the distribution system as a result of biofilm processes:

• decrease in chlorine residual (Larson, 1966; O'Connor et al., 1975);
• increased bacterial counts resulting from loss of chlorine residual (Larson, 1966; O'Connor et al., 1975);
• increased bacterial counts or "regrowth" in the distribution system resulting from detachment of bacteria from the biofilm (Becker, 1975; Russell, 1976);
• reduction in dissolved oxygen content resulting from microbial activity in the biofilm (O'Connor et al., 1975);
• taste and odor changes resulting from products of microbial metabolism within the biofilm or their reaction with chlorine (O'Connor et al., 1975; Silvey et al., 1975);
• "red water" resulting from the activity of iron bacteria (Larson, 1966; O'Connor et al., 1975; Russell, 1976);
• "black water" resulting from the activity of sulfate-reducing bacteria in anaerobic microenvironments within the conduits (Larson, 1966; Lee and O'Connor, 1975); and
• increased "hydraulic roughness," which increases turbulence in the conduit. Increased turbulence increases mass transfer rates at the conduit wall, influencing corrosion rates, leaching rates, and detachment of bacteria from the biofilm (Picologlou et al., 1980).

BIOFILM FORMATION

Biofilm formation is the net result of several physical, chemical, and biological processes including the following:

• transport of solutes to the wetted surface;
• adsorption of solutes at the wetted surface;
• transport of particles (including microbial cells) to the wetted surface;
• attachment of microorganisms to the surface; and
• metabolism and growth of microorganisms immobilized in the biofilm.

The rate of water flow and the concentration of growth-limiting nutrients (i.e., substrate) are the primary environmental variables influencing the rate and extent of biofilm formation. A general discussion of biofilm formation follows, with special attention to problems encountered in water supply distribution systems.

The formation of biofilm begins with transport to and adsorption of organic solutes at the pipe wall. The organic material may be of microbial origin or a component of the raw water supply. Algae and bacteria in the water treatment plant, on the open reservoirs, or within the conduits produce relatively high-molecular-weight organic compounds, primarily polysaccharide in nature. Raw waters frequently contain organic compounds such as tannins or lignins. These polyelectrolytes are surface active and adsorb readily, thereby conditioning the surface. Generally, the polyelectrolytes and the conduit surface are both negatively charged, and firm adsorption of the polyelectrolyte to the surface is mediated by inorganic cations such as calcium, magnesium, and iron.

Microbial cells are transported to the conditioned surface where they attach. Research by Marshall *et al.* (1971) and Zobell (1943) suggests the existence of a two-stage attachment process: reversible adhesion followed by an irreversible attachment. Reversible adhesion refers to an initially weak adhesion of a cell that can still exhibit Brownian motion. Conversely, irreversible attachment is a permanent bonding to the surface, usually aided by the production of extracellular polymers. Marshall (1976) and Corpe (1978) have implicated polysaccharides and glycoproteins in irreversible attachment.

Attached microorganisms assimilate nutrients, synthesize biomass, and produce extracellular products. In many cases, the rate of assimilation of nutrients is limited by the diffusion of nutrients through the biofilm. As a result, a significant concentration gradient exists between the bulk fluid and the pipe wall. When nutrients cannot penetrate the lower layers of the biofilm, the microorganisms in that region lyse. If dissolved oxygen becomes depleted in the biofilm, denitrification and sulfate reduction will occur when nitrate and sulfate are present. The sulfate-reducing organisms have been implicated in accelerated corrosion of pipelines.

At any point in its development, portions of biofilm peel away from the pipe surface and are reentrained in the fluid flow. Detachment is a continuous process of biofilm removal. It is highly dependent on hydrodynamic conditions and is characterized by particle sizes similar to microbial cell diameters. As the biofilm grows thicker, the fluid shear stress at the biofilm interface generally increases and the potential for substrate oxygen or nutrient limitation in the deeper portions is great. These limitations may weaken the biofilm matrix and cause detachment. When the flow is turbulent, the rate at which the biofilm detaches increases as the thickness of the biofilm increases (Trulear and Characklis, 1979). For a given biofilm thickness, detachment rate increases with increasing fluid shear stress. Sloughing, a random massive removal of biofilm, is generally attributed to oxygen/nutrient depletion deep within the biofilms. Sloughing occurs more frequently with thicker, dense films characteristic of laminar flow systems and results in the reentrainment of large aggregates of biofilm.

The detached material consists of microbial cells, their extracellular products, and any other adsorbed or entrapped material within the biofilm.

The rate of water flow and the concentration of growth-limiting nutrient (i.e., substrate) significantly influence the rate and extent of biofilm development. For example,

- high rate of water flow and high concentrations increase transport rate of soluble substrate to the pipe wall;
- high concentrations of substrate increase the rate of metabolic processes within the biofilm;
- high rates of water flow and low concentrations of substrate result in thinner biofilms; and
- high rates of water flow increase the detachment of material from the biofilm.

PROPERTIES AND COMPOSITION

Microorganisms, primarily bacteria, adhere to surfaces ranging from the human tooth and intestine to the metal surface of power plant condenser tubes exposed to turbulent flows of water. The microorganisms "stick" by means of extracellular polymer fibers, which are fabricated and oriented by the cell and extend from the cell surface to form a tangled matrix termed a "glycocalyx" (Costerton et al., 1978). The fibers may conserve and concentrate extracellular enzymes that are necessary for preparing substrate molecules for ingestion, especially high molecular weight or particulate substrate frequently found in natural waters.

The biofilm surface is highly adsorptive, especially because of its polyelectrolyte nature, and can collect significant quantities of silt, clay, or other detritus in natural waters. Biofilms can also accumulate large amounts of heavy metals (Dugan and Pickrum, 1972).

Physical, chemical, and biological properties of biofilms are dependent on the environment to which the attachment surface is exposed. The physical and chemical microenvironments combine to select the prevalent microorganisms which, in turn, modify the microenvironment of the surface.

As colonization proceeds and a biofilm develops, concentration gradients develop within the biofilm and "average" biofilm properties change.

PHYSICAL PROPERTIES

The most fundamental biofilm properties are volume (thickness) and mass. In turbulent flow systems, wet biofilm thickness seldom exceeds 1,000 mm (Picologlou *et al.*, 1980). In laminar flow, biofilms can be several millimeters thick. The biofilm mass can be determined from the wet biofilm thickness if the biofilm dry mass density is known. Biofilm dry mass density reflects the attached dry mass per unit wet biofilm volume. Measured mass values in turbulent flow systems range from 10 to 50 mg/cm^3. In laminar flow, higher values have been observed (Hoehn and Ray, 1973). Biofilm density increases with increasing turbulence (Characklis 1980) and increasing substrate loading (Trulear and Characklis, 1979). The increase in biofilm density with increasing turbulence may be caused by one of the following phenomena:

- selective attachment of only certain microbial species from the available population;
- microbial metabolic response to environmental stress; and
- "squeexing" of loosely bound water from the biofilm by fluid pressure forces.

The relatively low densities of biofilm mass compare well with observed water content of biofilm (Characklis, 1973, 1980; Nimmons, 1979).

The transport properties of biofilm are of critical importance in assessing its effects on mass, heat, and transfer of momentum. Diffusion coefficients for various compounds through microbial aggregates have been reported in the literature, mostly for microbial floc particles. Matson and Characklis (1976) reported variation in the diffusion coefficient for glucose and oxygen with growth rate and carbon-to-nitrogen ratio. The diffusion coefficient of biofilms is most probably related to its density. *In-situ* rheological measurements indicate that the biofilm is viscoelastic with a relatively high viscous modulus (Characklis, 1980). The thermal conductivity of biofilm is not significantly different from that of water (Characklis, 1980).

CHEMICAL PROPERTIES

The inorganic composition of biofilms undoubtedly varies with the chemical composition of the bulk water and probably affects the physical and

TABLE IV-1 Chemical Properties of Biofilms Obtained from Fouled Surfaces Experiencing Excessive Frictional Losses[a]

Water, %	Volatile Fraction, %	Fixed Fraction, %	Silicon, %	Iron, %	Aluminum, %	Calcium, %	Magnesium, %	Manganese, %	References
87	2.5	10.5	NR[b]	NR	NR	NR	NR	NR	Pollard and House, 1959
85.6	2.7	11.7	7.0	18.5	7.5	1.0	2.5	59.5	Minkus, 1954
90	1.9	8.1	11.8	7.9	NR	5.6	NR	56.3	Minkus, 1954
95	2.4	2.6	12.5	1.4	3.9	NR	3.2	4.9	Arnold, 1936
96	3.2	0.8	NR	NR	NR	NR	NR	NR	Characklis, 1980

[a] Adapted from Characklis, 1973.
[b] Not reported.

biological structure of the film. Calcium, magnesium, and iron affect intermolecular bonding of biofilm polymers, which are primarily responsible for the structural integrity of the deposit. Experimentally, ethylenediaminetetraacetic acid (EDTA) is effective in detaching biofilm (Characklis, 1980). Table IV-1 shows the range of inorganic composition observed in selected biofilms. Very little is known about the interaction between biological fouling and inorganic scaling (primarily calcium precipitation on the pipe wall). The combined process probably occurs in many water distribution systems.

The organic composition of the biofilm is strongly related to the energy and carbon sources available for metabolism. Herbert (1961) and Schaechter *et al.* (1958) demonstrated the effect of environment and microbial growth rate on the composition of the cells and their extracellular products. For example, nitrogen limitation can result in production of copious quantities of microbial extracellular polysaccharides. Table IV-2 presents data on the composition of biofilms developed in the field and in the laboratory. Other chemical analyses of biofilm from laboratory systems indicate relatively high levels of polysaccharide in the biofilm (Bryers and Characklis, 1980).

BIOLOGICAL PROPERTIES

The organisms that colonize the attachment surface strongly influence the rate at which biofilm develops and its chemical and physical properties. However, organism-organism and organism-environment interactions undoubtedly shift population distributions during biofilm accumulation. Several investigators have observed a succession of various microbial species during biofouling (Corpe, 1978; Marshall, 1976).

The first visible signs of microbial activity on a surface are usually small "colonies" of cells distributed randomly on the surface. If biofilm development continues, the colonies grow together forming a relatively uniform biofilm. The viable cell numbers are relatively low in comparison to the volume of biofilm. The cells occupy from 1% to 10% of the biofilm in dilute nutrient solutions (Characklis, 1980). Jones *et al.* (1969) presented photomicrographs to corroborate these data in natural and laboratory systems. Allen and Geldreich (1977) have measured bacterial populations exceeding 10^5 organisms per gram of deposit from a distribution pipeline. These deposits consisted of sediment accumulations and "encrustations." Figure IV-2 contains electron micrographs of encrustations collected from water distribution systems across the United States (Allen *et al.*, 1979, 1980).

A number of different genera of bacteria and fungi have been observed

TABLE IV-2 Chemical Composition of Biofilms Obtained in the Field and Laboratory Emphasizing the
Primary Constituents—Carbon, Nitrogen, and Phosphorus

| Source | Composition, Percent Dry Weight | | | | | | References |
	Carbon	Nitrogen	Phosphorus	Fixed Solids	Carbon/ Nitrogen	Carbon/ Phosphorus	
Biofilm—laboratory reactor	42.8	10.0	—	—	4.3	—	Kornegay and Andrews, 1968
Biofilm—laboratory	19.0	9.2	1.8	20	2.1	10.5	Characklis, 1980
Escherichia coli	50.0	14.0	3.0	—	3.6	16.7	Gunsalus and Stanier, 1960

in distribution systems (Table IV-3). Generally, these organisms grow well in oligotrophic environments. In many cases, observed filamentous forms may provide an ecological advantage since the cells extend into the flow to obtain needed nutrients or oxygen, which may be depleted in the region close to the pipe wall.

EFFECT OF BIOFILMS ON FLUID FRICTIONAL RESISTANCE

Increase in frictional resistance of fluid resulting from the accumulation of biofilm causes an increased drop in pressure and power requirements for pumping when flow rate remains constant. Conversely, if pressure loss is held constant, flow capacity is reduced (Picologlou et al., 1980). For example, Wiederhold (1949) observed a 45% decrease in flow capacity in a pipe [2.5 ft (65 cm) I.D.] caused by a 0.6-mm thick biofilm.

The frictional resistance of biofilms grown under constant pressure loss (i.e., constant shear stress) has been compared to the frictional resistance of pipes with a rigid roughness. Picologlou et al. (1980) reported the following:

• Frictional resistance due to biofilms is dependent on fluid velocity as is frictional resistance due to rough surfaces of commercial pipes.
• Frictional resistance is dependent on the thickness of the biofilm.
• Frictional resistance does not increase above that of "hydraulically smooth" pipe until a critical biofilm thickness is obtained.

Increases in the frictional resistance when the water flow rate is constant increases the fluid stress at the biofilm-water interface. The result is an increase in the rates at which nutrients and particles (including microbial cells) are transported to the wall. Increased fluid shear stress will also dramatically increase detachment rate.

DISPERSED GROWTH

Almost all growth of microorganisms in the water distribution system occurs at the water-pipe interface. The rate of this growth is limited by the low concentrations of organic and inorganic nutrients in potable water. Moreover, since the mean flow-through time in most water distribution systems rarely exceeds several days, the mean residence time for the dispersed microorganisms is correspondingly short. Thus, most of these cells wash out of the distribution system before they can multiply to any appreciable extent.

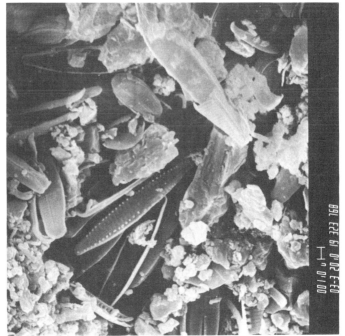

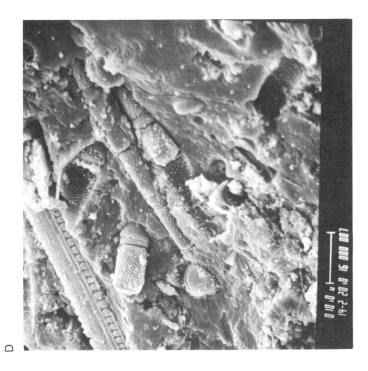

C

D

FIGURE IV-2 Electron micrographs of encrustations in water distribution systems. The variety of microorganisms found in the water distribution system is illustrated in panels A through D. The magnification is indicated for each picture (Allen *et al.*, 1979).

TABLE IV-3 Some Genera of Microorganisms Associated with Effects on the Quality of Water in Distribution Systems

Genera	Possible Effect	References
Acinetobacter	Potential indicator antagonist	Geldreich, 1980
Actinomyces	Taste and odors	Geldreich *et al.*, 1972; Larson, 1966
Arthrobacter	Color production (porphyrins); slime formation	Geldreich, 1980; Victoreen, 1969
Bacillus	Nitrate reduction; corrosion potential indicator antagonist	Geldreich *et al.*, 1972
Beggiatoa	"Red" water, sulfur oxidation	Ackerman and Lynde, 1944; Derby, 1947; Larson, 1966; Victoreen, 1974
Crenothrix	"Red" water (iron bacteria)	Ackerman and Lynde, 1944; Arnold, 1936; Larson, 1966
Desulfovibrio	Corrosion; hydrogen sulfide production ("black" water)	Larson, 1966; O'Connor *et al.*, 1975; Russell, 1976
Enterobacter	Regrowth	Geldreich, 1980; Lee and O'Connor, 1975
Escherichia	Fecal indicator	Geldreich *et al.*, 1972
Flavobacterium	Opportunistic pathogen; potential indicator antagonist	Geldreich *et al.*, 1972
Gallionella	"Red" water (iron bacteria)	Larson, 1966; Mackenthun and Keup, 1970; Ridgway and Olson, 1981

Klebsiella	Potential pathogen; regrowth	Geldreich, 1980; Lee and O'Connor, 1975
Leptothrix	"Red" water (iron bacteria)	Geldreich *et al.*, 1972; Larson, 1966; Mackenthun and Keup, 1970
Methylmonas (*Methanomonas*)	Methane oxidation	Larson, 1966
Micrococcus	Nitrate reduction; corrosion; potential indicator antagonist	Geldreich *et al.*, 1972
Mycobacterium	Potential pathogen	O'Connor *et al.*, 1975
Nitrobacter	Nitrate production; possible corrosion and slime formation	Kooijmans, 1966; Lee and O'Connor, 1975; Russell, 1976
Nitrosomonas	Nitrate production; possible corrosion and slime formation	Kooijmans, 1966; Larson, 1966; Russell, 1976; Victoreen, 1974
Nocardia	Potential pathogen	Water Research Centre, 1977
Proteus	Potential indicator antagonist	Geldreich *et al.*, 1972
Pseudomonas	Opportunistic pathogen; potential indicator antagonist	Geldreich *et al.*, 1972; O'Connor *et al.*, 1975
Serratia	Opportunistic pathogen	Geldreich, 1980
Sphaerotilus	"Red" water	Larson, 1966
Staphylococcus	Potential pathogen	Geldreich, 1980
Streptococcus	Fecal indicator	Ridgway and Olson, 1980
Streptomyces	Taste and odor	American Water Works Association Committee on Tastes and Odors, 1970; Russell, 1976

SOURCES OF BIOLOGICAL MATERIAL

Most genera of protists have been found in water distribution systems (Ridgway *et al.*, 1978; Water Research Centre, 1977). They range in size from picornaviruses (20-30 nm) to nematodes, crustaceans, and mollusks (1-20 mm). This living material can enter the distribution network in many ways: through raw water, treated water, reservoirs, tanks, and imperfections and perturbations in the water distribution system. Their growth can be influenced by the availability of suitable habitats, such as surface areas afforded by large pipe networks, and vehicles for their entry into the system, including those provided by imperfections such as cross-connections.

Table IV-3 lists some microorganisms found in water distribution systems and their effects on water quality.

Raw Water

A large portion of the flora and fauna in the water distribution system can also be found in the raw water. Clark and Pagel (1977) reported that the distribution of most bacteria was similar in raw and finished water. However, two exceptions were noted: Species of the genus *Escherichia* were more frequently isolated from raw water, and the oxidase-positive groups were more frequently isolated from the distribution system samples. Organisms in raw water may enter the distribution system in several ways. Unfiltered, turbid water may harbor solids that protect the microorganisms from disinfectants. Organic particulates have been shown to have a marked protective effect on both viruses and bacteria during disinfection (Hejkal *et al.*, 1979; Hoff, 1978; Tracey *et al.*, 1966). These particulates enter the distribution network, settle or adsorb, and continue to provide protection to the microorganisms. The sand filters at the water treatment plant provide an excellent niche from which many different microorganisms have been recovered (Geldreich *et al.*, 1972). Table IV-4 lists types of microorganisms and the density in which they have been found in sand taken from active filters. Intermittent or inadequate disinfection will also permit microorganisms to enter the pipe network.

Reservoir

Treated open water reservoirs and tanks may become contaminated by birds and other animals. Algae and other plants may grow in them, eventually providing nutrients to support bacterial growth in the distribution system.

An open reservoir was suspected of being the cause of an outbreak of di-

TABLE IV-4   Microorganisms in Filter-Bed Sand[a]

Organisms	Mean Density per Gram of Sand	
	Surface Sand	Deep Sand (25-150 cm)
Bacteria		
Coliforms	6,300	110
Fecal coliforms	75	51
Bacterial plate count (37°C)	770,000	350,000
Aerobic spores	430,000	350,000
Anaerobic spores	9,400	5,100
Protozoa		
Ciliates and flagellates	41,000	740
Amoebas	7,100	1,900

[a] From Geldreich *et al.*, 1972.

arrheal disease in Sewickley, Pennsylvania (Lippy and Erb, 1976). This is described in Chapter V. High standard plate counts were obtained from open reservoirs in Baltimore and Pittsburgh, although drinking water standards were not exceeded (Lippy, 1979).

Pipe Network

The distribution system itself may contribute microorganisms to the water. The joints between the pipe sections may provide protected habitats for large quantities of various kinds of microorganisms (Hutchinson, 1971). Gasket seals and joint packing are difficult to disinfect and sometimes serve as sources of nutrients. Many lubricants have high chlorine demand, which prevents the chlorine from gaining entrance to the joint. Hutchinson and Collingwood (1974) developed a bactericidal lubricant to minimize the bacteriological failure rate of new water main installation.

Construction and Repair

Microorganisms and nutrients supporting microbial growth may gain access to water distribution systems during installation and repair of components (Buelow *et al.*, 1976; Geldreich *et al.*, 1974). During these processes, unprotected pipe sections may become contaminated by soil, sewage, storm runoff, animal feces, and debris and can therefore contribute heavy loads of microorganims to the pipe network directly. Decontamination following construction and repair generally requires repeated high doses of chlorine before the system can be placed into service.

Cross-Connections

Cross-connections and back-siphonages provide another opportunity for large amounts of biological material to enter the distribution system. These events generally result in noticable change in water quality, including turbidity, increased content of solids, and undesirable tastes and odors.

In many cases, cross-connections are not obvious and the resulting changes in water quality are not detected by the consumer. Often, small intermittent flows through cross-connections can back-siphon and be responsible for outbreaks of disease.

CONTROL OF BIOLOGICAL CONTAMINATION

Chlorination has been the predominant means of controlling fouling biofilm formation in water distribution systems. Figure IV-3 illustrates the effectiveness of these processes in a segment of a water distribution conduit. There are three basic steps:

- Chlorine species entering the pipe segment react with chlorine-demanding components (viable cells and chemical compounds) in the bulk water.
- Chlorine species are transported through the bulk water to the water-biofilm interface.
- Chlorine species diffuse and react within the biofilm releasing soluble and particulate matter into the bulk water.

Since both "solid" and liquid phases are required, the chlorine-biofilm reaction is a heterogeneous process. Therefore, physical transport of reactants and products in each phase becomes important since transport limitations can significantly affect the rate of the overall process.

Transport of Chlorine

WATER PHASE

The rate at which chlorine is transported to the biofilm depends on the concentration of chlorine in the bulk water and the intensity of the turbulence.

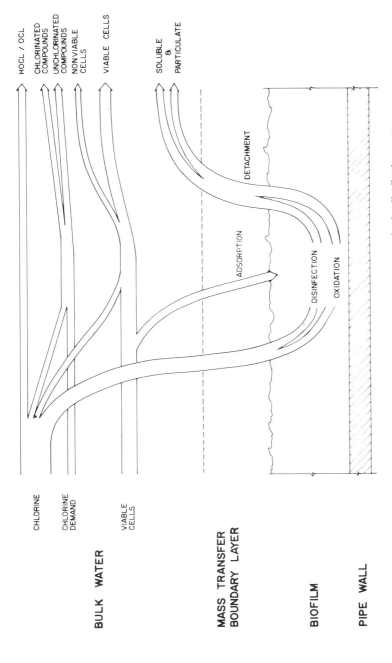

HOCL / OCL

CHLORINATED
COMPOUNDS

UNCHLORINATED
COMPOUNDS

NON VIABLE
CELLS

VIABLE CELLS

SOLUBLE
&
PARTICULATE

DETACHMENT

ADSORPTION

DISINFECTION

OXIDATION

CHLORINE

CHLORINE
DEMAND

VIABLE
CELLS

BULK WATER

MASS TRANSFER
BOUNDARY LAYER

BIOFILM

PIPE WALL

FIGURE IV-3   Schematic summary of chlorination processes in the distribution system.

The concentration of chlorine in the bulk water is related to the rate of its application minus the chlorine demand of the water. If the chlorine concentration at the biofilm interface is the same as its concentration in the bulk water, then the chlorine concentration in the water drives the reactions of chlorine within the biofilm. If chlorine reacts with biofilm relatively rapidly, the concentration at the interface will be low and the physical transport of the chlorine may limit the rate of the overall process within the biofilm.

By increasing the intensity of the turbulence through increased flow rate both the transport rates in the bulk water and the concentration at the interface will increase. In bulk water, chlorine is transported primarily by eddy diffusion.

BIOFILM

The transport of chlorine in biofilms occurs primarily by molecular diffusion. Since the composition of biofilms is from 96% to 99% water, the diffusivity of chlorine in biofilm is probably similar to its diffusivity in water. In biofilms of higher density or in those containing microbial matter associated with inorganic scale, tubercules, or sediment deposits, diffusion of chlorine may be relatively slow.

Chlorine reacts with various organic and reduced inorganic components within the biofilm, and it disrupts cellular material and inactivates cells in the biofilm to some extent. Its greatest apparent effect is its reaction with the extracellular polymers (primarily polysaccharides), which are responsible for the physical integrity of the biofilm (Characklis and Dydek, 1976).

Bacterial flocs or biofilms that are rich in polysaccharide material exhibit a more rapid and ultimately greater chlorine demand (Characklis and Dydek, 1976). One possible explanation is that hypochlorite ion attacks glucose polysaccharides with extensive oxidation at the C_2 and C_3 positions of D-glucose units, which results in cleavage of the C_2-C_3 bond (Hullinger, 1964; Whistler et al., 1956). Depolymerization can result from the inductive effects of this oxidation, from direct oxidative cleavage of the glucosidic bond, or from degradation of the intermediate carbonyl compound.

The reaction of chlorine with biofilm produces an immediate response in the bulk water by increasing turbidity and the soluble organic constituents (Characklis and Dydek, 1976). A significant removal of biofilm is evidenced by a decrease in biofilm thickness and a decrease in fluid frictional resistance (Characklis, 1980; Characklis and Dydek, 1976; Norrman et al., 1977). Inactivation of the biofilm with a nonoxidizing poison does not result in any biofilm removal (Characklis and Dydek, 1976). The results suggest that hypochlorite ion oxidizes the polysaccharides in the biofilm resulting in depolymerization, dissolution, and detachment.

Characklis *et al.* (1980) reported that biofilm detachment resulting from chlorination is much higher between pH 7.5 and 8.5 than between pH 6 and 7. These data correspond well with data for chlorination of polysaccharides such as starch, which is optimum at pH >7 (Whistler and Schweiger, 1957). On the other hand, disinfection with chlorine is more effective at lower pH (approximately pH 6-7). Similar data are not available for monochloramine, dichloramine, or other *N*-chloro compounds.

Fluid shear forces may play a major role in the removal of biofilm. Norrman *et al.* (1977) measured a higher rate of chlorine uptake by biofilms when the fluid shear stress was greater. The authors suggested that these greater shear forces disrupted the biofilm during chlorination, thereby reentraining reaction products and exposing new surfaces for chlorine reaction. Characklis *et al.* (1980) observed that the detachment of biofilm resulting from chlorination increased with increasing fluid stress.

In summary, when chlorine contacts biofilm, the following occurs: detachment of biofilm, dissolution of biofilm components, and consumption of chlorine. Limited observations suggest that the following factors influence the rate of the chlorine-biofilm reaction:

• Transport of chlorine from the water to the water-biofilm interface. Transport rate increases with increasing chlorine concentration and turbulence.

• Transport of chlorine within the biofilm or deposit. Transport rate can be increased by increasing the chlorine concentration at the water-biofilm interface.

• Reaction of chlorine within the biofilm, especially the abiotic components.

• Detachment and reentrainment of reacted biofilm primarily due to fluid shear stress.

Appropriate chlorine residuals are difficult to maintain throughout the distribution system on a continuing basis. Consequently, biofilms may frequently exist in various locations in the pipe network. Therefore, more studies should be conducted to define these fundamental process rates and the factors that influence them.

DISPERSED GROWTH

Finished water leaving a properly operated water treatment plant is relatively free of biological activity. Pipe networks designed specifically to minimize water stagnation and dead ends and regular cleaning and flushing programs are used to control contamination after treatment. In addition, chlorine and chloramines have been used almost exclusively as the residual disinfectants in water distribution systems.

Control of chlorination during the early days of water disinfection was based on the applied dose of chlorine. It was soon recognized that the dose of chlorine alone was not adequate to ensure good microbial inactivation. Folwell (1917) pointed out that "the only safe rule is to test the germicidal effect of different doses on the water in question." The concept of residual chlorination was suggested by Wolman and Enslow (1919). They recommended that the amount of chlorine applied should be based on the amount of chlorine consumed by the water at 20°C for 5 minutes (chlorine demand) plus an additional 0.2 mg/liter. However, they specifically did not recommend the maintenance of a chlorine residual in the distribution system because of anticipated taste and odor problems.

By the 1930's ammonia was sometimes added to reduce the tastes and odors produced by the chlorine. Baylis (1935) noted that the chlorammoniation process yielded a stable chlorine residual that produced minimum complaints and reduced bacterial growth in the distribution system. The practice of maintaining a chlorine residual throughout the distribution system was gradually adopted, and by 1941 the American Water Works Association water quality and treatment manual noted that the chlorine-ammonia treatment prevented the formation of tastes and odors in the distribution system and reduced the number of complaints pertaining to "red-water" in the dead ends of the system. However, the chlorammoniation process was quite ineffective in eliminating taste and odors in unfiltered water supplies. As the reaction between chlorine and ammonia became better understood and the superior disinfecting activity of free chlorine was recognized, the practice of maintaining a free chlorine residual in the distribution system evolved. The 1950 American Water Works Association water quality and treatment manual noted that high chlorination rates reduced bacterial content and eliminated some tastes and odors.

The value of residual chlorine in the distribution system has received considerable attention. At the request of the Department of the Army, the National Academy of Sciences/National Research Council (NAS/NRC) prepared the following statement in 1958:

Residual chlorine in the concentrations routinely employed in water utility practice will not ordinarily disinfect any sizeable amounts of contaminatory material entering the system, though this will depend on the amount of dilution occurring at the point of contamination, on the type and concentration of residual chlorine and on the time-of-flow interval between the point of contamination and the nearest consumer.... The NAS-NRC does not consider maintenance of a residual satisfactory substitute for good design, construction and supervision of a water distribution system, nor does it feel that the presence of a residual in the system constitutes a guarantee of water potability.

It was the opinion of the NAS/NRC committee responsible for this statement that the establishment of a universal standard for maintaining residual chlorine in the water in distribution systems was not desirable. Although the military had no policy concerning residual chlorine, all services recommended that chlorination be accomplished to levels of free residuals.

More recently Coene (1963) reported that the presence of some type of chlorine residual reduces the coliform content. In 1970, the results of a survey of community water supplies supported Coene's study (McCabe *et al.*, 1970). Buelow and Walton (1971) reported that the maintenance of a chlorine residual throughout the water system was effective in meeting the bacterial standards. Geldreich *et al.* (1972) showed that chlorine residuals were effective in controlling bacterial populations within the distribution lines. Snead *et al.* (1980) confirmed the earlier results and reported that the chlorine residual was the single most important factor influencing the level of microorganisms found in samples collected from distribution networks in Baltimore and Frederick, Maryland.

Cross-connections and back-siphonages have been implicated in numerous outbreaks attributed to waterborne microorganisms (Craun *et al.*, 1976; McCabe *et al.*, 1970). Snead *et al.* (1980) evaluated the protection afforded the water consumer by the maintenance of a free or combined chlorine residual when tap water was challenged with sewage containing enteric bacteria and viruses. An initial free chlorine residual was more effective than an equivalent initial combined chlorine residual. At pH 8.0, an initial free chlorine residual of 0.7 mg/liter, and a challenge of 1.0% sewage by volume, investigators observed inactivation of enteric bacteria at 3 logs or greater (>99.9% kill). Viral inactivation under these conditions was 2 logs (>99% kill.)

SUMMARY AND CONCLUSIONS

Living organisms can enter the water distribution system through insufficiently treated raw water, in-line reservoirs, and imperfections in the pipeline network. Microbial activity occurs predominantly at the pipe wall where nutrients gather in high concentrations. Flow rate, ratio of surface area to volume, and nutrient concentration all influence the microbial activity both at the wall and in the bulk water.

Microbial processes within the distribution system can significantly increase hydraulic roughness and corrosion in the pipes. Microbial activity can result in undesirable tastes and odors, "black" water (sulfide), and "red" water (iron). Detached portions of biofilms in the pipes provides a continuing source of microorganisms in the distribution system.

Disinfectant residual, usually chlorine, provides a relatively effective barrier to the growth of microorganisms in both the bulk water and the biofilm. Chlorine is also effective in removing existing biofilms and providing some protection against contamination of the water after treatment.

Distribution networks are dynamic systems. The flow rates and composition of water in the pipelines vary with the length of time they are in the system and the magnitude of the network as a result of changes in raw water characteristics, water treatment processes, reactions within the pipes, and water demand. Because chlorine residual is often low or even absent in some portions of the distribution system, microorganisms may proliferate.

Enteric pathogens are rarely found in distribution systems containing adequately disinfected water.

REFERENCES

Ackerman, T.V., and E.J. Lynde. 1944. Effect of storage reservoir detritus on groundwater. J. Am. Water Works Assoc. 36:315-322.

Allen, M.J., and E.E. Geldreich. 1977. Distribution line sediments and bacterial regrowth. Paper 3B-1 in Water Quality in the Distribution System, Proceedings, American Water Works Association Water Quality Technology Conference, Dec. 4-7, Kansas City, Mo. American Water Works Association, Denver, Colo. 6 pp.

Allen, M.J., E.E. Geldreich, and R.H. Taylor. 1979. The occurrence of microorganisms in water main encrustations. Pp. 113-117 in Advances in Laboratory Techniques for Quality Control. Presented at the 7th Annual American Water Works Association Water Quality Technology Conference, Dec. 9-12, 1979, Philadelphia, Pa. American Water Works Association, Denver, Colo.

Allen, M.J., R.H. Taylor, and E.E. Geldreich. 1980. The occurrence of microorganisms in water main encrustations. J. Am. Water Works Assoc. 72:614-625.

American Water Works Association Committee on Tastes and Odors. 1970. Research on tastes and odors. J. Am. Water Works Assoc. 62:59-62.

Arnold, G.E. 1936. Crenothrix chokes conduits. Eng. News-Rec. 116:774-775.

Baylis, J.R. 1935. Elimination of Taste and Odor in Water. McGraw-Hill Book Co., Inc., New York. 375 pp.

Becker, R.J. 1975. Bacterial regrowth within the distribution system. Paper 2B-4 in Water Quality, Proceedings, American Water Works Association Water Quality Technology Conference, Dec. 8-9, Atlanta, Ga. American Water Works Association and the American Water Works Association Research Foundation, Denver, Colo. 10 pp.

Bryers, J.D., and W.G. Characklis. 1980. Measurement of primary biofilm formation. Pp. 169-183 in J.F. Garey, ed. Condenser Biofouling Control. Ann Arbor Science Publishers, Inc., Ann Arbor, Mich.

Beulow, R.W., and G. Walton. 1971. Bacteriological quality vs. residual chlorine. J. Am. Water Works Assoc. 63:28.

Beulow, R.W., R.H. Taylor, E.E. Geldreich, A. Goodenkouf, L. Wilwerding, F. Holdren, M. Hutchinson, and I.H. Nelson. 1976. Disinfection of new water mains. J. Am. Water Works Assoc. 68:283.

Characklis, W.G. 1973. Attached microbial growths. I. Attachment and growth. Water Res. 7:1113-1127.

Characklis, W.G. 1980. Biofilm Development and Destruction. Final Report. Prepared by Rice University, Houston, Texas. EPRI CS-1554. Electric Power Research Institute, Palo Alto, Calif. 283 pp.

Characklis, W.G., and S.T. Dydek. 1976. The influence of carbon nitrogen ratio on the chlorination of microbial aggregates. Water Res. 10:515-522.

Characklis, W.G., M.G. Trulear, N. Stathopoulos, and L-C. Chang. 1980. Oxidation and destruction of microbial films. Pp. 349-368 in R.J. Jolley, W.A. Brungs, and R.B. Cumming, eds. Water Chlorination: Environmental Impact and Health Effects. Vol. 3. Proceedings of the 3rd Conference held in Colorado Springs, Colo., Oct. 28-Nov. 1, 1979. Ann Arbor Science Publishers, Ann Arbor, Mich.

Clark, J.A., and J.E. Pagel. 1977. Pollution indicator bacteria associated with municipal raw and drinking water supplies. Can. J. Microbiol. 23:465-470.

Coene, R.F. 1963. Relationship between Residual Chlorine and Coliform Density in Water Distribution Systems. M.S. Thesis, Oregon State University, Corvallis, Oreg.

Corpe, W.A. 1978. Ecology of microbial attachment and growth on solid surfaces. Pp. 57-65 in R.M. Gerhold, ed. Microbiology of Power Plant Thermal Effluents. Proceedings of the Symposium. The University of Iowa, Iowa City.

Costerton, J.W. 1979. The mechanism of primary fouling of submerged surfaces by bacteria. Condenser Biofouling Control Symposium, Electric Power Research Institute, Atlanta, Ga.

Costerton, J.W., G.G. Geesey, and K.J. Cheng. 1978. How bacteria stick. Sci. Am. 238(1): 86-95.

Craun, G.F., L.J. McCabe, and J.M. Hughes. 1976. Waterborne disease outbreaks in the US—1971-1974. J. Am. Water Works Assoc. 68:420-424.

Derby, R.L. 1947. Control of slime growths in transmission lines. J. Am. Water Works Assoc. 39:1107-1114.

Dugan, P.R., and H.M. Pickrum. 1972. Removal of mineral ions from water by microbially produced polymers. Pp. 1019-1038 in Proceedings of the 27th Industrial Waste Conference, May 2, 3, and 4, 1972, Purdue University, Lafayette, Ind.

Folwell, A.P. 1917. Water-Supply Engineering. John Wiley & Sons, New York. 562 pp.

Geldreich, E.E. 1980. Microbiological processes in water supply distribution. Presented at an American Society for Microbiology Seminar, Microbial Problems in Potable Water Distribution, May 14, 1980, Miami Beach, Fla. 22 pp.

Geldreich, E.E., H.D. Nash, D.J. Reasoner, and R.H. Taylor. 1972. The necessity of controlling bacterial populations in potable waters: Community water supply. J. Am. Water. Works Assoc. 64:596-602.

Geldreich, E.E., R.H. Taylor, and M.J. Allen. 1974. Bacteriological considerations in the installation and repair of water mains. Paper VIII-1 in Water Quality, Proceedings, American Water Works Association Water Quality Technology Conference, Dec. 2-3,

1974, Dallas, Tex. American Water Works Association and the American Water Works Association Research Foundation, Denver, Colo. 5 pp.

Gunsalus, I.C., and R.Y. Stanier, eds. 1960. Bacteria—Structure. Vol. 1. Academic Press, New York. 34 pp.

Hejkal, T.W., F.M. Wellings, P.A. LaRock, and A.L. Lewis. 1979. Survival of poliovirus within organic solids during chlorination. Appl. Environ. Microbiol. 38:114-118.

Herbert, D. 1961. The chemical composition of micro-organisms as a function of their environment. Pp. 391-416 in Microbial Reaction to Environment. Eleventh Symposium of the Society for General Microbiology held at the Royal Institution, London, April 1961. The University Press, Cambridge, England.

Hoehn, R.C., and A.D. Ray. 1973. Effects of thickness on bacterial film. J. Water Pollut. Control. Fed. 45:2302-2320.

Hoff, J.C. 1978. The relationship of turbidity to disinfection of potable water. Pp. 103-117 in C.W. Hendricks, ed. Evaluation of the Microbiology Standards for Drinking Water. EPA-570/9-78-00C. U.S. Environmental Protection Agency, Washington, D.C.

Hullinger, C.H. 1964. Oxidation. [74] Hypochlorite-oxidized starch. Pp. 313-315 in R.L. Whistler, R.J. Smith, and J.N. BeMiller, eds. Methods in Carbohydrate Chemistry. Academic Press, Inc., New York.

Hutchinson, M. 1971. The disinfection of new water mains. Chem. Ind. No. 1:139-142.

Hutchinson, M., and R.W. Collingwood. 1974. WRA MEDLUBE, A Bactericidal Lubricant for Assembly of Push-Fit Pipe Joints. TP 110. The Water Research Association, Medmenham, England.

Jones, H.C., I.L. Roth, and W.M. Sanders, III. 1969. Electron microscopic study of a slime layer. J. Bacteriol. 99:316-325.

Kooijmans, L.H. 1966. Occurrence, significance and control of organisms in distribution systems. Pp. C5-C32 in International Water Supply Congress and Exhibition. Vol. I. General Reports and Papers on Special Subjects. 7th Congress, 3rd to 7th Oct. 1966, Barcelona. International Water Supply Association, Barcelona, Spain.

Kornegay, B.H., and J.F. Andrews. 1968. Kinetics of fixed-film biological reactors. J. Water Pollut. Control Fed. 40:R460-R468.

Larson, T.E. 1966. Deterioration of water quality in distribution systems. J. Am. Water Works Assoc. 58:1307-1316.

Lee, S.H., and J.T. O'Connor. 1975. Biologically mediated deterioration of water quality in distribution systems. Paper No. 22-6. Presented at the American Water Works Association Annual Conference, Minneapolis, Minn. 9 pp.

Lippy, E.C. 1979. Reservoir Water Quality studies. Pp. 5A-1 in Proceedings, American Water Works Association Water Quality Technology Conference. American Water Works Association, Denver, Colo.

Lippy, E.C., and J. Erb. 1976. Gastrointestinal illness at Sewickley, Pa. J. Am. Water Works Assoc. 68:606-610.

Mackenthun, K.M., and L.E. Keup. 1970. Biological problems encountered in water supplies. J. Am. Water Works Assoc. 62:520-526.

Marshall, K.C. 1976. Interfaces in Microbial Ecology. Harvard University Press, Cambridge, Mass. 156 pp.

Marshall, K.C., R. Stout, and R. Mitchell. 1971. Mechanisms of the initial events in the sorption of marine bacteria to surfaces. J. Gen. Microbiol. 68:337-348.

Matson, J.V., and W.G. Characklis. 1976. Diffusion into microbial aggregates. Water Res. 10:877-885.

McCabe, L.J., J.M. Symons, R.D. Lee, and G.G. Robeck. 1970. Survey of community water supply systems. J. Am. Water Works Assoc. 62:670-687.

Minkus, A.J. 1954. Deterioration of the hydraulic capacity of pipelines. J. N. Engl. Water Works Assoc. 68:1-10.

National Academy of Sciences. 1958. Revised Statement on Maintaining a Trace of Residual Chlorine in Water Distribution Systems. Prepared for the Subcommittee on Water Supply of the Committee on Sanitary Engineering and the Environment, National Academy of Sciences-National Research Council, Washington, D.C. 4 pp.

Nimmons, M.J. 1979. Heat Transfer Effects in Turbulent Flow Due to Biofilm Development. M.S. Thesis, Rice University, Houston, Tex. 119 pp.

Norrman, G., W.G. Characklis, and J.D. Bryers. 1977. Control of microbial fouling in circular tubes with chlorine. Dev. Ind. Microbial. 18:581-590.

O'Connor, J.T., L. Hash, and A.B. Edwards. 1975. Deterioration of water quality in distribution systems. J. Am. Water Works Assoc. 67:113-116.

Picologlou, B.F., N. Zelver, and W.G. Characklis. 1980. Biofilm growth and hydraulic performance. J. Hydraulics Div. 106:733-746.

Pollard, A.L., and H.E. House. 1959. An unusual deposit in a hydraulic tunnel. J. Power Div. 85:163-171.

Ridgway, H.F., and B.H. Olson. 1981. Scanning electron microscope evidence for bacterial colonization of a drinking-water distribution system. Appl. Environ. Microbiol. 41:274-287.

Ridgway, J., R.G. Ainsworth, and R.D. Gwilliam. 1978. Water quality changes—Chemical and microbiological studies. In Proceedings of the Conference on Water Distribution Systems. Water Research Centre, Medmenham, England.

Russell, G.A. 1976. Deterioration of water quality in distribution systems—Dimensions of the problem. Pp. 5-11 in Proceedings, 18th Annual Public Water Supply Conference, Water Treatment, Part 1. University of Illinois, College of Engineering, Urbana, Ill.

Schaechter, M., O. Maale, and N.O. Kjeldgaard. 1958. Dependency on medium and temperature of cell size and chemical composition during balanced growth of *Salmonella typhimurium*. J. Gen. Microbiol. 19:592-606.

Silvey, J.K.G., D.E. Henley, R. Hoehn, and W.C. Nunez. 1975. Musty-earthy odors and their biological control. Paper 4B-1 in Water Quality, Proceedings, American Water Works Association Water Quality Technology Conference, Dec. 8-9. Atlanta, Ga. American Water Works Association and the American Water Works Association Research Foundation, Denver, Colo.

Snead, M.C., V.P. Olivieri, K. Kawata, and C.W. Krusé. 1980. Effectiveness of chlorine residuals in inactivation of bacteria and viruses introduced by post-treatment contamination. Water Res. 14:403-408.

Tracey, H.W., V.M. Camarena, and F. Wing. 1966. Coliform persistence in highly chlorinated waters. J. Am. Water Works Assoc. 58:1151-1159.

Trulear, M.G., and W.G. Characklis. 1979. Dynamics of biofilm processes. Pp. 838-853 in Proceedings of the 34th Industrial Waste Conference, May 8, 9, and 10, 1979, Purdue University, Lafayette, Ind. Ann Arbor Science Publishers, Inc., Ann Arbor, Mich.

Victoreen, H.T. 1969. Soil bacteria and color problem in distribution systems. J. Am. Water Works Assoc. 61:429-431.

Victoreen, H.T. 1974. Control of water quality in transmission and distribution mains. J. Am. Water Works Assoc. 66:369-370.

Water Research Centre. 1977. Deterioration of Bacteriological Quality of Water During Distribution. Notes on Water Research No. 6. Water Research Centre, Medmenham, England. 4 pp.

Whistler, R.L., and R. Schweiger. 1957. Oxidation of amylopectin with hypochlorite at different hydrogen-ion concentrations. J. Am. Chem. Soc. 79:6460-6464.

Whistler, R.L., E.G. Linke, and S.J. Kazeniac. 1956. Action of alkaline hypochlorite on corn-starch amylose and methyl 4-0-methyl-D-glucopyranosides. J. Am. Chem. Soc. 78: 4704-4709.

Wiederhold, W. 1949. Über den Einsluss von Rohrablagerungen auf den hydraulischen Druckabsall. GWF, Gas Wasserfach, 90:634-641.

Wolman, A., and L.H. Enslow. 1919. Chlorine absorption and the chlorination of water. J. Ind. Eng. Chem. 11:209-213.

Zobell, C.E. 1943. The effect of solid surfaces upon bacterial activity. J. Bacteriol. 46:39-56. Washington, D.C. 187 pp.

V

Health Implications of Distribution System Deficiencies

Although it is not the purpose of this report to review the optimum engineering design, construction, and operation of distribution systems, it is important to recognize that waterborne diseases may result from inadequate attention to any of those areas.

Outbreaks of acute disease associated with contaminated drinking water are reported to the Centers for Disease Control (CDC) by state health departments or to the Health Effects Research Laboratory of the U.S. Environmental Protection Agency (EPA) by state water supply agencies. These reports are made on a voluntary basis. The data are reviewed and summarized annually by representatives from CDC and EPA.

In the majority of these reports, the etiologic agent is not identified. However, the clinical and epidemiological evidence suggests that most of these outbreaks are caused by infectious agents. In many investigations of outbreaks of unknown etiology, appropriate laboratory specimens are not collected; in others, sophisticated laboratory procedures required for identification of some potential etiologic agents are not performed.

Well-documented cases of acute waterborne disease outbreaks in the United States have implicated bacteria, viruses, and protozoa. Some of the bacteria (e.g., *Salmonella* and *Shigella*) and the protozoa (e.g, *Giardia lamblia* and *Entamoeba histolytica*) can be identified by culture or microscopic examination of stool specimens, respectively. Identification of some other pathogenic bacteria (e.g., *Campylobacter fetus* subspecies *jejuni* and *Yersinia enterocolitica*) requires the use of special media or incubation conditions that are not available in all laboratories. Identification of enterotoxigenic *Escherichia coli* and viral causes of acute gastroenteritis (e.g., Norwalk-like agents and rotaviruses) requires the use of very sophisticated laboratory methodology generally accessible only in a research laboratory.

DEFINITIONS

A waterborne disease outbreak is defined by CDC and EPA as an incident in which (1) two or more persons experience similar illness after consumption or external use of water intended for drinking and (2) epidemiological evidence implicates water as the source of illness. A single case of acute chemical poisoning constitutes an outbreak if laboratory studies indicate that the water is contaminated by the suspect chemical. With the exception of acute chemical poisoning, data on single cases of acute disease that might be waterborne are rarely reported to CDC or EPA and are not tabulated.

Municipal or community systems are public or investor-owned water supplies that serve large or small communities, subdivisions, or trailer parks with at least 15 service connections or 25 year-round residents. Semipublic (noncommunity) water systems are those in institutions, industries, camps, parks, hotels, or service stations that may be used by the general public. Individual (private water) systems are those used by single or several residences or by persons such as backpackers who travel outside populated areas. These definitions correspond to those used in the Safe Drinking Water Act (PL 93-523).

ORIGINS OF WATERBORNE DISEASES

Sources of the contamination responsible for the outbreak include untreated surface water, untreated groundwater, treatment deficiencies (e.g., malfunction of a chlorinator), and deficiencies in the distribution system (e.g., cross-connections). Several well-known outbreaks have been caused by deficiencies in the distribution system. Examples include a large outbreak of amebiasis among guests at two Chicago hotels in 1933 (U.S. Treasury Department, Public Health Service, 1936) and infectious hepatitis in members of a college football team (Morse *et al.*, 1972). In both outbreaks, potable water was contaminated as a result of a defect in the distribution system.

INTERPRETATION OF DATA

One must be cognizant of the limitations of the data pertaining to these outbreaks in order to avoid inappropriate interpretation. Since some investigations were incomplete or were conducted long after the outbreak, the waterborne transmission hypothesis could not always be proven although it was the most logical explanation.

It is known that the reports of outbreaks received by the CDC and EPA represent only a fraction of those that occur, but the actual extent of these outbreaks is unknown. The likelihood of an outbreak coming to the attention of health authorities varies considerably from one locale to another depending largely upon consumer awareness, physician interest, and disease surveillance activities of state and local health and environmental agencies. The sequence of events leading to the reporting of an outbreak is summarized in Figure V-1, but this sequence can be interrupted at any stage.

Large interstate outbreaks and outbreaks of serious illness are most likely to come to the attention of health authorities. On occasion, initial investigation of a few cases of illness has led to the identification of a large outbreak. For example, investigation of 10 culture-proven cases of *Shigella* infection in a Miami suburb in 1974 led to identification of 1,000 cases of waterborne illness (Weissman *et al.*, 1976).

The number of reported outbreaks of different etiologies may depend

REPORTING OF AN OUTBREAK

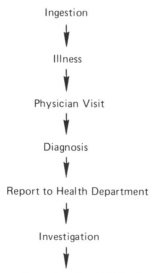

Ingestion

↓

Illness

↓

Physician Visit

↓

Diagnosis

↓

Report to Health Department

↓

Investigation

↓

Report to Centers for Disease Control and/or U.S. Environmental Protection Agency

FIGURE V-1   Sequence of events leading to the reporting of an outbreak.

upon the interest of a particular health department or individual. In addition, a few outbreaks involving very large numbers of persons may vastly alter the relative proportion of cases attributed to various etiologic agents.

For these reasons, the existing data should not be used as the basis for drawing firm conclusions about the true incidence of waterborne disease outbreaks or about the relative incidence of waterborne diseases of various etiologies. Nevertheless, these data can be useful in determining the causative agents and water system deficiencies that most frequently result in outbreaks.

More intensive surveillance and prompter reporting of suspected outbreaks to public health authorities are needed so that more timely and thorough epidemiological investigations can be conducted. By utilizing recent advances in diagnostic laboratory techniques, such investigations will increase knowledge of waterborne pathogens, identify factors responsible for the outbreaks, and provide a better estimate of the true magnitude of this route of disease transmission.

OUTBREAKS

From 1971 through 1978, 224 outbreaks of waterborne diseases were reported. Of these, 33 (15%), involving 10,010 cases, were attributed to deficiencies in distribution systems. Features of these 33 outbreaks are summarized in Tables V-1 and V-2. Municipal systems were responsible for a total of 68 outbreaks and 33,473 cases, of which 26 outbreaks and 9,298 cases were attributed to distribution system deficiencies (Table V-3). Thus, municipal systems accounted for 78% (26 of 33) of the outbreaks and 93% (9,298 of 10,010) of the cases associated with system deficiencies. In contrast, defects in semipublic and individual systems were responsible for less than 5% of the outbreaks and cases (Table V-3). The most frequently identified deficiencies were indirect cross-connections, which permitted wastewater or toxic chemicals to gain access to the water system by back-siphonage through hoses or through defects in water pipes during periods of low pressure. These defects accounted for 13 (50%) of the outbreaks involving municipal systems (Table V-4). Direct cross-connections between sewerage or wastewater systems and municipal potable water systems accounted for 5 (19%).

The etiology of outbreaks involving defects in municipal distribution systems differed from that of municipal outbreaks attributed to other sources (Table V-5). Outbreaks of chemical etiology were much more likely to be associated with such system defects; 10 (38%) of the 26 outbreaks resulting from distribution system deficiencies were caused by a chemical, while only two of the 42 (5%) outbreaks due to other deficiencies had a chemical etiology. In contrast, no outbreaks of giardiasis were caused by distribution system deficiencies.

The 33 outbreaks attributed to deficiencies in all systems were reported by 23 different states. Pennsylvania reported the most (5 outbreaks or 15%); however, during this period Pennsylvania also reported 44 (23%) of the 191 outbreaks caused by other deficiencies. This observation is consistent with the fact that Pennsylvania reports the largest number of outbreaks each year, reflecting that state's great interest in outbreaks of waterborne disease.

The number of outbreaks due to distribution system deficiencies by year is depicted in Figure V-2. The number of outbreaks involving municipal systems has remained fairly constant, while the semipublic system outbreaks were only reported in 1976–1978.

Sewickley, Pennsylvania

During the last 10 days of August 1975, an outbreak of diarrheal illness occurred in residents of Sewickley. A community survey indicated that approximately 60% of the people who obtained their water from the Sewickley municipal system had been ill. The illness occurred much more frequently in persons using water from this system than in those using well water or water from another, nearby municipal system.

Examination of the water system revealed that no free residual chlorine was detectable at several points in the distribution system on at least one of the days on which transmission occurred. The most likely source of the water contamination was an open holding reservoir, since the fence restricting access to it had been broken by falling trees the previous winter. Several soda bottles and golf balls were found in that reservoir, but no specific source of human excreta was identified. Despite extensive bacterial and viral laboratory studies, no specific etiologic agent was identified. A heavy growth of algae had been observed where contamination was thought to have occurred in the reservoir, but it is not known if the algae played any role in causing the disease (Lippy and Erb, 1976). Control measures included covering the reservoir and maintaining adequate chlorination of the system.

Suffolk County, New York

During the last week of March 1976, approximately 37% of the people who attended one of four functions at a large catering establishment developed a diarrheal illness caused by *Salmonella typhimurium*. Although foodborne transmission was initially suspected, epidemiological investigation suggested that the illness was transmitted by contaminated drinking

TABLE V-1 Reported Waterborne Outbreaks Involving Municipal Systems with Deficiencies in Distribution System, 1971–1978^a

Year	State	Etiology	No. of Cases	Location	Documented Contamination of Water^b	Chlorinated	Deficiency
1971	Mich.	*Shigella sonnei*	187	Camp	No	Yes	Low pressure activation of booster pump; three potential indirect cross-connections (hose in bathtub, no air gap in laundry room sinks, pipe leak) with possibilities for back-siphonage; and leaking sewer line identified.
1971	Mo.	?	2	Subdivision	No	No	Water from fire hydrant used to mix water, fertilizer, grass seed, and wood pulp; pumping system clogged with back-siphonage into water line.
1971	N.C.	?	38	Trailer park	Yes(B)	Yes	Potential indirect cross-connections (leaks) with back-siphonage.
1972	Ohio	Hepatitis	9	Trailer park	Yes(B)	?	Presumed indirect cross-connection with back-siphonage.
1972	Tenn.	?	19	School	?	Yes	Presumed contamination during construction of plumbing in new building.
1973	Fla.	?	194	Industry	Yes(B)	Yes	Direct cross-connection in new building.
1974	Ill.	Furadan insecticide	1	Fertilizer plant	Yes(C)	?	Direct cross-connection in fertilizer plant.

Year	State	Contaminant	No.	Location	Illness	Confirmed	Comments
1974	Oreg.	Hydrocarbons (lubricating oil)	18	Subdivision	Yes(C)	Yes	Contamination of pipes before or during installation.
1974	Oreg.	?	19	Residential area	No	No	Indirect cross-connection (leak) suspected.
1974	N.Y.	Chromate	20	Office building	Yes(C)	?	Direct cross-connection between water and air-conditioning systems.
1975	Ind.	?	1,400	City	Yes(B)	Yes	Heavy rains followed by contamination during construction.
1975	N.J.	Herbicide	4	Resort	Yes(C)	?	Probable indirect cross-connection with back-siphonage through hose during pesticide spraying during period of high demand.
1975	Pa.	?	5,000	City	No	Yes	Contamination of open finished water reservoir suspected.
1975	P.R.	?	550	Housing project	Yes(B)	?	Direct cross-connection with back-siphonage between sewage system and cistern.
1975	S.C.	Ethyl acrylate	7	City	Yes(C)	No	Direct cross-connection between industrial well and distribution system; malfunction of check valve with back-siphonage.
1976	N.Y.	Salmonella typhimurium	750	Catering facility	No	?	Temporary indirect cross-connection with back-siphonage through pipe in contaminated sink during period of high demand.
1976	Tenn.	Chlordane pesticide	13	City	Yes(C)	?	Temporary indirect cross-connection with back-siphonage through a hose used for dilution of pesticide solution following disruption of system by builders.

TABLE V-1 Continued

Year	State	Etiology	No. of Cases	Location	Documented Contamination of Water[b]	Chlori- nated	Deficiency
1977	Calif.	Hydroquinone (developer fluid)	531	Ship	No	?	Temporary indirect cross-connection with back-siphonage through a hose between developer tank and water system.
1977	Conn.	Copper	3	College dormitory	Yes(C)	?	Presumed leaching of copper from pipes.
1977	N.D.	?	25	Motel	?	?	Temporary indirect cross-connection with back-siphonage through a hose between drain and water system.
1977	Pa.	?	73	Restaurant	No	?	Temporary indirect cross-connection with back-siphonage between sewer line and ice machine.
1977	Tex.	?	12	City	No	No	Outbreak followed repair of broken transmission main; presumed contamination of water in auxiliary system in covered storage tank.
1977	Vt.	Copper	74	Restaurant	Yes(C)	?	Defective check valve permitted carbonated water backflow and leaching.
1978	Conn.	Copper	12	School	Yes(C)	?	Copper buildup in pipe to drinking fountain; electrolysis suspected.
1978	Minn.	?	137	Trailer park	Yes(B)	No	Unspecified type of cross-connections in plant.
1978	Pa.	?	200	College	No	Yes	Construction in area, but no specific defect found.

[a]From Center for Disease Control, 1978.
[b]B = bacterial; C = chemical.

TABLE V-2 Reported Waterborne Outbreaks Involving Semipublic and Individual Systems with Deficiencies in Distribution System, 1971–1978[a]

Year	State	Etiology	No. of Cases	Location	Documented Contamination of Water[b]	Chlorinated	Deficiency
Semipublic Systems							
1976	Calif.	?	60	State park	Yes(B)	No	Indirect cross-connection with back-siphonage from mineral water pool during period of high demand (cold water intake below water level).
1977	S.C.	Hepatitis A	47	Plant	No	No	Indirect cross-connection with back-siphonage (broken sewer and water lines).
1978	Pa.	*Salmonella weltevreden*	11	Camp	Yes(B)	No	Contamination of water in covered holding tanks, possibly by geckos.
1978	N.M.	Fluoride	34	School	Yes(C)	No	Faulty relay switch activated fluoridation unit while well pump not running, which discharged sodium fluoride solution into storage tanks.
1978	Pa.	?	91	Resort	Yes(B)	No	Defect not specified.
1978	Wash.	Norwalk-like agent	467	School	Yes(B)	No	Temporary indirect cross-connection between water pressure tank and floor drain; mechanical obstruction of sewage line with back-siphonage.
Individual System							
1976	Pa.	Lead	2	Home	Yes(C)	No	Leaching from lead pipe.

[a]From Center for Disease Control, 1978.
[b]B = bacterial; C = chemical.

TABLE V-3   Proportion of Reported Waterborne
Outbreaks and Cases Due to Deficiencies in
Distribution System by Type of System, 1971–1978[a]

System	Outbreaks	Cases
Municipal	26/68 (38%)	9,298/33,473 (28%)
Semipublic	6/129 (5%)	710/14,470 (5%)
Individual	1/27 (4%)	2/249 (1%)
TOTAL	33/224 (15%)	10,010/48,192 (21%)

[a]From Center for Disease Control, 1978.

water. Further investigation indicated that municipal water used to cool a
refrigerator compressor was discharged through a pipe submerged in a
clogged sink filled with wastewater containing *Salmonella typhimurium*.
The resulting indirect cross-connection resulted in back-siphonage during
a period of high demand caused by the operation of on-site pumps to pres-
surize the irrigation system for a nearby golf course. Control measures included removing the discharge pipe from the sink (Center for Disease
Control, 1976).

Chattanooga, Tennessee

On March 24, 1976, residents of a three-street area in Chattanooga com-
plained that their water turned white and smelled of insecticide. Epidemiological investigation identified 13 ill individuals. Extremely high concen-

TABLE V-4   Nature of Distribution System Deficiency
in Reported Outbreaks Involving Municipal Systems,
1971–1978[a]

Deficiency	No.	Percent[b]
Indirect cross-connections	13	50
Direct cross-connections	5	19
Contamination during construction	3	12
Leaching of copper from pipes	3	12
Contamination of open reservoir	1	4
Unknown	1	1
TOTAL	26	101

[a]From Center for Disease Control, 1978.
[b]Numbers are rounded off. Thus, total is not exactly 100%.

TABLE V-5 Etiology of Reported Outbreaks Due to Deficiencies in Municipal Distribution System or to Other Deficiencies, 1971–1978[a]

Etiology	Outbreaks Due to Deficiencies in Distribution System		Outbreaks Due to Other Deficiencies	
	No.	Percent	No.	Percent
Unknown	13	50	17	40
Chemical	10	38[b]	2	5[b]
Bacterial diarrhea (*Shigella sonnei, Salmonella typhimurium*)	2	8	9	21
Hepatitis	1	4	4	10
Giardia lamblia	0	0[c]	10	24[c]
TOTAL	26	100	42	100

[a] From Center for Disease Control, 1978.
[b] Fisher's two-tailed exact test, $p = 0.00067$.
[c] Fisher's two-tailed exact test, $p = 0.01$.

trations of chlordane were identified in the water of and soil surrounding a house in which chlordane had been used on March 24 to exterminate termites. The exact mode in which the municipal water supply in this three-street area was contaminated was not identified. However, the most likely explanation is that back-siphonage of chlordane occurred when the concentrated chlordane solution was diluted with water from a hose. This could have taken place during a period of low pressure resulting from the breakage of several nearby water mains the previous week by a building contractor. Control measures included replacement of all street pipes in the affected area and flushing of pipes to each house (Center for Disease Control, 1976).

Los Lunas, New Mexico

On the morning of November 17, 1978, 34 students at an elementary school developed an acute gastrointestinal illness. Epidemiological investigation indicated that the illness was related to contaminated drinking water from the semipublic supply at the school. Examination of the water system indicated a faulty electrical relay switch in the circuit from the pressure gauge for the storage tanks to the well pump and the fluoridator pump. This malfunction permitted the fluoridator to pump concentrated sodium fluoride solution into the storage tanks without simultaneously

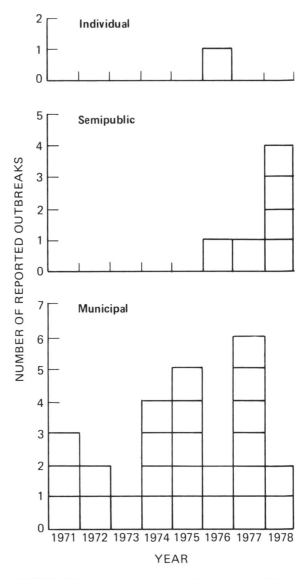

FIGURE V-2 Reported waterborne outbreaks due to deficiencies in distribution systems, by type of system and year, 1971–1978.

pumping an appropriate amount of water into the tanks. In addition, a toilet in the bathroom near a hallway drinking fountain continued to run following flushing. The continual flow of water into this building caused by this toilet defect accounted for the concentration of fluoride (275 mg/liter) in the school's water being higher than that in the water in an adjacent building (93.5 mg/liter). Control measures included repair of the electrical relay switch and the toilet (Center for Disease Control, 1978).

Pierce County, Washington

During the first week of May 1978, approximately 70% of the students and teachers at a rural elementary school developed an acute gastrointestinal illness. Epidemiological investigation suggested that the illness had been acquired by drinking water from the semipublic supply at the school. Serologic studies indicated that the outbreak was caused by a Norwalk-like agent. Further investigation revealed that a pipe had been installed to deliver overflow from the air outlet of a pressure tank to a nearby floor drain. On the day when transmission occurred, turbid foul-smelling water was noted on the floor around the drain. The overflow was caused by a jammed baffle at the point of entry of the drain line into the school septic tank. Control measures included removal of the cross connection and repair of the jammed baffle (Center for Disease Control, 1978).

HEALTH EFFECTS OF CHEMICAL CONTAMINANTS IN DISTRIBUTION SYSTEMS

Chemical contaminants that may be introduced into drinking water from the distribution system are listed in Table V-6. The adverse health effects of most of these agents have been reviewed in previous publications of the Safe Drinking Water Committee. For the convenience of the reader of this volume, references are provided to the appropriate *Drinking Water and Health* volume for each of the agents listed in the table.

SUMMARY AND CONCLUSIONS

Deficiencies in distribution systems were responsible for 15% of water-borne disease outbreaks reported from 1971 through 1978.

Municipal water systems were more likely than semipublic or individual water systems to be associated with outbreaks related to distribution system deficiencies; 38% of the outbreaks and 28% of the cases involving

TABLE V-6 Health Effects of Chemical Contaminants
Associated with the Distribution System

Contaminant	Source	References to Discussions of Health Effects in the *Drinking Water and Health* Series of Reports[a]
Lead	Corrosion	1:309–311
		1:258–260
		3:270–271
		4:179–183
Zinc	Corrosion and corrosion inhibitors	1:299–302
		1:315–316
Cadmium	Corrosion	1:238–240
		3:92–96
		3:271
		4:170–174
Iron	Corrosion, deposition, and resuspension	3:309–312
Copper	Corrosion	1:252–253
		1:308–309
		3:312–315
Nickel	Corrosion	1:287–288
		1:345–350
Chromium	Corrosion	1:242–246
		1:306–307
		3:364–369
Manganese	Deposition and resuspension	1:266–270
		1:311–312
		3:334–337
Phosphates	Corrosion inhibitors	3:277–278
Vinyl chloride	Plastic pipe	1:783–787
Asbestos	Asbestos-cement pipe	1:160–168
		1:189
Inorganic hydrated silicates	Asbestos-cement pipe	3:355–356
Polynuclear aromatic hydrocarbons and related substances	Pipe or tank lining	4:255–264
Tetrachlorethylene	Pipe or tank lining	1:769–780
		3:134–142

[a]References are cited as volume and page number(s), from this (volume 4) and the first three volumes of *Drinking Water and Health* (National Academy of Sciences, 1977, 1980a,b), e.g., 1:309–311 refers to pages 309–311 in the first volume (National Academy of Sciences, 1977).

municipal systems were caused by such defects. However, these data must be interpreted with caution since reporting of outbreaks is certainly not complete. That municipal systems were most frequently involved probably reflects both the fact that they have more complex distribution systems resulting in greater potential for cross-connections and the fact that outbreaks involving municipal systems are most likely to be recognized and reported. The most common defects were indirect cross-connections, which permitted wastewater or toxic chemicals to gain access to the water system by back-siphonage through hoses or defects in water pipes during periods of low pressure. Less frequent defects included direct cross-connections, contamination of the system during construction, leaching of copper from pipes, and contamination of an open reservoir. Outbreaks of chemical etiology involving municipal water systems were especially likely to be caused by distribution system deficiencies.

RECOMMENDATIONS

- Intensify surveillance, investigation, and reporting of outbreaks of waterborne diseases at the local, state, and federal levels.
- Maintain adequate pressure in distribution systems so that back-siphonage cannot occur.
- Develop public education programs that focus on the prevention of indirect cross-connections.
- Maintain a chlorine residual throughout the system.

REFERENCES

Center for Disease Control. 1976. Water Related Disease Outbreaks—Annual Summary. Center for Disease Control, Atlanta, Ga.

Center for Disease Control. 1978. Water Related Disease Outbreaks—Annual Summary. Center for Disease Control, Atlanta, Ga.

Lippy, E.C., and J. Erb. 1976. Gastrointestinal illness at Sewickley, Pa. J. Am. Water Works Assoc. 68:606–610.

Morse, L.J., J.A. Bryan, J.P. Hurley, J.F. Murphy, T.F. O'Brien, and W.E.C. Wacker. 1972. The Holy Cross College football team hepatitis outbreak. J. Am. Med. Assoc. 219: 706–708.

Weissman, J.B., G.F. Craun, D.N. Lawrence, R.A. Pollard, M.S. Saslaw, and E.J. Gangarosa. 1976. An epidemic of gastroenteritis traced to a contaminated public water supply. Am. J. Epidemiol. 103:391–398.

U.S. Treasury Department, Public Health Service. 1936. Epidemic Amebic Dysentery. The Chicago Outbreak of 1933. National Institute of Health Bulletin No. 166. U.S. Government Printing Office, Washington, D.C. 187 pp.

VI

Toxicity of Selected Inorganic Contaminants in Drinking Water

SELECTION OF CONTAMINANTS

In 1977, the Safe Drinking Water Committee examined health effects associated with microbiological, radioactive, particulate, inorganic, and organic chemical contaminants found in drinking water (National Academy of Sciences, 1977). Additional selected chemical contaminants were considered in a subsequent study (National Academy of Sciences, 1980b). The health effects of the organic and inorganic contaminants evaluated in Chapters VI and VII of this volume were selected for one or more of the following reasons:

• They are contaminants that have been identified in drinking water since the previous studies were conducted by the Safe Drinking Water Committee.
• Sufficient new data have become available to justify further attention to contaminants evaluated in the earlier studies.
• Several compounds were judged to be of concern because of potential spill situations.
• They are contamintants associated with the drinking water distribution system.
• They are structurally related to known toxic chemicals.

ACUTE AND CHRONIC EXPOSURE

The committee has evaluated the data concerning both acute and chronic exposures to selected chemicals. Information derived from studies of acute exposure provides a basis for judging health effects resulting from accidental spills of chemicals into drinking water supplies.

A suggested no-adverse-response level (SNARL) for acute exposures of 24 hours or 7 days has been calculated for these compounds for which sufficient data were available. These values were based on the assumption that 100% of the exposure to the chemical was supplied by drinking water during either the 24-hour or 7-day period. When the chemical was a known or suspected carcinogen, the potential for carcinogenicity after acute exposure was not considered. Acute SNARL's were calculated only when there were data on human exposures or data from oral tests in animals. LD_{50}'s were not used as a basis for calculation. If no-effect levels were not known, the lowest level producing an observed effect was used with an appropriate safety factor. Some 7-day values were derived by dividing the 24-hour SNARL by 7. The converse was not done, nor were data obtained from studies of lifetime exposures used to establish acute SNARL's.

The calculated acute SNARL's should not be used to estimate hazards from exposures exceeding 7 days. They are *not* a guarantee of absolute safety. Furthermore, SNARL's are based on exposure to a single agent and do not take into account possible interactions with other contaminants. In all cases, the safety or uncertainty factor used in the calculations of the SNARL's reflect the degree of confidence in the data as well as the combined judgment of the committee members.

As in the previous reports, the following assumptions were used when assigning an uncertainty factor to calculate either the acute or chronic SNARL's:

• An uncertainty (safety) factor of 10 was used when data on both human exposure and extensive chronic exposures of animals were available.

• A factor of 100 was used when chronic and acute toxicity data were available for one or more species.

• A factor of 1,000 was used when the acute or chronic toxicity data were limited or incomplete.

SNARL's for chronic exposure were calculated for chemicals that were not known or suspected to be carcinogens on the basis of data obtained

TABLE VI-1 Summation of Acute and Chronic
Exposure Levels for Inorganic Chemicals
Reviewed in this Chapter

Chemical	Suggested No-Adverse-Response Level (SNARL), mg/liter, by Exposure Period[a]		
	24-Hour	7-Day	Chronic
Aluminum	35.0	5.0	
Barium	6.0		4.7
Cadmium	0.15	0.021	0.005
Chlorate	0.125	0.125	
Chlorite	0.125	0.125	
Chlorine dioxide	1.2	0.125	
Chloramine	1.2	0.125	
Strontium		8.4	

[a]See text for details on individual compounds.

during a major portion of the lifetime of the laboratory animals. An arbitrary assumption was made that 20% of the intake of the chemical of concern was derived from drinking water. Therefore, it would be inappropriate to use these values as though they were maximum contaminant intakes. Table VI-1 summarizes the acute and chronic SNARL's for the inorganic chemicals reviewed in this chapter.

The 1977 Amendments to the Safe Drinking Water Act of 1974 (PL 93-523) authorized the committee to revise the earlier studies to reflect "new information which has become available since the most recent previous report [and which shall be reported to Congress each two years thereafter]."

Thus, the descriptions of some contaminants in Chapters VI and VII are limited to data generated since the last three volumes of *Drinking Water and Health* were published. Other contaminants and their health effects are evaluated for the first time in this series of reports. This is one reason why no significance should be attached to the length of the discussion devoted to each contaminant.

Included in this chapter is information on the toxicity of several metallic ions associated generally with drinking water distribution systems. Other contaminants, such as barium, lead, and strontium, pose problems only in certain local areas. The chlorine derivatives were evaluated because of their possible use as alternatives to chlorine in the disinfection of drinking water.

Recently, the EPA Criteria and Standards Division of the Office of Water Planning and Standards released a series of documents on Ambient Water Quality Criteria. Although the committee does not endorse all of the conclusions (e.g., numerical criterion formulations) reached in those documents, it does believe that they are a valuable source of general toxicological information. Several of the contamintants that are examined in Chapters VI and VII of this report were previously evaluated in one of these criteria documents.

This committee agrees with the following statement from *Drinking Water and Health*, Volume 3 (National Academy of Sciences, 1980, p. 68):

It was the belief of this subcommittee that it could perform a more valuable service to the Environmental Protection Agency (EPA) in the future if it evaluated criteria documents that were prepared by the EPA or other groups contracted to conduct these tasks. It will be necessary for the EPA to develop a mechanism for a comprehensive search and review of the literature in order to make in-depth hazard assessments for these chemicals. It is the consensus of this subcommittee that this cannot be done appropriately by the National Academy of Sciences because time and staff requirements far exceed those available. Neither can it be expected that the scientists who donate their services on these subcommittees will have the resources or time to carry out the routine aspects of this task.

In keeping with this philosophy, the committee drew heavily from criteria documents when one had already been prepared for the contaminant being studied. In such cases, the document was reviewed for accuracy and updated when additional information was available. For some of the contaminants reviewed here, appropriate parts of the criteria documents were condensed and included in the final report.

The committee commends the EPA for making this valuable material available for study and evaluation. It hopes that future committees with a similar mission will have the opportunity to review documents of this type prior to their general release. Because of the tremendous volume of data to evaluate for the hundreds of potential drinking water contaminants, this type of collaboration is beneficial to all concerned.

Aluminum (Al)

Aluminum, a silver-white, malleable, and ductile metal, is the third most abundant element in the earth's crust, comprising 8.3% of its volume. In nature, it is generally found in a combined state with various silicates, the most important of which are bauxite and cryolite (Norseth, 1979).

The world production of aluminum in 1974 was estimated to be approximately 14 million tons (Norseth, 1979). There are more than 4,000 terminal uses of this element in such fields as electrical engineering and the transport and air traffic industries and in such products as building materials, home furnishings, kitchen appliances, farm implements, containers for packaging material, and building structures. In powder form, aluminum is a component of paints, pigments, missile fuel, and chemical explosives. Medicinally, aluminum and its salts are used in antacids, antidiarrheals, and protective dermatological pastes. It is also found in cosmetics and deodorants. Aluminum compounds are applied in the processing, packaging, and preservation of foods. It is also used to line water storage vessels and in the purification of drinking water (Gilman *et al.*, 1980; Norseth, 1979; Sorenson *et al.*, 1974).

Concentrations of aluminum in soils vary widely, and its solubility is determined by pH. Concentrations of aluminum in water also vary. Since large amounts (> 100 μg/ml) occur only when the pH is less than 5, the concentration of aluminum in most natural waters is negligible (Sorenson *et al.*, 1974). In analyses of 1,577 U.S. water samples, Kopp and Korner (1970) found 456 samples positive for aluminum. Concentrations of soluble aluminum were as high as 2.76 μg/ml (mean, 0.074).

Aluminum compounds such as aluminum sulfate and potash aluminum and certain aluminum-bearing minerals are commonly used as major coagulants in the treatment of drinking water supplies. The principal coagulants are aluminum sulfate and potash aluminum. Aluminum sulfate is the principal coagulant and bentonite is a coagulating aid. Aluminum ammonium sulfate is used as a dechlorinating agent (Sorenson *et al.*, 1974). Sodium aluminate is added sometimes to remove fine turbidity. In modern purification practice, aluminum-based coagulants usually result in the presence of lower concentrations of aluminum in the drinking water than in the raw water (Sorenson *et al.*, 1974).

The major sources of aluminum in the normal human diet include plants and processed foods (Crapper and DeBoni, 1980). The concentrations in foods and beverages vary widely, depending upon the product, the type of processing, and the geographical areas in which the plants are raised (Sorenson *et al.*, 1974).

The daily intake of aluminum has been estimated in several studies. In general, the data pertaining to natural dietary intake indicate that concentrations range from approximately 10 to 50 mg/day (Sorenson *et al.*, 1974).

The use of aluminum in the processing and storing of food increases the aluminum content, but not enough to contribute significantly either to total body burden or the toxic effects (Norseth, 1979; Underwood, 1971).

In general, aluminum has largely been regarded as nontoxic. Neither the international nor the European standards for drinking water (World Health Organization 1970, 1973) lists aluminum among those substances for which limits are specified. The National Academy of Sciences' Committee on Water Quality Criteria recommended the following maximum concentrations of aluminum in agricultural and irrigation waters: 5.0 $\mu g/ml$ for waters used continuously on all soil and 20 $\mu g/ml$ for waters used not more than 20 years on fine textured neutral to alkaline soils (National Academy of Sciences, 1973).

Although the question of the essentiality of aluminum for biological function was raised as early as 1915, its function remains unknown (Sorenson et al., 1974). Failure to demonstrate this essentiality probably results from the difficulty of finding a diet that is deficient in the metal (Norseth, 1979; Underwood, 1971).

METABOLISM

The dynamics of absorption, distribution, and excretion of aluminum are poorly understood. Furthermore, little is known about its metabolism or the factors that determine burdens of aluminum in specific tissues. This is partially due to a lack of detection methodology and the universal contamination of laboratory reagents and chemicals with the metal (Crapper and DeBoni, 1980; Norseth, 1979; Sorenson et al., 1974). The human body burden of aluminum is estimated to range from 50 to 150 mg, most soft tissues containing approximately 0.2 to 0.6 $\mu g/g$ (Underwood, 1971).

Contrary to former opinion, studies by Kaehny et al. (1977a) have shown that aluminum is readily absorbed from the gastrointestinal tract by normal persons who consume one of several aluminum salts (e.g., hydroxide or carbonate) or dihydroxy aluminum aminoacetate, but not aluminum phosphate. In earlier studies, Clarkson et al. (1972) found a net gastrointestinal absorption of aluminum ranging from 100 to 568 mg/day in dialysis patients taking antacids containing 2 to 3.4 mg of aluminum daily for 20 to 32 days. In another study, Cam et al. (1976) studied the absorption of aluminum in both normal patients and patients suffering from chronic renal failure. Both groups of patients received approximately 2.5 g of aluminum daily for 23 to 27 days. In the normal group, the maximum absorption of aluminum was approximately 97 mg/day, while in the renal failure patients it was 256 mg/day. In balance studies conducted by Gorsky et al. (1979), the aluminum balance was usually negative in those patients receiving less than 5 mg of aluminum per day. However, when the diet was supplemented with antacids that contributed from 1 to 3 g of aluminum daily, an average positive balance of 23 to 313 mg of aluminum per day was observed over an 18- to 30-day period.

Studies by Mayor et al. (1977a,b) strongly suggest that aluminum in the gastrointestinal tract and its subsequent distribution in tissue can be influenced by increasing the concentration of parathyroid hormone (PTH). They fed male rats aluminum as 0.1% of their diet for 25 days. The ready absorption of aluminum from the gastrointestinal tract of these normal rats was enhanced by injections of PTH (17 U twice weekly). There was also increased deposition of the metal in the kidney, muscle, bone, and the gray matter of the brain, but not in the liver or in the white matter of the brain. Thus, the PTH exerted a specific effect on the absorption and distribution of aluminum. In 1977, these same investigators had found a positive correlation between increased serum PTH and serum aluminum levels in dialysis patients. The increase in serum PTH in these patients had been reported earlier by Kleeman and Better (1973).

In patients on dialysis, there are apparently two sources of extraneous aluminum: via the gastrointestinal tract from aluminum antacids, which are used to bind phosphate, and via the dialysate solution. Kaehny et al. (1977b) have shown that aluminum can also be transferred across the dialysis membranes. This transfer can occur even if the levels of aluminum in plasma are much higher than the levels of aluminum in the dialysate solution. Thus, aluminum has been shown to accumulate in the serum and in the tissues of chronic renal failure patients either after absorption from the gastrointestinal tract or from parenteral administration during dialysis with a solution that contains aluminum.

Following absorption or parenteral administration, aluminum distributes to nearly all of the organs including the brain (Crapper and DeBoni, 1980; Norseth, 1979; Sorenson et al., 1974). Lundin et al. (1978) have found that approximately 50% of the aluminum in the plasma of normal humans is bound to protein with a molecular weight greater than 8,000.

The major route of excretion of aluminum in humans appears to be the bile. Only a small amount is excreted via the urine (Gorsky et al., 1979). Parenteral administration of aluminum to laboratory animals increases urinary excretion (Norseth, 1979).

HEALTH ASPECTS

Since aluminum constitutes a substantial portion of the earth's crust and atmosphere and is a common contaminant in food and drinking water, environmental exposure is virtually universal (Bland, 1979; Goetz and Klawans, 1979; Sorenson et al., 1974). Its extensive uses in cosmetics, such as aluminum hexahydrate (aluminum chloride) in deodorants, and in medicines also provide opportunities for exposure of humans. In its predominant medical application it serves as an antacid to control gastric hyperacidity. Aluminum hydroxide is generally used for this purpose. In addition, aluminum is frequently combined with a magnesium-containing compound to prevent constipation (Sorenson *et al.*, 1974).

Aluminum hydroxide antacids are administered orally in large doses (5-10 g/day) in renal-failure patients to limit the accumulation of phosphate (hyperphosphatemia) and the consequent development of metastatic calcifications. The treatment induces phosphate loss by stopping the absorbability of phosphate in the gastrointestinal tract (Mallick and Berlyne, 1968).

In general, aluminum has been considered to be nontoxic (Sorenson *et al.*, 1974). However, toxic syndromes have been observed in animals injected with the element (Sorenson *et al.*, 1974). There is also a good deal of interest in the role of aluminum in various syndromes of the central nervous system in humans. Recent studies indicate that it may be selectively toxic to certain neurons in the central nervous system (Crapper and DeBoni, 1980; Goetz and Klawans, 1980; Norseth, 1979).

Observations in Humans

Recently reported adverse effects of aluminum in humans have resulted from inhalation or ingestion of aluminum in concentrations many times greater than the amounts present in normal circumstances. Following large oral doses of aluminum, toxic syndromes involve gastrointestinal tract irritation and, eventually, interference with phosphate absorption, which results in rickets (Casarett and Doull, 1977). Industrial exposure to high concentrations of aluminum-containing airborne dusts has resulted in a number of cases of occupational pneumoconiosis (Norseth, 1979; Sorenson *et al.*, 1974). Most of these exposures were chronic, and other substances were involved in nearly all instances. For example, an asthma-like disease has been reported in workers engaged in the production of aluminum from its oxide. This condition may result from the hydrogen fluoride that evolves from the use of fluorine-bearing materials in the production of metallic aluminum (Sorenson *et al.*, 1974). Silicosis, aluminosis, aluminum lung, and bauxite pneumoconiosis are the result of pulmonary fibrotic reactions to silica and aluminum-containing compounds, which have been observed in the lung tissue in humans (Sorenson *et al.*, 1974). Paradoxically, aluminum powder has been used in the prevention and therapy of silicosis. The rationale is that small amounts of metallic aluminum inhibit the solubility of siliceous materials in the lungs or diminish their fibrogenic properties (Casarett and Doull, 1977; Denny *et al.*, 1939). There is no unequivocable evidence that the procedure is clinically effective (Sorenson *et al.*, 1974).

In one of the earliest cases reported by McLaughlin *et al.* (1962), an aluminum-ball-mill worker died with encephalopathy and pulmonary fibrosis. After having been exposed to aluminum-containing compounds more than 13 years, the concentration of aluminum in his brain was 20 times greater than that in the brains of controls. In more recent studies, aluminum deposition in the brain has been implicated as an etiologic factor in two neurologic disorders: Alzheimer's disease and chronic renal failure accompanied by senile dementia (Alfrey et al., 1976; Crapper et al., 1973). Nonetheless, the importance of aluminum as a pathogenic factor in human disease has not yet been established (Crapper and DeBoni, 1980).

Alzheimer's disease usually occurs in humans after the age of 40. It is a slowly progressive, fatal encephalopathy associated with behavioral alterations, memory disturbances, spacial disorientation, agnosia, dysphasia, and seizures (Crapper and Dalton, 1973a,b; Crapper and DeBoni, 1980). The role of aluminum as an etiologic agent in Alzheimer's disease rests on circumstantial evidence such as the resemblance between aluminum-induced neurofilamentous aggregates and human neurofibrillar tangles that characterize Alzheimer's disease and senile dementia (Goetz and Klawans, 1980; Klatzo et al., 1965; Terry, 1963). However, there are important differences between the morphological changes induced in animals by aluminum and those observed in humans with Alzheimer's disease (Crapper and DeBoni, 1980). Additional circumstantial evidence has been provided by studies of Crapper et al. (1976), who reported elevated aluminum levels in some regions of the brains of patients who had died from Alzheimer's disease. For example, in 28% of the 585 brain regions sampled, aluminum levels exceeded 4 μg/g—the minimum concentration of metal associated with neurofibrillar degeneration in cats observed in the same laboratory (Crapper et al., 1973). Trapp et al. (1978) also reported increased aluminum levels in patients who had died from Alzheimer's disease. However, McDermott et al. (1978) did not find any significant differences in aluminum levels in brain samples taken from patients suffering from Alzheimer's disease and healthy, age-matched controls. Before aluminum is assigned a role in Alzheimer's disease, further investigations must be undertaken (Crapper and DeBoni, 1980).

Another encephalopathic syndrome in which aluminum has been suggested as an etiologic agent has been described as "dialysis encephalopathy" or "dialysis dementia," which is a relentlessly progressive form of dementia observed in chronic dialysis patients (Alfrey et al., 1976; Anonymous, 1976; Elliott et al., 1978; Goetz and Klawans, 1979). This disorder is characterized by an insidious onset of altered behavior, speech disturbances, dyspraxia, tremor, myoclonus, convulsions, personality changes, and psychoses. This syndrome, which results in death within approximately 6 to 7 months (Alfrey et al., 1976; Bland, 1979; Crapper and

DeBoni, 1980), has been reported to be the leading cause of death in long-term dialysis patients (Crapper and DeBoni, 1980; Goetz and Klawans, 1979). The majority of the patients in whom this syndrome developed had been on intermittent hemodialysis for 3 to 7 years before the onset of symptoms. All had routinely received aluminum-containing antacids for the purpose of binding gastrointestinal phosphates for at least 2 years.

The possible hazard of aluminum intoxication in dialysis patients was first described by Berlyne et al. (1970). Subsequent studies by Alfrey et al. (1976) showed that patients dying of the syndrome had significantly higher tissue concentrations of aluminum in their bones, skeletal muscles, and gray matter of the brain. These authors reported that the aluminum concentrations in the gray matter of the brain were approximately 4 times higher in these patients than in any other group.

The source of aluminum was not limited to the antacids given to these patients, but was contained in the water used to prepare the dialysate solution as well (Alfrey et al., 1976; Crapper and DeBoni, 1980; Elliott et al., 1978). Because only a few of the dialysis patients taking large doses of aluminum-containing antacids develop the syndrome, it has been suggested that the syndrome may be related to aluminum contamination of the water used for dialysis.

One outbreak occurring in Chicago between September 1972 and January 1976 affected 20 patients who had been maintained on long-term hemodialysis (Dunea et al., 1978). It was later established that the city's adoption of a water purification method using pure aluminum sulfate resulted in higher concentrations of aluminum in the water. The relationships of the onset of the dementia to documentations of aluminum in the water and changes in water treatment are shown in Figure VI-1. The first cases of dementia appeared in September 1972, 3 months after the change in water treatment. They coincided with a peak water concentration of aluminum in the water (360 μg/liter). Thirteen patients became demented between September 1973 and August 1974, the later cases appearing during the winters of 1974-1975 and 1975-1976, shortly after additional peaks in aluminum concentrations in the water. Before the method of water treatment was changed, aluminum concentrations varied from 0 to 150 μg/liter. After the change, concentrations of aluminum were higher, peaking between 300 and 400 μg/liter. The other constituents of the water were not significantly altered. Studies by Elliot et al. (1978), Flendrig et al. (1976), and Ward et al. (1978) also suggest that high concentrations of aluminum in dialysate are important etiologic factors in outbreaks of the dialysis dementia syndrome.

Dialysis patients often exhibit multiple osteomalacic fractures and myopathic changes, mostly in the proximal muscles (Flendrig et al., 1976;

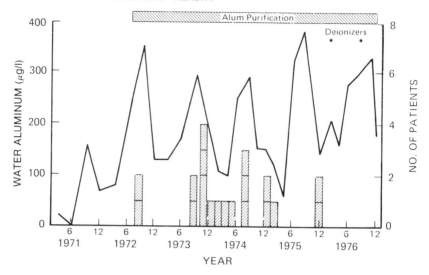

FIGURE VI-1 Relationship between changes in water treatment and dialysis dementia: ▨▨▨ = period of aluminum sulfate purification; ——— = water aluminum levels; ✫ ✫ = installation of deionizers at the two hospitals; ▨ = new cases of dialysis dementia.

Pierides, 1978; Platts *et al.*, 1977). The clinical features of this syndrome include progressive skeletal pain, proximal muscle weakness, and spontaneous fractures affecting primarily the ribs, pelvic rami, femoral necks, metatarsals, and other parts of the peripheral skeleton (Pierides, 1978). The skeletal demineralization may result from the binding of gastrointestinal phosphate by aluminum, leading to a decrease in phosphate absorption, decreased urinary phosphate levels, and an increase in urinary calcium (Spencer and Lender, 1979). In a second interaction, aluminum in the gut also binds with fluoride, thereby decreasing fluoride absorption (Spencer *et al.*, 1979). This may further contribute to the skeletal demineralization, since fluoride might play a role in the maintenance of normal bone structure.

The major etiologic factor associated with this syndrome is untreated aluminum-rich tap water that is used to prepare the dialysis fluid. Aluminum is known to accumulate in the serum and tissues of chronic renal failure patients either after it is absorbed from the gastrointestinal tract (Alfrey *et al.*, 1976) or after parenteral administration of a dialysis fluid containing a high concentration of aluminum (Elliott *et al.*, 1978; Kaehny *et al.*, 1977b). Interestingly, although many chronic renal failure patients consume large amounts of aluminum-containing antacids, this syndrome is distinctly absent in nondialyzed uremic patients, while exposure to repetitive hemodialysis for only 6 to 12 months may provoke this syndrome. The close relationship of this syndrome to dialysis is strengthened significantly by the repeated observation that in hemodialysis centers troubled by dialysis dementia or osteomalacic syndrome, a change to deionized water has helped to eliminate these complications (Dunea *et al.*, 1978; Flendrig *et al.*, 1976; Ward *et al.*, 1978). In another study, Pierides (1978) reported no new cases of the syndrome and a striking improvement in 12 patients after the introduction of a water-processing plant involving the use of a water softener, reverse osmosis, and deionization, in that order (Pierides, 1978).

Mayor *et al.* (1977a,b, 1978) indicated that PTH may also play an important role in this syndrome because of its ability to increase the absorption of aluminum in the gastrointestinal tract and because elevated levels of serum PTH have been found in most dialysis patients (Kleeman and Better, 1973).

Observations in Other Species

Severe aluminum intoxication following parenteral or oral administration of aluminum hydroxide, chloride, or sulfate to rats is characterized by lethargy, anorexia, or death (Berlyne *et al.*, 1972). Other authors have found that intratracheal instillation of aluminum salts or metallic aluminum powder has produced pulmonary fibroses (Stacey *et al.*, 1959). Injected intraperitoneally, aluminum compounds produce fibrotic peritonitis (Norseth, 1979; Sorenson *et al.*, 1974). The LD_{50}'s for several aluminum salts administered by the various routes to several animal species are given in Table VI-2.

The central nervous system is the major target organ for toxicity in mammals following administration of aluminum (Bland, 1978; Crapper and DeBoni, 1980; Norseth, 1979; Sorenson *et al.*, 1974). The neurotoxicity of aluminum has been demonstrated in the cat, rat, rabbit, and monkey following systemic administration subcutaneously or per os or after it was introduced directly into the central nervous system either intracisternally or intracerebrally (Crapper and Dalton, 1973a,b; Crapper *et al.*, 1976; DeBoni *et al.*, 1976; Klatzo *et al.*, 1965). The major pathologic lesion is neurofibrillar degeneration, which is similar but not identical to that observed in Alzheimer's disease (Crapper and DeBoni, 1980; Crapper *et al.*, 1976). It has been suggested that this could serve as a model for Alzheimer's disease (Crapper and DeBoni, 1980).

Administration of aluminum by oral or parenteral routes to uremic rats (5/6 nephrectomy) produced a clinical syndrome of lethargy, periorbital

TABLE VI-2   Acute Toxicity of Aluminum Compounds

Compound	Species	Route of Administration	LD_{50}, mg/kg	References
Aluminum	Rat	Oral	380	Krasovskii *et al.*, 1979
chloride	Guinea pig	Oral	400	Krasovskii *et al.*, 1979
	Rabbit	Oral	400	Krasovskii *et al.*, 1979
	Rat	Oral	757	Spector, 1956
	Mouse	Oral	780	Ondreicka *et al.*, 1966
Aluminum	Rat	Oral	542.5	Spector, 1956
nitrate	Mouse (male)	Intraperitoneal	37	Hart *et al.*, 1971
	Rat (female)	Intraperitoneal	37	Hart and Adamson, 1971
Aluminum	Mouse	Intraperitoneal	6.3	Bienvenu *et al.*, 1963
sulfate	Mouse	Oral	970	Christensen, 1971

bleeding, anorexia, and death (Berlyne *et al.*, 1972). Other neurological syndromes produced by aluminum include that of epilepsy. High-frequency repetitive firing patterns comprising interictal bursts are consistent with findings in aluminum-treated animals (Goetz and Klawans, 1979). Moseley *et al.* (1972) originally described such seizure activity in relation to focal hypothermia in a focus induced by aluminum oxide or alumina in experimental animals. Abnormal electrical activity has also been observed in animals given aluminum to induce neurofibrillar degenerative changes. Alterations in electroencephalograms did not occur until late in the encephalopathy, and sequential comparisons of photically evoked responses served as a more sensitive measure of progressive cortical pathology (Crapper, 1973). In the opinion of Ward (1972), the aluminum hydroxide model provides one of the most promising approaches for studying processes underlying the epileptic focus.

There have been few subacute or chronic studies of animals exposed to aluminum. Sorenson *et al.* (1974) reported long-term experiments in which laboratory mice were fed aluminum chloride in concentrations ranging from 100 to 200 mg/kg, which resulted in retarded growth and disturbances of phosphate and carbohydrate metabolism in the exposed animals. The same authors described studies of aluminum compounds as food additives. In small amounts (1%–2%), they stimulated growth, but higher amounts retarded growth and caused grave disturbances of phosphate and calcium metabolism (Sorenson *et al.*, 1974). The results of other studies in which aluminum was administered either subchronically or chronically are presented in Table VI-3.

Schroeder and Mitchener (1975) exposed weanling male and female Long-Evans rats to aluminum potassium sulfate salt in concentrations of 5 mg/liter in drinking water over the lifetime of the animals. Males fed aluminum grew significantly heavier, but the weight of the females were similar to those of the controls. Aluminum did not alter life span or the amount of glucose or protein in the urine. However, male rats at autopsy did have an increased incidence of gross tumors, but no increase in malignant tumors.

Mutagenicity   DiPaolo and Casto (1979) studied the effect of various metals on the *in-vitro* morphological transformation of Syrian hamster embryo cells. The results for aluminum chloride administered in concentrations up to 20 μg/ml were negative. In shorter experiments (20 to 30 days), aluminum chloride was given orally to rats, guinea pigs, and rabbits in doses ranging from 3 to 50 mg/kg/day, and in chronic experiments (6 to 12 months) it was given to rats in oral doses ranging from 0.025 to 2.5 mg/kg. No chromosomal aberrations were found in bone marrow cells as a result of these exposures (Krasovskii *et al.*, 1979).

Carcinogenicity   Studies of animals have failed to demonstrate carcinogenicity that is attributable to aluminum powder or aluminum salts as the hydroxide, phosphate, or oxide administered by various routes to rabbits, mice, or guinea pigs (Furst, 1971; Furst and Harro, 1969; Shubick and Hartwell, 1969).

Teratogenicity   In one study, concentrations of aluminum ranging from 500 to 1,000 μg/g body weight were added to the diets of pregnant rats from day 6 to day 19 of gestation, when the fetuses were removed by Caesarean section. Aluminum in the diet did not affect embryo or fetal mortality rate, litter size, fetal body weight, or length (McCormack *et al.*,

TABLE VI-3   Subchronic or Chronic Toxicity of Aluminum Chloride

Species	Route	Dose	Duration	Effects	References
Mice	Oral	100 mg/kg	6–12 mo.	No change in growth or reproduction	Ondreicka *et al.*, 1966
Rat	Oral	150 mg/kg		Negative phosphorus balance; decreased incorporation of ^{32}P into phospholipids; decrease in ATP	Ondreicka *et al.*, 1966
Rat	Oral	1 g/kg/day	18 days	Decrease in liver glycogen and coenzyme A	Kortus, 1967

1979). However, in a similarly designed experiment in which the pregnant mothers received subcutaneous injections of PTH (68 U/kg) on days 6, 9, 12, 15, or 18 of gestation, there was an increase only in the resorption rate in those animals receiving aluminum at 1,000 μg/g body weight (McCormack *et al.*, 1979).

CONCLUSIONS AND RECOMMENDATIONS

Suggested No-Adverse-Response Level (SNARL)

24-Hour Exposure   Kortus (1967) reported a minimum-effect dose for rats at 1 g/kg/day administered over an 18-day period (see Table VI-2). Using this value, applying a safety factor of 1,000, and assuming that a 70-kg human consumes 2 liters of drinking water daily and that 100% of exposure is from water during this period, one may calculate the 24-hour SNARL as:

$$\frac{1,000 \text{ mg/kg} \times 70 \text{ kg}}{1,000 \times 2 \text{ liters}} = 35.0 \text{ mg/liter}.$$

This value exceeds the solubility of aluminum in nonacidic solutions. Thus, it has only limited usefulness.

7-Day Exposure   Based on the 24-hour SNARL, the 7-day SNARL is calculated:

$$\frac{35.0 \text{ mg/liter}}{7} = 5.0 \text{ mg/liter}.$$

This value also exceeds the solubility of aluminum in nonacidic solutions and, thus, has only limited usefulness.

Chronic Exposure   There are no adequate data from which to calculate a chronic SNARL.

In view of the wide exposure of humans to aluminum in food, cosmetics, medicines, and water sources, it would appear that aluminum is relatively nontoxic to the majority of the population (Sorenson *et al.*, 1974). However, epidemiological studies indicate that chronic hemodialysis patients comprise a special population at risk. No studies have been conducted to determine what level of aluminum might be tolerated by this patient population. Pierides (1978) reported that some nephrologists believe that tap water containing aluminum concentrations of 50 μg/liter is safe. However, studies by Alfrey *et al.* (1976) have shown that a positive aluminum balance will occur even at this level. Therefore, it is best if the dialysis fluid is prepared with softened water treated by reverse osmosis and deionization, in that order (Pierides, 1978).

Further studies are needed to assess the molecular interaction of aluminum and the components of the central nervous system, which produce the pathological changes observed in patients with Alzheimer's disease.

Arsenic (As)

Arsenic compounds were evaluated in the first volume of *Drinking Water and Health* (National Academy of Sciences, 1977). The EPA standard for arsenic is 50 μg/liter for drinking water (U.S. Environmental Protection Agency, 1977). Although there is no reliable evidence that arsenic compounds produce tumors in laboratory animals, epidemiological studies show that the incidence of epidermoid carcinomas of the skin and lungs and precancerous dermal keratoses may be increased in humans who have been chronically exposed to arsenic compounds by oral or respiratory routes (Leonard and Lauwerys, 1980).

Because of the continuing uncertainty surrounding what role, if any, arsenic has in the etiology of epidermoid carcinomas of the skin and lungs and precancerous dermal keratoses this subject needs further evaluation. The followup study to this volume will include a thorough review of the epidemiologic association between arsenic in drinking water and these conditions.

Barium (Ba)

Barium was reviewed in the first volume of *Drinking Water and Health* (National Academy of Sciences, 1977). At that time the committee concurred with the reasoning of Stokinger and Woodward (1958), who concluded that a barium concentration of 2 mg/liter of water was safe for adults, but suggested a reduction to 1 mg/liter to provide an added margin of safety for children. This level was calculated from the threshold limit value (TLV) in industrial air, which remains at 0.5 mg/m^3 (American Conference of Governmental Industrial Hygienists, 1980). In the 1977 report, the committee pointed out that there had been no long-range feeding studies to confirm the safety of barium intake. This lack of data persists.

Since the 1977 report was published, information has come to light indicating that the basis on which the original, and current, drinking water standard (1 mg/liter) was established may have been in error. Stokinger and Woodward (1958) assumed that 90% of ingested barium was absorbed via the gastrointestinal tract. The rationale or documentation for using the 90% figure was not given in their report. Subsequently, Cuddihy and Ozog (1973) reported that the gastric absorption of barium-chloride-133 in Syrian hamsters was 11% ± 13%. Another report indicated that the intestinal absorption of barium was 5% (Committee II on Permissible Dose for Internal Radiation, 1960). Still another value of 20% can be interpolated from data on the absorption of strontium and radium, which have physical properties quite similar to those of barium (International Commission on Radiological Protection, 1972). Thus, it seems quite clear that the original figure of 90% for the gastrointestinal absorption of barium cannot be justified. Based on the conservative value of 20% gastrointestinal absorption, the oral intake limit (maximum allowable concentration) would increase from 1 mg/liter to 4.7 mg/liter. Calculations for the former oral intake limit were based on the original acceptable daily intake value of 3.75 mg derived from the 0.5 mg/m³ TLV by Stokinger and Woodward (1958), 90% gastrointestinal absorption, the consumption of 2 liters of water daily, and an additional safety factor of 2:

$$\frac{3.75\,\text{mg}}{0.9} = 4.17\,\text{mg}; \qquad \frac{4.17\,\text{mg}}{2\,\text{liters}} = 2\,\text{mg/liter};$$

$$\frac{2\,\text{mg/liter}}{2} = 1\,\text{mg/liter}.$$

Substituting the gastrointestinal absorption value of 20%, one may calculate the oral intake limit as follows:

$$\frac{3.75\,\text{mg}}{0.2} = 18.75\,\text{mg}; \qquad \frac{18.75\,\text{mg}}{2\,\text{liters}} = 9.375\,\text{mg/liter};$$

$$\frac{9.375\,\text{mg/liter}}{2} = 4.7\,\text{mg/liter}.$$

Therefore, the committee recommends that the current drinking water standard of 1 mg/liter be reevaluated.

One study in animals not reported in the first volume of *Drinking Water and Health* was conducted by Schroeder and Mitchener (1975). In this study, male and female weanling Long-Evans rats were given a 5-mg/liter concentration of barium as barium acetate in drinking water over a lifetime. In general, there was no toxicity, in terms of survival time or effect on growth rate. Minor changes were noted in fasting serum glucose and cholesterol values. There was an increase in proteinuria in males.

The above results were extended and confirmed when Tardiff *et al.*

(1980) studied the subchronic oral toxicity of barium chloride in adult rats. Groups of rats of both sexes were given barium chloride in their drinking water at levels of 0, 10, 50, or 250 mg/liter for 4, 8, or 13 weeks. The investigators observed no adverse effects on food consumption, body weight, hematologic indices, serum enzymes, serum ions, gross pathology, or histopathology. They noted a slight decrease in the relative weights of the adrenal glands at the highest doses ($p = >0.05$). This study provides further evidence of the low degree of toxicity resulting from the subchronic ingestion of barium.

Brenniman *et al*. (1979) studied death rates from cardiovascular disease in communities with elevated levels of barium in drinking water. They compared the rates in communities with barium levels ranging from 2.0 to 10.0 mg/liter with those from communities with 0.0 to 0.2 mg/liter. When age- and sex-adjusted death rates for cardiovascular disease in high- and low-barium communities were compared, there was a higher ($p > 0.05$) death rate for both males and females in the high-barium communities for "all cardiovascular deaths," "health disease" (atheroscelerosis), and "all causes." When male and female death rates were analyzed separately, only male deaths from "all cardiovascular disease" and female deaths from "all causes" were significant. The authors mentioned several confounding factors that make it difficult to interpret the results of this study. For example, the high-barium communities had a considerable population increase between 1960 and 1970, while the low-barium communities were more stable. This could influence the duration of exposure that would most likely play a role in any possible effect of barium. Moreover, it was not possible to control for the use of home water-softeners. Since there may be a relationship between softened water and cardiovascular disease (National Academy of Sciences, 1977), this confounding variable could be important.

Brenniman *et al*. (1981) also studied the effects of barium in public water supplies on blood pressure. They compared two populations in Illinois whose drinking water supplies contained mean barium drinking water levels of 7.3 mg/liter and 0.1 mg/liter. All other drinking water constituents were approximately equal in the supplies of the two communities. They found no significant differences ($p > 0.05$) in either systolic or diastolic blood pressures between the high- and low-barium communities. Adjustments for duration of exposure, use of home water-softeners, and treatment for hypertension did not alter the findings. This study is of interest because of the current general lack of information on health effects resulting from chronic exposure to barium. It also partially addresses several problems that were encountered in their original (1979) study. Further intensive study of these two populations is strongly recommended in light of the conflicting results obtained to date.

CONCLUSIONS AND RECOMMENDATIONS

Suggested No-Adverse-Response Level (SNARL)

24-Hour Exposure The reported lethal dose of barium chloride in humans is 800 to 900 mg (550 to 600 mg of barium) (Sollmann, 1957a). Threshold toxic doses range from 120 to 500 mg/day (Reeves, 1979). Based on a safety factor of 10 and the assumption that 100% of the exposure during this period comes from a 2-liter daily intake of drinking water, the SNARL would be:

$$\frac{120 \text{ mg}}{10 \times 2 \text{ liters}} = 6.0 \text{ mg/liter.}$$

7-Day Exposure If the 24-hour SNARL is divided by 7, the value derived (0.86 mg/liter) is less than the current drinking water standard. Therefore, there are no adequate data from which to calculate a reasonable 7-day SNARL.

Chronic Exposure The average concentration of barium in U.S. drinking water is 28.6 μg/liter (range, 1 to 172 μg/liter (National Academy of Sciences, 1977). The drinking water of many communities in Illinois, Kentucky, Pennsylvania, and New Mexico contains concentrations of barium that may be 10 times higher than the drinking water standard. The source of these supplies is usually well water. Because many people are exposed to those concentrations, it would be prudent to extend the observations of Brenniman *et al.* (1981) to potential effects other than those on cardiovascular disease and blood pressure. The data of Schroeder and Mitchener (1975) are the only chronic data available. Unfortunately, these investigators used only a single dose of barium (5 mg/liter). Although that dose produced no effects, it may be a low estimate of the no-effect level. Therefore, there are no adequate direct data from which to calculate a chronic SNARL for barium. However, the committee believes that the recalculated value of 4.7 mg/liter provides an adequate margin of safety for chronic exposure to barium.

Cadmium (Cd)

Cadmium was reviewed in the first and third volumes of *Drinking Water and Health* (National Academy of Sciences, 1977, 1980b) as well as in a recent EPA document (U.S. Environmental Protection Agency, 1979b). Since then, a plethora of research reports concerned with the toxicity of this element have been published. However, few of them deal directly with health effects that are relevant to establishing safe levels of cadmium in drinking water. The current drinking water standard is 10 μg/liter.

The following material is based only on reports not covered in the earlier volumes of this series. There is additional information on the possible relationship between cadmium and hypertension (Calabrese *et al.*, 1980), but it is not considered here since it goes beyond a general toxicological review.

HEALTH ASPECTS

Observations in Humans

In humans, acute oral doses of cadmium usually result from the ingestion of food or beverages that have been contaminated during storage in cadmium-plated containers. The initial symptoms include severe nausea, vomiting, diarrhea, muscle cramps, and salivation (Arena, 1963). When fatal intoxication occurs, these symptoms are followed either by shock due to the loss of liquid and death within 24 hours or by acute renal failure and cardiopulmonary depression and death within 7 to 14 days (Gosselin *et al.*, 1976).

According to McKee and Wolf (1963), punch containing cadmium concentrations of 67 mg/liter has caused sickness. If 200 to 500 ml of punch had been consumed, the cadmium intake would have been 13 to 35 mg.

Swedish schoolchildren were acutely poisoned after consuming a fruit drink from a distributing machine that had a cadmium-plated reservoir containing water in which cadmium concentrations ranged from 0.5 to 16 mg/liter (Friberg *et al.*, 1974).

Various estimates of acute oral toxicity to cadmium are as follows:

- 3 to 90 mg—emetic threshold (Arena, 1963; McKee and Wolf, 1963);
- 15 mg—experimentally induced vomiting (Browning, 1969; McKee and Wolf, 1963);
- 10 to 326 mg—severe toxic symptoms, but not fatal (Gosselin *et al.*, 1976); and
- 350 to 3,500 mg—estimated lethal doses (Gosselin *et al.*, 1976).

Observations in Other Species

The no-effect level for cadmium administered orally to animals in food or drinking water is approximately 10 mg/kg and 10 mg/liter, respectively. Kotsonis and Klaassen (1978) exposed male rats to cadmium at concentrations of 10, 30, and 100 mg/liter for 24 weeks. Testicular function, blood pressure, heart rate, electrocardiogram, hematocrit, blood hemoglobin, plasma glucose, aniline hydroxylase, hexobarbital oxidase, cytochrome P-450, organ weights, bone calcifications, and histopathology were examined at 3, 6, 12, and 24 weeks. The major toxicity noted was renal injury, which was indicated by an increase in urinary protein for the rats receiving cadmium in concentrations of 30 and 100 mg/liter but not at 10 mg/liter. The chronic exposure SNARL given in Volume 3 of *Drinking Water and Health* (National Academy of Sciences, 1980b) was based on a no-effect level of 10 mg/liter, which was reported by Decker *et al.* (1958).

After administering drinking water containing cadmium concentrations of 250 mg/liter to male rats for periods of 2 or 8 weeks, Hietanen (1978) reported alterations in hepatic and renal cytochrome P-450 levels. No other concentrations of cadmium were used in this study.

Mutagenicity Several reports suggest that cadmium is mutagenic. Deknudt and Gerber (1979) found chromosomal aberrations in bone marrow cells of male C57BL mice maintained on a low-calcium (0.03%) diet supplemented with cadmium (0.06%). DiPaolo and Casto (1979) found morphological transformations of Syrian hamster embryo cells induced by direct exposure to cadmium (0.1, 0.5, and 1.0 μg/ml). Watanabe *et al.* (1979) administered cadmium (1.0, 2.0, or 4.0 mg/kg) subcutaneously 5 hours prior to ovulation to study its mutagenic effects on the metaphase II oocyte chromosomes of virgin female golden hamsters. No structural anomalies were observed, but the frequencies of hyperhaploidy and diploidy increased in the cadmium-treated hamsters, especially in those given higher doses. After injecting hybrid (CBA × C57BL)F_1 mice with a cadmium dose of 4 μg/kg, Vilkina *et al.* (1978) observed no difference between the number of chromosomal aberrations in the bone marrow of the treated mice and in the controls.

Carcinogenicity Loser (1980) fed a diet containing cadmium chloride to male and female rats for 2 years. Concentrations of cadmium were 1, 3, 10, and 50 mg/kg. The results of the study showed no association between the oral administration of cadmium and an increased incidence of tumors or of any specific type of neoplasia.

CONCLUSIONS AND RECOMMENDATIONS

Suggested No-Adverse-Response Level (SNARL)

24-Hour Exposure From the studies cited by Arena (1963), the threshold emetic dose of cadmium in humans is approximately 3 mg.

Therefore, assuming a safety factor of 10, one may calculate the 24-hour SNARL as:

$$\frac{3 \text{ mg}}{10 \times 2 \text{ liters}} = 0.150 \text{ mg/liter.}$$

7-Day Exposure   Using the data for the 24-hour exposure and dividing by 7, one may calculate the 7-day SNARL as:

$$\frac{0.15 \text{ mg/liter}}{7} = 0.021 \text{ mg/liter.}$$

Benes (1978) has cited a "provisional tolerable weekly intake" of cadmium for humans as 6.7 to 8.3 μg/kg based on a report of the World Health Organization (1973). Using these data, applying a safety factor of 10, and assuming 100% intake from 2 liters of drinking water daily by a 70-kg human, one may calculate the 7-day SNARL's as:

$$\frac{6.7 \, \mu\text{g/kg} \times 70 \text{ kg}}{10 \times 2 \text{ liters}} = 0.0235 \text{ mg/liter}$$

and

$$\frac{8.3 \, \mu\text{g/kg} \times 70 \text{ kg}}{10 \times 2 \text{ liters}} = 0.0291 \text{ mg/liter.}$$

Thus, the 7-day SNARL's calculated on the basis of either human or animal data are in rather good agreement.

Chronic Exposure   These calculations are based on the data of Decker *et al.* (1958), who gave rats cadmium in water in a concentration of 10 mg/liter for 1 year without effect. Weight loss and anemia were observed when cadmium was administered in concentrations of 50 mg/liter for 3 months.

The data of Kotsonis and Klaassen (1978) support the 10 mg/liter concentration of cadmium as the no-effect level. Assuming that the rats consumed an average of 30 ml of water daily and that their average weight was 400 g, one may calculate the daily exposure as:

$$\frac{10 \text{ mg/liter} \times 0.03 \text{ liter/day}}{0.4 \text{ kg}} = 0.75 \text{ mg/kg.}$$

Using a safety factor of 1,000 for a 70-kg human consuming 2 liters of water daily and assuming a 20% exposure from drinking water, one may calculate the SNARL as:

$$\frac{0.75 \text{ mg/kg} \times 70 \text{ kg} \times 0.2}{1,000 \times 2 \text{ liters}} = 0.005 \text{ mg/liter.}$$

Chlorinated Disinfectants: Chlorine Dioxide (ClO_2), Chlorate (ClO_3^-), Chlorite (ClO_2^-), and Chloramines (NH_2Cl or $NHCl_2$)

Chlorine dioxide, chlorate, chlorite, and chloramines were reviewed in *Drinking Water and Health*, Volume 3 (National Academy of Sciences, 1980b, pp. 193-202). The chemistry of these agents was examined in detail in that volume. The following material, some of which became available after that volume was published, updates and, in some instances, reevaluates the information in the earlier report.

METABOLISM

Studies in rats suggest that chlorine dioxide is converted to chloride, chlorite, and chlorate. Chlorine dioxide is rapidly absorbed after oral administration, and plasma levels peak within 1 hour after dosing. Forty-three percent of the administered dose was excreted in urine and feces within 72 hours. None was detected in expired air. The plasma half-life was determined to be 44 hours in rats (Abdel-Rahman *et al.*, 1980a,b).

HEALTH ASPECTS

Observations in Humans

In recently completed experiments (Bianchine *et al.*, 1980), adult male volunteers were given water containing chlorine dioxide, chloramine, chlorite, or chlorate. The study was carefully controlled, and subjects were monitored by physical examination, measurement of vital signs, assessment of side-effects, and an extensive battery of clinical laboratory tests. Control subjects were given distilled water, and a positive control group was given water containing chlorine. A brief description of these studies follows.

Acute Effects Two adults ingested 250 ml of chlorine dioxide in water containing concentrations of 40 mg/liter. Within 5 minutes of ingestion, sudden headache, nausea, abdominal discomfort, and light-headedness were observed. These effects disappeared within 5 minutes.

Subchronic and Chronic Effects   In a "rising-dose tolerance study," chlorine dioxide was administered in two separate 500-ml doses of water consumed over 15-minute intervals, 4 hours apart. The concentrations of chlorine dioxide were 0.1, 1.0, 5.0, 10.0, 18.0, and 24.0 mg/liter on days 1, 4, 7, 10, 13, and 16 of the study, respectively. In a similar manner, both chlorite and chlorate were each administered in concentrations of 0.01, 0.1, 0.5, 1.0, 1.8, and 2.4 mg/liter, on the days indicated above, to two additional groups of 10 subjects. Chloramine was given to a sixth group at 0.01, 1.0, 8.0, 18.0, and 24.0 mg/liter on days 1, 4, 7, 10, and 13 of the study, respectively. Accumulated data, averaged for all dose ranges in the study, revealed no striking, clinically relevant changes among these groups.

In a subsequent study, groups of healthy adult males were given a 500-ml solution containing chlorine dioxide, chlorite, chlorate, chlorine, or chloramine in concentrations of 5 mg/liter. The solutions were consumed daily for 12 weeks and subjects were monitored for an additional 8 weeks after treatment. No clinically significant alterations were observed in any of the parameters studied. Nor were there serious objections to the taste of the disinfectants at these concentrations.

Additional studies were conducted in three subjects deficient in glucose-6-phosphate dehydrogenase activity who were given sodium chlorite at 5 mg/liter in the same manner as described above. Again, no adverse effect was noted. Other investigators have suggested that persons with this deficiency may be at a greater risk of oxidant damage (Moore *et al.*, 1978).

Observations in Other Species

Acute Effects   In one male cat given sodium chlorite at 64 mg/kg orally, methemoglobin reached 45% of total hemoglobin within 1 to 2 hours and was still at 20% of the total 6 hours later. In three other cats, given sodium chlorite at 20 mg/kg, methemoglobinemia reached 10% to 30% of total hemoglobin within 2 to 3 hours. In male rats, 20 mg/kg, but not 10 mg/kg, given intraperitonally caused slight but significant methemoglobinemia, which was short-lived (30 to 60 minutes). Higher doses produced much greater levels of methemoglobinemia, but these were also short-lived (Heffernan *et al.* 1979a).

Acute oral dosing of rats with chlorine dioxide concentrations of 0.18 to 0.72 mg/kg produced no methemoglobinemia but caused a slight decrease in blood glutathione concentration within 15 minutes. This progressed to an approximately 20% decrease within 2 hours (Abdel-Rahman *et al.*, 1980b).

Subchronic and Chronic Effects Sodium chlorite was administered to male cats in their drinking water for up to 90 days. No change in ratios of kidney, liver, or spleen to body weight were observed after 60 days of exposure to 25 mg/liter (Heffernan *et al.*, 1979a). In the same study, dose-dependent decreases in erythrocyte count, hemoglobin, and packed cell volume were observed after 30 days. Yet, these parameters returned to near-normal levels during 60 additional days of exposure. None of these effects were observed in animals consuming 50 mg/liter or less in their drinking water. In contrast, dose-related decreases in glutathione and increases in 2,3-diphosphoglyceric acid in the blood were observed in rats drinking 50 to 100 mg/liter (but not 10 mg/liter) sodium chlorite for up to 90 days. These effects rendered the cells more susceptible to oxidative damage and confirmed similar *in-vitro* observations (Heffernan *et al.*, 1979b).

Couri and Abdel-Rahman (1979) conducted similar studies over a 12-month period in male rats given chlorine dioxide, chlorate, and chlorite, and in male mice given chlorine dioxide. Their data suggest oxidative stress to erythrocytes. However, the effects were not clearly dependent on dose. Only four control rats were included, and in some cases both elevation and depression of a parameter were produced by different doses of the same disinfectant. Therefore, it is difficult to assess the biological importance of these results. They reported that chlorine dioxide, chlorite, and chlorate, adminstered for 3 months in water, decreased the incorporation of ^{3}H-thymidine into the nuclei of rat testes and kidneys and increased its incorporation into the intestine. No-effect levels and dose dependency of effects were not reported.

Cats given sodium chlorite in water concentrations of 500 mg/liter for 5 weeks experienced a signficiant decrease in hemoglobin and packed cell volume. When the concentration was increased to 1,000 mg/liter, hemoglobin decreased sharply. Removal of chlorite from the water was followed by a return toward control values within 3 weeks. Red cell half-life *in vivo* was shortened significantly by concentrations of chlorite at 100 mg/liter or more, but not by concentrations of 10 mg/liter. These latter concentrations were adjusted to account for water consumption variability, and dosages were estimated to be 0.6 mg/kg/day for 10 mg/liter and 3.0 mg/kg/day for 100 mg/liter (Heffernan *et al.*, 1979a).

Mutagenicity No available data.

Carcinogenicity   No available data.

Teratogenicity   No available data.

CONCLUSIONS AND RECOMMENDATIONS

Suggested No-Adverse-Response Level (SNARL)

Extensive studies of the effects of chlorinated disinfectants in humans permit estimation of SNARL's for chlorate, chlorite, chlorine dioxide, and chloramine. The calculations are based on a safety factor of 10 and an assumption that 100% of exposure is through the drinking water and that a 70-kg human consumes 2 liters daily. In order to make comparable calculations for chlorine, additional toxicity data are needed. A concentration of 5 mg/liter of each of the disinfectants was not considered to have a seriously objectional taste by the test subjects.

24-Hour Exposure   In the "rising-dose tolerance study," subjects consumed two 500-ml bolus doses, each containing *chlorate* in concentrations of 2.4 mg/liter, with no ill effects. In the chronic study, subjects consumed one 500-ml bolus dose daily containing 5 mg/liter without acute effects. Assuming a safety factor of 10 and that 100% of exposure is from drinking water during this period, one may calculate the 24-hour SNARL as:

$$\frac{5 \text{ mg/liter} \times 0.5 \text{ liter}}{10 \times 2 \text{ liters}} = 0.125 \text{ mg/liter.}$$

Concentrations of *chlorite* identical to those for chlorate were also well tolerated in the two studies:

$$\frac{5 \text{ mg/liter} \times 0.5 \text{ liter}}{10 \times 2 \text{ liters}} = 0.125 \text{ mg/liter.}$$

In the rising-dose tolerance study, subjects consumed two 500-ml bolus doses, each containing *chlorine dioxide* in concentrations up to 24 mg/liter without ill effect. Assuming a safety factor of 10, one may calculate the 24-hour SNARL as:

$$\frac{24 \text{ mg/liter} \times 1 \text{ liter}}{10 \times 2 \text{ liters}} = 1.2 \text{ mg/liter.}$$

Four of the 10 subjects considered concentrations of 10 mg/liter to be unpleasant in taste.

Concentrations of *chloramine* up to 24 mg/liter were also well tolerated in the same dosage regime as that for chlorine dioxide. Assuming a safety factor of 10, one may calculate the 24-hour SNARL as:

$$\frac{24 \text{ mg/liter} \times 1 \text{ liter}}{10 \times 2 \text{ liters}} = 1.2 \text{ mg/liter}.$$

Five of the 12 subjects considered concentrations of 8 mg/liter to be unpleasant in taste.

7-Day Exposure   Since concentrations of *chlorate, chlorite, chlorine dioxide*, and *chloramine* were administered to humans at 5 mg/liter (500 ml daily) for 12 weeks with no apparent adverse effect, this concentration has been selected for projection of a 7-day SNARL. Assuming a safety factor of 10, one may calculate the SNARL as:

$$\frac{5 \text{ mg/liter} \times 0.5 \text{ liter}}{10 \times 2 \text{ liters}} = 0.125 \text{ mg/liter}.$$

Chronic Exposure   No additional lifetime studies in animals have been reported since these disinfectants were reviewed in *Drinking Water and Health*, Volume 3 (National Academy of Sciences, 1980b). A 12-week study conducted by Bianchine *et al.* (1980) suggests that humans can tolerate daily doses of 500 ml of each of the disinfectants alone in water at 5 mg/liter. However, it would be premature to project this value for chronic exposure.

CONCLUSIONS AND RECOMMENDATIONS

In light of the evidence that both chlorate and chlorite appear in animals given chlorine dioxide in their drinking water, additional studies are needed to evaluate the effects of lifetime exposure to these agents and to determine no-effect levels. Additional studies are needed to determine if the studies in male laboratory animals and in humans are valid for females of both species. At present, there is not enough information to determine if persons with genetic disorders, such as hereditary methemoglobinemia and glucose-6-phosphate dehydrogenase deficiency, and other persons unusually susceptible to oxidants may be at greater risk than the general population. Additional studies are needed to resolve this.

Lead (Pb)

Lead was evaluated in the first volume of *Drinking Water and Health* (National Academy of Sciences, 1977, pp. 254–261) and more recently by the EPA (U.S. Environmental Protection Agency, 1979a). The following material, some of which became available after the 1977 publication, updates and, in some instances, reevaluates the information in the earlier report. Also included are some references that were not assessed in the original report. Since that first volume was published, the EPA standard for lead in water has continued at 50 μg/liter (U.S. Environmental Protection Agency, 1977, 1979a).

HEALTH ASPECTS

Observations in Humans

There are a number of recent reviews of the effects of exposure to lead on human health (Goyer, 1974; Goyer and Mushak, 1977; Hammond, 1977; Mahaffey, 1977; National Academy of Sciences, 1980a; Nordberg, 1976; Waldron and Stofen, 1974). Acute lead poisoning in humans is almost nonexistent today, but subchronic and chronic lead poisoning is common, especially among urban children.

In general, the concentration of lead in the blood has been measured to determine if there has been excessive absorption of lead. Specific, lead-induced biochemical or functional disorders are commonly associated with specific ranges of lead concentrations in blood. The concentrations of free erythrocyte porphyrin is becoming widely accepted as a very sensitive indicator of lead exposure and is currently used in many urban screening programs to detect excessive lead intake (Hammond and Beliles, 1980).

Studies of humans have demonstrated that infants and young children are more susceptible than adult females, who are more susceptible than adult males to biochemical effects of lead. Excessive lead intake results primarily in adverse effects on three target systems: the heme-hemoprotein system, the kidneys, and the nervous system. Effects in the first have been studied most, while effects on the nervous system, especially the developing nervous system, constitute a very active research area. In most cases, recommended maximum daily intakes of lead are based on studies of the heme synthetic pathway or the monitoring of lead concentrations in blood.

Concern about the contribution of drinking water to daily lead intake is not new. It has been well established that soft, acid water will extract lead from lead-containing supply pipes or water storage vessels. This may result in lead concentrations in drinking water that exceed the recommended EPA standard of 50 μg/liter (Wong and Berrang, 1976). Morse *et al.* (1979) suggested that lead leached from pipe may only pose a problem in urban areas where lead intake from sources other than water is significant. In a rural setting (Bennington, Vermont), they found no correlation between blood lead and lead concentrations in the water. On the other hand, there have been several recent studies of the relationship between concentrations of lead in water and those in blood.

Greathouse *et al.* (1976) studied 774 persons from 323 greater Boston area households. Their results suggested that lead concentrations in water exceeding 50 μg/liter contributed to elevations of lead in blood in excess of 30 μg/dl. Moore *et al.* (1977) also found that blood lead concentrations increased as a function of the level of lead in drinking water but that the relationship was curvilinear. Thus, increasing concentrations of lead in water from 50 to 100 μg/liter would elevate lead by only 11% above the value at 50 mg/liter. Calcium, phosphate, and iron in the water may affect lead absorption (Ziegler *et al.*, 1978), thereby contributing to disagreement among such studies.

In these studies, the water samples included both first-draw morning samples and daytime running water samples. This point is raised because Pocock (1980) recently reported that the lead content of water samples drawn in Great Britain from 1,071 households with lead plumbing varied greatly with the time of sampling. For example, the ratio of lead concentration in daytime samples to that in first-draw samples ranged from 0.25 to 2.0. This study emphasizes the need for standardized sampling techniques if predictions of lead ingestion from drinking water are based on tap water analyses. Many common problems that can affect the accuracy of measurements of lead in water and elsewhere are discussed in a recent review of lead (National Academy of Sciences, 1980a). It is clear that both analytical and water sampling methodology must be refined.

Infants and young children absorb ingested lead more readily than do older children and adults (Ziegler *et al.*, 1978). Mahaffey (1977) recommended that the lead intake for children less than 6 months of age should be no more than 100 μg/day, and for children between 6 months and 2 years of age, it should be no more than 150 μg/day. These estimates were based on a critical review of the health effects of lead ingestion in infants and young children, taking into consideration factors such as body weight, body surface area, and food and water consumption. Thus, the current standard of 50 μg/liter would permit a child to ingest one-half to one-third of the recommended maximum daily lead intake by consuming

1 liter of water daily. This would present no danger if exposure to lead from other sources were minimized (Mahaffey, 1977).

Of major concern today are the reported subtle effects of lead on behavior, especially in infants and young children. Bornschein *et al.* (1980) have recently prepared a critical review of the major studies of the effects of low-level chronic lead exposure on behavior in children. Adverse effects on behavior and intelligence have been reported to occur at exposure levels below those causing encephalopathy (Hammond and Beliles, 1980; Krigman *et al.*, 1980), but not at blood lead concentrations below 50 μg/100 ml (National Academy of Sciences, 1980a, p. 77). Thus, it would seem that alterations in heme synthesis are the most sensitive responses to lead exposure, since such disturbances have been reported in children with blood lead levels of 15 to 30 μg/100 ml (National Academy of Sciences, 1980a, p. 77).

Environmental and occupational exposure to lead has been associated with adverse effects on reproduction, e.g., premature births, miscarriages, sperm abnormalities, etc. However, there are *no* conclusive data indicating that lead is teratogenic in humans (Krigman *et al.*, 1980; National Academy of Sciences, 1980a, p. 127). This is a very serious potential problem and extensive effort should be directed toward a definitive solution.

Observations in Other Species

Acute Effects   The acute LD_{50} of lead acetate administered to rats intraperitonially is reported to be 150 mg/kg. Oral doses of 300 mg/kg have been reported to be lethal to dogs (Spector, 1956).

Absorption of lead was enhanced in rats made anemic by bleeding (Angle *et al.*, 1977). Iron deficiency anemia also results in enhanced lead absorption (Six and Goyer, 1972).

Subchronic and Chronic Effects   Free erythrocyte porphyrin was measured in adult male and female and suckling rats after oral dosing with lead in drinking water. Young rats were more susceptible than adult females, which were more susceptible than adult males to elevated free erythrocyte porphyrin (Buchet *et al.*, 1978). Krasovski *et al.* (1979) administered lead acetate to rats orally for up to 6 months. They found no adverse effects on biochemical behavior or gonadal function at 1.5 μg/kg/day. Yet, at dosages of 5 and 50 μg/kg/day, they observed dominant lethal, adverse behavioral, and gonadotoxic effects. They suggest that 1.5 μg/kg/day is equivalent to 30 μg/liter in the drinking water. No measurements of blood lead concentrations or free erythrocyte porphyrin were reported.

The effects of lead on the nervous system and behavior are being studied in many animal models. Evidence from such studies clearly indicates that pre- and perinatal exposure to lead may alter neurological development, behavior, and learning ability in laboratory animals. At present, however, there is insufficient evidence to characterize the dose-effect relationship between lead intake or lead concentrations in tissue with nervous system impairment (Bornschein *et al.*, 1980; Krigman *et al.*, 1980; National Academy of Sciences, 1980a, pp. 70–75).

Mutagenicity In mice, lead acetate was reported to be mutagenic in the sperm abnormality assay but not in the micronucleus or *Salmonella* tests (Heddle and Bruce, 1977).

Carcinogenicity Several studies have demonstrated that lead can cause renal tumors in rats. There is also some evidence of lead-induced brain tumors in rats, renal tumors in mice, and lung tumors in hamsters. Very high doses of lead were used in all of the tests.

The data produced by these studies are inadequate to permit estimates of risk to humans. There is no evidence of lead-induced carcinogenicity in humans (International Agency for Research on Cancer, 1972; National Academy of Sciences, 1980a, p. 128; U.S. Environmental Protection Agency, 1979a).

Teratogenicity Teratogenic effects of lead have been observed primarily in the nervous system only after high doses of lead were given to rats on day 9 of gestation. When administered at other times, lead was fetotoxic (Michaelson and Sauerhoff, 1974).

CONCLUSIONS AND RECOMMENDATIONS

The current Safe Drinking Water Committee agrees with the conclusion reached in the first edition of *Drinking Water and Health* (National Academy of Sciences, 1977, pp. 260–261):

... the present limit of 50 µg/liter may not, in view of other sources of environmental exposure, provide a sufficient margin of safety, particularly for fetuses and young growing children. Although further studies will be necessary to arrive at a reasonable limit, it is suggested that the limit be lowered. This recommendation is made with the assumption that analytical methodology will be sufficient to detect this value above background.

There is no evidence that lead is carcinogenic or teratogenic in humans, and evidence of mutagenicity is scant. But special consideration must be given to the greater susceptibility of infants and young children to lead accumulation and test results suggesting that absorption of lead is enhanced in anemic animals. Although it appears that 50 μg/liter may not provide adequate protection of certain high risk groups, in light of the report by Pocock (1980) and the problems of lead analysis and data interpretation (National Academy of Sciences, 1980a), this committee cannot now suggest a lower lead standard.

The committee recommends that the following actions be taken:

• Studies relating lead concentrations in drinking water to those in blood must be conducted in a way that permits accurate determination of lead ingested in the water consumed. Tap water analyses are too unreliable for this purpose.

• Action is required to minimize extraction of lead from supply system pipes into drinking water.

• Additional research is needed to determine whether or not lead is truly a carcinogen in laboratory animals. If it is, then appropriate dose-response data are needed to permit projection of such risks to the human population.

• Additional research is needed to determine no-effect levels for lead-induced alterations in behavior and other nervous system effects and to clarify the question of the suggested adverse effects of lead exposure on human intelligence.

• Additional research is needed to determine if humans are at increased risk of teratogenic or reproductive effects from lead exposure.

Suggested No-Adverse-Response Level (SNARL)

24-Hour and 7-Day Exposures   There are no adequate data from which to calculate a 24-hour or a 7-day SNARL.

Chronic Exposure   Since the carcinogenicity of lead has not yet been resolved, no chronic SNARL can be calculated.

Silver (Ag)

Silver was reviewed in the first volume of *Drinking Water and Health* (National Academy of Sciences, 1977) and more recently by the EPA (U.S. Environmental Protection Agency, 1979c).

This white, ductile metal occurs naturally in pure form and in ores, most commonly in argentite (Ag_2S). It is used principally as an electroconductor and in photographic materials, electroplating, dental alloys, solder and braying alloys, paints, jewelry, silverware, coinage, and mirrors (Goodman and Gilman, 1975). Silver nitrate (1%–2%) is used medicinally in the prophylaxis of ophthalmia neonatorum. Silver protein (Argyrol®) and silver sulfadiazine (Silvadene®) are used as topical antiinfectives (Martin, 1965; Pariser, 1978).

In some instances, silver has been used to purify water since silver concentrations from 0.001 to 500 μg/liter have been reported to be sufficient to sterilize water (McKee and Wolf, 1963).

Concentrations exceeding 150 μg/liter have been used to purify swimming pools, but because of the cost and the opalescence caused by colloidal silver chloride, the method is not practical nor is it recommended for public water supplies (National Academy of Sciences, 1977). Natural freshwaters contain an average silver concentration of 0.2 μg/liter, and seawater contains an average of 0.24 μg/liter (Boyle, 1968). Kopp and Kroner (1970) found silver in 6.6% (130) of 1,577 surface water samples collected in the United States. Concentrations in samples containing silver varied from 0.1 to 38 μg/liter, averaging 2.6 μg/liter.

Examination of finished water in public supplies of the 100 largest cities in the United States revealed trace quantities of silver as high as 7 μg/liter (median, 2.3 μg/liter) (Durfor and Becker, 1962). In another survey of finished water, silver was found in 6.1% of 380 samples in concentrations ranging from 0.3 to 5 μg/liter (mean, 2.2 μg/liter) (Kopp, 1969). In yet another study, a maximum silver concentration of 26 μg/liter was found in 2,595 samples from household taps within 959 public water supply systems (McCabe, 1970). After reviewing the literature, Snyder et al. (1975) estimated that the average daily intake of silver by Reference Man was 70 μg/day, 30 μg of which was ingested in food. In earlier balance studies, Kehoe et al. (1940) determined that the daily dietary intake of silver by humans in the United States was 88 μg. A source of dietary silver in addition to food and drinking water is possibly dental amalgams, which are dissolved in the mouth by saliva (Wyckoff and Hunter, 1956).

Until 1962, there were no restrictions on silver in drinking water. The current standard for silver in drinking water is 50 μg/liter (National Academy of Sciences, 1977).

METABOLISM

Silver may enter the body via the respiratory tract, the gastrointestinal tract, mucous membranes, or broken skin. Estimates of the amount of silver absorbed from the gastrointestinal vary widely. A value of 10% is reported by Hill and Pillsbury (1939), but they did not provide documentation. A more adequately supported value is given by Scott and Hamilton (1950), who showed that 4 days after administration of silver by stomach tube, 99% had been eliminated in the feces and 0.18% in the urine of rats. A similar value was reported by Jones and Bailey (1974), who fed some rabbits food containing 4.2 mg/kg of silver iodide and others a diet containing 10 mg/kg of silver nitrate. They found that 99% of the silver was eliminated in 3 days and essentially all of it in 6.3 days. They also noted that after 30 days, when rabbits maintained on a diet containing silver were compared with rabbits on a silver-free diet, the concentration of silver in the livers of both groups was the same.

Some silver is retained by virtually all body tissues. In persons not taking silver therapeutically, the primary sites of deposition are the liver, skin, adrenals, lungs, muscles, pancreas, kidney, heart, and spleen. Some silver is also deposited in blood vessel walls, testes, pituitary gland, nasal membrane, trachea, and bronchi (Furchner et al., 1968; Sax, 1963). It tends to accumulate in the body as one ages (Hill and Pillsbury, 1939).

Silver is transported primarily by the globulin fraction of the blood. Most of the absorbed silver is removed from the body via the reticuloendothelial system, especially the liver (Scott and Hamilton, 1950). Excretion in the urine is very low; only trace amounts ($< 1.0\%$) being present. The biological half-life of silver in rats is described by two exponential functions, giving half-life values of 8 days and 20 days (Phalen and Morrow, 1973). After inhalation, the half-life in the human lung is approximately 1 day (Newton and Holmes, 1966), and the half-life for the other tissues is 15 days (Phalen and Morrow, 1973).

HEALTH ASPECTS

While metallic silver is not regarded as toxic, most of its salts are toxic to many organisms. These salts can combine with certain biological molecules, subsequently altering their properties (Goodman and Gilman, 1975). Large oral doses of silver nitrate cause severe gastrointestinal irritation due to its caustic action. Ingestion of 10 g of silver nitrate is usually fatal.

Observations in Humans

The most common noticeable effects of chronic and subacute human exposure to silver or silver compounds are generalized argyria or localized argyria, involving primarily the eye. The most important causes of argyria are the medicinal application of silver compounds and industrial exposure (Goodman and Gilman, 1975; Hill and Pillsbury, 1939). Symptoms of generalized argyria include a slate-gray pigmentation of the skin, hair, and internal organs resulting from the deposition of silver in the tissues. The degree of pigmentation is highest in portions of skin exposed to light, even though the concentration of silver in the skin of other parts of the body is the same. Additional manifestations include silver coloration of fingernails and conjunctiva and a blue halo around the cornea.

In localized argyria, pigmentation is limited. Generalized argyria as an occupational disease was never common, occurring mainly among silver nitrate workers. Other toxic effects only indirectly attributable to the use of silver compounds in the treatment of burn patients include: electrolyte imbalance, from hypotonicity of silver nitrate dressings (Wood, 1965), and methemoglobinemia, from reduction of nitrate to nitrite (Strauch *et al.*, 1969).

Observations in Other Species

Acute toxic effects of silver in animals are usually associated with intravenous administration of silver nitrate (at approximately 32 mg/kg), which will produce pulmonary edema in dogs (Hill and Pillsbury, 1939). Other effects involve the central nervous system, producing symptoms such as weakness, rigidity, contractures in the legs, loss of voluntary movements, and interference with cardiac blood supply. The LD_{50} for silver nitrate administered intraperitoneally to male Swiss albino mice was 13.9 mg/kg (Bienvenu *et al.*, 1963). For silver sulfadiazine given to CF-1 mice, the LD_{90-100} was $> 1,050$ mg (Wysor, 1975).

In a subchronic study lasting 18 weeks, Cabe *et al.* (1979) gave silver to rats via the drinking water in a concentration of 1,000 mg/kg. They observed no effects on body weight, fluid intake, food consumption, or measures of forelimb or hindlimb strength, but water consumption was reduced by approximately 25%.

Mutagenicity Silver has not been found to be mutagenic in the *Salmonella* Ames test (McCoy and Rosenkrantz, 1978); in the "rec-assay," in which differential sensitivities to killing by chemicals are observed in wild-type and recombination-deficient strains of *Bacillus subtilis* (Nishioka, 1975); or in mutation tests in *Micrococcus aureus* (Clark, 1953) or *Escherichia coli* (Demerec *et al.*, 1951).

Carcinogenicity Some studies involving implanted foils, disks, or injected colloidal suspensions or metallic silver have been found to produce tumors or hyperplasia, but the interpretations of such findings have been questioned (Becker *et al.*, 1967; Northdurft, 1955; Saffiotti and Shubik, 1963). Furst and Schlauder (1977) did not find any tumor formation from silver powder administered subcutaneously. In summary, although the literature is replete with clinical reports of cases of argyria, the relationships between human cancer and silver as the causative agent are very tenuous.

Teratogenicity   No available data.

CONCLUSIONS AND RECOMMENDATIONS

Unless some new data become available, this committee remains in agreement with the authors of *Drinking Water and Health*, Volume 1 (National Academy of Sciences, 1977), who stated on page 292:

There seem to be no pressing research needs with regard to silver in drinking water. There seems to be little possibility that the addition of oligodynamic silver will have any place in public water supplies, and natural concentrations are so low that consideration should be given to taking silver off the list of substances included in primary drinking-water standards.

There are no adequate data from which to calculate 24-hour, 7-day, or chronic SNARL's.

Strontium (Sr)

Strontium is a silvery-white alkaline earth metal (Periodic Group IIA) that has a valence of two and exists in several isotopic states, some of which are radioactive. Strontium occurs naturally in two ores—strontium sulfate (celestite) and strontium carbonate (strontianite) (Browning, 1969).

Strontium and its salts have many industrial uses such as providing the red color in pyrotechnic devices as tracer bullets, distress signal rockets, flares, and fireworks. They are also used as rubber fillers, as corrosion inhibitors, in plastics, in ceramics, in luminous paints, in sugar refining, and in alloys of tin and lead (Browning, 1969; Venugopal and Luckey, 1978). In medicine, strontium bromide has been used as a sedative, an antiepileptic, and in the therapy of urticaria and skin rashes (Schroeder *et al.*, 1972; Venugopal and Luckey, 1978).

Strontium is the fifteenth most abundant element in nature (400-500 mg/kg in the earth's crust), and it is the most abundant trace element in seawater (8-10 mg/liter) (Schroeder *et al.*, 1972; Venugopal and Luckey, 1978). Thus, it has become incorporated into all plants and animal tissues since they have evolved in the presence of strontium. The amounts of strontium in natural freshwaters in the United States may vary from approximately 0.007 to 15 mg/liter, averaging about 0.5 mg/liter. The average concentrations of strontium in finished or municipal water supplies in the United States is approximately 10 mg/liter (range, 2.2 to 1,200 mg/liter) (Schroeder *et al.*, 1972). The daily intake of strontium varies from about 1.8 to 2.0 mg/day. Of this, a negligible quantity is supplied by air, approximately 60% to 90% by food, and the remaining 10% to 40% by water (Schroeder *et al.*, 1972; Tipton *et al.*, 1966). Strontium is present in many foods, e.g., spices, seafood, cereals, grains, and leafy vegetables (Beliles, 1979).

Since strontium and its salts are relatively nontoxic or of very low toxicity, they are not regarded as industrial health hazards (Beliles, 1979; Browning, 1969; Schroeder *et al.*, 1972; Venugopal and Luckey, 1978). There is some evidence that strontium is essential for the growth of animals, especially for the calcification of bone and teeth (Browning, 1969), but its role as a trace element has not been proven (Schroeder *et al.*, 1972).

A maximum ambient environmental level for strontium in potable water was set at 10 mg/liter (Dawson, 1974). This value was extrapolated from minimal lethal dose data obtained in animals and has a *very* low level of reliability.

METABOLISM

There is a paucity of recent information on the metabolism of strontium. From previous studies, it would appear that the metabolism of strontium closely resembles that of calcium, especially with regard to bone (Browning, 1969; Schroeder *et al.*, 1972). However, in most biological processes there is a distinct preference for calcium assimilation and utilization as compared to strontium (Browning, 1969; Chen *et al.*, 1961).

The gastrointestinal absorption of strontium is described as poor, varying from approximately 5% to 25% of the ingested dose (Browning, 1969; Schroeder *et al.*, 1972). However, absorption is affected by species, age, and other dietary constituents such as calcium (Browning 1969; Schroeder *et al.*, 1972; Venugopal and Luckey, 1978).

The 70-kg standard human described by Schroeder *et al.* (1972) contains approximately 320 mg of strontium, but this amount may vary with the geographical location. The skeleton contains more than 99% of the strontium. The rest is distributed among soft tissues, the largest concentrations residing in the aorta, larnyx, trachea, and lower gastrointestinal tract (Beliles, 1979; Schroeder *et al.*, 1972).

The pattern of excretion of strontium varies with the species and the route of exposure. Strontium administered parenterally or absorbed from the gastrointestinal tract is excreted primarily via the urine (Browning, 1969; Schroeder et al., 1972). When administered orally, it is excreted primarily in the feces (Browning, 1969). Strontium is also excreted in the sweat and in the milk of lactating females (Browning, 1969; Schroeder et al., 1972; Sollman, 1957).

HEALTH ASPECTS

Strontium poisoning is rare and in most instances is accidental (Venugopal and Luckey, 1978). Current interest in the toxicity of strontium is concerned primarily with the radioactive isotope, ^{90}Sr, which is present in radioactive fallout as a fission product from nuclear explosions. This isotope is a potential radiation hazard and has been implicated as a causative agent in bone cancers and leukemia (Chen et al., 1961; Schroeder et al., 1972).

This report is concerned with the chemical toxicity of the stable isotopes of strontium.

Observations in Humans

There is little evidence that strontium causes chronic disease in humans (Schroeder et al., 1972). As mentioned above, strontium compounds have been used medicinally for various purposes.

In an early study, McCance and Widdowson (1939) administered 47 mg of strontium lactate daily for 5 days by intravenous injection. They reported no symptoms of toxicity.

Although it has been proposed by some that strontium may be essential for the development of mammalian bone structure, nothing is known about its biochemical functions, if any, in bone or soft tissue (Schroeder et al., 1972). In balance studies conducted by Tipton et al. (1966), the average daily intake by adult subjects was approximately 1.8 mg daily, which seemed to be in balance with the amount that was excreted.

Observations in Other Species

Table VI-4 lists the acute toxicities of some strontium compounds in various species. As can be seen, the toxicity of these compounds vary with the anion. Acute poisoning in laboratory animals leads to excess salivation, vomiting, colic, and diarrhea. In rats, death is due to respiratory failure; in cats, it is due to cardiac arrest (Browning, 1969; Venugopal and

TABLE VI-4   Acute Toxicity of Strontium Salts[a]

Compound	Animal	Route[b]	Toxicity[c]	Compound, mg	Metal mg	mM
Strontium fluoride	Rat	iv	LD$_{100}$	625	436	4.98
	Guinea pig	oral	MLD	5,000	3,490	39.8
	Guinea pig	sc	MLD	5,000	3,490	39.8
Strontium chloride	Mouse	iv	LD$_{50}$	148	82	0.94
	Mouse	ip	LD$_{50}$	908	502	5.73
	Rat	ip	LD$_{50}$	405	224	2.56
	Rat	iv	MLD	123	68	0.78
	Rabbit	iv	LD$_{50}$	1,060	590	6.73
Strontium chloride	Rat	iv	MLD	400	221	2.52
Strontium bromide	Rat	ip	LD$_{50}$	1,000	246	2.81
	Rat	iv	MLD	500	177	2.02
Strontium iodide	Rat	ip	LD$_{50}$	800	156	1.78
Strontium nitrate	Rat	ip	LD$_{50}$	540	224	2.56
Strontium fluoroborate	Rat	oral	MLD	500	155	1.77
Strontium acetate	Mouse	iv	MLD	123	52.3	0.60
	Mouse	iv	LD$_{100}$	383	163	1.86
	Rat	iv	MLD	239	101	1.15
	Rat	iv	LD$_{100}$	238	101	1.15
	Rat	iv	LD$_{50}$	105	44.5	0.51
Strontium lactate	Rat	ip	LD$_{50}$	900	247	2.82
Strontium salicylate	Rat	ip	LD$_{50}$	363	88	1.00

[a]From Venugopal and Luckey, 1978.
[b]iv, intravenous; sc, subcutaneous; ip, intraperitoneal.
[c]LD, lethal dose; MLD, minimum lethal dose.

Luckey, 1978). Major signs of chronic toxicity, which involve the skeleton, have been labeled as "strontium rickets." Follis (1955) produced rickets in laboratory rats by feeding them strontium carbonate at 2% strontium in the diet.

Johnson (1973) has found that the bones of weanling male and female rats fed a diet high in strontium content (0.2%) for 8 weeks will generally exhibit severe aberrations. Gross examination revealed that bones were deformed and shorter than normal. Histologically, strontium-laden bone had widened epiphyseal cartilage plates of irregular outline and trabeculae with prominent osteoid seams. These changes were accompanied by a marked reduction in bone ash, elevated magnesium and potassium levels, and a depressed calcium content in bone.

Mechanism studies by Omdahl and DeLuca (1971, 1972) indicate that the bone aberrations result from an inhibition of calcium absorption by dietary strontium as a result of a block in the renal synthesis of 1,25-dihydroxycholecalciferol from 25-hydroxycholecalciferol (Omdahl and DeLuca, 1971, 1972). In 90-day studies, Kroes et al. (1977) fed male and female Wistar rats strontium in strontium chloride at 75, 300, 1,200, and 4,800 mg/kg diet. They did not find any changes in behavior, growth, food intake, or food efficiency, but observed minor changes in hematology and blood chemistry at the highest dose. In the female rats given the highest dose, the glycogen content of the liver was decreased at 12 weeks. Thyroid weights were increased in males in the 1,200 and 4,800 mg/kg groups.

Forbes and Mitchell (1957) fed adult male and weanling male and female rats strontium in the diet at levels of 10, 30, 100, and 1,000 mg/kg for 8 weeks. They found no differences in food intake, weight gain, total bone ash, calcium and phosphorus composition of the bone ash, or other signs of toxicity in the strontium-fed rats.

Mutagenicity   Loeb et al. (1977), using an *in-vitro* assay to measure the fidelity of DNA synthesis, observed no effects from strontium added *in vitro*.

Carcinogenicity   No data available for evaluation.

Teratogenicity   No data available for evaluation.

CONCLUSIONS AND RECOMMENDATIONS

The chemical toxicity of the stable isotopes of strontium is considered to be quite low. Although Dawson (1974) suggested that strontium in potable water should not exceed 10 mg/liter based on LD_{50} data, he evaluated this calculation as having the "lowest level of reliability."

Suggested No-Adverse-Response Level (SNARL)

24-Hour Exposure   There are no data from which to calculate the 24-hour SNARL for strontium. However, based on the 90-day study of Kroes et al. (1977), the 24-hour exposure level would be at least 8.4 mg/liter.

7-Day Exposure   Using the data of Kroes *et al.* (1977), who found the no-effect level of strontium to be 300 mg/kg after 90 days of exposure in the diet, and assuming that the rats consumed 20 g of food daily and that their average weight was 250 g, one may calculate the daily exposure level as:

$$\frac{300 \text{ mg/kg/day} \times 0.02 \text{ kg/day}}{0.25 \text{ kg}} = 24 \text{ mg/kg}.$$

Using a safety factor of 100 and assuming that a 70-kg human consumes 2 liters of water per day, and that 100% of exposure is from water during this period, one may calculate the 7-day SNARL as:

$$\frac{24 \text{ mg/kg} \times 70 \text{ kg}}{100 \times 2 \text{ liters}} = 8.4 \text{ mg/liter}.$$

Chronic Exposure   There are no data from which to make this calculation.

Sulfate (SO$_4$)

Sulfate was reviewed in the first volume of *Drinking Water and Health* (National Academy of Sciences, 1977). The no-adverse-health-effect level recommended at that time was 500 mg/liter, whereas the taste threshold may be as low as 200 mg/liter. No additional data pertaining to the effects of inorganic sulfates have been reported since that report was published.

REFERENCES

Abdel-Rahman, M.S., and D. Couri. 1980. Toxicity of chlorine dioxide in drinking water. P. A-29, No. 86 in Abstracts of Papers, Society of Toxicology. Nineteenth Annual Meeting, March 9–13. Washington, D.C.

Abdel-Rahman, M.S., D. Couri, and J.D. Jones. 1980a. Chlorine dioxide metabolism in rat. J. Environ. Pathol. Toxicol. 3:421–430.

Abdel-Rahman, M.S., D. Couri, and R.J. Bull. 1980b. Kinetics of ClO_2, and effects of ClO_2, ClO_2^-, and ClO_3^- in drinking water and blood glutathione and hemolysis in rat and chicken. J. Environ. Pathol. Toxicol. 3:431–449.

Alfrey, A.C., G.R. LeGendre, and W.D. Kaehny. 1976. The dialysis encephalopathy syndrome. Possible aluminum intoxication. N. Engl. J. Med. 294:184–188.

Angle, C.R., M.S. McIntire, and G. Brunk. 1977. Effect of anemia on blood and tissue lead in rats. J. Toxicol. Environ. Health 3:557–563.

American Conference of Governmental Industrial Hygienists. 1980. Threshold limit values for chemical substances and physical agents in the workroom environment with intended changes for 1980. American Conference of Governmental Industrial Hygienists, Cincinnati, Ohio. 93 pp.

Anonymous. 1976. Dialysis dementia: Aluminium again? Lancet 1:349.

Arena, J.M. 1963. Poisoning: Chemistry—Symptoms—Treatments. Charles C Thomas, Baltimore, Md. 440 pp.

Becker, T., E. Markgraf, H. Oswald, B. Sachyra, and K. Winnefeld. 1967. Behavior of metallic foreign bodies in animals. Pp. 1722-1727 in Th. Matthes, ed. Wissenschaftliche Chirurgen-Tagung der Deutschen Demokratischen Republik mit Internationaler Beteiligung, 6th, Berlin, 1966, volume 2, Barth, Leipzig. [Chem. Absts. 70:076383t, 1969.]

Beliles, R.P. 1979. The lesser metals: Strontium. Pp. 556-557 in F.W. Oehme, ed. Toxicity of Heavy Metals in the Environment. Part 2. Marcel Dekker, New York.

Benes, V. 1978. Toxicological aspects of the water we drink. Pp. 35-45 in G.L. Plaa and W.A.M. Duncan, eds. Proceedings of the First International Congress on Toxicology. Toxicology as a Predictive Science. Academic Press, New York.

Berlyne, G.M., J. Ben-Ari, D. Pest, J. Weinberger, M. Stern, G.R. Gilmore, and R. Levine. 1970. Hyperaluminemia from aluminum resins in renal failure. Lancet 2:494-496.

Berlyne, G.M., J. Ben-Ari, E. Knopf, R. Yagil, G. Weinberger, and G.M. Danovitch. 1972. Aluminium toxicity in rats. Lancet 1:564-568.

Bianchine, J.R., J.R. Lubbers, S. Chavhan, and J. Miller. 1980. The safety study of chlorine dioxide and its metabolites in man. Summary Report. Grant No. 805643. Submitted to U.S. Environmental Protection Agency, Cincinnati, Ohio.

Bienvenu, P., C. Nofre, and A. Cier. 1963. [In French] Toxicité générale comparée des ions métalliques. Relation avec la classification périodique. C.R. Acad. Sci. 256:1043-1044.

Bland, J. 1979. Trace elements in human health and disease: IV. Influence of trace elements on development and as environmental toxicants. Osteopath. Med. 4(10):105-108, 110-111, 113.

Bornschein, R., D. Pearson, and L. Reiter. 1980. Behavioral effects of moderate lead exposure in children and animal models: Part 1, Clinical studies. Crit. Rev. Toxicol. 8:43-99.

Boyle, R.W. 1968. Geochemistry of silver and its deposits with notes on geochemical prospecting for the element. Geol. Surv. Can., Bull. No. 160. 264 pp. [Chem. Absts. 71:5300y, 1969.]

Brenniman, G.R., T. Namekata, W.H. Kojola, B.W. Carnow, and P.S. Levy. 1979. Cardiovascular disease death rates in communities with elevated levels of barium in drinking water. Environ. Res. 20:318-324.

Brenniman, G.R., W.H. Kojola, P.S. Levy, B.W. Carnow, and T. Namekata. 1981. High barium levels in public drinking water and its association with elevated blood pressure. Arch. Environ. Health 36(1):28-32.

Browning, E., ed. 1969. Toxicity of Industrial Metals. Second edition. Appleton-Century-Crofts, New York.

Buchet, J.P., H. Roels, and R. Lauwerys. 1978. Influence of sex hormones on free erythrocyte protoporphyrin response to lead in rats. Toxicology 9:361-369.

Cabe, P.A., N.G. Carmichael, and H.A. Tilson. 1979. Effects of selenium, alone and in combination with silver or arsenic, in rats. Neurobehav. Toxicol. 1:275-278. [Chem. Absts. 92:192218w, 1980.]

Calabrese, E.J., G.S. Moore, R.W. Tuthill, and T. L. Sieger, eds. 1980. Drinking Water and Cardiovascular Disease. Pathotox Publishers, Inc., Park Forest South, Illinois.

Cam, J.M., V.A. Luck, J.B. Eastwood, and H.E. De Wardener. 1976. The effect of aluminum hydroxide orally on calcium, phosphorus and aluminum metabolism in normal subjects. Clin. Sci. Mol. Med. 51:407–414.

Casarett, L.J., and J. Doull, eds. 1977. Toxicology—The Basic Science of Poisons. Macmillan Publishing Co., Inc., New York.

Chen, P.S., Jr., A.R. Terepka, and H.C. Hodge. 1961. The pharmacology and toxicology of the bone seekers. Annu. Rev. Pharmacol. 1:369–396.

Christensen, H.E., ed. 1971. Toxic Substances Annual List. 1971. U.S. National Institute for Occupational Safety and Health, Rockville, Md. 512 pp.

Clark, J.B. 1953. The mutagenic action of various chemicals on *Micrococcus pyogenes* var. *aureus*. Proc. Okla. Acad. Sci. 34:114–118. [Chem. Absts. 49:8373f, 1955.]

Clarkson, E.M., V.A. Luck, W.V. Hynson, R.R. Bailey, J.B. Eastwood, J.S. Woodhead, V.R. Clements, J.L.H. O'Riordan, and H.E. De Wardener. 1972. The effects of aluminium hydroxide on calcium phosphorus and aluminium balances, the serum parathyroid hormone concentration and the aluminium content of bone in patients with chronic renal failure. Clin. Sci. 43:519–531.

Committee II on Permissible Dose for Internal Radiation. 1960. International Commission on Radiological Protection. Health Phys. 3:1–380.

Couri, D., and M.S. Abdel-Rahman. 1979. Effect of chlorine dioxide and metabolites on glutathione dependent system in rat, mouse and chicken blood. J. Environ. Pathol. Toxicol. 3:451–460.

Crapper, D.R. 1973. Experimental neurofibrillary degeneration and altered electrical activity. Electroencephalogr. Clin. Neurophysiol. 35:575–588.

Crapper, D.R., and A.J. Dalton. 1973a. Alterations in short-term retention, conditioned avoidance response acquisition and motivation following aluminum induced neurofibrillary degeneration. Physiol. Behav. 10:925–933.

Crapper, D.R., and A.J. Dalton. 1973b. Aluminum induced neurofibrillary degeneration, brain electrical activity and alterations and acquisition and retention. Physiol. Behav. 10:935–945.

Crapper, D.R., and U. DeBoni. 1980. Aluminum. Pp. 326–335 in P.S. Spencer and H.H. Schaumburg, eds. Experimental and Clinical Neurotoxicology. Williams & Wilkins, Baltimore, Md.

Crapper, D.R., S. S. Krishnan, and A.J. Dalton. 1973. Aluminum distribution in Alzheimer's disease and mental neurofibrillary degeneration. Science 180:511–513.

Crapper, D.R., S.S. Krishnan, and S. Quittkat. 1976. Aluminium, neurofibrillary degeneration and Alzheimer's disease. Brain 99:67–80.

Cuddihy, R.G., and J.A. Ozog. 1973. Nasal absorption of $CsCl_2$, $SrCl_2$, $BaCl_2$, and $CeCl_3$ in Syrian hamsters. Health Phys. 25:219–224.

Dawson, G.W. 1974. The Chemical Toxicity of Elements. Report Prepared for the U.S. Atomic Energy Commission under Contract AT(45-1):1830. Battelle, Pacific Northwest Laboratories, Richland, Wash. 25 pp. [BNWL-1815, UC-70.]

DeBoni, U., A. Otvos, J.W. Scott, and D.R. Crapper. 1976. Neurofibrillary degeneration induced by systemic aluminum. Acta Neuropathol. 35:285–294.

Decker, L.E., R.U. Byerrum, C.F. Decker, C.A. Hoppert, and R.F. Langham. 1958. Chronic toxicity studies. I. Cadmium administered in drinking water to rats. AMA Arch. Ind. Health 18:228–231.

Deknudt, Gh., and G.B. Gerber. 1979. Chromosomal aberrations in bone-marrow cells of mice given a normal or a calcium-deficient diet supplemented with various heavy metals. Mutat. Res. 68:163–168.

Demerec, M., G. Bertani, and J. Flint. 1951. A survey of chemicals for mutagenic action on *E. coli*. Am. Nat. 85:119–136.

Denny, J.J., W.D. Robson, and D.A. Irwin. 1939. The prevention of silicosis by metalic aluminum. II. Can. Med. Assoc. J. 40:213-228.

Dipaolo, J.A., and B.C. Casto. 1979. Quantitative studies of *in vitro* morphological transformation of Syrian hamster cells by inorganic metal salts. Cancer Res. 39:1008-1013.

Dunea, G., S.D. Mahurkar, B. Mamdani, and E.C. Smith. 1978. Role of aluminum in dialysis dementia. Ann. Intern. Med. 88:502-504.

Durfor, C.N., and E. Becker, eds. 1962. Public Water Supplies of the 100 Largest Cities in the United States, 1962. U.S. Department of the Interior, Geological Survey Water-Supply Paper 1812. Washington, D.C. 364 pp.

Elliott, H.L., F. Dryburgh, G.S. Fell, S. Sabet, and A.I. MacDougall. 1978. Aluminium toxicity during regular haemodialysis. Br. Med. J. 1:1101-1103.

Flendrig, J.A., H. Kruis, and H.A. Das. 1976. Aluminium intoxication: The cause of dialysis dementia? Pp. 355-363 in B.H.B. Robinson, ed. Dialysis, Transplantation, Nephrology. Proceedings of the Thirteenth Congress of the European Dialysis and Transplant Association, held in Hamburg, Germany. 1976. Pitman Medical Publishing Co., Tunbridge Wells, England.

Follis, R.H., Jr. 1955. Bone changes resulting from parenteral strontium administration. Fed. Proc. Am. Soc. Exp. Pathol. 14:403, Abstr. No. 1301.

Forbes, R.M., and H.H. Mitchell. 1957. Accumulation of dietary boron and strontium in young and adult albino rats. Arch. Ind. Health. 16:489-492.

Friberg, L., M. Piscator, G.F. Nordberg, and T. Kjellstrom, eds. 1974. Cadmium in the Environment. Second edition. CRC Press, Inc., Cleveland, Ohio. 248 pp.

Furchner, J.E., C.R. Richmond, and G.A. Drake. 1968. Comparative metabolism of radionuclides in mammals. IV. Retention of silver-110m in the mouse, rat, monkey, and dog. Health Phys. 15:505-514.

Furst, A. 1971. Trace elements related to specific chronic diseases: Cancer. Geol. Soc. Am., Mem. No. 123:109-130.

Furst, A., and R.T. Haro. 1969. Survey of metal carcinogenesis. Prog. Exp. Tumor Res. 12:102-133.

Furst, A., and M.C. Schlauder. 1977. Inactivity of two noble metals as carcinogens. J. Environ. Pathol. Toxicol. 1:51-57.

Gilman, A.G., L.S. Goodman, and A. Gilman, eds. 1980. The Pharmacological Basis of Therapeutics. Sixth edition. MacMillan, New York. 1,843 pp.

Goetz, C.G., and H.L. Klawans. 1979. Neurologic aspects of other metals. Pp. 319-345 in P.J. Vinken and G.W. Bruyn, eds. Handbook of Clinical Neurology. Vol. 36. North-Holland, New York.

Goodman, L.S., and A. Gilman, eds. 1975. Silver. Pp. 930-931 in The Pharmacological Basis of Therapeutics. Fifth edition. MacMillan, New York.

Gorsky, J.E., A.A. Dietz, H. Spencer, and D. Osis. 1979. Metabolic balance of aluminum studied in six men. Clin. Chem. 25:1739-1743.

Gosselin, R.E., H.C. Hodge, R.P. Smith, and M.N. Gleason, eds. 1976. Section III. Therapeutics Index: Cadmium. Pp. 69-74 in Clinical Toxicology of Commercial Products: Acute Poisoning. Fourth edition. Williams & Wilkins, Baltimore, Md.

Goyer, R.A., ed. 1974. Low Level Lead Toxicity. Environ. Health Perspect. Issue No. 7. 252 pp.

Goyer, R.A., and P. Mushak. 1977. Lead toxicity, laboratory aspects. Pp. 41-77 in R.A. Goyer and M.A. Mehlman, eds. Advances in Modern Toxicology: Toxicology of Trace Elements. Vol. 2. John Wiley & Sons, New York.

Greathouse, D.G., G.F. Craun, and D. Worth. 1976. Epidemiologic study of the relationship between lead in drinking water and blood lead levels. Pp. 9-24 in D.D. Hemphill, ed.

Trace Substances in Environmental Health: A Symposium. Vol. 10. University of Missouri, Columbia, Mo.

Hammond, P.B. 1977. Exposure of humans to lead. Ann. Rev. Pharmacol. Toxicol. 17:197-214.

Hammond, P.B., and R.P. Beliles. 1980. Metals: Lead. Pp. 415-421 in J. Doull, C. Klaassen, and M.O. Amdur, eds. Casarett and Doull's Toxicology: The Basic Science of Poisons. Second edition. MacMillan, New York.

Hart, M.M., and R.H. Adamson. 1971. Antitumor activity and toxicity of salts of inorganic Group IIIa metals: Aluminum, gallium, indium, and thallium. Proc. Natl. Acad. Sci. USA 68:1623-1626.

Hart, M.M, C.F. Smith, S.T. Yancey, and R.H. Adamson. 1971. Toxicity and antitumor activity of gallium nitrate and periodically related metal salts. J. Natl. Cancer Inst. 47:1121-1127.

Heddle, J.A., and W.R. Bruce. 1977. Comparison of tests for mutagenicity of carcinogenicity using assays for sperm abnormalities, formation of micronuclei, and mutations in *Salmonella*. Pp. 1549-1557 in H.H. Hiatt, J.D. Watson, and J.A. Winsten, eds. Origins of Human Cancer: Book C. Human Risk Assessment. Cold Spring Harbor Conferences on Cell Proliferation, Vol. 4. Cold Spring Harbor Laboratory, Cold Spring Harbor, N.Y.

Heffernan, W.P., C. Guion, and R.J. Bull. 1979a. Oxidative damage to the erythrocyte induced by sodium chlorite, in vivo. J. Environ. Pathol. Toxicol. 2:1487-1499.

Heffernan, W.P., C. Guion, and R.J. Bull. 1979b. Oxidative damage to the erythrocyte induced by sodium chlorite, in vitro. J. Environ. Pathol. Toxicol. 2:1501-1510.

Hill, W.R., and D.M. Pillsbury. 1939. Argyria: The Pharmacology of Silver. Williams & Wilkins, Baltimore, Md. 172 pp.

International Agency for Research on Cancer. 1972. Lead salts. Pp. 40-50 in IARC Monographs on the Evaluation of Carcinogenic Risk of Chemicals to Man, Vol. 1. World Health Organization/International Agency for Research on Cancer, Lyon, France.

International Commission on Radiological Protection. 1972. Alkaline earth metabolism in adult man. ICRP Publication 20. Pergamon Press, New York.

Johnson, A.R. 1973. The influence of strontium on characteristic factors of bone. Calcif. Tissue Res. 11:215-221.

Jones, A.M., and J.A. Bailey. 1974. Effect of silver from cloud seeding on rabbits. Water Air Soil Pollut. 3(3):353-363.

Just, J., and A. Szniolis. 1936. Germicidal properties of silver in water. J. Am. Water Works Assoc. 28:492-506.

Kaehny, W.D., A.P. Hegg, and A.C. Alfrey. 1977a. Gastrointestinal absorption of aluminum from aluminum-containing antacids. N. Engl. J. Med. 296:1389-1390.

Kaehny, W.D., A.C. Alfrey, R.E. Holman, and W. J. Shorr. 1977b. Aluminum transfer during hemodialysis. Kidney Int. 12:361-365.

Kehoe, R.A., J. Cholak, and R.V. Story. 1940. A spectrochemical study of the normal ranges of concentration of certain trace metals in biological materials. J. Nutr. 19:579-592.

Klatzo, I., H. Wisniewski, and E. Streicher. 1965. Experimental production of neurofibrillary degeneration. 1. Light microscopic observations. J. Neuropathol. Exp. Neurol. 24:187-199.

Kleeman, C.R., and O.S. Better. 1973. Disordered divalent ion metabolism in kidney disease: Comments on pathogenesis and treatment. Kidney Int. 4:73-79.

Kopp, J.F. 1969. The occurrence of trace elements in water. Pp. 59-73 in D.D. Hemphill, ed. Trace Substances in Environmental Health—III. Proceedings of the University of

Missouri's Third Annual Conference on Trace Substances in Environmental Health, June 24-26. University of Missouri, Columbia, Mo.

Kopp, J.F., and R.C. Kroner. 1970. Trace Metals in Waters of the United States. A Five Year Summary of Trace Metals in Rivers and Lakes of the United States (Oct. 1, 1962-Sept. 30, 1967). U.S. Department of the Interior, Federal Water Pollution Control Administration, Division of Pollution Surveillance, Cincinnati, Ohio. [207 pp.]

Kortus, J. 1967. The carbohydrate metabolism accompanying intoxication by aluminium salts in the rat. Experientia 23:912-913.

Kotsonis, F.N., and C.D. Klaassen. 1978. The relationship of metallothionein to the toxicity of cadmium after prolonged oral administration to rats. Toxicol. Appl. Pharmacol. 46:39-54.

Krasovskii, L., Y. Vasukovich, and O.G. Chariev. 1979. Experimental study of biological effects of lead and aluminum following oral administration. Environ. Health Perspect. 30:47-51.

Krigman, M.R., T.W. Bouldin, and P. Mushak. 1980. Lead. Pp. 490-507 in P.S. Spencer and H.H. Schaumburg, eds. Experimental and Clinical Neurotoxicology. Williams & Wilkins, Baltimore, Md.

Kroes, R., E.M. Den Tonkelaar, A. Minderhoud, G.J.A. Speijers, D.M.A. Vonk-Visser, J.M. Berkvens, and G.J. Van Esch. 1977. Short-term toxicity of strontium chloride in rats. Toxicology 7:11-21.

Leonard, A., and R.R. Lauwerys. 1980. Carcinogenicity, teratogenicity, and mutagenicity of arsenic. Mutat. Res. 75:49-62.

Loeb, L.A., M.A. Sirover, L.A. Weymouth, D.K. Dube, G. Seal, S.S. Agarwal, and E. Katz. 1977. Infidelity of DNA synthesis as related to mutagenesis and carcinogenesis. J. Toxicol. Environ. Health 2:1297-1304.

Loser, E. 1980. A 2 year oral carcinogenicity study with cadmium on rats. Cancer Lett. 9:191-198.

Lundin, A.P., C. Caruso, M. Sass, and G.M. Berlyne. 1978. Ultrafilterable aluminum in serum of normal man. Clin. Res. 26:636A.

Mahaffey, K.R. 1977. Relation between quantities of lead ingested and health effects of lead in humans. Pediatrics 59:448-456.

Mallick, N.P., and G.M. Berlyne. 1968. Arterial calcification after vitamin-D therapy in hyperphosphataemic renal failure. Lancet 2:1316-1320.

Martin, E.W., ed.-in-chief. 1965. Remington's Pharmaceutical Sciences. Thirteenth edition. Mac Publishing Co., Easton, Pa.

Mayor, G.H., J.A. Keiser, D. Markdani, and P.K. Ku. 1977a. Aluminum absorption and distribution: Effect of parathyroid hormone. Science 197:1187-1189.

Mayor, G. H., D.D. Makdani, and J.A. Keiser. 1977b. The effect of parathyroid hormone (PTH) on the gastrointestinal (GI) absorption and distribution of aluminum. Pp. 41-44 in S.S. Brown, ed. Clinical Chemistry and Chemical Toxicology of Metals: Proceedings of the First International Symposium organized by the Commission on Toxicology, IUPAC Section on Clinical Chemistry, held at Monte Carlo, March 2-5. Elsevier/North-Holland, New York.

Mayor, G.H., J.A. Keiser, T.V. Sanchez, S.M. Sprague, and J.B. Hook. 1978. Factors affecting tissue aluminum concentration. J. Dialysis 2:471-481.

McCabe, L.J. 1970. Metal levels found in distribution samples. In Control of Corrosion by Soft Waters, presented by Education Committee of American Water Works Association and U.S. Public Health Service, Washington, D.C. 6 pp.

McCance, R.A., and E.M. Widdowson. 1939. The fate of strontium after intravenous administration to normal persons. Biochem. J. 33:1822–1825.

McCormack, K.M., L.D. Ottosen, V.L. Sanger, S. Sprague, G.H. Mayor, and J.B. Hook. 1979. Effect of prenatal administration of aluminum and parathyroid hormone on fetal development in the rat. Proc. Soc. Exp. Biol. Med. 161:74–77.

McCoy, E.C., and H.S. Rosenkranz. 1978. Silver sulfadiazine: Lack of mutagenic activity. Chemotherapy 24:87–91.

McDermott, J.R., A.I. Smith, M.K. Ward, I.S. Parkinson, and D.N.S. Kerr. 1978. Brain-aluminium concentration in dialysis encephalopathy. Lancet 1:901–904.

McKee, J.E., and H.W. Wolf. 1963. Reprinted 1971. Water Quality Criteria. Second edition. Publ. No. 3-A. The Resources Agency of California State Water Resources Control Board, Sacramento, Calif. 548 pp.

McLaughlin, A.I.G., G. Kazantzis, E. King, D. Teare, R.J. Porter, and R. Owen. 1962. Pulmonary fibrosis and encephalopathy associated with the inhalation of aluminium dust. Br. J. Ind. Med. 19:253–263.

Michaelson, I.A., and M.W. Sauerhoff. 1974. An improved model of lead-induced brain dysfunction in the suckling rat. Toxicol. Appl. Pharmacol. 28:88–96.

Moore, G.S., E.J. Calabrese, S.R. DiNardi, and T.W. Tuthill. 1978. Potential health effects of chlorine dioxide as a disinfectant in potable water supplies. Med. Hypotheses 4:481–496.

Moore, M.R., P.A. Meredith, B.C. Campbell, A. Goldberg, and S.J. Pocock. 1977. Contribution of lead in drinking water to blood-lead. Lancet 2:661–662.

Morse, D.L., W.N. Watson, J. Houseworth, L.E. Witherell, and P.J. Landrigan. 1979. Exposure of children to lead in drinking water. Am. J. Public Health 69:711–712.

Moseley, J.I., G.A. Ojemann, and A.A. Ward, Jr. 1972. Unit activity in experimental epileptic foci during focal cortical hypothermia. Exp. Neurol. 37:164–178.

National Academy of Sciences. 1973. Water Quality Criteria 1972. A report prepared by the Committee on Water Quality Criteria, Environmental Studies Board, Commission on Natural Resources, National Research Council, National Academy of Sciences. EPA-R3-73-003. U.S. Government Printing Office, Washington, D.C. 594 pp.

National Academy of Sciences. 1977. Drinking Water and Health. A report prepared by the Safe Drinking Water Committee, Advisory Center on Toxicology, Assembly of Life Sciences, National Research Council. National Academy of Sciences, Washington, D.C. 939 pp.

National Academy of Sciences. 1980a. Lead in the Human Environment. A report prepared by the Committee on Lead in the Human Environment, Environmental Studies Board, Commission on Natural Resources, National Research Council. National Academy of Sciences, Washington, D.C. 525 pp.

National Academy of Sciences. 1980b. Drinking Water and Health, Volume 3. A report prepared by the Safe Drinking Water Committee, Board on Toxicology and Environmental Health Hazards, National Research Council. National Academy of Sciences, Washington, D.C. 415 pp.

Newton, D., and A. Holmes. 1966. A case of accidental inhalation of zinc-65 and silver-110m. Radiat. Res. 29:403–412.

Nishioka, H. 1975. Mutagenic activities of metal compounds in bacteria. Mutat. Res. 31:185–189.

Nordberg, G.F., ed. 1976. Effects and Dose-Response Relationships of Toxic Metals. Elsevier, New York. 559 pp.

Norseth, T. 1979. Aluminum. Pp. 275-281 in L. Friberg, G.F. Nordberg, and V.B. Vouk, eds. Handbook on the Toxicology of Metals. Elsevier/North-Holland Biomedical Press, New York.

Northdurft, H. 1955. Die experimentelle Erzeugung von Sarkomen bei Ratten und Mäusen durch Implantation von Rundscheiben aus Gold, Silber, Platin oder Elfenbein. Naturwiss. 42:75-76.

Omdahl, J.L., and H.F. DeLuca. 1971. Strontium induced rickets: Metabolic basis. Science 174:949-951.

Omdahl J.L., and H.F. DeLuca. 1972. Rachitogenic activity of dietary strontium. I. Inhibition of intestinal calcium absorption and 1,25-dihydroxycholecalciferol synthesis. J. Biol. Chem. 247:5520-5526.

Ondreicka, R., E. Ginter, and J. Kortus. 1966. Chronic toxicity of aluminium in rats and mice and its effects on phosphorus metabolism. Br. J. Ind. Med. 23:305-312.

Pariser, R.J. 1978. Generalized argyria. Clinicopathologic features and histochemical studies. Arch. Dermatol. 114:373-377.

Phalen, R.F., and P.E. Morrow. 1973. Experimental inhalation of metallic silver. Health Phys. 24:509-518.

Pierides, A.M. 1978. Dialysis dementia, osteomalacic fractures and myopathy: A syndrome due to chronic aluminum intoxication. Int. J. Artif. Organs 1:206-208.

Platts, M.M., G.C. Goode, and J.S. Hislop. 1977. Composition of the domestic water supply and the incidence of fractures and encephalopathy in patients on home dialysis. Br. Med. J. 2:657-660.

Pocock, S.J. 1980. Factors influencing household water lead: A British national survey. Arch. Environ. Health 35:45-51.

Reeves, A.L. 1979. Barium. Pp. 321-328 in L. Friberg, G.F. Nordberg, and V.B. Vouk, eds. Handbook on the Toxicology of Metals. Elsevier/North Holland Biomedical Press, Amsterdam, The Netherlands.

Saffiotti, U., and P. Shubik. 1963. Pp. 489-507 in F. Urbach, ed. The First International Conference on the Biology of Cutaneous Cancer. Monograph No. 10. National Cancer Institute, Washington, D.C.

Sax, I.N. 1963. Silver—Silver thioarsenite. Pp. 1174-1178 in Dangerous Properties of Industrial Materials. Second edition. Reinhold Publishing Corp., New York.

Schroeder, H.A., and M. Mitchener. 1975. Life-term studies in rats: Effects of aluminum, barium, beryllium, and tungsten. J. Nutr. 105:421-427.

Schroeder, H.A., I.H. Tipton, and A.P. Nason. 1972. Trace metals in man: Strontium and barium. J. Chronic Dis. 25:491-517.

Scott, K.G., and J.G. Hamilton. 1950. The metabolism of silver in the rat with radio-silver used as an indicator. Univ. Calif. Berkeley Publ. Pharmacol. 2:241-261.

Shubik, P., and J.L. Hartwell, eds. 1969. Pp. 3-4 in Survey of Compounds Which Have Been Tested for Carcinogenic Activity. U.S. Public Health Service Publication No. 149, Supplement 2. National Cancer Institute, Bethesda, Md.

Six, K.M., and R.A. Goyer. 1972. The influence of iron deficiency on tissue content and toxicity of ingested lead in the rat. J. Lab. Clin. Med. 79:128-136.

Snyder, W.S., M.J. Cook, E.S. Nasset, L.R. Karhausen, G.P. Howells, and I.H. Tipton, eds. 1975. Report of the Task Group on Reference Man. A Report prepared by a Task Group of Committee 2 of the International Commission on Radiological Protection. ICRP No. 23. Pergamon Press, New York. 480 pp.

Sollman, T., ed. 1957a. Barium. Pp. 665-667 in A Manual of Pharmacology and Its Application to Therapeutics and Toxicology. W. B. Saunders, Philadelphia, Pa.

Sollmann, T., ed. 1957b. Strontium. Pp. 1101-1102 in A Manual of Pharmacology and Its Applications to Therapeutics and Toxicology. Eighth edition. W. B. Saunders, New York.

Sorenson, J.R.J., I.R. Campbell, L.B. Tepper, and R.D. Lingg. 1974. Aluminum in the environment and human health. Environ. Health Perspect. 8:3-95.

Spector, W.S., ed. 1956. Handbook of Toxicology: Acute Toxicities of Solids, Liquids and Gases to Laboratory Animals. Vol. 1. W.B. Saunders, Philadelphia, Pa. 408 pp.

Spencer, H., and M. Lender. 1979. Adverse effects of aluminum-containing antacids on mineral metabolism. Gastroenterology 76:603-606.

Spencer, H., L. Kramer, C.A. Gatza, and M. Lender. 1979. Calcium loss, calcium absorption and calcium requirement in osteoporosis. Pp. 65-90 in U.S. Barzel, ed. Osteoporosis II. Grune and Stratton, New York.

Stacy, B.D. E.J. King, C.V. Harrison, G. Nagelschmidt, and S. Nelson. 1959. Tisse changes in rats' lungs caused by hydroxides, oxides and phosphates of aluminum and iron. J. Pathol. Bacteriol. 77:417-426.

Stokinger, H.E., and R.L. Woodward. 1958. Toxicologic methods for establishing drinking water standards. J. Am. Water Works Assoc. 50(4):515-529.

Strauch, B., W. Buch, W. Grey, and D. Laub. 1969. Successful treatment of methemoglobinemia secondary to silver nitrate therapy. N. Engl. J. Med. 281:257-258.

Tardiff, R.G., M. Robinson and N.S. Ulmer. 1980. Subchronic oral toxicity of $BaCl_2$ in rats. J. Environ. Pathol. Toxicol. 4:267-275.

Terry, R.D. 1963. The fine structure of neurofibrillary tangles in Alzheimer's disease. J. Neuropathol. Exp. Neurol. 22:629-634.

Tipton, I.H., P.L. Stewart, and P.G. Martin. 1966. Trace elements in diets and excreta. Health Phys. 12:1683-1689.

Trapp, G.A., G.D. Miner, R.L. Zimmerman, A.R. Mastri, and L.L. Heston. 1978. Aluminum levels in brain in Alzheimer's disease. Biol. Psychiatry 13:709-718.

Underwood, E.J., ed. 1971. Other elements. 1. Aluminum. Pp. 425-427 in Trace Elements in Human and Animal Nutrition. Third edition. Academic Press, New York.

U.S. Environmental Protection Agency. 1977. National Interim Primary Drinking Water Regulations. EPA-570/9-76-003. U.S. Environmental Protection Agency, Office of Water Supply. Washington, D.C. 159 pp.

U.S. Environmental Protection Agency. 1979a. Lead: Ambient Water Quality Criteria. [PB-292-437.] Criteria and Standards Division, Office of Water Planning and Standards. U.S. Environmental Protection Agency, Washington, D.C. 151 pp.

U.S. Environmental Protection Agency. 1979b. Cadmium: Ambient Water Quality Criteria. [PB-292-423.] Criteria and Standards Division, Office of Water Planning and Standards. U.S. Environmental Protection Agency, Washington, D.C. 108 pp.

U.S. Environmental Protection Agency. 1979c. Silver: Ambient Water Quality Criteria. [PB-292-441.] Criteria and Standards Division, Office of Water Planning and Standards. U.S. Environmental Protection Agency, Washington, D.C. 161 pp.

Venugopal, B., and T.D. Luckey, eds. 1978. Toxicity of group II metals: Strontium (Sr). Pp. 58-63 in Metal Toxicity in Mammals. 2. Chemical Toxicity of Metals and Metalloids. Plenum Press, New York.

Vilkina, G.A., M.D. Pomerantzeva, and L.K. Ramaya. 1978. Lack of mutagenic effect of cadium and zinc salts in somatic and germ mouse cells. Genetika 14:2212-2214.

Waldron, H.A., and D. Stofen, eds. 1974. Sub-Clinical Lead Poisoning. Academic Press, New York. 224 pp.

Ward, A.A. 1972. Topical convulsant metals. Pp. 13-35 in D.P. Purpura, J.K. Penny, D.B. Tower, D.M. Woodbury, and R.D. Walter, eds. Experimental Models of Epilepsy—A Manual for the Laboratory Worker. Raven Press, New York.

Ward, M.K., T.G. Feest, H.A. Ellis, I.S. Parkinson, D.N.S. Kerr, J. Herrington, and G.L.

Goode. 1978. Osteomalacic dialysis osteodystrophy: Evidence for a water-borne aetiological agent, probably aluminum. Lancet 1:841–845.

Watanabe, T., T. Shimada, and A. Endo. 1979. Mutagenic effects of cadmium on mammalian oocyte chromosomes. Mutat. Res. 67:349–356.

Wong, C.S., and P. Berrang. 1976. Contamination of tap water by lead pipe and solder. Bull. Environ. Contam. Toxicol. 15:530–534.

Wood, M. 1965. Silver nitrate and burns—caution!!! Ariz. Med. 22:817.

World Health Organization. 1970. European Standards for Drinking Water, 2nd ed. Geneva, Switzerland.

World Health Organization. 1971. International Standards for Drinking Water, 3rd ed. Geneva, Switzerland.

World Health Organization. 1973. Health Aspects Relating to the Use of Polyelectrolytes in Water Treatment for Community Water Supply. Tech. Paper No. 5. WHO International Reference Center for Community Water Supply, The Hague, The Netherlands. 32 pp.

Wyckoff, R.C., and F.R. Hunter. 1956. A spectrographic analysis of human blood. Arch. Biochem. Biophys. 63:454–460.

Wysor, M.S. 1975. Orally-administered silver sulfadiazine. Chemotherapy and toxicology in CF-1 mice. *Plasmodium berghei* (malaria) and *Pseudomonas aeruginosa*. Chemotherapy (Basel) 21:298-306. [Chem. Absts. 83:71889w, 1975.]

Ziegler, E.E., B.B. Edwards, R.L. Jensen, K.R. Mahaffey, and S.J. Fomon. 1978. Absorption and retention of lead by infants. Pediatr. Res. 12:29-34.

VII

Toxicity of Selected Organic Contaminants in Drinking Water

The compounds evaluated in this chapter were selected for essentially the same reasons as those enumerated at the beginning of Chapter VI. Chloroform is included because new information has become available since it was evaluated in the first volume of *Drinking Water and Health* (National Academy of Sciences, 1977). Dibromochloropropane appears for the first time in this report because of its occurrence in drinking water resulting from its use in agriculture.

Toxicological information is required for a large number of solvents that are appearing with greater frequency in wastewater, thereby posing a real or potential hazard for contamination of drinking water. Among them are nitrophenols, nitrobenzene, petroleum products, and polynuclear aromatic hydrocarbons, which are also evaluated in this chapter. Table VII-1 summarizes the acture and chronic SNARL's for the compounds reviewed in this chapter.

Acetonitrile (CH₃CN)

Nitriles characteristically contain a cyano group, $C \equiv N$. Acetonitrile—a mononitrile having the formula CH_3CN—is also known as methylcyanide, cyanomethane, or ethanenitrile (National Institute for Occupational Safety and Health, 1978a). A colorless liquid, acetonitrile is infinitely soluble in water and has a molecular weight of 41.1. Because of their versatile chemical reactivity, nitriles have many industrial uses, such as in the manufacture of plastics, synthetic fibers, and elastomers, and as a solvent

TABLE VII-1   Summation of Acute and Chronic
Exposure Levels for Organic Chemicals Reviewed
in this Chapter

| Chemical | Suggested No-Adverse-Response Level (SNARL), mg/liter, by Exposure Period[a] | | |
	24-Hour	7-Day	Chronic
Nitrobenzene	0.035	0.005	
Mononitrophenol		0.29	
Dinitrophenol			0.11[b]
Trinitrophenol	4.9	0.2	
Benzene		0.25	
2,4,6-Trichlorophenol	17.5	2.5	

[a] See text for details on individual compounds.
[b] This is the average from two calculated SNARL's; see text for details.

in the extractive distillation that separates olefins from diolefins, butadiene
from butylene, and isoprene from isopentene (Merck Index, 1976; National
Institute for Occupational Safety and Health, 1978a; Pozzani *et al.*, 1959).
In 1964 approximately 1,575 metric tons of acetonitrile were used in the
United States (National Institute for Occupational Safety and Health, 1978a).

The major occupational exposures to nitriles occur primarily by the dermal and inhalation routes. Depending upon the amount absorbed, nitriles
may cause hepatic, renal, cardiovascular, gastrointestinal, and central
nervous system disorders, regardless of the route of administration.
Although these effects are usually attributed to the metabolic release of
cyanide, they may also be partly due to the intact molecule (National Institute for Occupational Safety and Health, 1978a).

The time-weighted average (TWA) standard for nitriles published by
the National Institute for Occupational Safety and Health (NIOSH) is
based on reports indicating that certain nitriles are sources of cyanide
ions. The TWA for acetonitrile is 20 ppm for up to a 10-hour workshift in
a 40-hour work week (National Institute for Occupational Safety and
Health, 1978a).

METABOLISM

There has been little work concerned with the metabolism and disposition
of acetonitrile. In studies by Dequidt and Haguenoer (1972) and Haguenoer and Dequidt (1975a), rats received intraperitoneal injections of

acetonitrile in doses ranging from 600 to 2,340 mg/kg. The tissues were analyzed for acetonitrile and both free and combined hydrogen cyanide content. In general, acetonitrile was found to be rather evenly distributed among the various organs, and hydrogen cyanide was found in nearly all organs in varying concentrations. In subsequent studies, Haguenoer and Dequidt (1975b) obtained similar results following the administration of acetonitrile to rats via the inhalation route.

A series of studies have shown that humans absorb nitriles through the skin (Sunderman and Kincaid, 1953; Wolfsie, 1960) and through the respiratory tract (Amdur, 1959; Dalhamn *et al.*, 1968; McKee *et al.*, 1962; Pozzani *et al.*, 1959). After absorption, nitriles may be metabolized to an alpha-cyanohydrin or to inorganic cyanide, which is oxidized to thiocyanate and excreted in the urine. Nitriles also undergo other types of reactions depending on the moiety to which the cyano group is attached. The cyano group may be converted to a carboxylic acid derivative and ammonia or may be incorporated into cyanocobalamin (National Institute for Occupational Safety and Health, 1978a).

HEALTH ASPECTS

In general, adverse effects resulting from exposure to the nitriles, including acetonitrile, occur primarily by the dermal and inhalation routes. Depending on the amount absorbed, nitriles may cause toxic effects involving the hepatic, renal, cardiovascular, gastrointestinal, and central nervous systems. These effects may be due in part to the intact molecules, but are also attributed to the metabolic release of cyanide. There are substantial differences among the various nitriles with regard to the amounts necessary to cause poisoning, the durations of exposure, and the time intervals between exposure and manifestation of the adverse effects. These differences are associated with the rate and extent of the release of cyanide ion (Amdur, 1959; National Institute for Occupational Safety and Health, 1978a).

Observations in Humans

Acute exposure of humans to acetonitrile by inhalation results in headache, dizziness, profuse sweating, vomiting, giddiness, hypernea, difficulty in breathing, palpitations, irregular pulse, convulsions, loss of consciousness, and death, usually resulting from respiratory arrest (Amdur, 1959; Grabois, 1955; National Institute for Occupational Safety and Health, 1978a). Most deaths have followed industrial exposures, and effects have generally been observed anywhere from 3 to 12 hours after exposure (National Institute for Occupational Safety and Health, 1978a). This delayed onset of effects has been explained by Amdur (1959) as a slow release of cyanide and its metabolism to thiocyanate. There are apparently no reports of toxicity in humans following ingestion of acetonitrile.

Observations in Other Species

Acute toxic effects observed in animals include labored breathing, anuria, ataxia, cyanosis, coma, and death. Tissue distribution studies indicate that mononitriles are distributed uniformly in the various organs and that cyanide metabolites are found in the spleen, stomach, and skin, smaller amounts being present in the liver, lungs, kidneys, heart, brain, muscle, intestines, and testes (Dequidt and Haguenoer, 1972; Pozzani et al., 1959).

Most studies conducted in animals have been concerned with toxicity following inhalation. Studies of orally adminstered acetonitrile have shown LD_{50}'s in various species as follows: Sherman rats, 3.8 g/kg (Smyth and Carpenter, 1948); rats, 1.34-6.68 g/kg (Pozzani et al., 1959); and guinea pigs, 0.14 g/kg (Pozzani et al., 1959). Kimura et al. (1971) found that the oral toxicity of acetonitrile varied according to the age of the rat. The acute oral LD_{50}'s for 14-day-old, young adult, and adult rats were 0.16 g/kg, 3.1 g/kg, and 3.5 g/kg, respectively. Acetonitrile was significantly more toxic in the 14-day-old rat than in the adult.

There are no studies dealing with subacute or chronic toxicity of acetonitrile administered orally to animals.

Carcinogenicity, Mutagenicity, and Teratogenicity There are no reports indicating any possible carcinogenic, mutagenic, or teratogenic effects of acetonitrile (National Institute for Occupational Safety and Health, 1978a). Acrylonitrile (vinyl cyanide) is suspected of inducing cancer in both animals and humans (National Institute for Occupational Safety and Health, 1978c).

CONCLUSIONS AND RECOMMENDATIONS

Suggested No-Adverse-Response Level (SNARL)

24-Hour Exposure There are no adequate data from which to calculate a 24-hour or 7-day SNARL.

,

Chronic Exposure There are no adequate data from which to calculate a chronic exposure SNARL.

Chloroform (CHCl₃)

Chloroform was evaluated in the first and third volumes of *Drinking Water and Health* (National Academy of Sciences, 1977, pp. 713-717; 1980a, pp. 203-204). The following material, which became available after these volumes were published, updates and, in some instances, reevaluates the information in the earlier reports. Also included are some references that were not assessed in the original report.

HEALTH EFFECTS

Observations in Humans

No new data.

Observations in Other Species

Hewitt *et al.* (1979) observed an increased uptake of glutamate-pyruvate transaminase (GPT) and decreased uptake of indicator organic anions and cations in kidney slices from male Swiss-Webster mice exposed to chloroform. Pretreatment of the animals with mirex did not markedly alter either the hepatotoxic or nephrotoxic effects of chloroform. However, pretreatment with kepone potentiated chloroform hepatotoxicity and may have increased chloroform-induced kidney damage. The authors concluded that ingestion of kepone may increase the sensitivity of the liver and kidneys to chloroform toxicity.

The toxicity of chloroform was more pronounced in males than in females of the following barrier-reared strains of mice: Tif:MAG$_f$, Tif:MF2$_f$, C3H/TifBom$_f$, DBA/JBom$_f$, C57BL/6J/Bom$_f$, and A/JBom$_f$ strains. The C3H/TifBom$_f$ strain proved to be the most sensitive of the several strains tested (Pericin and Thomann, 1979). 2,3,7,8-Tetrachloro-dibenzo-*p*-dioxin did not alter the acute toxicity of chloroform (Hook *et al.*, 1978), but Cornish *et al.* (1977) showed that the toxicity of chloroform can be markedly potentiated by prior treatment with ethanol or phenobarbital.

Mutagenicity In studies by Agustin and Lim-Sylianco (1978), chloroform showed DNA-damaging and chromosome-breaking (clastogenic) activity; however, it had no direct effect on base-pair and frameshift mutations. Chloroform also caused frameshift mutations in male mice after metabolic activation. Vitamin E treatment decreased the mutagenicity and clastogenicity of chloroform.

Clemens *et al.* (1979) reported genotypic differences in responses to the toxic effects of chloroform that were manifestations of differences in renal rather than hepatic responses or the ability to repair renal damage. In these studies, the authors showed that DBA/2J male mice were more sensitive to the 10-day lethal effect of chloroform than were C57BL/6J males, whereas the sensitivity of B6D2F$_1$ (C57BL/6J $\times$ DBA/2J) mice was intermediate. This relative order of sensitivity was preserved following sublethal doses of labelled chloroform with respect to accumulation in subcellular fractions and renal (but not hepatic) dysfunction. Kidneys from mice of the three genotypes were able to repair tubular damage from chloroform. Prior to toxic exposure to chloroform, covalent binding of labeled chloroform to renal microsomes was greater in DBA than in C57BL mice. Pretreatment with phenobarbital enhanced covalent binding by renal microsomes from DBA, but not from C57BL mice. Testosterone propionate and medroxyprogesterone acetate sensitized the kidneys of both sexes in DBA/2J and C57BL/6J mice. Progesterone and hydrocortisone sodium phosphate sensitized the kidneys to chloroform in DBA/2J males but not in DBA/2J females or in C57BL/6J mice of either sex.

In the presence of metabolically active mouse liver microsomes and bacteria, chloroform was not activated to mutagenic species (Greim *et al.*, 1977). It also gave negative results in the Ames test and failed to increase the frequency of sister chromatid exchange (SCE) in fibroblasts of Chinese hamsters (Li *et al.*, 1979). Results from a study by White *et al.* (1979) also indicated that chloroform did not increase SCE values. Simmon (1977) reported that bromoform, dibromochloromethane, and bromodichloromethane are mutagenic whereas chloroform is not mutagenic in *Salmonella typhimurium* strains TA1535 and TA100.

Carcinogenicity Reuber (1979) recently reviewed the literature concerning the carcinogenicity of 14 organochlorine pesticides in mice. Carcinomas of the liver were observed most frequently in mice ingesting chloroform, among other organochlorine compounds. When administered orally in doses of 0.15 mg/kg/day in drinking water, chloroform did not enhance the growth or metastasis of Lewis lung carcinoma or increase the number of Ehrlich ascites tumor cells in mice inoculated with tumor cells (Capel and Williams, 1978). However, when administered at 15 mg/kg/day in similar experiments it caused increases in pulmonary tumor foci after inoculation with Lewis lung carcinoma cells and in the number of Ehrlich ascites tumor cells. At both doses, it led to more organ invasions by B16 melanoma after inoculation with the tumor cells. When administered by oral intubation, it produced kidney tumors in male Osborne-Mendel rats (Weisburger, 1977).

A series of studies was conducted at the Huntington Research Center in England, using beagle dogs, specific pathogen-free Sprague-Dawley rats, and three stocks (C57BL, CBA, and CSI) of mice, which were given chloroform in a toothpaste base (Heywood et al., 1979; Palmer et al., 1979; Roe et al., 1979). The beagle dogs were given the mixture orally in gelatin capsules 6 days/week for 7.5 years, followed by a 20- to 24-week recovery period (Heywood et al., 1979). Groups of males and females received 0.5 ml/kg/day of the vehicle (toothpaste without chloroform), and eight dogs of each sex remained untreated. The treated groups were composed of eight dogs of both sexes, each receiving chloroform in doses equivalent to 15 and 30 mg/kg/day in the toothpaste vehicle. Another group of the same size received an equivalent amount of toothpaste (0.5 ml/kg/day) without chloroform. At the end of the exposure, a small number of macroscopic and microscopic neoplasms were observed. One dog in each chloroform-treated group had a malignant tumor, but there were no tumors in the livers or kidneys of any dog. Overall, exposure to chloroform in a toothpaste base was not associated with any effects on the incidence of any kind of neoplasia.

Groups of 50 cesarean-derived specific pathogen-free male and female Sprague-Dawley rats received either chloroform in doses equivalent to 60 mg/kg/day in a toothpaste base or the vehicle only by gavage 6 days/week for 80 weeks. They were then observed for as long as 15 weeks more (Palmer et al., 1979). Chloroform-treated rats of both sexes survived better than the controls, although both groups had a high incidence of non-neoplastic respiratory and renal diseases. There were consistent observations of decreases in plasma cholinesterase in female rats, which were shown to be related to activity against butyrylcholine but not to acetyl-β-methylcholine. Tumors of various sites were observed in 39% of chloroform-treated rats of both sexes examined histologically, compared with 38% of the vehicle controls. There were no treatment-related effects on the incidence of liver or kidney tumors. However, histological observations of malignant mammary tumors were reported in more treated than control rats, but these differences were not statistically different.

In another study, mice were given chloroform in a toothpaste base by gavage or in arachis oil in doses up to 60 mg/kg/day, 6 days/week for 8 weeks (Roe et al., 1979). Control groups were left untreated or given the vehicle only. In general, there were more survivors in the chloroform-treated groups than in the control group. Treatment was not associated with any type of neoplasia. In male, but not female, ICI mice receiving doses of 60 mg/kg/day, but not in those given 17 mg/kg/day, chloroform in a toothpaste base was associated with an increased incidence of epithelial tumors of the kidney. A more pronounced effect of the same kind was observed in mice given chloroform at 60 mg/kg/day in an arachis oil vehicle. This treatment was also associated with a higher incidence and severity of nonneoplastic renal disease. At the dose levels tested, namely 113 and 400 times greater than the average human exposure resulting from the use of toothpaste containing 3.5% chloroform, no adverse effects were seen in the liver and there was no increased incidence of liver tumors, even in the CBA strain with the greatest susceptibility to liver tumor formation. At the 17 mg/kg/day level, which is 113 times greater than the average exposure of humans from toothpaste, no excess of renal tumors was observed in males of the particularly susceptible ICI strain.

Teratogenicity   No new data.

CONCLUSIONS AND RECOMMENDATIONS

Suggested No-Adverse-Response Level (SNARL)

The following calculations are for *noncarcinogenic* effects only.

24-Hour Exposure   A SNARL of 22 mg/liter was calculated in *Drinking Water and Health*, Volume 2 (National Academy of Sciences, 1980a). Details of the calculation are contained in that volume.

7-Day Exposure   This was calculated to be one-seventh (3.2 mg/liter) of the 24-hour SNARL.

Chronic Exposure   This value cannot be calculated because chloroform is a carcinogen in animals.

1,2-Dibromo-3-chloropropane ($C_3H_5Br_2Cl$)

1,2-Dibromo-3-chloropropane (DBCP) is an amber-brown liquid with a low vapor pressure and solubility (0.1% w/w), but it is miscible with aliphatic and aromatic hydrocarbons and other solvents and oils. Its molecular weight is 236.36.

Since the 1950's, DBCP has been used as a soil fumigant and nematocide in emulsifiable concentrates, liquid concentrates, powders, granules, and other formulations. It has been marketed under such trade names as Negmagon, Fumazone, Nemaset, Nematox, and Nemafume.

DBCP is produced primarily by the bromination of allyl chloride at room temperature. Technical grade DBCP has been shown to contain up to 10% impurities, including epichlorohydrin and allyl chloride. The levels of these compounds and 14 other identified impurities may vary among batches. In contrast to the other impurities, epichlorohydrin is added intentionally as a stabilizer.

Observations in Humans

In August 1977, at the request of the Oil, Chemical, and Atomic Workers Union (OCAW), the National Institute for Occupational Safety and Health (NIOSH) inspected manufacturing facilities in California. In September of that year, an emergency temporary standard for exposure to DBCP was issued by the Occupational Safety and Health Administration (OSHA). A permanent standard for DBCP exposure, which was established on March 17, 1978, limits employee exposure to 1 ppb as an 8-hour time-weighted average concentration. This OSHA standard also prohibited eye and skin contact and provided for monitoring of employee exposure, engineering controls, safe work practices, and various other regulatory requirements. A rebuttable presumption against registration (RPAR) and continued registration of pesticide products containing DBCP was issued by the U.S. Environmental Protection Agency (EPA) on September 22, 1977 (U.S. Environmental Protection Agency, 1977).

Both the OSHA standard and the EPA RPAR were based primarily on toxicological findings in animals, suggesting that DBCP causes sterility and is carcinogenic. The NIOSH recommendation for an occupational exposure standard for DBCP was based not only on its carcinogenic and sterilizing potential, but also on its ability to cause diminished renal function, degeneration and cirrhosis of the liver, and mutagenesis in chronically exposed employees.

Observations in Other Species

Acute Effects Studies by Torkelson *et al.* (1961) and by Rakhmatullaev (1971) indicate that the acute oral LD_{50} for DBCP in rats and other animals such as guinea pigs, mice, rabbits, and chickens ranges from 170 to 350 mg/kg. Mice and rabbits appear to be somewhat less sensitive than chickens. Effects preceding death following lethal exposures to DBCP included depression, analgesia, skeletal muscle incoordination, and paralysis. DBCP produced slight irritation when applied to the eye, but corneal irritation was not noted. Dermal application of DBCP produced only transient erythema in rabbits, but both single and repeated dermal exposure produced subcutaneous necrosis with polymorphonuclear leucocyte infiltration. Using a modified Draize technique, Torkelson *et al.* (1961) reported a dermal LD_{50} of 1,400 mg/kg in rabbits exposed for 24 hours to undiluted DBCP at 60 ppm. Inhalation exposure to vaporized DBCP produced respiratory irritation, apathy, and ataxia. Clouding of the lens and cornea and mortality occurred at higher concentrations. A 1-hour LC_{50} of 368 ppm was observed in rats, but delayed deaths and kidney pathology were noted following inhalation exposures to concentrations as low as 50 ppm.

Subchronic Effects   Torkelson *et al.* (1961) fed diets containing DBCP concentrations of 0, 5, 20, 150, 450, and 1,350 mg/kg to male and female rats for 90 days. Female rats exhibited increased kidney weights at 20 mg/kg and at higher doses, retarded weight gain at doses of 150 mg/kg and higher, and increased liver weight at 450 mg/kg. There were no growth effects in male rats fed diets containing less than 450 mg/kg. Histological effects were minimal at all dosage levels in both sexes.

In contrast to the diet exposure studies, repeated inhalation exposure produced poor growth, increased susceptibility to secondary infection, and both gross and histological changes in the testes of male rats at the lowest exposure rate tested (50 exposures of 7 hours daily, 5 days a week to DBCP at 5 ppm). Higher concentrations of DBCP produced mortality, and similar findings were observed in monkeys, guinea pigs, and rabbits. Intramuscular injection of testosterone, cortisone, and ACTH (adrenocorticotropic hormone) failed to protect male rats against the testicular effects of exposure to DBCP (Torkelson *et al.*, 1961).

Mutagenicity   DBCP was shown to be directly mutagenic to *Salmonella typhimurium* TA1530 and *Escherichia coli* Pol. A by Rosenkrantz (1975). Prival *et al.* (1977) reported that the compound is a direct weak mutagen in *Salmonella* TA1535. Blum and Ames (1977) reported mutagenic effects with DBCP in *Salmonella* TA100 with metabolic activation. The observation of Vogel and Chandler (1974) that 1,2-dibromopropane was also mutagenic in *Drosophila* could have been due to the ability of vicinal 1,2-dibromides to rearrange in solution to form reactive bromonium ion. The substitution of a chlorine atom on the third carbon of propane would probably not alter this property significantly. Thus, DBCP would be expected to be mutagenic on the basis of its 1,2-dibromide configuration. However, Biles *et al.* (1978), in a more recent reevaluation of the mutagenicity of DBCP, suggest that most, if not all, of the mutagenic effects attributed to the technical grade of DBCP used in previous mutagenesis assays is due to epichlorohydrin or to other highly mutagenic contaminants in the technical product. Using *Salmonella typhimurium* TA1535 with and without S-9 activation, these investigators demonstrated mutagenic effects (increased revertants at doses ranging from 0 to 1,600 μg/plate) with technical DBCP, pure epichlorohydrin, and distillates from the technical product. Pure (redistilled) DBCP did not produce mutagenic effects even at high dosage levels. On the basis of the mutagenesis assay data, these authors calculated that the mutagenic effect of technical DBCP can be attributed almost entirely to the presence of the stabilizer epichlorohydrin in the technical product. They also observed that the use of S-9 activation in the mutagenesis assay eliminated the mutagenic activity of epichlorohydrin and produced a mutagenic effect from pure DBCP, suggesting the formation of a mutagenic metabolite. Allyl chloride, which is also an impurity in technical DBCP, was found to be mutagenic in these studies, but the mutagenic potency of this contaminant is less than that of either epichlorohydrin or technical DBCP.

Carcinogenicity   The EPA RPAR Final Position Document for DBCP (U.S. Environmental Protection Agency, 1978) describes four studies that attribute carcinogenic effects to DBCP in laboratory animals. The first of these is the National Cancer Institute (NCI) (1978) bioassay of DBCP for possible carcinogenicity. Partial results of this study have also been published by Weisburger (1977), and preliminary observations on the carcinogenicity of DBCP were reported by Olson *et al.* (1973). Two additional studies, which were sponsored by Dow Chemical, were conducted at the Hazelton Laboratories. The fourth study was a skin bioassay study conducted by Van Duuren at the New York Medical Center. An earlier report by Van Duuren (1977) describes the carcinogenicity of epichlorohydrin, allyl chloride, and other DBCP-related halohydrocarbons.

When the NCI carcinogenicity bioassay was initiated in 1972, DBCP was only one of several halohydrocarbons under test. It was administered by gavage 5 days a week to male and female Osborne-Mendel rats at dosage levels of 12 and 24 mg/kg for 14 weeks, after which the dosages were increased to 15 and 30 mg/kg for a period of 73 or 64 weeks, respectively. Similar studies with male and female B6C3F$_1$ mice were also conducted at higher concentrations of DBCP. The major conclusions of this study were that, "In rats and mice of both sexes, statistically significant incidences of squamous-cell carcinomas of the forestomach occurred in each dosed group with a positive association between dose level and tumour incidence." The NCI also concluded that DBCP is carcinogenic to the mammary gland of female rats. Toxic nephropathy was observed in the treated rats and mice, but testicular damage was not prominent. Initial reports from the two Dow/Hazelton studies and the Van Duuren study also indicated an increased incidence of "possible neoplasms" or "raised areas or nodules" in the forestomach of male and female rats. Squamous cell carcinoma of the forestomach of female Swiss mice was also observed in the Van Duuren study.

All of these studies have been vigorously criticized for various defects in protocol, e.g., multiple agents on test in same room, inappropriateness of the control groups, study deficiencies, etc., but the conclusion of the EPA's final position document (U.S. Environmental Protection Agency, 1978) is that the carcinogenicity trigger for DBCP had not been rebutted. However, the question of whether "pure" DBCP is a carcinogen requires further study in view of the demonstration by Biles *et al.* (1978) that some of the adverse effects of technical DBCP can be attributed to its epichlorohydrin content. Van Duuren (1977) has also demonstrated that allyl chloride, a contaminant of technical DBCP formulations, may be carcinogenic, which could result from the presence of the known carcinogens epichlorohydrin and glycidaldehyde in the metabolic pathway of allyl chloride. In previous NIOSH documents relating to epichlorohydrin (National Institute for Occupational Safety and Health, 1976, 1978b), evidence has suggested that epichlorohydrin produces carcinogenic effects in both laboratory animals and in humans. The 1978 NIOSH document also reports mutagenic effects (chromosomal aberrations) in humans, and the 1976 NIOSH document described the ability of epichlorohydrin to induce sterility in rats.

Teratogenicity   No data available.

REPRODUCTIVE AND FERTILITY STUDIES

A conventional three-generation reproduction study in mammals does not appear to have been conducted with DBCP. However, several reports describe the adverse effects on the testes and the production of sterility in DBCP-exposed humans. Torkelson *et al.* (1961) reported that testicular atrophy occurred in rats repeatedly exposed to DBCP vapors at 20 ppm and higher and that there was a decreased testes weight in rats exposed to DBCP vapors at levels as low as 5 ppm. Similar effects have been reported in a series of Russian papers (Faidysh, 1973; Faidysh and Avkhimenko, 1974; Faidysh *et al.*, 1970; Rakhmatullaev, 1971; Reznik and Sprinchan, 1975). Prolongation of the estrous cycle was also noted by Reznik and Sprinchan (1975).

Rao *et al.* (1979) and Burek *et al.* (1979) reported inhalation studies in which male rats and rabbits were exposed to DBCP at levels of 0.1 and 1 ppm for 14 weeks or 10 ppm for 10 weeks. The results of these studies indicated that rabbits are somewhat more susceptible to the adverse testicular effects of inhaled DBCP and that the no-effect level for DBCP by this route is 0.1 ppm.

Sterility in a group of pesticide formulation workers exposed to DBCP was initially observed in December 1977 (Whorton *et al.*, 1977). These investigators described azoospermia or oligospermia in 14 of 25 nonvasectomized men and an increased serum level of follicle-stimulating hormone (FSH) and luteinizing hormone (LH) in these individuals. Additional results of these and related studies have been reported subsequently by the same group of investigators (Biava *et al.*, 1978; Marshall *et al.*, 1977). In a recent 1-year followup report on 21 of the original subjects, Whorton and Milby (1980) indicated that recovery occurred in most of the oligospermic individuals but not in the azoospermic men.

Several additional epidemiological studies of DBCP-exposed workers have been initiated by the EPA, and preliminary reports from these studies are generally consistent with the Whorton study. Similar observations have also been reported by Glass *et al.* (1979) and Potashnik *et al.* (1978).

Two major questions remain unanswered: first, does repeated exposure to DBCP, even at low levels from which apparent recovery could occur, produce cumulative damage in the male reproductive tract and, eventually, a nonrecoverable azoospermia? Second, are the adverse effects of DBCP on the testes due to DBCP itself or to a contaminant such as epichlorohydrin, which is known to cause sterility as well as mutagenic and oncogenic effects (National Institute for Occupational Safety and Health, 1978b)?

CONCLUSIONS AND RECOMMENDATIONS

In view of the possibility that epichlorohydrin, allyl chloride, or one of the other contaminants of technical DBCP may be responsible for the adverse toxicological effects observed in both animals and in humans exposed to DBCP, it is premature to recommend a suggested no-adverse-response level (SNARL) for pure DBCP.

Dimethylformamide [$HCON(CH_3)_2$]

Dimethylformamide (DMF) has a variety of applications in industrial processes, primarily as a solvent for liquids, gases, Orlon, and similar polyacrylic fibers, and in the formulation of organic compounds. It also is used as a solvent in Spandex fiber-lengthening reactions, for polyacrylonitrile, vinyl chloride polymers, epoxy polymers, cellulose-derived polymers, urea-formaldehyde polymers, polyamides, and paint strippers, and in the production of acrylic fibers (Zaebst and Robinson, 1977). Its solvent properties are also useful in pigments and dyes and in gasoline anti-icing additives.

DMF is a colorless liquid that is miscible with water and with most organic solvents. It is only slightly soluble in petroleum ether. It has an unpleasant, fishy odor, a vapor density of 3.7 mm mercury at 25°C, and a freezing point of −61°C (Deichmann and Gerarde, 1969).

Inhalation exposures to DMF are moderately hazardous to human health. The compound is moderately irritating to the skin and is a definite hazard when absorbed through the skin (Patty, 1963). There does not appear to have been injury in humans who have inhaled DMF, at least at low concentrations (50 ppm) (Patty 1963). According to Gosselin et al. (1976), the probable lethal dose in humans for DMF ranges from 500 mg to 5 g/kg. The current threshold limit value (TLV) is 10 ppm.

METABOLISM

During the 24 hours following oral administration of DMF to rats at 4 to 400 mg/kg, nonmetabolized DMF was detected in the blood at concentrations proportional to the dose given. Following DMF doses less than 200 mg/kg, the urinary concentration of N-methylformamide, the primary metabolite of DMF, was greater than that of the parent compound. After DMF doses higher than 200 mg/kg, the reverse was observed. Excretion of DMF and N-methylformamide was similar following administration of DMF at 200 mg/kg. Essentially nontoxic doses are associated with greater excretion of N-methylformamide than DMF, whereas toxic doses are associated with higher concentrations of DMF than N-methylformamide in urine (Sanotskii et al., 1978).

Krivanek et al. (1978) exposed eight healthy male humans to DMF vapor at a concentration of 8.79 ± 0.33 ppm for 6 hours daily for 5 consecutive days. All urine voided by the subjects was collected from the beginning of the first exposure to the 24th hour after the end of the last exposure. Each sample was analyzed for N-methylformamide. The investigators observed that N-methylformamide was rapidly eliminated from the body, concentrations in urine peaking within a few hours after the end of each exposure period. Very little N-methylformamide was found in a sample examined 24 hours after exposure, and none of the compound was detected in a sample examined 48 hours after exposure. There was no increased excretion of N-methylformamide in the urine following repetitive exposure. The mean for the 7-hour (end of exposure) sample was 4.7 μg/ml, or 436.8 μg total. Lower and upper one-sided 95% tolerance limits for 95% of a population were 1.2 μg/ml (367 μg total) and 13.9 μg/ml (1,625 μg total). The coefficient of variation (CV) for the micrograms of N-methylformamide per milliliter was approximately 25 times more variable than the CV for total micrograms (Krivanek et al., 1978).

Maxfield et al. (1975) reported a study of workers oocupationally exposed to DMF. Urine samples were collected at the beginning and at the end of the workshift. Measurable amounts of DMF metabolites appeared in the urine after a single exposure to a TLV dose (10 ppm) of DMF. The metabolites were present within 2 to 3 hours after an exposure, but generally maximum concentrations were not obtained for 6 to 12 hours. Thereafter, the concentration declined and generally reached an undetectable level 24 hours after the exposure ended. DMF was absorbed through the skin and lungs when men were exposed to TLV concentrations of the vapor.

A series of studies dealing with the metabolism of DMF in rats, dogs, and humans was conducted by Kimmerle and Eben (1975a,b) and Eden and Kimmerle (1976). In acute and subacute inhalation studies, rats and dogs were exposed to DMF. Dogs were also subjected to subchronic inhalation tests. The rats were subjected to DMF concentrations of 21, 146, or 2,005 ppm during a 3-hour trial. During a 6-hour exposure, they were exposed to DMF at 29 or 170 ppm. When repeated exposures were administered to rats, the average concentration was 350 ppm. In a 6-hour test, dogs were exposed to 20, 32, 143, or 172 ppm. In a 5-day test (6 hours/day), they were exposed to 23 or 59 ppm. In a 4-week test (6 hours/day), the concentration was 20 ppm. In addition to the known metabolite N-methylformamide, another metabolite, formadine, was found in the urine of rats and dogs. The elimination rates for N-methylformamide and formadine were slower in dogs than in rats. An accumulation of N-methylformamide was detected in the blood and urine of dogs subjected to repeated inhalation exposures to DMF at 59 ppm. In rats exposed to substantially higher subacute concentrations of DMF (350 ppm), this phenomenon was not observed. In the 20-ppm repeat study, the dogs in the subacute and subchronic groups showed no sign of accumulating metabolite(s). The results of the liver and kidney function tests in dogs exposed to DMF at 20 ppm for 4 weeks were also normal (Kimmerle and Eben, 1975a).

In an acute inhalation test, Kimmerle and Eben (1975b) exposed four persons to DMF at concentrations of approximately 26 or 87 ppm. Another four persons were exposed daily to a concentration of approximately 21 ppm for 4 hours daily on 5 consecutive days. The behavior of the DMF and its metabolites (N-methylformamide and formadine) in blood and urine was examined. DMF was no longer detectable in the blood a few hours after exposure. It was detectable in the urine only after acute exposure to 87 ppm. The N-methylformamide levels in the blood and liver increased continuously or remained for several hours at the level recorded immediately after inhalation. N-Methylformamide was detected in the urine 4 hours after exposure to DMF. Most of the substance was eliminated within 24 hours. Elimination of formadine, however, was delayed. After workers were exposed repeatedly to the maximum allowable concentration in the working area, there was no accumulation of N-methylformamide in the blood or urine. The investigators suggested that determination of N-methylformamide in a 24-hour urine sample be used as a routine monitoring procedure for employees exposed to DMF. Concentrations above 50 μg in a 24-hour urine sample indicated that exposure exceeded the maximum allowable concentration of 10 ppm (Kimmerle and Eben, 1975b).

Delayed catabolism of DMF was observed in rats and dogs after oral administration of ethanol prior to inhalation exposure to DMF. This was also true for humans. During repeated exposure and daily pretreatment with ethanol, the metabolism of DMF was inhibited. The metabolism of ethanol was also influenced by the presence of DMF (Eben and Kimmerle, 1976).

DMF was absorbed through the skin and lungs when workmen were exposed voluntarily to its vapor (Maxfield *et al.*, 1975). Application of DMF to the skin also resulted in absorption. After these exposures, N-methylformamide appeared in the urine in small but measurable concentrations. The estimated dose recovered ranged from 0.5% to 2% of the administered DMF. Individual variation in the metabolite(s) excreted was marked, probably resulting from difference in the actual amount absorbed and such other factors as the rate of metabolism and of renal clearance. Muravieva *et al.* (1975) have also shown that free DMF appears in the blood and urine regardless of the route of administration (i.e., via the gastrointestinal tract, by inhalation, or by contact with the skin).

Oral administration of ethanol to rats at 2.0 g/kg before inhalation exposures to DMF at 87, 104, or 209 ppm for 2 hours only or for 2 hours daily for 5 days was investigated by Eben and Kimmerle (1976). They also examined the effects of DMF in dogs subjected to 2-hour inhalation exposures to 210-240 ppm. In both experiments there was a delayed effect on the demethylation of DMF. A dose of ethanol at 2 g/kg before inhalation did not influence DMF metabolism in rats. The metabolism of N-methylformamide was inhibited by ethanol.

In humans exposed to 50 to 80 ppm DMF for 2 hours prior to oral administration of 19 g/person ethanol, the blood level of DMF did not increase. However, N-methylformamide concentrations were slightly lower and were not detected in the blood immediately after exposure. Excretion of formamide in the urine was increased by ethanol when measured 24 hours after the start of DMF administration by inhalation and was detected for up to 32 hours. The metabolism of ethanol was also influenced by the presence of DMF (Eben and Kimmerle, 1976).

HEALTH ASPECTS

Observations in Humans

Krivanek *et al.* (1978) exposed eight healthy men to DMF vapor at a concentration of 8.79 ± 0.33 ppm for 6 hours daily for 5 consecutive days. All urine voided by the subjects was collected from the beginning of the first exposure to 24th hour after the end of the last exposure. Each sample was analyzed for N-methylformamide. The investigators observed that N-methylformamide was rapidly eliminated from the body via the urine and that the concentrations peaked within a few hours following the end of each exposure. Very little N-methylformamide was found in the sample collected 24 hours after the exposure ended, and none was found 48 hours after. There was no increase in N-methylformamide in the urine following repetitive exposures. The mean value for the 7-hour (end of exposure) sample was 4.7 μg/ml, or 786.8 μg total. Lower and upper one-sided 95% tolerance limits for 95% of the population were 1.2 μg/ml (367 μg total) and 13.9 μg/ml (1,625 μg total) (Krivanek *et al.*, 1978).

Lyle and his colleagues (1979) reported facial flushing and other symptoms in 19 of 102 men who worked with DMF. The highest concentration of DMF measured in the air of the workplace was 200 ppm. Twenty-six of the 34 episodes occurred after the workers had consumed alcoholic drinks. The metabolite N-methylformamide was detected in the urine of these workers on 45 occasions, the highest concentration recorded at 75 μl/liter. The DMF-ethanol reaction is possibly attributable to the inhibition of acetaldehyde metabolism, probably by N-methylformamide.

Stamova *et al.* (1976) examined workers occupied in the production of polyacrylonitrile fibers near Burgas, Bulgaria. There was a tendency toward elevation of morbidity due to neuroses and diseases of the peripheral and autonomic nervous system, stomach and duodenum, and skin. There was a neurasthenic syndrome in 41.5% of the patients as well as skin changes such as toxic dermatitis, itching dermatosis, and chronic eczema. No definite correlation between exposure to DMF and these outbreaks was established. However, Chary (1974) presented evidence to support the presence of acute pancreatitis in two patients exposed to DMF. Symptoms included upper abdominal pain, nausea, vomiting, and erythema of exposed parts. Potter (1973) reported that an accidental dermal and respiratory exposure to DMF by a single patient produced severe abdominal pain, hypotension, leukocytosis, and hepatic damage. Pain began 62 hours after exposure to DMF and was associated with positive results obtained from a Watson-Schwartz test for urine porphobilinogen.

A 34-year old, healthy maintenance fitter spent 4 hours repairing a blocked pipe under a DMF reaction vessel. Since the worker noticed an unusual smell during the job, the concentration of DMF in the atmosphere was measured and found to be 30 ppm. During the next several days, the worker developed dyspnea, tightness of the chest, and a generalized red blotchiness of the skin after alcohol consumption (Chivers, 1978).

When humans were exposed by inhalation to 10 ppm DMF vapor for 6 hours daily for 5 consecutive days, absorbed DMF could be correlated with urinary N-methylformamide (Krivanek et al., 1977). The rate of urinary excretion increased rapidly during the exposure period, peaked within 3 hours after the end of exposure, and was nearly zero by the beginning of the next exposure period. The best index of DMF exposure was the total amount of urinary N-methylformamide excreted within 24 hours. The concentrations excreted were related to the duration and level of exposure and the subject's physical activity.

Es'kova-Soskovets (1973) observed eight volunteers exposed to DMF and styrene for 60 days. The combined effect of DMF and styrene absorbed through the skin resulted in inhibited activity of the hematopoietic system, e.g., reduced content of mature formed elements in the peripheral blood and shifts in the protein fraction of the blood plasma, indicating an unfavorable effect.

Exposure of workers to DMF along with acrylonitrile and methyl methacrylate led to occasional eczema, toxic dermatitis, and vertigo, but the incidence of skin lesions was low (Bainova, 1975). Delayed skin sensitivity and allergenic dermatitis were observed in 11 of the 28 workers exposed (Bainova, 1975).

Observations in Other Species

Acute Effects   The acute oral LD_{50} for DMF in rats is 2,800 mg/kg, while its percutaneous LD_{50} in rats and rabbits is approximately 5,000 mg/kg (Deichmann and Gerarde, 1969). The oral LD_{50} in mice is 1,122 mg/kg. The acute LD_{50} in gerbils ranges from 3,000 to 4,000 mg/kg after a single intraperitoneal or subcutaneous injection or after stomach intubation. The threshold limit value for DMF in air is 10 ppm (American Conference of Governmental Industrial Hygienists, 1971, pp. 3, 90, 71).

In rats, acute inhalation of DMF resulted in hemorrhage and edema of the lungs, hemorrhage and degeneration of the liver, and other, less severe alterations in the kidneys and heart. The greatest damage was found in the liver (Cruz and Corpino, 1978).

Subchronic and Chronic Effects Although the combined action of 5 mg/m^3 inhaled DMF and a 30% aqueous solution of DMF cutaneously applied was negative, 10 mg/m^3 inhaled DMF and a 60% aqueous solution of DMF disturbed phagocytosis and decreased glycogen content in neutrophils of rats in a chronic test (Medyankin, 1975). Cruz and Corpino (1978) reported myocardial changes in rats after exposure to DMF vapor for 0.5 hour daily for 30 days followed by sacrifice immediately or 60 days after the end of the treatment. The effects were related to the concentration and length of exposure, neither of which were reported.

Chronic LD$_{50}$'s for DMF in female Mongolian gerbils ranged from 3,800 to 4,000 mg/kg within 3 to 6 days after consuming DMF in drinking water at 34,000 to 66,000 mg/liter and ranged from 90,000 to 100,000 mg/kg within 80 to 200 days after consuming DMF in drinking water at 10,000 to 17,000 mg/liter (Llewellyn et al., 1974).

Mutagenicity DMF was negative in the Ames *Salmonella typhimurium* assay both with or without metabolic activation (McCann et al., 1975). Thus, it is recommended as a carrier solvent for compounds being tested in the Ames system that are not water soluble. DMF was also negative in a transplacental host-mediated hamster cell culture system (Quarles et al., 1979). Williams and Laspia (1979) were unable to induce DNA repair in a hepatocyte primary culture/DNA repair system with DMF.

DMF treatment of a cell culture established from a transplantable murine rhabdomyosarcoma induced morphologic differentiation and caused a marked reduction in the tumorigenicity of the sarcoma cells. Fourteen of 17 CE/J mice receiving injections of inducer-treated cells did not develop tumors after 6 months, whereas all 21 mice receiving inocula of untreated sarcoma cells died of the disease between the 11th and 31st day. The drug-treated cells did not grow in soft agar. The untreated tumor cells grew in the semisolid medium, showed a reduced serum requirement, and had a higher saturation density than did the drug-treated cells. Thus, the reduction in tumorigenicity of DMF-treated cells correlates with certain *in-vitro* growth properties that are more characteristic of normal, mesenchymally derived cells than of sarcoma cells (Dexter, 1977).

Borenfreund and colleagues (1975) reported that the combined action of DMF and 5-bromodeoxyuridine reversed the random, irregular growth pattern of cultured tumor cells to a regular pattern typical of nonmalignant cells. The effect was eliminated by removal of the DMF, which altered the components of the surface membrane glycoprotein whereas 5-bromodeoxyuridine did not. The morphologic alterations induced by 5-bromodeoxyuridine were reversed by excess thymidine, while those induced by DMF were not. Furthermore, DMF appeared to act on the cell membrane, whereas 5-bromodeoxyuridine may interact directly with the genetic material.

Reproductive Effects and Teratogenicity   When applied to the skin of pregnant rabbits during organogenesis, DMF induced slight embryo mortality but had no apparent teratogenic effects (Stula and Krauss, 1977). In another study, Filimonov *et al.* (1974) observed that DMF produced no effect on the function of the maternal heart during acute asphyxia when DMF was inhaled by rats in concentrations of 400 mg/m^3 for 5 to 7 hours at various stages of gestation or during the entire gestation period.

Sheveleva *et al.* (1979) reported that inhalation of DMF at 10.7 mg/m^3 for 4 hours daily for 20 days increased embryonic mortality in pregnant rats, disturbed the estrous cycle in nonpregnant rats, and inhibited urinary elimination of hippuric acid after loading with sodium benzoate. No mutagenic effects or alterations in the functioning of the testes were reported. Scheufler (1976), however, reported that DMF was teratogenic in the rat, but only after repeated administration. Scheufler and Freye (1975) observed that DMF was embryotoxic and teratogenic in pregnant mice following intraperitoneal injections for 10 or 14 days during gestation. Four percent of the pups were deformed, the major defects occurring in the occipital area of the osseous skull.

Kimmerle and Machemer (1975) reported that fetal development was not influenced by exposure of pregnant rats to DMF at approximately 18 ppm; however, fetuses taken by cesarean section from dams exposed to 172 ppm weighed significantly less than those from control dams. Skeletal development of these fetuses was normal, and all other reproductive parameters were within the normal range for this strain of rat. The authors concluded that inhalation of DMF in concentrations up to approximately 10 times more than the maximum allowable concentration was not teratogenic in rats.

Carcinogenicity   No available data.

CONCLUSIONS AND RECOMMENDATIONS

Suggested No-Adverse-Response Level (SNARL)

24-Hour Exposure   There are no adequate data from which to calculate this SNARL.

7-Day Exposure   There are no adequate data from which to calculate this SNARL.

Chronic Exposure   This SNARL cannot be calculated since there is a lack of adequate chronic exposure data.

Nitrobenzene ($C_6H_5NO_2$)

This compound was reviewed previously by the Criteria and Standards Division, Office of Water Planning and Standards, U.S. Environmental Protection Agency (1979c). The committee reviewed and discussed that document for accuracy and completeness. In this section, the committee summarizes the pertinent data in that document and provides additional material where necessary.

Ninety-seven percent of nitrobenzene is used to reduce aniline, which has wide application in the manufacture of dyes, rubber, and medicines. Nitrobenzene is also an intermediate in the production of explosives and organic chemicals and is used as an industrial solvent, a combustible propellent, a paint solvent, and an ingredient of perfumes and shoe and metal polishes (Dorigan and Hushon, 1976). It is produced by the nitration of benzene with nitric and sulfuric acids.

Annual production of nitrobenzene in the United States ranges from 90,000 to 315,000 metric tons (Dorigan and Hushon, 1976; Lu and Metcalf, 1975). The greatest loss of nitrobenzene during production (estimated at 3,600 metric tons annually) occurs in the effluent wash (Dorigan and Hushon, 1976). The compound may also form spontaneously in the atmosphere from the photochemical reaction of benzene with oxides of nitrogen (Dorigan and Hushon, 1976).

Nitrobenzene, also referred to as nitrobenzol, oil of mirbane, or oil of bitter almond, is a pale yellow, oily liquid with an almond-like odor. It has a melting point of 6°C, a boiling point of 210-211°C, and at 25°C its vapor pressure is 0.340 mm of mercury (Windholz *et al.*, 1976). It is slightly soluble in water, 0.1 per 100 parts of water (1,000 mg/liter) at

20°C (Kirk and Othmer, 1967). Its odor is detectable in water at concentrations as low as 30 μg/liter (Austern *et al.*, 1975).

The threshold limit value (TLV) of nitrobenzene in the air of industrial plants is set at 5 mg/m^3 (1 ppm) (American Conference of Governmental Industrial Hygienists, 1980).

METABOLISM

Nitrobenzene is a very lipid-soluble compound, having an oil to water partition coefficient of 800. In a study conducted in rats, the ratio of the concentration of nitrobenzene in adipose tissue to that in the blood of internal organs and muscles was approximately 10:1 1 hour after an intravenous dose (Piotrowski, 1977). In rabbits receiving an oral dose of 0.25 ml of nitrobenzene, 50% of the compound had accumulated unchanged in tissues within 2 days after the intubation (Dorigan and Hushon, 1976). In humans, the rate of nitrobenzene turnover is sufficiently slow to result in its accumulation in tissues under conditions of daily exposure (Piotrowski, 1967).

Nitrobenzene is metabolized via two main pathways: reduction to aniline followed by hydroxylation to aminophenols and direct hydroxylation of nitrobenzene to form nitrophenols. Further reduction of nitrophenols to aminophenols may also occur (Piotrowski, 1977). Reduction of nitrobenzene to aniline occurs via the unstable intermediates nitrosobenzene and phenyl hydroxylamine, both of which are toxic and have pronounced ability to form methemoglobin. The reductions occur in the cytoplasmic and endoplasmic reticulum regions of the cell catalyzed by the nitroreductase enzyme system (Fouts and Brodie, 1957). The resulting aniline is then acetylated to acetanilide or is hydroxylated and excreted as aminophenol. Metabolism of nitrobenzene to nitroso and hydroxylamino derivatives by microsomal nitroreductase apparently plays an important role in methemoglobin formation, since treatment of rats with inhibitors such as SKF-525A causes a significant reduction in methemoglobin levels after dosing with nitrobenzene (Kaplan and Khanna, 1975). However, induction of microsomal enzymes by phenobarbital and similar inducers decreases nitrobenzene-induced methemoglobinemia, presumably as a result of greater rates of nitrobenzene metabolism and excretion (Kaplan *et al.*, 1974). Reddy *et al.* (1976) showed that the gut flora of rats also contributed to the reduction of nitrobenzene and the subsequent formation of methemoglobin.

Robinson *et al.* (1951a,b) studied the metabolism of ^{14}C-nitrobenzene in the rabbit. Approximately 55% of the dose was excreted as metabolites in the urine during the 2 days after dosing—20% in the form of nitro compounds and 35% as amino compounds. The nitro compounds found in urine were nitrobenzene, o-nitrophenol, and 4-nitrocatechol in very small amounts, and m- and p-nitrophenol in relatively large amounts. Amino compounds included the major (35%) urinary metabolite p-aminophenol as well as o- and m-aminophenol. All of the phenols were excreted as either glucuronide or sulfate conjugates. Approximately 1% of the dose was expired from the rabbits as $^{14}CO_2$.

Parke (1956) investigated the fate of ^{14}C-nitrobenzene in rabbits. Radioactivity was distributed as follows: 1% in respiratory carbon dioxide, 60% in the urine, 9% in the feces, and between 15% and 20% in the tissues. Unchanged nitrobenzene was eliminated by expiration (0.5%) and in the urine (<0.1%). Major urinary metabolites included p-aminophenol (31%), m-aminophenol (4%), o-aminophenol (3%), aniline (0.3%), o-nitrophenol (0.1%), m-nitrophenol (9%), p-nitrophenol (9%), 4-nitrocatechol (0.7%), nitroquinol (0.1%), and p-nitrophenol mercapturic acid (0.3%).

HEALTH ASPECTS

Observations in Humans

Nitrobenzene is readily absorbed by contact with the skin, inhalation of the vapor, or by ingestion. There are reports of nitrobenzene poisoning resulting from ingestion of synthetic almond oil in baked products and toothache relievers applied to the gums and from its contamination of alcoholic drinks and food (Nabarro, 1948).

Leader (1932) reported a case of nitrobenzene poisoning in a child who was given "oil of almonds" for relief of a cold. Acute nitrobenzene poisoning has also resulted from ingestion of denatured alcohol (Donovan, 1920; Wirtschafter and Wolpaw, 1944) and from its use as an abortifacient (von Oettingen, 1941).

Nitrobenzene is also readily absorbed through the lungs, which can retain up to 80% of the chemical (Piotrowski, 1967; Salmowa et al., 1963). Poisoning has occurred after inhalation of a solution containing the compound, which was sprayed on a child's mattress to exterminate bedbugs (Nabarro, 1948; Stevenson and Forbes, 1942), and after inhalation of nitrobenzene used as a scent in perfume and soap (Dorigan and Hushon, 1976). Chronic and acute poisoning from exposure to nitrobenzene fumes in production plants are well documented (Browning, 1950; Dorigan and Hushon, 1976; Hamilton, 1919; Zeligs, 1929). In an 8-hour workday, a worker exposed to the TLV for nitrobenzene of 5 mg/m^3 (1 ppm) could absorb 24 mg through the lungs (Piotrowski, 1967). Since nitrobenzene is also absorbed through the skin, industrial poisoning cannot be attributed to inhalation alone.

Nitrobenzene is highly fat-soluble and can be absorbed through the human skin at rates as high as 2 mg/cm^2/hour (Dorigan and Hushon, 1976). The medical literature contains many reports of poisoning from absorption of nitrobenzene in shoe dyes and laundry marking ink. These reports were common during the 19th century and the first half of this century. Poisoning following the wearing of newly dyed wet shoes were reported as early as 1900 (Levin, 1927). The poisoning can result from nitrobenzene or aniline, both of which were used in shoe dyes and cause the same toxic symptoms. There have been reports of shoe dye poisoning in an army camp (Levin, 1927), in children who were given freshly dyed shoes (Graves, 1928; Levin, 1927; Zeitoun, 1959), and in adults. Generally, the affected people were brought to the physician's attention because of dizziness, bluish lips and nails (cyanosis), headache, and sometimes coma. All of these effects were due to methemoglobin formation from the absorbed nitrobenzene and/or aniline.

Cyanosis and poisoning of newborn who came into contact with diapers or pads containing marking ink were also very common. This generally occurred when the diapers or pads were freshly stamped by the hospital laundry (Etteldorf, 1951; MacMath and Apley, 1954; Ramsay and Harvey, 1959; Zeligs, 1929). The toxicity was often severe in premature infants who were in an incubator and surrounded by fumes as well as the dye in the cloth (Etteldorf, 1951).

General absorption of nitrobenzene is the cause of many of the chronic and acute toxic effects observed in nitrobenzene workers. The amount of cutaneous absorption is the function of the ambient concentration, the amount of clothing worn, and the relative humidity, which increases absorption as it becomes higher (Dorigan and Hushon, 1976). A worker exposed to the TLV of 5 mg/m^3 could absorb up to a total of 33 mg/day, approximately 9 mg of which is absorbed cutaneously (Piotrowski, 1967). Pacseri and Magos (1958), who measured ambient nitrobenzene in industrial plants, found levels up to 8 times higher than the current TLV.

There is a latent period of 1 to 4 hours before signs and symptoms of nitrobenzene poisoning appear. The chemical affects the central nervous system, producing fatigue, headache, vertigo, vomiting, and general weakness. In some cases, severe depression, unconsciousness, and coma also result (Browning, 1950; Hamilton, 1919; Pacseri and Magos, 1958; Piotrowski, 1967, 1977). Nitrobenzene is a powerful methemoglobin former, cyanosis appearing when methemoglobin levels reach 15%. Blood methemoglobin levels from nitrobenzene have ranged from 0.6 g/100 ml in industrial chronic exposures to 10 g/100 ml in acute poisoning (Myslak *et al.*, 1971; Pacseri and Magos, 1958). Normal methemoglobin levels are approximately 0.5 g/100 ml. Chronic exposure to nitrobenzene may lead to spleen and liver damage, jaundice, liver impairment, methemoglobinemia, sulfhemoglobinemia, dark-colored urine, anemia, the presence of Heinz bodies in erythrocytes, and hemolytic icterus.

Reported fatal doses of nitrobenzene in humans have varied widely—from less than 1 ml to more than 500 ml (Dorigan and Hushon, 1976; von Oettingen, 1941; Wirtschafter and Wolpaw, 1944). A minimum lethal dose of 4.0 ml has been reported by von Oettingen (1941). For a 70-kg adult, this would approximate 69 mg/kg.

Metabolic transformation and excretion of nitrobenzene and its metabolites in humans are slower by an order of magnitude than they are in rats and rabbits. Measurements of nitrobenzene concentrations in the blood of an acutely exposed person indicate that the compound is cumulative, remaining in the human body for a prolonged period (Piotrowski, 1967, 1977). There have been similar observations of persistence of the two major urinary metabolites, *p*-aminophenol and *p*-nitrophenol, in patients treated for acute or subacute poisoning. Because of the slow rate of nitrobenzene metabolism in humans, the concentration of *p*-nitrophenol in urine increases for approximately 4 days during exposure, eventually reaching a value 2.5 times that found during the first day. The half-life for the urinary excretion of *p*-nitrophenol from humans after a single dose was approximately 60 hours (Salmowa *et al.*, 1963); 84 hours was observed in a female who attempted suicide (Myslak *et al.*, 1971). The amount of nitrobenzene to which an individual has been exposed can therefore be estimated from the level of total (free and conjugated) *p*-nitrophenol in urine (Ikeda and Kita, 1964; Piotrowski, 1977). The urinary metabolites in humans account for only 20% or 30% of the nitrobenzene dose. The fate of the remaining nitrobenzene and its metabolites is not known (Piotrowski, 1977).

Ikeda and Kita (1964) measured the urinary excretion of *p*-nitrophenol and *p*-aminophenol in a patient admitted to a hospital with toxic symptoms resulting from a 17-month chronic industrial exposure to nitrobenzene. The rate of excretion of these two metabolites was similar and paralleled the level of methemoglobin in blood.

Observations in Other Species

Acute Effects   The acute oral LD_{50} for nitrobenzene in the rat is 640 mg/kg, while the LD_{50} in rats for intraperitoneal and percutaneous doses are 640 and 2,100 mg/kg, respectively (Fairchild, 1977b). The lowest published lethal oral doses in the dog, cat, and rabbit were 750, 2,000, and 700 mg/kg, respectively. Effects were loss of reflexes, methemoglobinemia, tremors, paralysis of hind legs, and labored respiration.

Subchronic and Chronic Effects Levin (1927) demonstrated *in-vivo* production of methemoglobin by nitrobenzene in dogs, cats, and rats, but not in guinea pigs or rabbits. Reddy *et al.* (1976) reported a delay in methemoglobin formation in germ-free rats by nitrobenzene and postulated that the gut flora of the rats was responsible for the *in-vivo* reduction and for the methemoglobin-forming capacity of nitrobenzene.

Yamada (1958) did a chronic toxicity study in rabbits that received a subcutaneous dose of 0.8 mg/kg nitrobenzene per day for 3 months. He found a decrease in erythrocyte number and hemoglobin content early in the exposure, but these values increased during the 3 months and did not return to the normal levels. Urinary excretion of detoxification products was variable in the early stages of the exposure, but then all the detoxification reactions (reduction, hydroxylation, and assimilation) were depressed. As a result of these observations, Yamada divided the response of rabbits to nitrobenzene into three stages: initial response, resistance, and exhaustion. Daily subcutaneous exposure of rats to nitrobenzene at doses of 50 mg/kg for 1 month had no effect on nitroreductase or aniline hydroxylase activity or length of hexobarbital-induced sleeping time, but the antipyretic effect of phenacetin was decreased (Wisniewska-Knypl *et al.*, 1975).

Mutagenicity Chiu *et al.* (1978) tested nitrobenzene using the Ames assay with *Salmonella typhimurium* strains TA98 and TA100. They found the compound not to be mutagenic. Since other nitrobenzene derivatives demonstrated mutagenicity in *in-vitro* assays, however, additional testing of the parent compound may still need to be done.

Carcinogenicity No available data. Nitrobenzene is currently undergoing testing for carcinogenicity in the National Toxicology Program.

Reproduction and Teratogenicity Kazanina (1968a,b) administered nitrobenzene in doses of 125 mg/kg/day subcutaneously to pregnant rats during preimplantation and placentation. Delay of embryogenesis, alteration of normal placentation, and abnormalities in the fetus were observed. Gross morphologic defects were seen in 4 of the 30 fetuses examined. There were changes in the tissues of the chorion and placenta of pregnant women whose work involved rubber catalysis with nitrobenzene. Men-

TABLE VII-2 Toxicity of Nitrobenzene

Species	Duration of Study (Exposure)	Route of Exposure	Dosage Levels and Number of Animals Per Group	Highest No-Adverse-Effect Level or Lowest-Minimal-Effect Level	Effect Measured	Reference
Human	6 hours	Inhalation	0.2-0.5 mg/liter (40-100 ppm)	0.010-0.026 mg/kg[a]	Slight effects: headache, fatigue	von Oettingen, 1941
Rabbit	Single dose	Oral	NR[b]	0.1 mg/kg	Threshold toxic dose	Kazakova, 1956
Guinea pig	Single dose	Oral	NR	0.1 mg/kg	Threshold toxic dose	Kazakova, 1956
Rabbit	3 months	Subcutaneous	NR	0.8 mg/kg/day	Maximum dose not causing death	Yamada, 1958
Human	NR	Oral	0.4 ml (482 mg) 1 subject	6.89 mg/kg	Minimal effect level	von Oettingen, 1941
Rabbit	Single dose	Subcutaneous	NR	10-14 mg/kg	Minimum single dose producing observable effects—slow and lasting methemoglobinemia	von Oettingen, 1941
Mouse	Single dose	Intraperitoneal	NR	20 mg/kg	Lethal dose	Brown et al., 1975
Rabbit	Single dose	Oral	NR	50 mg/kg	Tissue degeneration, especially heart, liver, kidney	Papageorgiou and Argoudelis, 1973
Guinea pig	1 year	Oral	NR	50 mg/kg	Tissue generation, especially heart, liver, kidney	Kazakova, 1956
Guniea pig	6 months	Subcutaneous	NR	200 mg/kg	Hemolytic anemia weight loss, decreased motor activity	Makotchenko and Akhmetov, 1972

[a] Assume average weight of human adult to be 70 kg.
[b] Not reported.

strual disturbances after chronic exposure to nitrobenzene have also been reported (Dorigan and Hushon, 1976).

CONCLUSIONS AND RECOMMENDATIONS

The toxicity of nitrobenzene is great, and there is a pressing need for adequate chronic toxicity data, from both short-term studies and longer-term studies in several animal species. Similarly, the compound has not been adequately tested for carcinogenicity, mutagenicity, reproductive effects, or teratogenicity.

Current data on human toxicity and acute and subacute toxicity of nitrobenzene are summarized in Table VII-2.

Suggested No-Adverse-Response Level (SNARL)

24-Hour Exposure   The minimal lethal dose for humans appears to be 69 mg/kg (von Oettingen, 1941). Since the water solubility of nitrobenzene is approximately 1,000 mg/liter, humans could theoretically consume a lethal dose in an acute spill situation. However, the minimal detectable odor level in water is quite low (30 μg/liter). The minimal effect level for humans is reported to range between 0.010 and 0.026 mg/kg (von Oettingen, 1941). Using this value, a safety factor of 10, and assuming that 2 liters of drinking water daily provide the only source during this period to a 70-kg human, one may calculate the 24-hour SNARL as:

$$\frac{0.010 \text{ mg/kg} \times 70 \text{ kg}}{2 \text{ liters} \times 10} = 0.035 \text{ mg/liter}.$$

7-Day Exposure   No data are available for calculation. Using the acute 24-hour SNARL of 0.035 mg/liter and dividing by 7 days, one may derive the SNARL as:

$$\frac{0.035 \text{ mg/liter}}{7} = 0.005 \text{ mg/liter}.$$

Chronic Exposure   This SNARL cannot be calculated due to a lack of adequate chronic exposure data.

Nitrophenols ($C_6H_5NO_3OH$)

These compounds were reviewed previously by the Criteria and Standards Division, Office of Water Planning and Standards, U.S. Environmental

Protection Agency (1979d). The committee has reviewed and discussed that document for accuracy and completeness. The following paragraphs summarize those findings and are augmented by additional information deemed necessary by the committee.

There are three isomeric forms of mononitrophenol, namely 2-nitrophenol, 3-nitrophenol, and 4-nitrophenol. 2-Nitrophenol and 4-nitrophenol are synthesized commercially by hydrolysis of the appropriate chloronitrobenzene isomer with aqueous sodium hydroxide at elevated temperatures (Howard *et al.*, 1976). Production of 3-nitrophenol is achieved through diazotization and hydrolysis of 3-nitroaniline (Matsuguma, 1967). The mononitrophenol isomers are used in the United States primarily as intermediates for the production of dyes, pigments, pharmaceuticals, rubber, lumber preservatives, photographic chemicals, and pesticides (U.S. International Trade Commission, 1976). The mononitrophenols may also be produced by a microbial or photodegradation of pesticides, which contain those moieties. Approximately 4,500 to 6,750 metric tons of 2-nitrophenol are produced annually (Howard *et al.*, 1976). Although production figures for 3-nitrophenol are not available, Hoecker *et al.* (1977) estimate that production is less than 450 metric tons annually.

4-Nitrophenol is probably the most important of the mononitrophenols in terms of quantities used and potential environmental contamination. Approximately 15,750 metric tons of 4-nitrophenol were used in 1976 (Chemical Marketing Reporter, 1976). Most (87%) of the 4-nitrophenol produced is used in the manufacture of ethyl and methyl parathions, but the compound has itself been used as a fungicide. Possible sources of human exposure to 4-nitrophenol can also result from the microbial or photodegradation of the parathions or from *in-vivo* metabolism following ingestion of parathion or other similar organophosphate insecticides.

The physical and chemical properties of mononitrophenols are summarized in Table VII-3.

Threshold concentrations for the mononitrophenols have been determined by Makhinya (1964). For odor, taste, and color, these concentrations were reported as follows: 2-nitrophenol, 3.83, 8.6, and 0.6 mg/liter; 3-nitrophenol, 389, 164.5, and 26.3 mg/liter; and 4-nitrophenol, 58.3, 43.4, and 0.24 mg/liter, respectively.

Six isomeric forms of dinitrophenols are possible, but 2,4-dinitrophenol is the most important commercially. Approximate annual usage of 2,4-dinitrophenol is estimated at 450 metric tons (Howard *et al.*, 1976). It is used primarily as a chemical intermediate for the production of sulfur dyes, azo dyes, photochemicals, pesticides, wood preservatives, and explosives (Matsuguma, 1967; Springer *et al.*, 1977a,b). 2,4-Dinitrophenol is synthesized commercially by the hydrolysis of 2,4-dinitro-1-chloro-

TABLE VII-3   Properties of Mononitrophenols[a]

Property	2-Nitrophenol	3-Nitrophenol	4-Nitrophenol
Melting point	44–45°C	97°C	113–114°C
Boiling point	214–216°C	194°C	279°C
Density	1.485 g/cm^3	1.485 g/cm^3	1.479 g/cm^3
Water solubility at 40°C	3.3 g/liter	30.28 g/liter	32.8 g/liter
Vapor pressure at 49.3°C	1 mm Hg	—	—
K_a[b]	7.5×10^{-8}	5.3×10^{-9}	7×10^{-8}

[a]Data from Stephen and Stephen, 1963, and Windholz et al., 1976.
[b]Dissociation constant.

benzene with sodium hydroxide at 95° to 100°C (Matsuguma, 1967). Production figures and usage data for the remaining five dinitrophenol isomers are not available, but it is reasonable to assume that usage of these compounds in the United States is very limited.

The physical and chemical properties of the dinitrophenol isomers are summarized in Table VII-4.

Six isomeric forms of trinitrophenol are possible, but significant commercial usage of these compounds is apparently limited to 2,4,6-trinitrophenol (picric acid). Picric acid is used as an explosive, germicide, fungicide, and tanning agent, in electroplating, and in the pharmaceutical and chemical industries. Annual production and the extent to which picric acid is applied in any of these areas is not known.

The properties of 2,4,6-trinitrophenol are summarized in Table VII-5.

TABLE VII-4   Properties of Dinitrophenol Isomers[a]

Isomer	Melting Point, °C	K_a[b] $\times 10^{-5}$, 25°C	Water Solubility, g/liter	Density, g/cm^3
2,3-Dinitrophenol	144	1.3	2.2	1.681
2,4-Dinitrophenol	144–115	10	0.79	1.683
2,5-Dinitrophenol	104	0.7	0.68	—
2,6-Dinitrophenol	63.5	27	0.42	—
3,4-Dinitrophenol	134	4.2	2.3	1.672
3,5-Dinitrophenol	122–123	21	1.6	1.702

[a]From Stephen and Stephen, 1963, and Windholz et al., 1976.
[b]Dissociation constant.

TABLE VII-5 Properties of 2,4,6-Trinitrophenol
(Picric Acid)[a]

Property	Value
Melting point	122–123°C
Boiling point	Sublimes, explodes at 300°C
Vapor pressure	1 mm Hg at 195°C
Density	1.763 g/cm^3
Water solubility at 25°C	1.25 g/liter

[a]From Stephen and Stephen, 1963, and Windholz et al., 1976.

Knowles *et al.* (1975) have demonstrated the production of a large number of monophenols, including 2-nitrophenol, in a model system simulating gastric digestion of smoked bacon. Under these conditions, in which nitrosation is favored, their results indicate that nitrosation of phenols in smoked bacon may occur in the stomach with resultant formation of 2-nitrophenol.

4-Nitrophenol may be produced in the atmosphere through the photochemical reaction between benzene and nitrogen monoxide. Nojima *et al.* (1975) irradiated a combination of benzene vapor and nitrogen monoxide gas, which resulted in the production of nitrobenzene, 2-nitrophenol, 4-nitrophenol, 2,4-dinitrophenol, and 2,4,6-dinitrophenol. The authors suggested that these nitro compounds may have affected seriously stricken victims of photochemical smog in Japan, whose symptoms characteristically included headache, breathing difficulties, vomiting, elevated body temperature, and numbness in the extremities.

METABOLISM

Mononitrophenols

Mononitrophenols are readily absorbed by the gastrointestinal tract and rapidly excreted, primarily in the urine. Lawford *et al.* (1954) showed that elimination of 4-nitrophenol by the monkey following oral and intraperitoneal doses of 20 mg/kg was complete within 5 hours. Excretion by mice, rats, rabbits, and guinea pigs is also rapid. Most doses were completely eliminated from the blood within 2 hours after administration. Rates at which 4-nitrophenol disappeared from the blood decreased in the following descending order: mouse, rabbit, guinea pig, rat, and monkey.

Metabolism of the mononitrophenols occurs via one of three mechanisms, primarily by conjugation, resulting in the formation of either glucuronide or sulfate conjugates. Other mechanisms include reduction to amino compounds or oxidation to diphenols. Sulfate and glucuronide conjugation processes are major detoxification mechanisms in many species, including mammals (Quebbemann and Anders, 1973).

4-Nitrophenol is used as a preferred substrate for analysis of UDP-glucuronyl transferase (Aitio, 1973; Litterst et al., 1975), which is localized primarily in the microsomal fraction of the liver of most species. Sulfate conjugation of 4-nitrophenol also occurs, but is decreased during pregnancy in rabbits (Pulkkinen, 1966b) and increases with age in the rat, guinea pig, and humans (Pulkkinen, 1966a). The relative rates of glucuronide versus sulfate conjugation of 4-nitrophenol may depend on the levels of phenol present (Moldeus et al., 1976).

Robinson et al. (1951a) studied the metabolic detoxification of the mononitrophenol isomers in rabbits. These workers showed that at doses of 0.2 to 0.3 g/kg, conjugation in vivo with glucuronic and sulfuric acids was almost complete, and only small amounts (< 1%) of the unchanged free phenols were excreted. With all three of the mononitrophenol isomers, the major conjugation product was nitrophenyl glucuronide, which accounted for approximately 70% of the dose. The corresponding sulfate conjugates were also excreted. Reduction of the nitrophenols occurred to a small extent, and there was a small amount of additional oxidation. Thus, 2-nitrophenol yielded traces of nitroquinol; 3-nitrophenol yielded nitroquinol and 4-nitrocatechol; and 4-nitrophenol yielded 4-nitrocatechol.

The following distributions of metabolites in the rabbit were noted by Robinson et al. (1951a,b): 2-nitrophenol gave 82% nitro compounds and 3% amino compounds, 71% of the dose excreted as glucuronide conjugates and 11% as ethereal sulfates; 3-nitrophenol resulted in 74% nitro compounds and 10% amino compounds in the urine, present as glucuronides (78%) and ethereal sulfates (19%); and 4-nitrophenol was excreted in the urine, 87% as nitro compounds and 14% as amino compounds, 65% of which occurred as glucuronic conjugates and 16% as ethereal sulfates.

Dinitrophenols

Dinitrophenol isomers are readily absorbed from the gastrointestinal tract and through the skin and lungs (Gehring and Buerge, 1969b; Harvey, 1959; von Oettingen, 1949). The dinitrophenol isomers are not stored to any significant extent in the tissues of humans or laboratory animals following absorption, but are readily excreted, primarily via the urine. Gehring and Buerge (1969b) have studied the elimination of 2,4-dinitrophenol from the serum of ducklings, mature rabbits, and immature rabbits following intraperitoneal administration of the compound. Serum levels of 2,4-dinitrophenol in mature rabbits declined to less than 1% of the original maximum value within 7 hours. The rate of elimination is significantly reduced in immature rabbits. Lawford *et al.* (1954) also studied the pharmacokinetics of the other dinitrophenol isomers and showed that elimination from the blood of mice, rabbits, guinea pigs, rats, and monkeys was complete within 30 hours. Harvey (1959) determined the half-lives for all six dinitrophenol isomers from the blood of mice and rats following a single large dose given intraperitoneally (Table VII-6).

Examination of the urine of a man fatally poisoned by 2,4-dinitrophenol showed that it contained 2-amino-4-nitrophenol, 4-amino-2-nitrophenol, and diaminophenol (Perkins, 1919). Williams (1959) stated that 2,4-dinitrophenol is excreted by mammals in the following forms: partially unchanged, partially conjugated with glucuronic acid, and reduced to 2-amino-4-nitrophenol, 2-nitro-4-aminophenol, and probably 2,4-diaminophenol. Rats orally dosed with 2,4-dinitrophenol excreted both free dinitrophenol (78%) and 2-amino-4-nitrophenol (17%) (Senczuk *et al.*, 1971). Parker (1952) examined the enzymatic reduction of 2,4-dinitrophenol by rat liver homogenates and found 4-amino-2-nitrophenol to be the major metabolite (90%) along with 2-amino-4-nitrophenol (10%) and trace amounts of 2,4-diaminophenol. In contrast, Eiseman *et al.* (1974) reported 2-amino-4-nitrophenol as a major metabolite (75% of total amine) in the same system. Considerably smaller amounts of 4-amino-2-

TABLE VII-6   Rates at Which Dinitrophenol Isomers Are Eliminated from the Blood of Mice and Rats Following a Single Large Intraperitoneal Dose[a]

	Half-time for Elimination, min	
Isomer	Mice	Rats
2,3-Dinitrophenol	2.7	12.5
2,4-Dinitrophenol	54.0	225
2,5-Dinitrophenol	3.3	13.0
2,6-Dinitrophenol	238	210
3,4-Dinitrophenol	3.5	11.5
3,5-Dinitrophenol	2.7	2.1

[a]From Harvey, 1959. Doses ranged between 20 to 180 mg/kg for mice and 20 to 90 mg/kg for rats.

nitrophenol (23%) was found following enzymatic reduction by rat liver homogenates. These investigators also detected only trace quantities of diaminophenol.

All six dinitrophenol isomers are uncouplers of oxidative phosphorylation. 2,4-Dinitrophenol is considered to be the classic uncoupler and, hence, is widely used by biochemists. The relative potency of the 6-nitrophenols toward the uncoupling of rat liver mitochondria was found to be in the following declining order: 3,5- > 2,4- > 2,6- = 3,4- > 2,4- = 2,5-dinitrophenol (Burke and Whitehouse, 1967). Since the order of *in-vivo* toxicities of the dinitrophenol isomers shown in Table VII-7 differs somewhat from that of the relative uncoupling potency reported by Burke and Whitehouse (1967), there are apparently differential rates of absorption and/or the metabolism of the various isomers *in vivo*. Both 2,4- and 3,5-dinitrophenol inhibit porcine heart maleate dehydrogenase *in vitro* (Wedding *et al.*, 1967), but at concentrations 10 to 100 times greater than those causing uncoupling.

Trinitrophenols

Autopsy examination of dogs after lethal doses of picric acid (2,4,6-trinitrophenol) revealed yellow staining of the subcutaneous fat, lungs, intestines, and blood vessels (Dennie *et al.*, 1929). The results indicate that picric acid is distributed to many tissues of the body. Dennie *et al.* (1929) reported the presence of picric acid in the blood and urine of dogs administered a lethal dose of the trinitrophenol, and Harris *et al.* (1946) reported the presence of the trinitrophenol in the urine of humans following oral exposure.

In a review of the early literature, Burrows and Dacre (1975) indicated that picric acid is eliminated from humans in both the free form and as picramic acid. In perfusion experiments with liver, kidney, and spleen, the liver exhibited the strongest capacity for reduction of 2,4,6-trinitrophenol to picramic acid.

HEALTH ASPECTS

Observations in Humans

Mononitrophenols

Myslak *et al.* (1971) reported on the excretion of 4-nitrophenol from a 19-year-old female following a suicidal oral dose of nitrobenzene. Large

TABLE VII-7 Acute Toxicity of Dinitrophenol Isomers[a]

| Species | Route of Administration | LD$_{50}$, mg/kg | | | | | |
		2,3-Dinitrophenol	2,4-Dinitrophenol	2,5-Dinitrophenol	2,6-Dinitrophenol	3,4-Dinitrophenol	3,5-Dinitrophenol
Rat	Oral	—	30	—	—	—	—
Rat	Intraperitoneal	190	28.5, 35	150	38	98	45
Mouse	Intraperitoneal	200	26, 36	273	45	112	50
Rabbit	Oral	—	30	—	—	—	—
Dog	Oral	—	20–30	—	—	—	—
Dog	Intramuscular	—	20	—	—	—	—

[a]Data from Harvey, 1959; Lawford et al., 1954; National Institute for Occupational Safety and Health, 1978d; Spector, 1956.

quantities of 4-nitrophenol and 4-aminophenol were detected in the urine, and urinary excretion of 4-nitrophenol showed a half-life of approximately 84 hours.

Dinitrophenols

Numerous cases of human poisoning by 2,4-dinitrophenol have been reported in the literature. The earliest cases of fatal dinitrophenol intoxication relate to its usage as a component of explosives during World War I. For example, 36 cases of fatal occupational dinitrophenol poisoning occurred among the employees of the munitions industry in France between 1916 and 1918 (Perkins, 1919). In a literature review, von Oettingen (1949) stated that there had been 27 reported cases of fatal occupational dinitrophenol poisoning in the United States between 1914 and 1916. Later, Gisclard and Woodward (1946) reported two fatal cases of dinitrophenol poisoning during manufacture of picric acid, when 2,4-dinitrophenol was produced as an intermediate. Swamy (1953) described a case of suicidal poisoning by 2,4-dinitrophenol.

Lethal doses for orally ingested 2,4-dinitrophenol in humans have been reported to be 14-43 mg/kg (Sax, 1968) and 61 mg/kg (Geiger, 1933). The toxic manifestations of 2,4-dinitrophenol exposures, which have been reviewed by Horner (1942), include subacute signs and symptoms such as gastrointestinal disturbances (nausea, vomiting, colic, diarrhea, anorexia), profuse sweating, weakness, dizziness, headache, and loss of weight. Acute poisoning has resulted in the sudden onset of pallor, burning thirst, agitation, dyspnea, profuse sweating, and hyperpyrexia. Intense and rapid onset of rigor mortis after death has also been observed. A physician who ingested a fatal overdose of dinitrophenol, estimated to be 4.3 g, died of hyperpyrexia with rectal temperatures at death exceeding 43.3°C (Geiger, 1933).

Early in the 1930's, 2,4-dinitrophenol was highly recommended for the treatment of obesity. During the first 15 months following the introduction of this use, an estimated 100,000 persons took the drug for weight reduction (Horner, 1942). Typical treatment regimen for weight control consisted of one capsule containing 75 mg of 2,4-dinitrophenol or 100 mg of the sodium salt taken 3 times daily after meals (2 to 5 mg/kg/day). Despite warnings of harmful side-effects caused by disruption of intermediary metabolism, usage of dinitrophenol became very widespread. Horner (1942) reported a total of nine deaths resulting from the use of dinitrophenol as a weight-reducing agent. In the wake of reports of cataract development in humans taking the drug, dinitrophenol was finally withdrawn from use in 1937 (Horner, 1942; Parascandola, 1974).

Tainter *et al.* (1933) administered 2,4-dinitrophenol to 113 obese patients for as long as 4 months without evidence of cumulative or toxic effects. The most important side-effect noted was a maculopapular or urticarial skin rash, which occurred in 7% of the patients. Symptoms subsided, however, within 2 to 5 days following withdrawal of the drug. Other effects noted were loss of taste and occasional gastrointestinal upset. No effects on liver or kidney function, pulse, blood pressure, or hematological paramaters were seen.

In a review of the acute and chronic toxicity of 2,4-dinitrophenol in humans, Horner (1942) indicated that nausea, vomiting, and loss of appetite were common in patients receiving dinitrophenol. Cutaneous lesions were the most common side-effect (8% to 23%), responses ranging from mild to severe. Bone marrow effects in patients treated with 2,4-dinitrophenol also occurred, and eight cases of agranulocytosis were reported, three resulting in death. There were also 30 cases of neuritis, including aberrations of taste and neurological impairment affecting, particularly, the feet and legs. Symptoms appeared after an average of 10 weeks of ordinary therapeutic doses and persisted for weeks and months. Electrocardiographic evidence of heart damage in some patients was also observed.

The development of cataracts following 2,4-dinitrophenol therapy was first described by Horner *et al.* (1935). Subsequently, more than 100 cases of 2,4-dinitrophenol-induced cataract formation were reviewed by Horner (1942). The cataracts occurred mainly in young women, and appeared during 2,4-dinitrophenol treatment or months or years afterward. The duration of 2,4-dinitrophenol treatment and the amount consumed varied tremendously. The length of treatment varied from 3 months to 24 months, averaging 11 months. Individual susceptibility rather than the length of treatment and the total dose seemed to be the most important factors in determining cataract formation. Horner (1942) estimated that that incidence of cataracts in patients taking 2,4-dinitrophenol was 1%.

Trinitrophenols

Gosselin *et al.* (1976) reported that severe poisoning has resulted from the ingestion of 14 mg/kg picric acid (2,4,6-trinitrophenol); however, details of the poisoning episode were not provided. According to Windholz *et al.* (1976), ingestion or percutaneous absorption of picric acid may cause nausea, vomiting, diarrhea, abdominal pain, oliguria, anuria, yellow staining of the skin, pruritus, skin eruptions, stupor, convulsions, and death. Perkins (1919) noted that picric acid was considerably less hazardous than 2,4-dinitrophenol in the munitions industry during World War I.

An outbreak of hematuria among U.S. Navy personnel aboard ships anchored at Wakayama, Japan, was attributed to the ingestion of picric acid in drinking water (Harris *et al.*, 1946). Approximately 3 weeks prior to the outbreak, more than 90 metric tons of confiscated Japanese ammunition containing picric acid had been dumped in the immediate vicinity of the anchorage. The trichlorophenol was apparently carried over in the vapor phase into the freshwater supply upon distillation of the seawater. Levels of picric acid ranging from 2 to 20 mg/liter were found in the drinking water.

During the 1920's and 1930's, picric acid was used both alone and in combination with butyl aminobenzoate as an antiseptic surgical dressing for the treatment of burns. A serious dysfunction of the central nervous system following the topical application of picric acid was reported by Dennie *et al.* (1929). The major effect of nonlethal doses of trinitrophenol appears to be an allergic or irritative dermatitis (Anonymous, 1937; Ehrenfried, 1911). According to Dennie *et al.* (1929), approximately 4% of the patients treated with picric acid were sensitive and developed a local dermatitis, which also appeared on unexposed areas. Intense itching, burning skin eruptions, and irritability were common. More severe reactions led to diffuse, often severe erythema and desquamation of affected areas (American Conference of Governmental Industrial Hygienists, 1971; Sulzberger and Wise, 1933). These reactions lasted from several weeks to almost a year after exposure (Sulzberger and Wise, 1933).

Effects on the skin are apparent when picric acid is applied in concentrations well below those necessary for oral systemic poisoning. Of 71 individuals exposed to concentrations ranging from 0.0088 to 0.1947 mg/m^3, dermatitis developed only among those exposed to the lower concentrations, indicating that desensitization or adaptation reactions may occur (American Conference of Governmental Industrial Hygienists, 1971).

Observations in Other Species

Mononitrophenol

Acute Effects   4-Nitrophenol is the most toxic of the mononitrophenols, followed by 3-nitrophenol and 2-nitrophenol. The acute oral LD$_{50}$ for 2-, 3-, and 4-nitrophenol in the rat are 2,830, 930, and 350 mg/kg, respectively (Fairchild, 1977a; Vernot *et al.*, 1977). In the mouse, oral LD$_{50}$'s were 1,300, 1,410, and 470 mg/kg (Spector, 1956; Vernot *et al.*, 1977). Symptoms of 4-nitrophenol intoxication in animals include methemoglobinemia, shortness of breath, and initial stimulation followed by progressive depression (von Oettingen, 1949). Grant (1959), however, was unable to detect methemoglobin formation after oral administration of 3-nitrophenol and 4-nitrophenol to rats. However, Smith *et al.* (1967) demonstrated that 2-aminophenol and 4-aminophenol, the reduction products of mononitrophenols, would produce methemoglobin in female mice. Methemoglobin formation, therefore, may depend upon the capacity of the animal to reduce the mononitrophenol to amines.

Dinitrophenols

The acute toxicity data for the six dinitrophenol isomers are summarized in Table VII-7.

Formation of cataracts resulting from acute exposure to 2,4-dinitrophenol was first demonstrated in animals almost 10 years after the problem was known to exist in humans (Bettman, 1946; Feldman *et al.*, 1959, 1960; Gehring and Buerge, 1969a; Ogino and Yasukura, 1957). The 2,4-dinitrophenol-induced cataracts, first produced in ducks and chickens, differ from human cataracts in that they can be formed in acute exposures and appear within less than 1 hour. Furthermore, these lesions will disappear spontaneously in animals within 25 hours (Howard *et al.*, 1976). Therefore, the utility of the animal model for 2,4-dinitrophenol-induced cataracts is questionable.

Trinitrophenols

The toxicity data on trinitrophenols in animals are limited to 2,4,6-trinitrophenol (picric acid). The lowest published lethal doses (LDLo) for picric acid in the rabbit and cat are 120 and 500 mg/kg, respectively (von Oettingen, 1949), while the lethal dose in the dog is reported to be 100-125 mg/kg following subcutaneous injection (Dennie *et al.*, 1929). After an acute lethal dose of picric acid, dogs died from respiratory paralysis (Dennie *et al.*, 1929). Autopsy results demonstrated the presence of yellow staining of the subcutaneous fat, lungs, intestines, and blood vessels. Swelling of the liver and glomerulitis were also observed.

Sublethal doses of picric acid less than or equal to 50 mg/kg in dogs have resulted in transitory changes in the kidney, including glomerulitis and other changes in the kidney ultrastructure.

Guinea pigs develop allergic reactions following topical treatment with picric acid (Chase and Maguire, 1972; Landsteiner and DiSomma, 1940; Maguire, 1973; Maguire and Chase, 1972).

Mononitrophenols

Subchronic and Chronic Effects   Ogino and Yasukura (1957) reported the development of cataracts in vitamin-C-deficient guinea pigs following the administration of 4-nitrophenol. Cataracts developed in two of three guinea pigs on day 7 and 11 following daily intraperitoneal administration of 4-nitrophenol in doses of 8.3 to 12.5 mg/kg. Administration of 4-nitrophenol over a 20-day test period produced cataracts while similar dosing with 2- and 3-nitrophenol did not. However, these investigators failed to report the results obtained from the control animals—neither those totally untreated nor those treated with nitrophenols and a vitamin C supplement. Thus, their results must be viewed with caution.

In contrast, Dietrich and Beutner (1946) found 2- and 4-nitrophenol to be devoid of cataract-forming activity in 7-day-old chicks. Animals in this study were fed a commercial brand of chick food containing 0.25% nitrophenol. Cataracts developed rapidly, within 24 to 48 hours after the animals were fed 2,4-dinitrophenol, but no cataracts developed with 3 weeks in animals fed the mononitrophenol isomers.

Both 2-and 4-nitrophenol have been shown to inhibit porcine heart maleate dehydrogenase *in vitro* (Wedding *et al.*, 1967), and depressed rectal temperatures have been observed in rats receiving any of the three isomeric nitrophenols (Cameron, 1958). Thus, these compounds presumably are not potent uncouplers of oxidative phosphorylation, in contrast to the chemically similar 2,4-dinitrophenol.

Makhinya (1969) indicated that 2-, 3-, and 4-nitrophenol possess distinct cumulative properties. Chronic administration of any of the mononitrophenols to mammals caused alterations of neurohumoral regulation and pathological changes including colitis, enteritis, hepatitis, gastritis, hyperplasia of the spleen, and neuritis. Limiting doses for the disruption of conditioned reflex activity were established as 0.003 mg/kg for 2-nitrophenol and 3-nitrophenol and 0.00125 mg/kg for 4-nitrophenol. However, this reference is retrievable only in abstract form.

Dinitrophenols

Spencer *et al.* (1948) studied chronic toxicity in rats fed diets containing 2,4-dinitrophenol at 0, 100, 200, 500, 1,000, and 2,000 $\mu g/g$ for 6 months. Both hematological and pathological investigations were conducted on surviving animals. Rats maintained on diets containing 2,4-dinitrophenol at 200 $\mu g/g$ (10 mg/kg/day) grew at a normal rate, and no adverse changes were noted at autopsy. Pathological changes were not found upon microscopic examination of tissues from rats receiving diets containing 2,4-dinitrophenol at 500 μg/g (25 mg/kg/day); however, growth of these rats was 5% to 10% less than that of controls. There was also a slight depletion of body fat and a slight increase in kidney weight. At higher doses of 2,4-dinitrophenol (50 and 100 mg/kg/day), some rats died and survivors rapidly lost weight. Enlarged dark spleens, pathological lesions of the liver and kidney, and testicular atrophy were also observed.

Trinitrophenols

No subchronic or chronic toxicity data in animals are available.

Mutagenicity Szybalski (1958) obtained negative results in tests to determine the ability of the three mononitrophenol isomers to induce streptomycin independence in streptomycin-dependent *Escherichia coli*. 4-Nitrophenol showed negative mutagenic activity in host-mediated activity in mice using *Salmonella typhimurium* and *Serratia marcescens* indicator organisms (Buselmaier *et al.*, 1973). Both 2- and 4-nitrophenol failed to induce mutations in *Salmonella*, both with and without microsomal activation (Chiu *et al.*, 1978; McCann *et al.*, 1975). However, Fahrig (1974) demonstrated weak mutagenic activity with 4-nitrophenol in tests for mutagenic gene conversion in *Saccharomyces cerevisiae*. This test system allows the detection of a genetic alteration whose molecular mechanism is presumably based on the formation of single-strand breaks of DNA. Adler *et al.* (1976) showed some evidence of DNA damage by 4-nitrophenol in wild-type and repair-deficient strains of *Proteus mirabilis*.

There have been some reports of effects on mitosis and chromosome fragmentation in plants. Sharma and Ghosh (1965) examined the mitotic effect of mononitrophenol isomers in root tips of *Allium cepa*. All three compounds induced mitosis in root tips, but only 4-nitrophenol induced detectable chromosome fragmentations. Nonetheless, the data indicate that the mononitrophenols do not pose a significant mutagenic hazard to humans.

A severalfold increase in mutation frequency was produced by 2,4-dinitrophenol in tests for back mutations from streptomycin dependence to independence in *E. coli* (Demerec *et al.*, 1951). Using a system that measured the induction of unscheduled DNA synthesis in testes, Friedman and Staub (1976) found no evidence for the mutagenicity of 2,4-dinitrophenol. Intraperitoneal injection of 2,4-dinitrophenol in mice produced chromatid-type breaks in bone marrow cells (Mitra and Manna, 1971); however, there was no linear relationship between the frequency of chromosome aberrations and the dose of 2,4-dinitrophenol. 2,4-Di-nitrophenol also failed to induce DNA damage in an *in-vitro* alkaline elution assay with Chinese hamsters V79 cells with or without P-450 or microsomal activation (Swenberg *et al.*, 1976) and was negative in the *Salmonella* system (Chiu *et al.*, 1978).

Streptomycin-independent mutants were produced in streptomycin-requiring *E. coli* after preincubation in the presence of picric acid (Demerec *et al.*, 1951). Yoshikawa *et al.* (1976) reported that mutation was induced in the *Salmonella* system when picric acid was tested in the presence of microsomes, but no activity was observed in their absence (Chiu *et al.*, 1978). In contrast, Auerbach and Robson (1949) failed to show mutagenicity in *Drosophila*.

Carcinogenicity   There are no data on the carcinogencity of mononi-trophenols; however, 4-nitrophenol has been selected by the National Cancer Institute for testing under its Carcinogenesis Bioassay Program. Boutwell and Bosch (1959) have studied the ability of a number of phenolic compounds to promote tumor formation in mouse skin following a single initiating dose of dimethylbenz[α]anthracene. Although phenol was shown to have promoting activity in this system, both 2- and 4-nitro-phenol and 2,4-dinitrophenol failed to promote tumor development in the mice (Boutwell and Bosch, 1959; Stenback and Garcia, 1975). In other experiments in mice, Spencer *et al.* (1948) did not detect tumor formation during a 6-month oral administration of 2,4-dinitrophenol.

The committee found no data on carcinogenic effects of picric acid.

Teratogenicity   No information on the teratogenicity of the mononitro-phenols is available.

The effects of 2,4-nitrophenol on fertility and gestation of female and fetal rats were examined by Wulff *et al.* (1935). They administered 2,4-nitrophenol (20 mg/kg/day) to female rats for 8 days before introduc-ing the males. 2,4-Dinitrophenol was then administered orally twice daily until the litters were weaned. There was no effect on the weight gain of the mothers during pregnancy, the average number of offspring in each litter, nor were neonatal malformations detected. However, 25% of the offspring of treated females were stillborn, compared to only 6.8% of those born to the controls. Moreover, the mortality during the nursing period among the viable offspring of the treated mothers was 30.9%, compared to 13.4% for the young of the control mothers.

Intraperitoneal (7.7 or 13.6 mg/kg) or oral (25.5 or 38.3 mg/kg) admin-istration of 2,4-dinitrophenol to pregnant mice during early organogenesis did not produce morphologic defects in the young, but embryotoxicity occurred at the higher dosage levels (Gibson, 1973). The higher concentrations also produced overt signs of toxicity, including hyperexcitability and hyperthermia in the dams, but they were not lethal.

Bowman (1967) studied the effect of 2,4-dinitrophenol on the developing chick embryo *in vitro*. Concentrations of 8 mg/liter or 370 mg/liter resulted in degeneration and sometimes complete absence of neural tissue accompanied by a reduction in the number of somites. Malformations such as hemiophthalmus and cross beak were induced in chick embryos following administration of 0.5 μg of 2,4-dinitrophenol per egg into the yolk sac at the 48th hour of incubation (Miyamoto *et al.*, 1975). Following examination of purified myelin in the malformed embryos, these investigators suggested that exposure to dinitrophenol resulted in impaired embryonic myelination.

No information on possible teratogenic effects of 2,4,6-trinitrophenol was found.

CONCLUSIONS AND RECOMMENDATIONS

Despite their high rates of production and use in a variety of products, data on the subacute and chronic toxicity of the nitrophenols are inadequate.

Suggested No-Adverse-Response Level (SNARL)

Mononitrophenols

24-Hour Exposure There are no adequate data from which to calculate this SNARL.

7-Day Exposure Ogino and Yasukura (1957) observed the development of cataracts in guinea pigs given daily intraperitoneal doses of 4-nitrophenol at 8.3 to 12.5 mg/kg for 6 to 11 days. Despite the absence of control animals and other shortcomings of these data, they will still be used for the SNARL calculation. Using the 8.3 mg/kg/day dosage, assuming all the mononitrophenol came from the water during this period, a 70-kg human, and an uncertainty factor of 1,000, one may calculate the 7-day SNARL as:

$$\frac{8.3 \text{ mg/kg} \times 70 \text{ kg}}{1,000 \times 2 \text{ liters}} = 0.29 \text{ mg/liter.}$$

Chronic Exposure   This cannot be calculated due to the lack of adequate subacute or chronic data for any of the mononitrophenols.

Dinitrophenols

24-Hour Exposure   No data are available for calculation.

7-Day Exposure   No data are available for calculation.

Chronic Exposure   No good chronic toxicity data for 2,4-dinitrophenol are available. However, one can estimate an approximate chronic exposure limit from information on toxicity in humans and animals (Table VII-8). Several investigators (Horner, 1942; Horner *et al.*, 1935; Tainter, 1933) have summarized the side-effects observed during the therapeutic use of 2,4-dinitrophenol for the treatment of obesity. At daily dosages as low as 2 mg/kg/day, skin lesions, hematological effects, neuritis, and cataracts developed in some patients over treatment periods as long as 4 months. Using this value and an uncertainty factor of 100 (since this is not a "no-toxic-effect" dose), and assuming a 20% intake from water and a daily consumption of 2 liters by a 70-kg adult, one may calculate the chronic SNARL as:

$$\frac{2 \text{ mg/kg} \times 70 \text{ kg} \times 0.2}{100 \times 2 \text{ liters}} = 0.14 \text{ mg/liter.}$$

Spencer (1948) fed 2,4-dinitrophenol to rats for 6 months and observed no toxic effect at a dose of 10 mg/kg/day. Using this value and an uncertainty factor of 1,000, and assuming a 20% intake from water and a daily consumption of 2 liters by a 70-kg adult, one may calculate the chronic SNARL as:

$$\frac{10 \text{ mg/kg} \times 70 \text{ kg} \times 0.2}{1,000 \times 2 \text{ liters}} = 0.07 \text{ mg/liter,}$$

which is in good agreement with the chronic SNARL calculated from exposure data on humans.

Trinitrophenol

24-Hour Exposure   Only acute toxicity data on 2,4,6-trinitrophenol (picric acid) are available. Severe poisoning in humans results from an

TABLE VII-8 Toxicity of 2,4-Dinitrophenol

Species	Duration of Study	Dosage Levels and Number of Animals per Group	Highest No-Adverse-Effect Level or Lowest-Minimal-Effect Level	Effect Measured	References
Human	4 months	2–5 mg/kg/day	2 mg/kg/day[a]	Cataracts, skin lesions, hematological effects, neuritis	Horner et al., 1935; Horner, 1942; Tainter et al., 1933
Rat	6 months	0–2,000 μg/g, 10–20 animals/group	200 μg/g (10 mg/kg/day)	No toxic effect	Spencer et al., 1948
Rat	Duration of pregnancy	20 mg/kg/day	20 mg/kg/day	Fetotoxicity	Wulff et al., 1935

[a]Value from which the chronic SNARL level was calculated.

oral dose as low as 14 mg/kg (Gosselin *et al.*, 1976). Using this value and an uncertainty factor of 100 (since this is not a "no-toxic-effect" dose) and assuming 100% of intake during this period from a daily water consumption of 2 liters by a 70-kg adult, one may estimate the 24-hour SNARL as:

$$\frac{14 \text{ mg/kg} \times 70 \text{ kg}}{100 \times 2 \text{ liters}} = 4.9 \text{ mg/liter}.$$

7-Day Exposure   Harris *et al.* (1946) reported that U.S. Navy personnel developed hematuria upon drinking water that contained picric acid in concentrations ranging from 2 to 20 mg/liter. Assuming that this exposure occurred over several days and that 2 mg/liter represents the minimum concentration in water, one may estimate a 7-day SNARL, using an uncertainty factor of 10, as:

$$\frac{2 \text{ mg/liter}}{10} = 0.2 \text{ mg/liter}.$$

Chronic Exposure   This cannot be calculated due to the lack of adequate chronic exposure data.

Petroleum Products (Crude and Refined)

The increasing demand for and consumption of petroleum and its by-products have greatly increased the risk of contamination of drinking water supplies. In 1974, world and U.S. crude oil production was estimated at 20,538 and 3,203 million barrels, respectively (U.S. Bureau of Mines, 1976). In the same year, the estimated U.S. demand for refined petroleum products was: residual fuel oil, 963 million barrels; gasoline, 2,402 million barrels; distillate fuel oil 1,016 million barrels; kerosene and jet fuel, 427 million barrels; and lubricants, including grease, 56.7 million barrels.

Crude oils vary widely in both physical and chemical properties. They are generally considered to be a complex mixture of hydrocarbons ranging in molecular weight from that of methane (e.g., 16.04) to possibly 100,000 or more (Kallio, 1976). In petroleum, there are fewer compounds containing nitrogen (amines), sulfur (sulfides), and oxygen (phenols). Kallio (1976) estimated that there may be as many as 1 million discrete compounds in crude oil.

The hydrocarbon portion of petroleum is composed of three major classes of hydrocarbons—alkanes, alicyclics, and aromatics. Alkanes or paraffins average approximately 20% of the oil fraction of crude oils but range in amounts from practically zero to close to 100% in different oils. About one-half of the alkane fraction is comprised of normal or straight-chain hydrocarbons, and the other half contains branched-chain hydrocarbons, both ranging from C_1 to approximately C_{40}. The content of alicyclic hydrocarbons (naphthenes, cycloalkanes, or cycloparaffins) also varies among crudes, but it is generally considered to be about 50% of the oil fraction, consisting mostly of cyclopentane or cyclohexane types and smaller amounts of seven- and eight-membered ring hydrocarbons. Aromatics generally do not account for more than 20% of the oil fraction. Benzene predominates in the aromatic fraction, but polynuclear aromatic compounds of up to nine rings have been identified.

Refined petroleum solvents that may contaminate drinking water supplies may be classified according to the following major divisions: petroleum ether, rubber solvent, varnishmakers' or painters' naphtha, mineral spirits, Stoddard solvents, and kerosene (National Institute for Occupational Safety and Health, 1977a). Petroleum ether is a refined petroleum solvent with a boiling point ranging from 30°C to 60°C and is typically composed of 80% pentane and 20% isohexane. Rubber solvent is a refined petroleum solvent with a boiling point ranging from 45°C to 125°C and is composed of hydrocarbons whose carbon chain lengths range from C_5 to C_7. Varnishmakers' or painters' naphtha is a refined petroleum solvent with a boiling point ranging from 95°C to 160°C and contains hydrocarbons of chain lengths from C_5 to C_{11}. Mineral spirits comprise a fraction with a boiling point ranging from 150°C to 200°C, while that of Stoddard solvents boils in the range of 160°C to 210°C and contains mainly C_7 to C_{12} hydrocarbons. Kerosene is a refined petroleum solvent with a boiling point ranging from 175°C to 325°C.

Gasoline, the major refined petroleum solvent, normally contains more than 200 different hydrocarbons, mainly in the C_5 to C_9 fraction. Its boiling point ranges from 26°C to 204°C (PEDCo. Environmental, Inc., 1977). Alkanes and aromatic compounds generally constitute the largest fraction of gasoline, but olefins and alicyclic compounds are also present. Analysis showed the mean composition of 15 premium grade gasolines to be: alkanes, 50%; aromatic compounds, 27%; olefins, 11%; and alicyclic compounds, 11% (PEDCo. Environmental, Inc., 1977). In addition, gasoline typically contains a variety of additives for improving engine performance, of which lead alkyls are predominant. The composition of gasoline varies as a function of the crude oil, the refinery process, the gasoline blending makeup for different grades, the grade of the gasoline, the climate of the marketing region, and the brand.

Thus, gasoline is a blend consisting of a mixture of various blending stocks, notably catalytically cracked gasoline, light, straight-run gasoline, hydrocracked gasoline, and thermally cracked gasoline, reformate, and alkylate. Since the highest octane blending components in gasoline are aromatics and branched-chain alkanes, refineries attempt to produce a blending stream rich in these components. Lower octane blending stocks can be used in the production of leaded gasoline because alkyl lead additives increase gasoline octane ratings. However, the increasing demands for unleaded gasoline are forcing refineries to produce more fractions rich in aromatics and branched-chain alkanes since the octane of unleaded gasoline depends solely on the natural octane rating of its blending components.

Approximately 325 inorganic and organic fuel additives were registered in 1972 (National Academy of Sciences, 1976a). These compounds, which can be classified into about 15 different chemical types, are added for such purposes as antiknock components, antioxidants, surfactants, and deposit modifiers. They are usually added to fuel in very small amounts ranging from a few micrograms per milliliter to a few hundred micrograms per liter. The average tetraethyl lead content, however, is one part per 1,300 parts of gasoline. EPA analyses of trace elements in 50 gasolines showed that only lead and sulfur were present in concentrations greater than a few micrograms per milliliter (Jungers *et al.*, 1975). Concentrations of lead in these gasoline samples ranged from 132 to 763 μg/ml, whereas the sulfur concentration fell between 4 and 720 μg/ml.

Drinking water may be contaminated by crude oil or its products, either accidentally or operationally, wherever oil is produced, transported, stored, processed, or used. Although there is a greater probability of freshwater contamination by refined petroleum products than by crude oil itself, the pollutants encountered in freshwater inevitably include the complete range of chemicals present in oils and their products as well as various chemical additives. In nearly all cases, the petroleum-derived pollutants have undergone some degree of weathering.

Crude oils and refined petroleum products exposed on surface waters are subjected simultaneously to several physical and chemical processes that can diminish their volume as well as alter their composition. In general, components with lower boiling points evaporate. The remaining pollutants may emulsify with water while undergoing dissolution, oxidation, and biological degradation. The hydrocarbons in petroleum are affected at different rates, depending on their molecular weights and structures, and the rates at which these processes occur, in turn, are dependent to a considerable extent on environmental conditions including temperature and wind velocities.

When studying the toxic hazards resulting from contamination of drinking water by crude and refined petroleum, one must consider the relative solubilities of the various constituents. With the exception of C_2-C_4 compounds, the aliphatic, olefinic, and alicyclic hydrocarbons are relatively insoluble in water (Anderson *et al.*, 1974). By contrast, the solubility of the aromatic constituents of petroleum, especially benzene and substituted benzenes, is quite high. Although hydrocarbons are not highly soluble in water, this property should be considered because of the volume of water that is available to the compounds. Solubilities are highest for the low-molecular-weight aromatic compounds, then decrease through the series: aromatics, alicyclic compounds, branched-chain alkanes, and *n*-alkanes. Within each series, solubility decreases with increasing molecular weight. An example of these differences is shown in Table VII-9, in which the hydrocarbon contents of water that has been equilibrated with two different crude oils and No. 2 fuel oil are compared. The solubility of hexane, a typical alkane, in the aqueous fraction is substantially lower than that of either benzene or toluene, two of the prominent components of the aromatic fraction. These results are in line with the relative water solubilities of the three pure hydrocarbons. In studies of experimental oil spills, benzene is solubilized and removed from the surface oil slick most rapidly of all of the major petroleum components (McAuliffe, 1977).

The chemical processes affecting petroleum constituents are extremely complex and not well understood. They are most likely photochemical oxidations and polymerizations. The products of oxidation are generally more soluble than the parent hydrocarbons and, hence, are more easily removed from the aquatic environment by further oxidation and by microbial degradation.

Microbial metabolism initially affects only the *n*-alkanes. Resistance to

TABLE VII-9 Specific Hydrocarbon Content (μ/ml) of Water-Soluble Fractions Equilibrated with Crude and Refined Oils

Compound	Crude Oil No. 1 in Seawater[a]	Crude Oil No. 2 in Seawater[a]	No. 2 Fuel Oil in Seawater[a]	Water Solubility in Freshwater at 25°C[b]
Hexane	0.09	0.29	0.014	9.5
Total saturates	9.86	11.62	0.54	
Benzene	6.75	3.36	0.55	1,780
Toluene	4.13	3.62	1.04	515
Total aromatics	13.90	10.03	5.74	

[a]Data from Anderson *et al.*, 1974.
[b]Data from McAuliffe, 1966.

microbial attack increases through the series of n-alkanes, branched-chain cycloalkanes, and alicyclic and aromatic compounds. This biological process, unlike the physical processes, is not necessarily concentrated on the lower-molecular-weight components, but the rate of attack is quite slow.

HEALTH ASPECTS

An in-depth consideration of the hazards associated with contamination of drinking water by crude oil or refined petroleum products is a very complex and difficult undertaking that is beyond the scope of this volume. Not only are there literally tens of thousands of different hydrocarbons present in crude oil and various refined petroleum products, but crude oil also contains countless numbers of oxygen, nitrogen, and sulfur compounds. Moreover, hydrocarbons are rearranged by catalytic processes during refining to form new compounds, and hundreds of different chemicals are also added to petroleum solvents, lubricating oils, and other by-products to impart desirable qualities. These substances all have different solubilities, volatilities, and, most importantly, toxicological properties. Since most of the toxicity data on the constituents of petroleum and petroleum solvents involve inhalation exposure, there is relatively limited information concerning the oral toxicity of these compounds. Despite this deficiency, one can make approximations that greatly simplify the estimation of toxic hazards.

Crude oil and refined petroleum products contain four major groups of hydrocarbon components: alkanes, olefins, and alicyclic and aromatic compounds (PEDCo. Environmental, Inc., 1977). Various types of chemical additives are also present in gasoline and other refined petroleum products. Small amounts of nitrogen, sulfur, and oxygen compounds are present in crude petroleum, but most of them are removed during the refining process.

The alkane or paraffin fraction, containing primarily aliphatic hydrocarbons from C_3 to C_8, has relatively low toxicity. Alkanes of five or more carbons have strong narcotic properties following inhalation exposure. Recent toxicological and epidemiological evidence suggests that acute intoxication by these alkanes involves a transient depression of the central nervous system. Chronic intoxication with alkanes may lead to development of a more persistent polyneuropathy (National Institute for Occupational Safety and Health, 1977b). Polyneuropathy has been observed in workers in shoe factories and various leather industries following inhalation of C_5-C_7 aliphatic hydrocarbons, which are generally used as solvents for leather adhesives (Buiatti et al., 1978). Although polyneuropathy has been attributed to exposure to n-hexane, recent evidence suggests that such neuropathies can be caused by other alkanes and their isomers (National Institute for Occupational Safety and Health, 1977b). Animal studies have shown that peripheral neuropathies can be produced with n-hexane (Schaumburg and Spencer, 1976). Recent studies suggest that the hydrocarbon-induced polyneuropathies can be attributed primarily to the neurotoxic effect of 2,5-hexanedione, which is a metabolite of n-hexane (Perbellini et al., 1980; Spencer et al., 1978). Presumably, similar ketone metabolites of other hydrocarbons also produce neuropathy. In general, straight-chain alkanes appear to be more toxic than the branched-chain isomers.

The olefin or alkene fraction contains unsaturated aliphatic hydrocarbons. These compounds exhibit little toxicity other than weak anesthetic properties (PEDCo. Environmental, Inc., 1977).

The naphthenes or cycloparaffins are saturated and unsaturated alicyclic hydrocarbons that resemble aliphatic hydrocarbons in their toxicity since they act as general anesthetics and have depressant effects on the central nervous system with a relatively low degree of acute toxicity (PEDCo. Environmental, Inc., 1977). These compounds are not cumulative and little if any significant toxicity has been noted upon prolonged exposure to naphthene vapors.

Aromatic hydrocarbons have generally been regarded as the most toxic fraction of petroleum and petroleum solvents (PEDCo. Environmental, Inc., 1977). They are also the most soluble in water. The aromatic fraction contains benzene, alkyl derivatives of benzene, and small quantities of various polynuclear aromatic hydrocarbons. Benzene, because of its volatility, unique myelotoxicity, and carcinogenic potential, is the most toxic component. The toxicity of toluene, the xylenes, and other alkylated benzene derivatives is considerably lower.

Tetraethyl and tetramethyl lead and organic halogen compounds are added to gasolines as antiknock agents to improve performance. Although these compounds have a fairly high degree of toxicity, their concentrations in gasolines are quite low. Moreover, these additives have a relatively low solubility in water. Ethylene dibromide, one of the organic halogens added to gasoline, has been identified as an animal carcinogen and is also mutagenic (National Academy of Sciences, 1980a).

Thus an assessment of the toxicity of drinking water contaminated by crude oil or refined petroleum products should focus on the aromatic fraction. Since benzene is the most acutely toxic member of the aromatic fraction and also has the highest solubility in water, the toxicity of drinking water polluted by crude or refined petroleum will be determined largely on the basis of benzene content. Since toluene is also found in high concentrations in such contaminated water, it is also considered in this section.

METABOLISM

Benzene

The metabolism of benzene, which has been reviewed by the U.S. Environmental Protection Agency (1979a), Rusch *et al.* (1977), Snyder and Kocsis (1975), and Snyder *et al.* (1977), is widely accepted as a prerequisite to its toxicity. It is metabolized by cytochrome P-450 monooxygenases to form the highly reactive arene-oxide-type metabolite, benzene oxide. The oxide can spontaneously rearrange to form phenol, undergo enzymatic hydration followed by dehydrogenation to catechol, react enzymatically to form a glutathione conjugate, or bind covalently with cellular macromolecules. Sulfate and glucuronide conjugates are also formed. The specific metabolite(s) of benzene that induce leukemia or other toxicities have not yet been identified, but likely candidates include benzene oxide, catechol, and hydroquinone or the corresponding semiquinones (U.S. Environmental Protection Agency, 1979a).

HEALTH ASPECTS

Observations in Humans

Chronic Effects   The toxicity of benzene has been reviewed in several reports (National Academy of Sciences, 1976b, 1977, 1980a; Snyder and Kocsis, 1975; U.S. Environmental Protection Agency, 1979a). The hematological toxicity following chronic exposure to benzene in humans is well established. Reported effects include myelocytic anemia, thrombocytopenia, or leukopenia and acute myelogenous and monocytic leukemia. The data thus suggest that benzene is a leukemogen in humans.

Observations in Other Species

The toxicity of benzene in laboratory animals has been summarized in the first and third volumes of *Drinking Water and Health* (National Academy of Sciences, 1977, 1980a) and by the U.S. Environmental Protection Agency (1979a).

Acute Effects   No new information has become available since those reports were published.

Chronic Effects   In most of the studies on the chronic toxicity of benzene to animals, investigators used inhalation exposures. An exception was the study of Wolfe *et al.* (1956), who administered benzene orally to rats 5 days/week for 6 months at daily doses of 1, 10, 50, and 100 mg/kg body weight. Leukopenia and erythrocytopenia were observed at the 50 mg/kg dosage, while slight leukopenia was seen at 10 mg/kg/day.

Mutagenicity There is no information in addition to that previously published (National Academy of Sciences, 1977, 1980a; U.S. Environmental Protection Agency, 1979a).

Carcinogenicity No new information has become available.

Toluene

Toluene, as well as several other alkyl benzenes, were recently reviewed in depth (National Academy of Sciences, 1980b). Because of that review, another review by the U.S. Environmental Protection Agency (1979b) and the calculations for acute and chronic SNARL's in *Drinking Water and Health, Vol. 3* (National Academy of Sciences, 1980a), no further consideration is necessary at this time.

CONCLUSIONS AND RECOMMENDATIONS

One may estimate the toxicity of drinking water contaminated by a crude oil or a refined petroleum solvent on the basis of its benzene and toluene contents. However, such estimates must be regarded only as approximations. More precise estimates of risk can be made only after there have been much more detailed and thorough evaluations of acute and chronic toxicities of all of the thousands of chemicals present in crude and refined petroleum products, singly and in combination. There are obviously still many unknown factors associated with the toxicity of petroleum products. This is illustrated by the recent, puzzling finding of a high frequency of brain tumors among workers in the petrochemical industry (Fox, 1980).

Other substantial limitations associated with the calculation of 24-hour and 7-day SNARL's for both benzene and toluene include the inadequacy of the oral toxicity data and the lack of data on synergistic interactions among petroleum constituents. These short-term SNARL calculations also ignore the carcinogenicity of benzene in humans. No chronic SNARL has been calculated since benzene is probably a leukemogen in humans.

Suggested No-Adverse-Response Level (SNARL)

24-Hour Exposure There are no adequate data from which to calculate a 24-hour SNARL.

7-Day Exposure   Oral administration of benzene to rats 5 days/week for 6 months produced a minimal toxic effect at a dose of 10 mg/kg body weight. Adjusting to a 7-day exposure, 10 mg/kg/day $\times$ 5/7 days = 7.1 mg/kg/day. Applying a safety factor of 1,000, assuming that 2 liters/day of drinking water is the only source of benzene during this period for a 70-kg human, one may calculate the 7-day SNARL for humans as:

$$\frac{7.1 \text{ mg/kg} \times 70 \text{ kg}}{1,000 \times 2 \text{ liters}} = 0.25 \text{ mg/liter}.$$

This committee has reevaluated the data on benzene to arrive at this 7-day SNARL. It elected to use the threshold dose rather than the leukopenic dose. This, coupled with a more conservative safety factor, results in a 7-day SNARL of 0.25 mg/liter as compared to the value of 12.6 mg/liter in *Drinking Water and Health, Vol. 3* (National Academy of Sciences, 1980a).

Chronic Exposure   No chronic SNARL can be calculated because benzene may be a leukemogen in humans.

Polynuclear Aromatic Hydrocarbons

These compounds were reviewed previously by the Criteria and Standards Division, Office of Water Planning and Standards, U.S. Environmental Protection Agency (1979e). The committee has reviewed and discussed that document for accuracy and completeness. The following pages summarize those findings and are augmented, when necessary, by additional information.

Polynuclear aromatic hydrocarbons (PAH's) are a diverse class of compounds consisting of substituted and unsubstituted polycyclic and heterocyclic aromatic rings. PAH's are formed as a result of incomplete combustion of organic compounds in the presence of insufficient oxygen. This leads to the production of C-H free radicals, which can polymerize to produce various PAH's. Among the PAH's, benzo[a]pyrene (BaP) is the most thoroughly studied because of its ubiquitous presence in the environment and its high carcinogenic activities in laboratory animals. The toxicity of BaP was reviewed in the first volume of *Drinking Water and Health* (National Academy of Sciences, 1977).

Although small amounts of PAH's originate from natural or endogenous sources, most of the PAH's in surface waters are derived from human activity. Discharges of raw and industrial wastewater, atmospheric fallout and precipitation, road runoff, and leachate from polluted soils all contain substantial concentrations of PAH's (Andelman and Suess, 1970), thereby contributing to the contamination of surface waters by these compounds.

The PAH's are extremely insoluble in water. For example, in relatively clean water, the solubility of BaP is only approximately 10 ng/liter (Andelman and Snodgrass, 1974). Despite the relative insolubility of the PAH's, their concentrations in surface waters can be increased by the action of detergents and other surfactants. Total PAH concentrations in surface waters have been found to range from 0.14 to 2.5 μg/liter, whereas BaP concentrations range from 0.0006 to 0.35 μg/liter (Borneff and Kunte, 1964, 1965; Harrison et al., 1975). Similar concentrations exist in surface waters used for drinking water supplies; however, water treatment in the United States significantly lowers these concentrations to a range of 0.003 to 0.14 μg/liter (Basu and Saxena, 1977, 1978; Borneff and Kunte, 1964; Harrison et al., 1975). In surface waters, one-third of the total PAH's is bound to large suspended particles, one-third is bound to finally dispersed particles, and the remainder is present in dissolved form (U.S. Environmental Protection Agency, 1980). The usual sedimentation, flocculation, and filtration process removes a good share of the PAH's present in the water. In addition, from 50% to 60% of PAH's such as BaP are removed by chlorination of the water (U.S. Environmental Protection Agency, 1979e).

PAH's are generally quite stable in water, remaining in solution over long periods. Ilnitsky et al. (1971) showed that after 35 to 40 days, 5% to 20% of an initial BaP concentration of 10 μg/liter remained in water.

As described in the earlier chapters on distribution systems, finished waters from various treatment sites are transported to the consumers through a variety of pipelines. PAH's leach from the tar or asphalt linings of these pipes (Basu and Saxena, 1977, 1978; Sorrell et al., 1980; U.S. Environmental Protection Agency, 1979e), resulting in increased concentrations of these compounds in water reaching the consumers. On the other hand, cement-lined pipes produce lower PAH concentrations, possibly because PAH's are adsorbed from the water.

Basu and Saxena (1977, 1978) analyzed BaP and five other PAH's in finished drinking water from 15 U.S. cities. BaP levels ranged from <0.1 to 2.1 ng/liter. The total concentration of carcinogenic PAH's ranged from 0.2 to 11.3 ng/liter, whereas levels of total PAH's ranged from 0.3 to 138 ng/liter. Sorrell et al. (1980) surveyed other data on the concentrations of PAH's in finished and distributed drinking waters. Phenanthrene was found in the highest concentrations in drinking water (3–3,300 ng/liter), whereas concentrations of most other PAH's were less than 1 ng/liter.

Levels of PAH's detected in U.S. drinking waters are well below the limit of 200 ng/liter recommended by the World Health Organization (1970). Furthermore, Shabad and Il'nitskii (1970) stated that the amount of carcinogenic PAH's in water ingested by humans is typically only 0.1% of the amount consumed in foods. Thus, if the total PAH uptake from food is 4.15 mg/year (U.S. Environmental Protection Agency, 1979e), the uptake of PAH's in drinking water by humans would probably not exceed 4 μg/year.

METABOLISM

Studies in animals indicate that structurally related PAH's, such as BaP, chrysene, 7,12-dimethylbenz[a]anthracene (DMBA), benz[a]anthracene, and 3-methylcholanthrene (3MC), are readily absorbed from the intestinal tract and tend to localize primarily in body fat and fatty tissues such as the breast (Bock and Dao, 1961; Kotin et $al.$, 1959; Schlede et $al.$, 1970a,b).

Disappearance of BaP from the blood and liver of rats following a single intravenous injection is very rapid (Schlede et $al.$, 1970a), having a half-life in blood of less than 5 minutes and a half-life in liver of 10 minutes. In both blood and liver, however, the initial rapid elimination phase is followed by a slower disappearance phase, lasting 6 hours or more. Schlede and coworkers (1970a) concluded that a rapid equilibrium is established between BaP in blood and that in liver and that the compound's fast disappearance from the blood is due to both metabolism and distribution in tissues.

The distribution of radioactivity in rats after administration of labeled dibenz[a]anthracene, DMBA, and 3MC by stomach tube was comprehensively studied by Daniel et $al.$ (1967). The major route of excretion was found to occur via the bile into the feces. There was a rather prolonged retention of radioactivity in body fat, ovaries, and adrenals.

Early physicochemical calculations to explain the carcinogenicity of various PAH's were based on the chemical reactivity of certain regions of the molecule (Pullman and Pullman, 1955). This concept, however, did not appear to hold true for many of the PAH's. More recently, it was learned that PAH's are metabolized by enzyme-mediated oxidative mechanisms to form reactive electrophiles (Lehr et $al.$, 1978). These reactive metabolites can then covalently interact with cellular constituents such as RNA, DNA, and proteins, ultimately leading to tumor formation (Miller, 1978).

The necessity for metabolic activation to express the carcinogenesis of PAH has prompted the investigation of PAH metabolism in numerous animal models and human tissues. From these studies has emerged a general understanding of the mechanisms involved in the biotransformation of these compounds. It is now known that PAH's are metabolized initially by the cytochrome-P-450-dependent monooxygenases, which are localized in the endoplasmic reticulum. These enzymes are often designated as aryl hydrocarbon hydroxylases (Conney, 1967). Their activity is readily induced by exposure to various chemicals. Although they are found in most mammalian tissues, they are located predominantly in the liver. In the initial step of the activation process, the hepatic cytochrome-P-450-dependent monooxygenases oxidize PAH's to reactive epoxide metabolites (Lehr *et al.*, 1978; Levin *et al.*, 1977a; Selkirk *et al.*, 1971, 1975; Sims and Grover, 1974; Thakker *et al.*, 1977). The PAH epoxides can undergo various further reactions, including hydration by the enzyme epoxide hydrolase, which is also located in the endoplasmic reticulum, to form *trans*-dihydrodiols. These in turn are oxidized by the cytochrome-P-450-dependent monooxygenases to form the highly reactive diol epoxides, the ultimate carcinogens. A schematic representation of the principal metabolic pathways involved in the activation of BaP is shown below.

Benzo[*a*]pyrene
  ↓   Cytochrome P-450 enzymes
Benzo[*a*]pyrene-7,8-oxide
  ↓   Epoxide hydrolase
Benzo[*a*]pyrene-7,8-dihydrodiol
  ↓   Cytochrome P-450 enzymes
Benzo[*a*]pyrene-7,8-diol-9,10-oxide
  ↓
Carcinogenesis

The metabolic profile of BaP, the most representative and well-studied compound of the PAH's, has been fairly well established. Known metabolites of BaP include five phenols, 1-, 3-, 6-, 7-, and 9-hydroxy BaP; three dihydrodiols, the (−)−enantiomers of BaP-4,5-, 7,8-, and 9,10-*trans*-dihydrodiols; and three quinones, BaP-1,6-quinone, BaP-3,6-quinone, and BaP-6,12-quinone (Holder *et al.*, 1974; Selkirk *et al.*, 1974; Sims, 1970; Thakker *et al.*, 1976; Yang *et al.*, 1978a,b). Considerable new evidence implicates the diol epoxide (+)−7β,8α-dihydroxy-9α,10α-epoxy-7,8,9,10-tetrahydro-BaP as the ultimate carcinogen derived from BaP (Huberman *et al.*, 1976; Jerina *et al.*, 1976; Kapitulnik *et al.*, 1978a,b; Levin *et al.*, 1976a,b, 1977b; Thakker *et al.*, 1977, 1979; Yang *et al.*, 1978a,b). Epoxides are the initial cytochrome-P-450-catalyzed oxidation products of BaP (Jerina and Daly, 1974; Sims and Grover, 1974). They rearrange nonenzymatically to form phenols, are hydrated by epoxide hydrolase to *trans*-dihydrodiols, or form glutathione conjugates catalyzed by glutathione *S*-transferase (Bend *et al.*, 1976; Sims and Grover, 1974). Some phenols are converted to glucuronide conjugates, a reaction that is catalyzed by UDP-glucuronyl transferase. Others form sulfate conjugates by the action of sulfotransferases (Cohen *et al.*, 1976).

Certain epoxides on saturated, angular benzo-rings that form part of a "bay-region" are important in the activation of various PAH's (Jerina *et al.*, 1978; Lehr and Jerina, 1977; Lehr *et al.*, 1978; Wood *et al.*, 1979). The bay region is typified by the hindered region in the 10 and 11 positions of BaP. Diol epoxides on saturated benzo-rings that form part of a bay region of a hydrocarbon are very active chemically and are more readily converted to carbonium ions than are epoxides not located in the bay region. Therefore, they are more potent alkylating agents with greater mutagenic and carcinogenic activities. Molecular orbital calculations can be used to predict the relative carcinogenic potential of a series of PAH's from their relative tendencies to form carbonium ion from their bay region diol epoxides.

HEALTH ASPECTS

Observations in Humans

Although exposure to PAH's occurs predominantly by direct ingestion of the compounds in food and in drinking water, there are no studies to document the possible carcinogenic risk to humans by these routes of exposure. It is known only that significant quantities of PAH's can be ingested by humans and that ingestion by animals of similar amounts may result in cancers at various sites in the body.

Convincing evidence from air pollution studies indicates an excess of mortality from lung cancer among workers exposed to large amounts of PAH-containing materials such coal gas, tars, soot, and coke-oven emissions (Doll *et al.*, 1965, 1972; Hammond *et al.*, 1976; Henry *et al.*, 1931; Kawai *et al.*, 1967; Kennaway, 1925; Kennaway and Kennaway, 1936; Kuroda, 1937; Mazumdar *et al.*, 1975; Redmond *et al.*, 1972, 1976; Reid and Buck, 1956). However, there is no definite proof that the PAH's present on these materials are responsible for the observed lesions. Nevertheless, our understanding of the characteristics of PAH-induced tumors in animals and their close resemblance to carcinomas of the same target organs in humans strongly suggests that PAH's pose a carcinogenic threat to humans, regardless of the route of exposure. There is now also good evidence of the overwhelming importance of cigarette smoking in the etiology of lung cancer in humans, and cigarette smoke is known to contain PAH's.

Observations in Other Species

Acute Effects There is little information on the acute toxicity of PAH's. It has been reported that the acute oral LD_{50} for DMBA in mice is 350 mg/kg (National Institute for Occupational Safety and Health, 1978d). Most adult male mice in a dominant lethal study survived intraperitoneal doses of BaP administered in tricaprylin in doses of 500, 750, and 1,000 mg/kg (Epstein *et al.*, 1972). Robinson *et al.* (1975) found that mouse strains that were "responsive" to the induction of cytochrome-P-450 and related monooxygenases by PAH's had significantly shorter survival times following 500 mg/kg intraperitoneal doses of BaP, 3MC, or DMBA than did "nonresponsive" mouse strains. At lower, single intraperitoneal doses of BaP at 100 mg/kg BaP and 3MC at 300 mg/kg, however, the differences in survival times were not evident.

Subchronic and Chronic Effects Almost all mice strains that were "responsive" to induction to cytochrome P-450 by PAH's were still alive at 180 days following daily oral intake of BaP, 3MC, or DMBA at doses of 120 mg/kg/day, whereas most of the "nonresponsive" strains died within 20 days after the start of the experiment (Robinson *et al.*, 1975). The mechanism for this effect is not known, but the PAH-exposed nonresponsive mice showed a rapid loss in body weight, increased binding of BaP metabolites to DNA, and leukopenia accompanied by a marked decrease in myeloid precursors in bone marrow.

PAH's at doses of 150 mg/kg or more produce systemic toxicity, which is manifested by the inhibition of body growth in rats and mice (Haddow *et al.*, 1937). Tissue damage resulting from the administration of various PAH's to laboratory animals is often widespread and severe, although there may be selective organ destruction such as adrenal necrosis and lymphoid tissue damage. Current opinion favors a concept that normally proliferating tissues, e.g., intestinal epithelium, bone marrow, lymphoid organs, and testes, are preferential targets for PAH's and that this susceptibility may be due to the specific attack on DNA by cells in the S-phase of mitosis (Philips *et al.*, 1973).

Target organs for the toxic action of PAH's are diverse because of the extensive distribution of these compounds within the body and because of their selective attack on proliferating cells. Damage to the hematopoietic and lymphoid systems of laboratory animals resulting from exposure to

PAH's is a particularly interesting observation. Yasuhira (1964) described severe degeneration of the thymus and markedly reduced weight of the spleen and mesenteric lymph nodes of CF1, Swiss, and C57BL mice given a single intraperitoneal injection of 3MC (0.3-1.0 mg/animal, i.e., approximately 150-500 mg/kg body weight) between 12 hours and 9 days after birth. Degeneration of young cells in the bone marrow and retardation of thyroid gland development were also noted. Newborn mice were highly susceptible to the toxic effects of the PAH's; many of them died from wasting disease following treatment.

After 50-day-old female Sprague-Dawley rats were fed one dose of DMBA at either 112 or 133 mg/kg body weight, pancytopenia accompanied by severe depression of hematopoietic and lymphoid precursors developed within weeks (Cawein and Sydnor, 1968). Female Sprague-Dawley rats receiving oral doses of DMBA at 300 mg/kg and male rats receiving an intravenous injection of DMBA at 50 mg/kg incurred injury to the intestinal epithelium, extreme atrophy of portions of the hematopoietic system, shrinkage of the lymphoid organs, agranulocytosis, lymphopenia, and progressive anemia (Philips et al., 1973). Mortality among female rats was approximately 65%. Sixty-day-old adult rats that were given 20 mg of DMBA orally and 5 mg intravenously developed transient degenerative changes in the testes, which were most evident between 38 and 40 days after treatment. Lesions of the testes were highly specific, involving destruction of spermatogonia and resting spermatocytes—the only testicular cells that actively synthesize DNA. Neither the remaining germinal cells nor the interstitial cells were damaged. Surprisingly, no testicular damage was produced by single oral doses of BaP at 100 mg and 3MC at 105 mg.

Numerous investigators have demonstrated that carcinogenic PAH's can produce an immunosuppressive effect. This was first observed by Malmgren et al. (1952), who administered high doses of 3MC and dibenz[a,h]anthracene to mice. Subsequent studies established that single carcinogenic doses of 3MC, DMBA, and BaP given to sheep caused prolonged depression in the immune response of red blood cells (Stjernsward, 1966, 1969). Noncarcinogenic hydrocarbons, such as benzo[e]pyrene and anthracene, produced no immunosuppressive activity. There is substantial evidence indicating that the degree of immunosuppression is correlated with the carcinogenic potency of the PAH's (Balwin, 1973).

Mutagenicity   The results obtained with several *in-vitro* mutagenesis test systems, especially the Ames *Salmonella typhimurium* assay, support the belief that most carcinogenic chemicals are mutagenic as well. For the PAH's, the Ames assay has been very effective in detecting the parent structures and biotransformation products that possess carcinogenic activity (Brookes, 1977; McCann and Ames, 1976; McCann *et al.*, 1975; Teranishi *et al.*, 1975; Wislocki *et al.*, 1976b; Wood *et al.*, 1976a). The use of *S. typhimurium* strains to detect chemically induced mutagens and microsomal preparations to provide metabolic activation has also made possible investigations of the mechanism of PAH-induced mutagenesis. In particular, an exhaustive survey of the mutagenicity of all the possible oxidative metabolites of BaP has helped to confirm the belief that diol epoxide intermediates are the ultimate mutagens/carcinogens derived from PAH's (Jerina *et al.*, 1976; Levin *et al.*, 1977a,b; Thakker *et al.*, 1976; Wislocki *et al.*, 1976a,b; Wood *et al.*, 1976a,b).

The mutagenic activity of the PAH's and their derivatives has also been examined in various mammalian cell line cultures. These studies have been conducted primarily in Chinese hamster cell lines, either V79 cells derived from male lung tissue or CHO cells derived from the ovary. Using mammalian cells, Huberman and Sachs (1974, 1976) have demonstrated the mutagenicity of a number of carcinogenic PAH's. In later studies, Huberman *et al.* (1977) showed a correlation between the degree of carcinogenicity and the frequency of induced somatic mutations.

The Chinese hamster V79 cells have also served to clarify the metabolism of BaP and the formation of the highly mutagenic and carcinogenic BaP-7,8-diol-9,10-epoxide metabolites as the ultimate mutagens/carcinogens (Brookes, 1977; Huberman *et al.*, 1976, 1977; Jerina *et al.*, 1976; Levin *et al.*, 1976a; Wood *et al.*, 1976a,b).

Carcinogenicity Many PAH's produce tumors in the skin and most epithelial tissues of practically all species of animals tested. Malignancies are often induced by acute exposure to microgram quantities of these PAH's. Latency periods can be short (4-8 weeks), and the tumors produced may resemble carcinomas in humans. Historically, studies of the carcinogenicity of PAH's have focused primarily on effects on the skin or lungs. Moreover, the compounds are frequently injected subcutaneously or intramuscularly to produce sarcomas at the injection site. Ingestion has not been a preferred route of administration for the bioassay of PAH's.

The tumorigenic effects of PAH's when applied to the skin of animals have been known for decades. Iball (1939) compared the carcinogenicity of a series of PAH's and observed that tumorigenic potency of the compounds in mouse skin to be: DMBA > 3MC > BaP > cholanthrene, etc. An additional compilation of tumorigenicity of the PAH's is provided in a monograph by the International Agency for Research on Cancer (1973).

The carcinogenicity of PAH's resulting from oral intake has not been studied as thoroughly as it has been for other routes of administration. Nevertheless, tumors at various sites do result when BaP is administered orally to rodents (International Agency for Research on Cancer, 1973). Tumors appeared in mice after a 0.2 mg single oral dose of BaP and after concentrations ranging from 50 to 250 μg/g had been fed to them in the diet for approximately 100 days. Stomach tumors, leukemias, and lung adenomas were produced in these animals. Other studies showed the carcinogenicity of BaP in the rat and hamster following oral administration. However, BaP produced carcinomas less effectively than other PAH's, notably DMBA, 3MC, and dibenz[a,h]anthracene.

An examination of comparative carcinogenicity within the same tumor model system can provide valuable insight concerning relative risks of various PAH's. Shimkin and Stoner (1975) attempted this by injecting mice intravenously with one, approximately 0.25-mg dose of aqueous dispersions of PAH's. In this test system, 3MC displayed the greatest lung-tumor-forming capability, followed closely by dibenz[a,h]anthracene. BaP was considerably less potent.

Teratogenicity   BaP had little effect on developing embryos in several mammalian and nonmammalian species, although there appeared to be resorption of embryos in the rat (Rigdon and Rennels, 1964). Mice fed 1 μg/g BaP in the diet over their entire life-span reproduced normally, no malformations were observed in their offspring, and no resorption of embryos was evident (Ridgon and Neal, 1965). BaP, 3MC, and DMBA administered in single intraperitoneal doses of 80 mg/kg in corn oil destroyed primordial oocytes in mouse ovaries. Thus, these PAH's are capable of producing premature ovarian failure in rodents. DMBA and its hydroxymethyl derivatives are teratogenic in the rat (Bird *et al.*, 1970; Currie *et al.*, 1970).

CONCLUSIONS AND RECOMMENDATIONS

The attempt to develop a drinking water criteria for PAH's as a class is hindered by several deficiencies in the scientific data base:

- The PAH's are comprised of many compounds capable of inducing diverse biological effects and having different carcinogenic potential. A "representative" PAH mixture has not been defined.
- The extrapolation to humans of results obtained from studies with BaP (or any other pure PAH) in animals may not be valid given the diverse nature of PAH mixtures.
- Few acute, subchronic, or chronic toxicity studies in animals have been conducted with oral exposure to defined PAH mixtures.

- No definitive acute toxicity data are available for pure PAH's.
- There are no data concerning the effects on humans resulting from exposure to defined PAH mixtures or to individual PAH's.

In the absence of data for oral exposure to defined PAH mixtures, assessment of exposure to such mixtures must be based on or derived from exposure to a single PAH. However, it is not possible to determine 24-hour or 7-day SNARL's for this class of compounds because the acute toxicity data for pure PAH's and PAH mixtures are inadequate. Moreover, because many of the PAH's are highly mutagenic and potent carcinogens in animals and good evidence implicates them in human cancer, chronic SNARL's also cannot be determined. However, the solubilities of the PAH's are quite low, approximately 10 ng/liter for BaP (Andelman and Snodgrass, 1974), and their presence in drinking water probably constitutes only a small percentage (0.1%) of the daily exposure of humans to PAH's (Shabad and Il'nitskii, 1970).

24-Hour Exposure   Insufficient data are available for calculation.

7-Day Exposure   Insufficient data are available for calculation.

Chronic Exposure   No chronic SNARL can be calculated because many of the PAH's are proven carcinogens in animals and are strongly suspected as being carcinogenic in humans.

2,4,6-Trichlorophenol ($C_6H_3Cl_3O$)

This compound was reviewed previously by the Criteria and Standards Division, Office of Water Planning and Standards, U.S. Environmental Protection Agency (1979b). The committee has reviewed and discussed that document for accuracy and completeness. The following pages summarize those findings and are augmented by additional information deemed necessary by the committee.

2,4,6-Trichlorophenol, also called Dowcide 2S, Penaclor, and Omal, is used commercially as a fungicide, slimicide, and bactericide, as a preservative for wood and glue, and as a protection against mildew in textiles (Windholz *et al.*, 1976). Production of this chemical was discontinued in 1975 by the Dow Chemical Company, the only manufacturer of 2,4,6-trichlorophenol in the United States, because of the high cost of removing highly toxic dioxin impurities.

2,4,6-Trichlorophenol was prepared commercially by direct chlorination of phenol (Kirk and Othmer, 1967). Polychlorinated dioxins and dibenzofurans may be formed during the chemical synthesis of certain chlorophenols, and these highly toxic contaminants were present in technical 2,4,6-trichlorophenol (Rappe *et al.*, 1979). Heating or burning 2,4,6-trichlorophenol also resulted in the formation of dioxins (Langer *et al.*, 1973; Rappe *et al.*, 1979).

2,4,6-Trichlorophenol is formed along with other chlorophenols by the chlorination of water or sewage containing phenol (Burttschell *et al.*, 1959). In the Netherlands, Piet and De Grunt (1975) found unspecified isomers of trichlorophenols in surface waters in concentrations ranging from 0.003 to 0.1 μg/liter. 2,4,6-Trichlorophenol is also a prominant constituent of effluent from pulp mills, where it is formed during the multistep bleaching processes that remove colored breakdown products of lignin from the pulp (Landner *et al.*, 1977; Lindström and Nordin, 1976). In addition, it is found as a degradation or metabolism product of the pesticides hexachlorobenzene (Engst *et al.*, 1976) and lindane and its isomers (Foster and Saha, 1978; Stein *et al.*, 1977; Tanaka *et al.*, 1977).

2,4,6-Trichlorophenol has a strong phenolic odor. In water, the threshold for this odor is 100 μg/liter at 30°C (Hoak, 1957). This compound is acidic, having a pKa of 6.4 (Dodgson *et al.*, 1950). It has a melting point of 69°C and a boiling point of 246°C, and is soluble in water to 90 mg/liter (Roberts *et al.*, 1977; Windholz *et al.*, 1976). Its vapor pressure is 1 mm Hg at 75°C (Weast and Astle, 1978).

METABOLISM

As to be expected from its high octanol-water partition coefficient of 4898:1 (Roberts *et al.*, 1977), 2,4,6-trichlorophenol readily accumulates in fish (Landner *et al.*, 1977) and penetrates the human epidermis (Roberts *et al.*, 1977) and the rabbit eye (Ismail *et al.*, 1975).

Little information is available on the absorption, distribution, excretion, and metabolism of 2,4,6-trichlorophenol in mammals. Korte *et al.* (1978) showed that it cleared rapidly from rats, most if it being excreted in the urine. They added a 1 μg/g concentration of labeled phenol to the diet of rats for a 3-day period. Eighty-two percent of the dose was excreted in the urine and 22% in the feces. Radioactive trichlorophenol was not detected in liver, lung, or fat samples examined 5 days after the last dose was administered. Daly *et al.* (1965) reported that the phenol is metabolized to 3,5-dichlorocatechol in the rabbit. Studies by Dodgson *et al.* (1950) in the rabbit have shown that 2,4,6-trichlorophenol does not form a sulfate conjugate *in vivo* because of its low pK value.

HEALTH ASPECTS

Observations in Humans
No data are available.

Observations in Other Species

Acute Effects   The acute oral LD_{50} for 2,4,6-trichlorophenol in the rat is 820 mg/kg, whereas the LD_{50} for an intraperitoneal dose in the same species is 276 mg/kg (Farquharson *et al.*, 1958; Lewis and Tatken, 1978). In other studies in the rat, the compound produced convulsions when injected intraperitoneally (Farquharson *et al.*, 1958) and lethal doses produced restlessness, hyperpyrexia, increased rates of respiration, tremors, dyspnea, and coma, continuing until death (Patty, 1963). All of the trichlorophenol isomers stimulate oxygen consumption by the rat brain *in vitro* and produce hyperpyrexia *in vivo* (Farquharson *et al.*, 1958). Onset of rigor mortis in 2,4,6-trichlorophenol-intoxicated animals is said to be characteristically rapid.

2,4,6-Trichlorophenol is a potent uncoupler of oxidative phosphorylation, as reflected by the 18 μM value for 50% inhibition of mitrochondrial ATP formation *in vitro* (Mitsuda *et al.*, 1963). Hexokinase and lactate dehydrogenase are also inhibited by low concentrations of 2,4,6-trichlorophenol *in vitro* (Stockdale and Selwyn, 1971).

Subchronic and Chronic Effects   In preliminary subchronic feeding studies, diets containing 2,4,6-trichlorophenol were given *ad libitum* to groups of male and female F334 rats and B6C3F$_1$ mice for 7 weeks (National Cancer Institute, 1979). The investigators continued to observe the animals for an additional week after the feeding was stopped. The diets given to the rats contained from 10,000 to 46,000 μg/g technical grade 2,4,6-trichlorophenol; those given to the mice contained from 6,800 to 31,500 μg/g. A significant reduction in growth rate was observed in rats fed 10,000 μg/g and in male mice receiving 14,700 μg/g. Assuming the rats weighed 0.4 kg and that they consumed 0.02 kg food per day (National Academy of Sciences, 1977), the minimum toxic dose for rats was 500 mg/kg/day.

Adult male Sprague-Dawley rats were given daily oral doses of 2,4,6-trichlorophenol at 0, 25, 100, and 200 mg/kg for 14 days with no adverse effect on hepatic monooxygenase and UDP-glucuronyl transferase activities or on cytochrome P-450 levels (Carlson, 1978). *In vitro*, the compound inhibited the pesticide *O*-ethyl *O-p*-nitrophenyl phenylphosphonothioate

(EPN) detoxification and demethylation of *p*-nitroanisole. Measurement of hepatic glucose-6-phosphatase and serum sorbitol dehydrogenase provided no evidence of hepatotoxicity.

Mutagenicity   The mutagenicity of 2,4,6-trichlorophenol was tested in *Salmonella typhimurium* strains TA98, TA100, TA1535, and TA1537 (Räsänen *et al.*, 1977). The compound failed to produce a significant increase in revertant colonies, either in the presence or absence of rat liver S-9 fraction. Fahrig *et al.* (1978), however, found that 2,4,6-trichlorophenol concentrations of 400 mg/liter increased the mutation rate in the strain of *Saccharomyces cerevisiae*, but there was no effect on the rate of intragenic recombination. By contrast, Simmon *et al.* (1978) failed to detect mutagenicity of 2,4,6-trichlorophenol in assays with *S. cerevisiae* or in the standard *Salmonella* microsome assay with strains TA1535, TA1537, TA1538, TA98, and TA100.

Carcinogenicity   Boutwell and Bosch (1959) showed that application of 2,4,6-trichlorophenol to the skin over a 15-week period failed to increase the incidence of papillomas in mice pretreated with the initiator, 7,12-dimethylbenzo(*a*)anthracene. Oral administration of technical 2,4,6-trichlorophenol to C57BL/6 and C3H/Anf mice at a dose of 32 to 100 mg/kg/day for approximately 18 months resulted in an elevation of tumor incidence, but the results were not regarded as definitive (Innes *et al.*, 1969).

In a more recent study, technical 2,4,6-trichlorophenol was administered in the diet of male and female F344 rats and male B6C3F$_1$ mice at concentrations of 5,000 and 10,000 μg/g for 105 to 107 weeks (National Cancer Institute, 1979). Female B6C3F$_1$ mice were initially fed 2,4,6-trichlorophenol at 10,000 or 20,000 μg/g, but at 38 weeks, because of reduced weight gain, the dietary levels were reduced to 2,500 and 5,000 μg/g, respectively. Administration of the lowered dosage rate was continued for 67 weeks. The time-weighted average doses for the female mice was either 5,214 or 10,428 μg/g, respectively. Mean body weights of dosed rats and mice of each sex were lower than the corresponding controls and were dose related. The investigators concluded that under the conditions of this bioassay technical 2,4,6-trichlorophenol was carcinogenic in male F344 rats, inducing lymphomas or leukemias. The test chemical was carcinogenic in both sexes of B6C3F$_1$ mice, inducing hepatocellular carcinomas or adenomas. The dioxin content of the 2,4,6-trichlorophenol used in these studies was not reported.

Teratogenicity   No data available.

CONCLUSIONS AND RECOMMENDATIONS

Suggested No-Adverse-Response Level (SNARL)

The acute toxicity of 2,4,6-trichlorophenol is relatively low, but there is only very limited information on its subchronic or chronic toxicity. Technical 2,4,6-trichlorophenol has been shown to be carcinogenic to rats and mice; however, it is not clear whether this activity is derived from dioxins or other impurities present in the commercial preparation.

24-Hour Exposure The minimum toxic dose for 2,4,6-trichlorophenol in the rat is 500 mg/kg (National Cancer Institute, 1979). Using this value, an uncertainty factor of 1,000, assuming that 2 liters of drinking water daily provides the only source during this period for a 70-kg human, one may calculate the 24-hour SNARL as:

$$\frac{500 \text{ mg/kg} \times 70 \text{ kg}}{1,000 \times 2 \text{ liter}} = 17.5 \text{ mg/liter.}$$

7-Day Exposure No data are available for calculation. Using the acute 24-hour SNARL of 17.5 mg/liter for 2,4,6-trichlorophenol and dividing by 7 days:

$$\frac{17.5 \text{ mg/liter}}{7} = 2.5 \text{ mg/liter.}$$

Chronic Exposure No chronic SNARL can be calculated because tests with technical 2,4,6-trichlorophenol have yielded positive results in animal carcinogenicity bioassays.

REFERENCES

Adler, B., R. Braun, J. Schoeneich, and H. Boehme. 1976. Repair-defective mutants of *Proteus mirabilis* as a prescreening system for the detection of potential carcinogens. Biol. Zentralbl. 95:463-469. [Chem. Absts. 86:26749, 1977.]

Agustin, J.S., and C.Y. Lim-Sylianco. 1978. Mutagenic and clastogenic effects of chloroform. Bull. Philipp. Biochem. Soc. 1:17-23.

Aitio, A. 1973. Glucuronide synthesis in the rat and guinea pig lung. Xenobiotica 3:13-22.

Amdur, M.L. 1959. Accidental group exposure to acetonitrile—A clinical study. J. Occup. Med. 1:627-633.

American Conference of Governmental Industrial Hygienists. 1971. Documentation of the Threshold Limit Values for Substances in Workroom Air. Vol. 1. Third edition. American Conference of Governmental Industrial Hygienists, Cincinnati, Ohio. 91 pp.

American Conference of Governmental Industrial Hygienists. 1974. Documentation of the Threshold Limit Values for Substances in Workroom Air. American Conference of Governmental Industrial Hygienists, Cincinnati, Ohio. 352 pp.

American Conference of Governmental Industrial Hygienists. 1980. Threshold Limit Values for Chemical Substances in Workroom Air Adopted by ACGIH for 1980. American Conference of Governmental Industrial Hygienists, Cincinnati, Ohio. 93 pp.

Andelman, J.B., and M.J. Suess. 1970. Polynuclear aromatic hydrocarbons in the water environment. Bull. WHO 43:479–508.

Andelman, J.B., and J.E. Snodgrass. 1974. Incidence and significance of polynuclear aromatic hydrocarbons in the water environment. Crit. Rev. Environ. Control 4:69–83.

Anderson, J.W., J.M. Neff, B.A. Cox, H.E. Tatem, and G.M. Hightower. 1974. Characteristics of dispersions of water-soluble extracts of crude and refined oils and their toxicity to estuarine crustaceans and fish. Mar. Biol. 27:75–88. [Chem. Absts. 82:11894p, 1975.]

Anonymous. 1937. Editorial: Sensitivity to butesin picrate. J. Am. Med. Assoc. 108:992.

Auerbach, C., and J.M. Robson. 1949. XXXIII. Tests of chemical substances for mutagenic action. Proc. R. Soc. Edinburgh B62:284–291.

Austern, B.M., R.A. Dobbs, and J.M. Cohen. 1975. Gas chromatographic determination of selected organic compounds added to wastewater. Environ. Sci. Technol. 9:588–590.

Bainova, A. 1975. Assessment of skin lesions in the production of Bulana polyacrylonitrile fibers. Dermatol. Venerol. (Sofia) 14:92–97. [Chem. Absts. 84:126187u, 1976.]

Balwin, R.W. 1973. Immunological aspects of chemical carcinogenesis. Adv. Cancer Res. 18:1–75.

Basu, D.K., and J. Saxena. 1977. Analysis of raw and drinking water samples for polynuclear aromatic hydrocarbons. EPA P.O. Nos. CA-7-299-A and CA-8-2275-B, Exposure Evaluation Branch, Health Effects Research Laboratory, Cincinnati, Ohio.

Basu, D.K., and J. Saxena. 1978. Polynuclear aromatic hydrocarbons in selected U.S. drinking waters and their raw water sources. Environ. Sci. Technol. 12:795–798.

Bend, J.R., Z. Ben-Zvi, J.V. Anda, P.M. Dansette, and D.M. Jerina. 1976. Hepatic and extrahepatic glutathione S-transferase activity toward several arene oxides and epoxides in the rat. Pp. 63–75 in R. Freudenthal and P.W. Jones, eds. Carcinogenesis—A Comprehensive Survey. Polynuclear Aromatic Hydrocarbons: Chemistry, Metabolism, and Carcinogenesis. Vol. 1. Raven Press, New York.

Bettman, J.W. 1946. Experimental dinitrophenol cataract. Am. J. Ophthalmol. 29: 1388–1395.

Biava, C.G., E.A., Smuckler, and M.D. Whorton. 1978. The testicular morphology of individuals exposed to dibromochloropropane. Exp. Mol. Pathol. 29:448–458.

Biles, R.W., T.H. Connor, N.M. Trieff, and M.S. Legator. 1978. The influence of contaminants on the mutagenic activity of dibromochloropropane (DBCP). J. Environ. Pathol. Toxicol. 2:301–312.

Bird, C.C., A.M. Crawford, A.R. Currie, and B.F. Stirling. 1970. Protection from the embryopathic effects of 7-hydroxymethyl-12-methylbenz(a)anthracene by 2-methyl-1,2-bis-(3-pyridyl)-1-propanone (Metopirone, CIBA) and beta-diethylaminoethyldiphenyl-N-propyl acetate (SKF 525-A). Br. J. Cancer 24:548–553.

Blum, A., and B.N. Ames. 1977. Flame-retardant additives as possible cancer hazards. Science 195:17–23.

Bock, F.G., and T.L. Dao. 1961. Factors affecting the polynuclear hydrocarbon level in rat mammary glands. Cancer Res. 21:1024–1029.

Borenfreund, E., M. Steinglass, G. Korngold, and A. Bendich. 1975. Effect of dimethyl sulfoxide and dimethylformamide on the growth and morphology of tumor cells. Ann. N.Y. Acad. Sci. 243:164–171.

Borneff, J., and H. Kunte. 1964. [In German; English summary.] Kanzerogene Substanzen in Wasser und Boden. XVI. Nachweis von polyzyklischen Aromaten in Wasserproben durch direkte Extraktion. Arch. Hyg. Bakteriol. 148:585–597.

Borneff, J., and H. Kunte. 1965. [In German; English summary.] Kanzerogene Substanzen in Wasser und Boden. XVII. Über die Herkunft und Bewertung der polyzyklischen, aromatischen Kohlenwasserstoffe im Wasser. Arch. Hyg. Bakteriol. 149:226–243.

Boutwell, R.K., and D.K. Bosch. 1959. The tumor-promoting action of phenol and related compounds for mouse skin. Cancer Res. 19:413–424.

Bowman, P. 1967. The effect of 2,4-dinitrophenol on the development of early chick embryos. J. Embryol. Exp. Morphol. 17:425–431.

Brookes, P. 1977. Mutagenicity of polycyclic aromatic hydrocarbons. Mutat. Res. 39:257–284.

Brown, S.L., F.Y. Chan, J.L. Jones, D.H. Liu, and K.E. McCaleb. 1975. P. 23A-1 in Research Program on Hazard Priority Ranking of Manufactured Chemicals. SRI Project ECU-3386. Stanford Research Institute, Menlo Park, Calif.

Browning, E. 1950. Occupational jaundice and anaemia. Practitioner 164:397–403.

Buiatti, E., S. Cecchini, O. Ronchi, P. Dolara, and G. Bulgarelli. 1978. Relationship between clinical and electromyographic findings and exposure to solvents, in shoe and leather workers. Br. J. Ind. Med. 35:168–173.

Burek, J.D., F.J. Murray, K.S. Rao, A.A. Crawford, J.S. Beyer, R.R. Albee, and B.A. Schwetz. 1979. Pathogenesis of inhaled 1,2-dibromo-3-chloropropane (DBCP) induced testicular atrophy in rats and rabbits. Toxiocol. Appl. Pharmacol. 48:A121. [Abstr. No. 241.]

Burke, J.F., and M.W. Whitehouse. 1967. Concerning the differences in uncoupling activity of isomeric dinitrophenols. Biochem. Pharmacol. 16:209–211.

Burrows, D., and J.C. Dacre. 1975. Toxicity to aquatic organisms and chemistry of nine selected waterborne pollutants from munitions manufacture—A literature evaluation. U.S. Army Med. Bioeng. Res. Dev. Lab. Tech. Rep. 7503. Fort Detrick, Frederick, Md. 97 pp.

Burttschell, R.H., A.A. Rosen, F.M. Middleton, and M. B. Ettinger. 1959. Chlorine derivatives of phenol causing taste and odor. J. Am. Water Works Assoc. 51:205–214.

Buselmaier, W., G. Rohrborn, and P. Propping. 1973. Comparative investigations on the mutagenicity of pesticides in mammalian test systems. Mutat. Res. 21:25–26.

Cameron, M.A.M. 1958. The action of nitrophenols on the metabolic rate of rats. Br. Jr. Pharmacol. 13:25–29.

Capel, I.D., and D.C. Williams. 1978. The effect of chloroform ingestion on the growth of some murine tumours. IRCS Med. Sci. 6:435.

Carlson, G.P. 1978. Effect of trichlorophenols on xenobiotic metabolism in the rat. Toxicology 11:145–151.

Cawein, M.J., and K.L. Sydnor. 1968. Suppression of cellular activity in the reticuloendothelial system of the rat by 7,12-dimethylbenz(a)anthracene. Cancer Res. 28:320–327.

Chary, S. 1974. Dimethylformamide: A cause of acute pancreatitis? Lancet 2:356.

Chase, M.W., and H.C. Maguire, Jr. 1972. Picric acid hypersensitivity: Cross-reactivity and cellular transfer. Clin. Res. 20:638.

Chemical Marketing Reporter. 1976. Chemical profile: p-Nitrophenol. May 24, p. 9.

Chiu, C.W., L.H. Lee, C.Y. Wang, and G.T. Bryan. 1978. Mutagenicity of some commercially available nitro compounds for *Salmonella typhimurium*. Mutat. Res. 58:11-22.

Chivers, C.P. 1978. Disulfiram effect from inhalation of dimethylformamide. Lancet 1:331.

Clemens, T.L., R.N. Hill, L.P. Bullock, W.D. Johnson, L.G. Sultatos, and E.S. Vesell. 1979. Chloroform toxicity in the mouse: Role of genetic factors and steroids. Toxicol. Appl. Pharmacol. 48:117-130.

Cohen, G.M., S.M. Haws, B.P. Moore, and J.W. Bridges. 1976. Benzo(a)pyren-3-yl hydrogen sulphate. A major ethyl acetate-extractable metabolite of benzo(a)pyrene in human, hamster and rat lung cultures. Biochem. Pharmacol. 25:2561-2570.

Conney, A.H. 1967. Pharmacological implications of microsomal enzyme induction. Pharmacol. Rev. 19:317-366.

Cornish, H.H., M.L. Barth, and B. Ling. 1977. Influence of aliphatic alcohols on the hepatic response to halogenated olefins. Environ. Health Perspect. 21:149-152.

Cruz, G.S., and P. Corpino. 1978. Morphological observations on experimental acute poisoning by dimethylformamide inhalation in the rat. Boll. Soc. Ital. Biol. Sper. 54:1710-1716. [Chem. Absts. 90:181102m, 1979.]

Currie, A.R., C.C. Bird, A.M. Crawford, and P. Sims. 1970. Embryopathic effects of 7,12-dimethylbenz(a)anthracene and its hydroxymethyl derivatives in the Sprague-Dawley rat. Nature 226:911-914.

Dalhamn, T., M.L. Edfors, and R. Rylander. 1968. Retention of cigarette smoke components in humans lungs. Arch. Environ. Health 17:746-748.

Daly, J., J.K. Inscoe, and J. Axelrod. 1965. The formation of O-methylated catechols by microsomal hydroxylation of phenols and subsequent enzymatic catechol O-methylation. Substrate specificity. J. Med. Chem. 8:153-157.

Daniel, P.M., O.E. Pratt, and M.M.L. Prichard. 1967. Metabolism of labelled carcinogenic hydrocarbons in rats. Nature 215:1142-1146.

Deichmann, W.B., and H.W. Gerarde, eds. 1969. Pp. 655-656 in Toxicology of Drugs and Chemicals. Academic Press, New York.

Demerec, M., G. Bertani, and J. Flint. 1951. A survey of chemicals for mutagenic action on *Escherichia coli*. Am. Nat. 85:119-135.

Dennie, C.C., W.L. McBride, and P.E. Davis. 1929. Toxic reactions produced by the application of trinitrophenol (picric acid). Arch. Dermatol. Syphilol. 20:698-704.

Dequidt, J., and J.-M. Haguenoer. 1972. Étude toxicologique expérimentale de l'acétonitrile chez le rat. 1ere note: Intoxication aigüe par voie intrapéritonéale. Bull. Soc. Pharm. Lille 4:149-154.

Dexter, D.L. 1977. N,N-Dimethylformamide-induced morphological differentiation and reduction of tumorigenicity in cultured mouse rhabdomyosarcoma cells. Cancer Res. 37:3136-3140.

Dietrich, W.C., and R. Beutner. 1946. Failure of o- or p-mononitrophenol to produce cataract. Fed. Proc. Soc. Pharmacol. Exp. Ther. 5:174.

Dodgson, K.S., J.N. Smith, and R.T. Williams. 1950. Studies in detoxication. 29. The orientation of glucuronic acid conjugation in chloroquinol. Biochem. J. 46:124-128.

Doll, R., R.E.W. Fisher, E.J. Gammon, W. Gunn, G.O. Huges, F.H. Tyrer, and W. Wilson. 1965. Mortality of gasworkers with special reference to cancers of the lung and bladder, chronic bronchitis, and pneumoconiosis. Br. J. Ind. Med. 22:1-12.

Doll, R., M.P. Vessey, R.W.R. Beasley, A.R. Buckley, E.C.Fear, R.E.W. Fisher, E.J. Gammon, W. Gunn, G.O. Hughes, K. Lee, and B. Norman-Smith. 1972. Mortality of gasworkers—Final report of a prospective study. Br. J. Ind. Med. 29:394-406.

Donovan, W.M. 1920. The toxicity of nitrobenzene with report of a fatal case. J. Am. Med. Assoc. 74:1647.

Dorigan, J., and J. Hushon. 1976. Air Pollution Assessment of Nitrobenzene. MTR-7228. Prepared for U.S. Environmental Protection Agency. Mitre Corporation, McLean, Va. 86 pp.

Eben, A., and G. Kimmerle. 1976. Metabolism studies of N,N-dimethyl-formamide. III. Studies about the influence of ethanol in persons and laboratory animals. Int. Arch. Occup. Environ. Health 36:243-265.

Ehrenfried, A. 1911. Picric acid and its surgical applications. J. Am. Med. Assoc. 56:412-415.

Eiseman, J.L., P.J. Gehring, and J.E. Gibson. 1974. Kinetics of *in vitro* reduction of 2,4-dinitrophenol by rat liver homogenates. Toxicol. Appl. Pharmacol. 27:140-144.

Engst, R., R.M. Macholz, and M. Kujawa. 1976. The metabolism of hexachlorobenzene (HCB) in rats. Bull. Environ. Contam. Toxicol. 16:248-252.

Epstein, S.S., E. Arnold, J. Andrea, W. Bass, and Y. Bishop. 1972. Detection of chemical mutagens by the dominant lethal assay in the mouse. Toxicol. Appl. Pharmacol. 23:288-325.

Es'kova-Soskovets, L.B. 1973. Biological action of a complex of chemical substances separated from shoes during use. Gig. Sanit. (USSR) No. 12:101-103. [Chem. Absts. 80:78919c, 1974.]

Etteldorf, J.N. 1951. Methylene blue in the treatment of methemoglobinemia in premature infants caused by marking ink. A report of eight cases. J. Pediatr. 38:24-27.

Fahrig, R. 1974. Comparative mutagenicity studies with pesticides. Pp. 161-181 in R. Montesano and L. Tomatis, eds. Chemical Carcinogenesis Essays. Proceedings of a Workshop on Approaches to Assess the Significance of Experimental Chemical Carcinogenesis Data for Man Organized by IARC and the Catholic University of Louvain, Brussels, Belgium. IARC Scientific Publication No. 10. International Agency for Research on Cancer/World Health Organization, Lyon, France.

Fahrig, R., C.A. Nilsson, and C. Rappe. 1978. Genetic activity of chlorophenols and chlorophenol impurities. Pp. 325-338 in K.R. Rao, ed. Pentachlorophenol. Chemistry, Pharmacology, and Environmental Toxicology. Plenum Press, New York.

Faidysh, E.V. 1973. [In Russian; English summary] Organism immunological reactivity during peroral administration of harmful substances during high environmental temperature. Gig. Vody Sanit. Okhr. Vodoemov:91-95.

Faidysh, E.V., and M.G. Avkhimenko. 1974. [In Russian; English summary.] Effect of the nematocide Nemagon on the reproductive function of an organism. Tr. Uzb. Nauchno-Issled. Inst. Sanit. Gig. Profzabol. 8:42-43.

Faidysh, E.V., N.N. Rakhmatullaev, and V.A. Varshavskii. 1970. [In Russian; English summary.] The cytotoxic action of Nemagon in a subacute experiment. Med. Zh. Uzb. No. 1:64-65. [Health Aspects Pest. 4:584, Abstr. No. 71-2205.]

Fairchild, E.J., ed. 1977a. Agricultural Chemicals and Pesticides: A Subfile of the NIOSH Registry of Toxic Effects of Chemical Substances. U.S. Department of Health, Education, and Welfare, National Institute for Occupational Safety and Health, Cincinnati, Ohio. 227 pp.

Fairchild, E.J., ed. 1977b. Suspected Carcinogens. Second edition. A Subfile of the NIOSH Registry of Toxic Effects of Chemical Substances. U.S. Department of Health, Education, and Welfare, Public Health Service, Center for Disease Control, National Institute for Occupational Safety and Health. U.S. Government Printing Office, Washington, D.C. 251 pp.

Farquharson, M.E., J.C. Gage, and J. Northover. 1958. The biological action of chlorophenols. Br. J. Pharmacol. 13:20-24.

Feldman, G.L., T.M. Ferguson, and A.J. Couch. 1959. Dinitrophenol-induced cataracts in the chick embryo. J. Exp. Zool. 140:191–206.

Feldman, G.L., T.M. Ferguson, and J.R. Couch. 1960. Dinitrophenol-induced cataracts in the avian embryo. Am. J. Ophthalmol. 49:1168–1174.

Filimonov, V.G., L.S. Finikova, and G.A. Sheveleva. 1974. Mechanism of the embryotropic action of dimethylformamide inhaled in low concentrations. Farmakol. Toksikol. (Moscow) 37:208–211. [Chem. Absts. 81:34132g, 1974.]

Foster, T.S., and J.G. Saha. 1978. The in vitro metabolism of lindane by an enzyme preparation from chicken liver. J. Environ. Sci. Health B13:25–45.

Fouts, J.R., and B.B. Brodie. 1957. The enzymatic reduction of chloramphenicol, p-nitrobenzoic acid and other aromatic nitro compounds in mammals. J. Pharmacol. Exp. Ther. 119:197–207.

Fox, J.L. 1980. Brain tumor risk in petrochemical workers. Chem. Eng. News 58:33–36.

Friedman, M.A., and J. Staub. 1976. Inhibition of mouse testicular DNA synthesis by mutagens and carcinogens as a potential simple mammalian assay for mutagenesis. Mutat. Res. 37:67–76.

Gehring, P.J., and J.F. Buerge. 1969a. The cataractogenic activity of 2,4-dinitrophenol in ducks and rabbits. Toxicol. Appl. Pharmacol. 14:475–486.

Gehring, P.J., and J.F. Buerge. 1969b. The distribution of 2,4-dinitrophenol relative to its cataractogenic activity in ducklings and rabbits. Toxicol. Appl. Pharmacol. 15:574–592.

Geiger, J.C. 1933. Letter to the Editor: A death from alpha-dinitrophenol poisoning. J. Am. Med. Assoc. 101:1333.

Gibson, J.E. 1973. Teratology studies in mice with 2-sec-butyl-4,6-dinitrophenol (dinoseb). Food Cosmet. Toxicol. 11:31–43.

Gisclard, J.B., and M.M. Woodward. 1946. 2,4-Dinitrophenol poisoning: A case report. J. Ind. Hyg. Toxicol. 28:47–51.

Glass, R.I., R.N. Lyness, and D.C. Mengle. 1979. Sperm count depression in pesticide applicators. Am. J. Epidem. 3:346–351.

Gosselin, R.E., H.C. Hodge, R.P. Smith, and M.N. Gleason. 1976. Clinical Toxicology of Commercial Products: Acute Poisoning. Fourth edition. Williams & Wilkins, Baltimore, Md. 1,785 pp.

Grabois, B. 1955. Fatal exposure to methyl cyanide. N.Y. State Dept. Labor, Div. Ind. Hyg., Mon. Rev. 34:1,7–8.

Grant, C.M. 1959. The action of nitrophenols on the pulmonary ventilation of rats. Br. J. Pharmacol. Chemother. 14:401–403.

Graves, G.W. 1928. Shoe-dye poisoning. Med. Clin. N. Am. 12:673–677.

Greim, H., D. Bimboes, G. Egert, W. Goggelmann, and M. Kramer. 1977. Mutagenicity and chromosomal aberrations as an analytical tool for in vitro detection of mammalian enzyme-mediated formation of reactive metabolites. Arch. Toxicol. 39:159–169.

Haddow, A., C.M. Scott, and J.D. Scott. 1937. The influence of certain carcinogenic and other hydrocarbons on body growth in the rat. Proc. R. Soc. Lond., Ser. B, 122:477–507.

Haguenoer, J.-M., and J. Dequidt. 1975a. Intoxications expérimentales par l'acétonitrile. 1ere note: Intoxications aiguës par voie intrapéritonéale. Eur. J. Toxicol. 8:94–101.

Haguenoer, J.-M., and J. Dequidt. 1975b. Intoxications expérimentales par l'acétonitrile. 2 note: Intoxications aiguës par voie pulmonaire. Eur. J. Toxicol. 8:102–106.

Hamilton, A. 1919. Industrial poisoning by compounds of the aromatic series. J. Ind. Hyg. 1:200–212.

Hammond, E.C., I.J. Selikoff, P.L. Lawther, and H. Seidman. 1976. Inhalation of benzpyrene and cancer in man. Ann. N.Y. Acad. Sci. 271:116–124.

Harris, A.H., O.F. Binkley, and B.M. Chenoweth, Jr. 1946. Hematuria due to picric acid poisoning at a naval anchorage in Japan. Am. J. Public Health 36:727-733.

Harrison, R.M., R. Perry, and R.A. Wellings. 1975. Polynuclear aromatic hydrocarbons in raw, potable and waste waters. Review paper. Water Res. 9:331-346.

Harvey, D.G. 1959. On the metabolism of some aromatic nitro compounds by different species of animal. Part III. The toxicity of the dinitrophenols, with a note on the effects of high environmental temperatures. J. Pharm. Pharmacol. 11:462-474.

Henry, S.A., N.M. Kennaway, and E.L. Kennaway. 1931. The incidence of cancer of the bladder and prostate in certain occupations. J. Hyg. 31:125-137.

Hewitt, W.R., H. Miyajima, M.G. Cote, and G.L. Plaa. 1979. Acute alteration of chloroform-induced hepato- and nephrotoxicity by mirex and Kepone. Toxicol. Appl. Pharmacol. 48:509-527.

Heywood, R., R.J. Sortwell, P.R.B. Noel, A.E. Street, D.E. Prentice, F.J.C. Roe, P.F. Wadsworth, A.N. Worden, and N.J. Van Abbe. 1979. Safety evaluation of toothpaste containing chloroform. III. Long-term study in beagle dogs. J. Environ. Pathol. Toxicol. 2:835-851.

Hoak, R.D. 1957. The causes of tastes and odors in drinking water. Water & Sewage Works 104:243-247.

Hoecker, J.E., P.R. Durkin, A. Hanchett, L.N. Davis, and W.M. Meylan. 1977. Information Profiles on Potential Occupational Hazards. Prepared by Syracuse Research Corp., Syracuse, N.Y. Report No. TR-77-565. (Available from National Technical Information Service, Springfield, Va., as PB-276 678.) U.S. Department of Health, Education, and Welfare, National Institute for Occupational Safety and Health, Rockville, Md. 334 pp.

Holder, G., H. Yagi, P. Dansette, D.M. Jerina. W. Levin, A.Y.H. Lu, and A.H. Conney. 1974. Effects of inducers and epoxide hydrase on the metabolism of benzo[α]pyrene by liver microsomes and a reconstituted system: Analysis by high pressure liquid chromatography. Proc. Natl. Acad. Sci. USA 71:4356-4360.

Hook, J.B., K.M. McCormack, and W.M. Kluwe. 1978. Renal Effects of 2,3,7,8-tetra-chlorodibenzo-p-dioxin. Pp. 381-388 in K.R. Rao, ed. Environmental Science Research. Vol. 12. Pentachlorophenol: Chemistry, Pharmacology, and Environmental Toxicology. Plenum Press, New York.

Horner, W.D. 1942. Dinitrophenol and its relation to formation of cataract. Arch. Ophthalmol. 27:1097-1121.

Horner, W.D., R.B. Jones, and W.W. Boardman. 1935. Cataracts following the use of dinitrophenol. Preliminary report of three cases. J. Am. Med. Assoc. 105:108-110.

Howard, P.H., J. Santodonato, J. Saxena, J. Malling, and D. Greninger. 1976. Investigation of Selected Potential Environmental Contaminants: Nitroaromatics. Prepared by Syracuse Research Corp., Syracuse, N.Y. Report No. TR-76-573. (Available from National Technical Information Service, Springfield, Va., as PB-275 078.) U.S. Environmental Protection Agency, Office of Toxic Substances, Washington, D.C. 618 pp.

Huberman, E., and L. Sachs. 1974. Cell-mediated mutagenesis of mammalian cells with chemical carcinogens. Int. J. Cancer 13:326-333.

Huberman, E., and L. Sachs. 1976. Mutability of different genetic loci in mammalian cells by metabolically activated carcinogenic polycyclic hydrocarbons. Proc. Natl. Acad. Sci. USA 73:188-192.

Huberman, E., L. Sachs, S.K. Yang, and H.V. Gelboin. 1976. Identification of mutagenic metabolites of benzo[a]pyrene in mammalian cells. Proc. Natl. Acad. Sci. USA 73:607-611.

Huberman, E., S.K. Yang, D.W. McCourt, and H.V. Gelboin. 1977. Mutagenicity to mammalian cells in culture by (+) and (−) trans-7,8-dihydroxy-7-8-dihydrobenzo(a)pyrenes and the hydrolysis and reduction products of two stereoisomeric benzo(a)pyrene 7,8-diol-9,10-epoxides. Cancer Lett. 4:35-43.

Iball, J. 1939. The relative potency of carcinogenic compounds. Am. J. Cancer 35:188-190.

Ikeda, M., and A. Kita. 1964. Excretion of p-nitrophenol and p-aminophenol in the urine of a patient exposed to nitrobenzene. Br. J. Ind. Med. 21:210-213.

Ilnitsky, A.P., K.P. Ershova, A.Ya. Khesina, L.G. Rozhkova, V.G. Klubkov, and A.A. Korolev. 1971. The stability of cancerogenic substances in water and the efficacy of methods of its decontamination. Gig. Sanit. 36(4):8-12. [In Russian, English summary.]

Innes, J.R.M., B.M. Ulland, M.G. Valerio, L. Petrucelli, L. Fishbein, E.R. Hart, A.J. Pallotta, R.R. Bates, H.L. Falk, J.J. Gart, M. Klein, I. Mitchell, and J. Peters. 1969. Bioassay of pesticides and industrial chemicals for tumorigenicity in mice: A preliminary note. J. Natl. Cancer Inst. 42:1101-1114.

International Agency for Research on Cancer. 1973. IARC Monographs on the Evaluation of Carcinogenic Risk of the Chemical to Man: Certain Polycyclic Aromatic Hydrocarbons and Heterocyclic Compounds. Vol. 3. Lyon, France. 271 pp.

Ismail, R., O. Hockwin, F. Korte, and W. Klein. 1975. Permeability of the isolated bovine lens capsule for environmental chemicals. Exp. Eye Res. 20:179.

Jerina, D.M., and J.W. Daly. 1974. Arene oxides: A new aspect of drug metabolism. Science 185:573-582.

Jerina, D.M., R.E. Lehr, H. Yagi, O. Hernandez, P.M. Dansette, P.G. Wislocki, A.W. Wood, R.L. Chang, W. Levin, and A.H. Conney. 1976. Mutagenicity of benzo[a]pyrene derivatives and the description of a quantum mechanical model which predicts the ease of carbonium ion formation from diol epoxides. Pp. 159-177 in F.J. de Serres, J.R. Fouts, J.R. Bend, and R.M. Philpot, eds. In Vitro Metabolic Activation in Mutagenesis Testing. Proceedings of the Symposium on the Role of Metabolic Activation in Producing Mutagenic and Carcinogenic Environmental Chemicals, Research Triangle Park, North Carolina, February 9-11, 1976. Elsevier/North-Holland Biomedical Press, Amsterdam, The Netherlands.

Jerina, D.M., D.R. Thakker, H. Yagi, W. Levin, A.W. Wood, and A.H. Conney. 1978. Carcinogenicity of benzo[a]pyrene derivatives: The bay region theory. Pure Appl. Chem. 50:1030-1044.

Jungers, R.H., R.E. Lee, Jr., and D.J. von Lehmden. 1975. The EPA National Fuels Surveillance Network. I. Trace constituents in gasoline and commercial gasoline fuel additives. Environ. Health Perspect. 10:143-150.

Kallio, R.E. 1976. The variety of petroleum and their degradations. Pp. 215-223 in Sources, Effects & Sinks of Hydrocarbons in the Aquatic Environment. Proceedings of the Symposium, American University, August 9-11. American Institute of Biological Sciences, Washington, D.C.

Kapitulnik, J., P.G. Wislocki, W. Levin, H. Yagi, D.R. Thakker, H. Akagi, M. Koreeda, D.M. Jerina, and A.H. Conney. 1978a. Marked differences in the carcinogenic activity of optically pure (+)- and (−)-trans-7,8-dihydroxy-7,8-dihydrobenzo(a)pyrene in newborn mice. Cancer Res. 38:2661-2665.

Kapitulnik, J., P.G. Wislocki, W. Levin, H. Yagi, D.M. Jerina, and A.H. Conney. 1978b. Tumorigenicity studies with diol-epoxides of benzo(a)pyrene which indicate that (±)-trans-7β, 8α-dihydroxy-9α, 10α-epoxy-7,8,9,10-tetrahydrobenzo(a)pyrene is an ultimate carcinogen in newborn mice. Cancer Res. 38:354-358.

Kaplan, A.M., and K.L. Khanna. 1975. The role of microsomal metabolism of nitrobenzene in methemoglobin formation. Toxicol. Appl. Pharmacol. 33:131, Abstr. no. 22.

Kaplan, A.M., K.L. Khanna, and H.H. Cornish. 1974. Methemoglobinemia and metabolism of nitro compounds. Toxicol. Appl. Pharmacol. 29:113, Abstr. No. 98.

Kawai, M., H. Amamoto, and K. Harada. 1967. Epidemiologic study of occupational lung cancer. Arch. Environ. Health 14:859–864.

Kazakova, M.I. 1956. Sanitary-hygienic evaluation of nitrobenzene in water reservoirs. Gig. Sanit. 21:7–10.

Kazanina, S.S. 1968a. The effect of nitrobenzene on the development of the fetus and placenta in the rat. Nauch. Tr. Novosib. Med. Inst. 48:42.

Kazanina, S.S. 1968b. Effect of maternal nitrobenzene poisoning on morphology and histochemistry of hemochorial placentas of albino rats. Bull. Exp. Biol. Med. 65:679–681.

Kennaway, E.L. 1925. The anatomical distribution of the occupational cancers. J. Ind. Hyg. 7:69–93.

Kennaway, N.M., and E.L. Kennaway. 1936. A study of the incidence of cancer of the lung and larynx. J. Hyg. 36:236–267.

Kimmerle, G., and A. Eben. 1975a. Metabolism studies of N,N-dimethylformamide. I. Studies in rats and dogs. Int. Arch. Arbeitsmed. 34:109–126.

Kimmerle, G., and A. Eben. 1975b. Metabolism studies of N,N-dimethylformamide. II. Studies in persons. Int. Arch. Arbeitsmed. 34:127–136.

Kimmerle, G., and L. Machemer. 1975. Studies with N,N-dimethylformamide for embryotoxic and teratogenic effects on rats after dynamic inhalation. Int. Arch. Arbeitsmed. 34:167–175.

Kimura, E.T., D.M. Ebert, and P.W. Dodge. 1971. Acute toxicity and limits of solvent residue for sixteen organic solvents. Toxicol. Appl. Pharmacol. 19:699–704.

Kirk, R.E., and D.F. Othmer, eds. 1967. Kirk-Othmer Encyclopedia of Chemical Technology. Vol. 1. Second edition. John Wiley & Sons, New York.

Knowles, M.E., J. Gilbert, and D.J. McWeeny. 1975. Phenols in smoked, cured meats: Nitrosation of phenols in liquid smokes and in smoked bacon. J. Sci. Food Agric. 26:267–276.

Korte, F., D. Freitag, H. Geyer, W. Klein, A.G. Kraus, and E. Lahaniatis. 1978. Ecotoxicologic profile analysis: A concept for establishing ecotoxicologic priority lists for chemicals. Chemosphere 7:79–102.

Kotin, P., H.L. Falk, and R. Busser. 1959. Distribution, retention, and elimination of C^{14}-3,4-benzpyrene after administration to mice and rats. J. Natl. Cancer Inst. 23:541–555.

Krivanek, N.D., M. McLaughlin, and W.E. Fayerweather. 1977. Repetitive human exposures to dimethylformamide vapor. Pp. 232-240 in Proceedings of the 8th Annual Conference on Environmental Toxicology. Aerosp. Med. Res. Lab. Tech. Rep. AMRL-TR-77-97. [AD-AO51 334] [Chem. Absts. 89:141405k, 1978.]

Krivanek, N.D., M. McLaughlin, and W.E. Fayerweather. 1978. Monomethylformamide levels in human urine after repetitive exposure to dimethylformamide vapor. J. Occup. Med. 20:179–182.

Kuroda, S. 1937. Occupational pulmonary cancer of generator gas workers. Ind. Med. 6:304–306.

Landner, L., K. Lindstrom, M. Karlsson, J. Nordin, and L. Sorensen. 1977. Bioaccumulation in fish of chlorinated phenols from kraft pulp mill bleachery effluents. Bull. Environ. Contam. Toxicol. 18:663–673.

Landsteiner, K., and A.A. DiSomma. 1940. Studies on the sensitization of animals with simple chemical compounds. VIII. Sensitization to picric acid; subsidiary agents and mode of sensitization. J. Exp. Med. 72:361–366.

Langer, H.G., T.P. Brady, and P.R. Briggs. 1973. Formation of dibenzodioxins and other condensation products from chlorinated phenols and derivatives. Environ. Health Perspect. 5:3–7.

Lawford, D.J., E. King, and D.G. Harvey. 1954. On the metabolism of some aromatic nitro-compounds by different species of animal. Part II. The elimination of various nitro-compounds from the blood of different species of animal. J. Pharm. Pharmacol. 6:619-624.

Leader, S.D. 1932. Nitrobenzene poisoning. Report of an unusual case in a child. Arch. Pediatr. 49:245-250.

Lehr, R.E., and D.M. Jerina. 1977. Relationships of quantum mechanical calculations, relative mutagenicity of benzo[α]-anthracene diol epoxides, and "bay region" concept of aromatic hydrocarbon carcinogenicity. J. Toxicol. Environ. Health 2:1259-1265.

Lehr, R.E., H. Yagi, D.R. Thakker, W. Levin, A.W. Wood, A.H. Conney, and D.M. Jerina. 1978. The bay region theory of polycyclic aromatic hydrocarbon-induced carcinogenicity. Pp. 231-241 in P.W. Jones and R.I. Freudenthal, volume eds. Carcinogenesis—A Comprehensive Survey. Volume 3. Polynuclear Aromatic Hydrocarbons: Second International Symposium on Analysis, Chemistry, and Biology. Raven Press, New York.

Levin, S.J. 1927. Shoe-dye poisoning—Relation to methemoglobin formation. Report of a case in a two-year-old child. J. Am. Med. Assoc. 89:2178-2180

Levin, W., A.W. Wood, H. Yagi, P.M. Dansette, D.M. Jerina, and A.H. Conney. 1976a. Carcinogenicity of benzo[a]pyrene 4,5-, 7,8-, and 9,10-oxides on mouse skin. Proc. Natl. Acad. Sci. USA 73:243-247.

Levin, W., A.W. Wood, H. Yagi, D.M. Jerina, and A.H. Conney. 1976b. ($\pm$)-trans-7,8-Dihydroxy-7,8-dihydrobenzo[a]pyrene: A potent skin carcinogen when applied topically to mice. Proc. Natl. Acad. Sci. USA 73:3867-3871.

Levin, W., A.W. Wood, A.Y.H. Lu, D. Ryan, S. West, A.H. Conney, D.R. Thakker, H. Yagi, and D.M. Jerina. 1977a. Role of purified cytochrome P-448 and epoxide hydrase in the activation and detoxification of benzo[a]pyrene. Pp. 99-106 in D.M. Jerina, ed. Drug Metabolism Concepts. ACS Symposium Series No. 44. American Chemical Society, Washington, D.C.

Levin, W., A.W. Wood, R.L. Chang, T.J. Slaga, H. Yagi, D.M. Jerina, and A.H. Conney. 1977b. Marked differences in the tumor-initiating activity of optically pure (+)- and (−)-trans-7,8-dihydroxy-7,8-dihydrobenzo(a)pyrene on mouse skin. Cancer Res. 37: 2721-2725.

Lewis, R.J., Sr., and R.L. Tatken. 1978. Registry of Toxic Effects of Chemical Substances. U.S. Department of Health, Education, and Welfare, Public Health Service, Center for Disease Control, National Institute for Occupational Safety and Health, Cincinnati, Ohio. 1,363 pp.

Li, C., C. Chao, X. Chiu, and J. Hseuh. 1979. Feasibility of mammalian sister chromatid exchanges in the detection of chemical mutagenicity as compared to the Ames test. Shih Yen Sheng Wu Hsueh Pao 12:131-137. [Chem. Absts. 91:169691r, 1979.]

Lindström, K., and J. Nordin. 1976. Gas chromoatography-mass spectrometry of chlorophenols in spent bleach liquors. J. Chromatogr. 128:13-26.

Litterst, C.L., E.G. Mimnaugh, R. L. Reagan, and T.E. Gram. 1975. Comparison of in vitro drug metabolism by lung, liver, and kidney of several common laboratory species. Drug. Metab. Dispos. 3:259-265.

Llewellyn, G.C., W.S. Hastings, T.D. Kimbrough, F.W. Rea, and C.E. O'Rear. 1974. The effects of dimethylformamide on female Mongolian gerbils, Meriones unguiculatus. Bull. Environ. Contam. Toxicol. 11:467-473.

Lu, P.Y., and R.L. Metcalf. 1975. Environmental fate and biodegradability of benzene derivatives as studied in a model aquatic ecosystem. Environ. Health Perspect. 10:269-284.

Lyle, W. H., T.W.M. Spence, W.M. McKinneley, and K. Duckers. 1979. Dimethylformamide and alcohol intolerance. Br. J. Ind. Med. 36:63-66.

MacMath, I.F., and J. Apley. 1954. Cyanosis from absorption of marking-ink in newborn babies. Lancet 2:895-896.

Maguire, H.C., Jr. 1973. The bioassay of contact allergens in the guinea pig. J. Soc. Cosmet. Chem. 24:151-162.

Maguire, H.C., Jr., and M.W. Chase. 1972. Studies on the sensitization of animals with simple chemical compounds. XIII. Sensitization of guinea pigs with picric acid. J. Exp. Med. 135:357-375.

Makhinya, A.P. 1964. Effect of certain nitrophenols on the organoleptic qualities of water and the sanitary conditions of water basins. Vopr. Gigieny Nasalen. Mest, Kiev, Sb. 5:43-46. [Chem. Absts. 64:15580c, 1966.]

Makhinya, A.P. 1969. Comparative hygienic and sanitary-toxicological studies of nitrophenol isomers in relation to their normalization in river waters. Prom. Zagryazeniya Vodoemov (9):84-95. [Chem. Absts. 72:047231c, 1970.]

Makotchenko, V.M, and Zh.B. Akhmetov. 1972. [in English summary] Adrenal cortex function in chronic nitrobenzene poisoning of guinea pigs and the effect of hydrocortisone on the course of poisoning. Farmakol. Toksikol. 35:247-249.

Malmgren, R.A., B.E. Bennison, and T.W. McKinley, Jr. 1952. Reduced antibody titers in mice treated with carcinogenic and cancer chemotherapeutic agents. Proc. Soc. Exp. Biol. Med. 79:484-488.

Marshall, S., M.D. Whorton, R.M. Krauss, and W. Palmer. 1977. The effects of pesticides on testicular function. J. Urol. 11:257-259.

Matsuguma, H.J. 1967. Nitrophenols. Pp. 888-894 in R.E. Kirk and D.F. Othmer, eds. Kirk-Othmer Encyclopedia of Chemical Toxicology. Vol. 13. Second edition. Wiley-Interscience, New York.

Maxfield, M.E., J.R. Barnes, A. Azar, and H.T. Trochimowicz. 1975. Urinary excretion of metabolite following experimental human exposures to DMF or to DMAC. J. Occup. Med. 17:506-511.

Mazumdar, S., C. Redmond, W. Sollecito, and N. Sussman. 1975. An epidemiological study of exposure to coal tar pitch volatiles among coke oven workers. J. Air Pollut. Control. Assoc. 25:382-389.

McAuliffe, C. 1966. Solubility in water of paraffin, cycloparaffin, olefin, acetylene, cycloolefin, and aromatic hydrocarbons. J. Phys. Chem. 70:1267-1275.

MaAuliffe, C.D. 1977. Evaporation and solution of C_2 to C_{10} hydrocarbons from crude oils on the sea surface. Pp. 363-372 in D.A. Wolfe, J.W. Anderson, D.K. Button, D.C. Malins, T. Roubal, and U. Varanasi, eds. Fate and Effects of Petroleum Hydrocarbons in Marine Organisms and Ecosystems. Pergamon Press, New York.

McCann, J., and B.N. Ames. 1976. Detection of carcinogens as mutagens in the *Salmonella*/microsome test: Assay of 300 chemicals: Discussion. Proc. Natl. Acad. Sci. USA 73:950-954.

McCann, J., E. Choi, E. Yamasaki, and B.N. Ames. 1975. Detection of carcinogens as mutagens in the *Salmonella*/microsome test: Assay of 300 chemicals. Proc. Natl. Acad. Sci. USA 72:5135-5139.

McKee, H.C., J.W. Rhoades, J. Campbell, and A.L. Gross. 1962. Acetonitrile in body fluids related to smoking. Public Health Rep. 77:553-554.

Medyankin, A.V. 1975. Complex action of dimethyl formamide under conditions of a long-term experiment. Gig. Sanit. (USSR) No. 9:39-42. [Chem. Absts. 83:202471d, 1975.]

Miller, E.C. 1978. Some current perspectives on chemical carcinogenesis in humans and experimental animals: Presidential address. Cancer Res. 38:1479-1496.

Mitra, A.B., and G.K. Manna. 1971. Effect of some phenolic compounds on chromosomes of bone marrow cells of mice. Indian J. Med. Res. 59:1442-1447.

Mitsuda, H., K. Mrakami, and F. Kawai. 1963. Effect of chlorophenol analogues on the oxidative phosphorylation in rat liver mitochondria. Agr. Biol. Chem. 27:366-372.

Miyamoto, K., Y. Ikeda, and K. Kurata. 1975. Deficient myelination by 2,4-dinitrophenol administration in the early stage of development. Teratology 12:204.

Moldeus, P., H. Vadi, and M. Berggren. 1976. Oxidative and conjugative metabolism of p-nitroanisole and p-nitrophenol in isolated rat liver cells. Acta Pharmacol. Toxicol. 39:17-32.

Muravieva, S.I., G.N. Zaeva, K.P. Stasenkova, and N.N. Ordynskaya. 1975. [In Russian; English summary.] Passage of dimethylformamide with urine depending upon the levels and duration of its action. Gig. Tr. Prof. Zabol. 12:36-39.

Myslak, Z., J.K. Piotrowski, and E. Musialowicz. 1971. Acute nitrobenzene poisoning: A case report with data on urinary excretion of p-nitrophenol and p-aminophenol. Arch. Toxicol. 28:208-213.

Nabarro, J.D.N. 1948. A case of acute mononitrobenzene poisoning. Br. J. Med. 1:929-931.

National Academy of Sciences. 1976a. Fuels and Fuel Additives for Highway Vehicles and Their Combustion Products: A Guide to Evaluation of Their Potential Effects on Health. Committee on Toxicology, Assembly of Life Sciences, National Research Council. National Academy of Sciences, Washington, D.C. 43 pp. (Available from National Technical Information Service, Springfield, Va., as PB-254 088.)

National Academy of Sciences. 1976b. Health Effects of Benzene: A Review. Committee on Toxicology, Assembly of Life Sciences, National Research Council. National Academy of Sciences, Washington, D.C. (Available from National Technical Information Service, Springfield, Va., as PB-254-388.)

National Academy of Sciences. 1977. Drinking Water and Health. Safe Drinking Water Committee, Advisory Center on Toxicology, Assembly of Life Sciences, National Research Council. National Academy of Sciences, Washington, D.C. 939 pp.

National Academy of Sciences. 1980a. Drinking Water and Health, Vol. 3. Safe Drinking Water Committee, Board on Toxicology and Environmental Health Hazards, Assembly of Life Sciences, National Research Council. National Academy Press, Washington, D.C. 1980. 415 pp.

National Academy of Sciences. 1980b. The Alkyl Benzenes. Committee on Alkyl Benzene Derivatives, Board on Toxicology and Environmental Health Hazards, Assembly of Life Sciences, National Research Council. National Academy Press, Washington, D.C.

National Cancer Institute. 1978. Bioassay of Dibromochloropropane for Possible Carcinogenicity. CAS No. 1836-75-5. National Cancer Institute Carcinogenesis Technical Report Series No. 28. U.S Department of Health, Education, and Welfare, Public Health Service. National Institutes of Health, Bethesda, Md. [DHEW (NIH) Publ. No. 78-828.]

National Cancer Institute. 1979. Bioassay of 2,4,6-Trichlorophenol for Possible Carcinogenicity. CAS No. 88-06-2. National Cancer Institute Carcinogenesis Technical Report Series No. 155. U.S. Department of Health, Education, and Welfare, Public Health Service, National Cancer Institute. National Institutes of Health, Washington, D.C. 115 pp. [DHEW (NIH) Publ. No. 79-1711.]

National Institute for Occupational Safety and Health. 1976. Criteria for a Recommended Standard ... Occupational Exposure to Epichlorohydrin. U.S. Department of Health, Education, and Welfare, Public Health Service, Center for Disease Control. National Institute for Occupational Safety and Health, Washington, D.C. [DHEW (NIOSH) Publ. No. 76-206.]

National Institute for Occupational Safety and Health. 1977a. Criteria for a Recommended

Standard ... Occupational Exposure to Refined Petroleum Solvents. U.S. Department of Health, Education, and Welfare, Public Health Service, Center for Disease Control. National Institute for Occupational Safety and Health, Washington, D.C. 247 pp. [DHEW (NIOSH) Publ. 77-192.]

National Institute for Occupational Safety and Health. 1977b. Criteria for a Recommended Standard ... Occupational Exposure to Alkanes (C5-C8). U.S. Department of Health, Education, and Welfare, Public Health Service, Center for Disease Control. National Institute for Occupational Safety and Health, Cincinnati, Ohio. 129 pp. [DHEW (NIOSH) Publ. No. 77-151.]

National Institute for Occupational Safety and Health. 1978a. Criteria for Recommended Standard ... Occupational Exposure to Nitriles. U.S. Department of Health, Education, and Welfare, Public Health Service, Center for Disease Control. National Institute for Occupational Safety and Heath, Washington, D.C. 155 pp. [DHEW (NIOSH) Publication No. 78-212.]

National Institute for Occupational Safety and Health. 1978b. Current Intelligence Bulletin 30: Epichlorohydrin. U.S. Department of Health, Education, and Welfare, Public Health Service, Center for Disease Control. National Institute for Occupational Safety and Health, Cincinnati, Ohio. 12 pp.

National Institute for Occupational Safety and Health. 1978c. A Recommended Standard for Occupational Exposure to ... Acrylonitrile. U.S. Department of Health, Education, and Welfare, Public Health Service, Center for Disease Control. National Institute for Occupational Safety and Health, Cincinnati, Ohio. 14 pp. [DHEW (NIOSH) Publication No. 78-116.]

National Institute for Occupational Safety and Health. 1978d. Registry of Toxic Effects of Chemical Substances. U.S. Department of Health, Education, and Welfare, Public Health Service. National Institute for Occupational Safety and Health, Cincinnati, Ohio.

Nojima, K., K. Fukaya, and S. Kanno. 1975. Studies on photochemistry of aromatic hydrocarbons. II. The formation of nitrophenols and nitrobenzene by the photochemical reaction of benzene in the presence of nitrogen monoxide. Chemosphere No. 2:77–82.

Ogino, S., and K. Yasukura. 1957. Biochemical studies on cataracts. VI. Production of cataracts in guinea pigs with dinitrophenol. Am. J. Ophthalmol. 43:939–946.

Olson, W.A., R.T. Habermann, E.K. Weisburger, J.M. Ward, and J.H. Weisburger. 1973. Induction of stomach cancer in rats and mice by halogenated aliphatic fumigants. J. Natl. Cancer Inst. 51:1993–1995

Pacseri, I., and L. Magos. 1958. Determination of the measure of exposure to aromatic nitro and amino compounds. J. Hyg. Epidemiology. Microbiol. Immunol. 2:92–110.

Palmer, A.K., A.E. Street, F.J.C. Roe, A.N. Worden, and N.J. Van Abbe. 1979. Safety evaluation of toothpaste containing chloroform. II. Long term studies in rats. J. Environ. Pathol. Toxicol. 2:821–833.

Papageorgiou, G., and C. Argoudelis. 1973. Cation-dependent quenching of the fluorescence of chlorophyll a[2] in vivo by nitroaromatic compounds. Arch. Biochem. Biophys. 156:134–142.

Parascandola, J. 1974. Dinitrophenol and bioenergetics: An historical perspective. Mol. Cell. Biochem. 5:69–77.

Parke, D.V. 1956. Studies in detoxication. 68. The metabolism of [14C]nitrobenzene in the rabbit and guinea pig. Biochem. J. 62:339–346.

Parker, V.H. 1952. Enzymic reduction of 2,4-dinitrophenol by rat-tissue homogenates. Biochem. J. 51:363–370.

Patty, F.A., ed. 1963. Industrial Hygiene and Toxicology. Toxicology. Vol. 2. Second edition. John Wiley & Sons, New York. 2,377 pp.

PEDCo. Environmental, Inc. 1977. Assessment of Gasoline Toxicity. Prepared for U.S. Environmental Protection Agency, Strategies and Air Standards Division, Research Triangle Park, N.C. under Contact No. 68-02-2515, Task No. 12. PEDCo. Environmental, Inc., Cincinnati, Ohio. 107 pp.

Perbellini, L., F. Brugnone, and I. Pavan. 1980. Identification of the metabolites of n-hexane, cyclohexane, and their isomers in men's urine. Toxicol. Appl. Pharmacol. 53:220-229.

Pericin, C., and P. Thomann. 1979. Comparison of the acute toxicity of clioquinol, histamine, and chloroform in different strains of mice. Arch. Toxicol. ISS Suppl. 2:371-373. [Chem. Absts. 92:122863d, 1980.]

Perkins, R.G. 1919. A study of the munitions intoxications in France. Public Health Rep. 34:2335-2374.

Philips, F.S., S.S. Sternberg, and H. Marquardt. 1973. In vivo cytotoxicity of polycyclic hydrocarbons. Pp. 75-88 in T.A. Loomis, ed. Pharmacology and the Future of Man. Vol. 2. Toxicological Problems. Proceedings of the Fifth International Congress on Pharmacology, San Francisco, Calif., July 23-28, 1972. S. Karger, Basel.

Piet, G.J., and F. De Grunt. 1975. Organic chloro compounds in surface and drinking water of the Netherlands. Pp. 81-92 in M. Barthelemy and P. Recht, eds. Problems Raised by the Contamination of Man and his Environment by Persistent Pesticides and Organohalogenated Compounds, European Colloquium, Luxembourg, 1974. Commission of the European Communities, Luxembourg.

Piotrowski, J. 1967. Further investigations on the evaluation of exposure to nitrobenzene. Br. J. Ind. Med. 24:60-65.

Piotrowski, J. 1977. Exposure Tests for Organic Compounds in Industrial Toxicology. U.S. Department of Health, Education, and Welfare, Public Health Service, Center for Disease Control, National Institute for Occupational Safety and Health, Washington, D.C. 138 pp. [DHEW (NIOSH) Publ. No. 77-144.]

Potashnik, G., N. Ben-Aderat, R. Israeli, I. Yanaiinbar, and I. Sober. 1978. Suppressive effect of 1,2-dibromo-3-chloropropane on human spermatogenesis. Fertil. Steril. 30:444.

Potter, H.P. 1973. Dimethylformamide-induced abdominal pain and liver injury. Case report. Arch. Environ. Health 27:340-341.

Pozzani, U.C., C.P. Carpenter, P.E. Palm, C.S. Weil, and J.H. Nair, III. 1959. An investigation of the mammalian toxicity of acetonitrile. J. Occup. Med. 1:634-642.

Prival, M.J., E.C. McCoy, B. Gutter, and H.S. Rosenkranz. 1977. Tris(2,3-dibromopropyl) phosphate: Mutagenicity of a widely used flame retardant. Science 195:76-78.

Pulkkinen, M.O. 1966a. Sulphate conjugation during development, in human, rat and guinea pig. Acta Physiol. Scand. 66:115-119.

Pulkkinen, M.O. 1966b. Sulphate conjugation during pregnancy and under the influence of cortisone. Acta Physiol. Scand. 66:120-122.

Pullman, A., and B. Pullman. 1955. Electronic structure and carcinogenic activity of aromatic molecules. New developments. Adv. Cancer Res. 3:117-169.

Quarles, J.M., M.W. Sega, C.K. Schenley, and R.W. Tennant. 1979. Rapid screening for chemical carcinogens: Transforming activity of selected nitroso compounds detected in a transplacental host-mediated culture system. Natl. Cancer Inst. Monogr. 51:257-263. [Chem. Absts. 91:169290j, 1979.]

Quebbemann, A.J., and M.W. Anders. 1973. Renal tubular conjugation and excretion of phenol and p-nitrophenol in the chicken: Differing mechanism of renal transfer. J. Pharmacol. Exp. Ther. 184:695-708.

Rakhmatullaev, N.N. 1971. Hygienic features of nematocide-Nemagon in connection with sanitary protection of water reservoirs. Gig. Sanit. 36:19-23.

Ramsay, D.H.E., and C.C. Harvey. 1959. Marking-ink poisoning: An outbreak of methaemoglobin cyanosis in newborn babies. Lancet 1:910–912.

Rao, K.S., F.J. Murray, A.A. Crawford, J.A. John, W.J. Potts, B.A. Schwetz, J.D. Burek, and C.M. Parker. 1979. Effects of inhaled 1,2-dibromo-3-chloropropane (DBCP) on the semen of rabbits and the fertility of male and female rats. Toxicol. Appl. Pharmacol. 48:A137, Abstr. No. 273.

Rappe, C., H.R. Buser, and H.-P. 1979. Dioxins, dibenzofurans and other polyhalogenated aromatics: Production, use, formation, and destruction. Ann. N.Y. Acad. Sci. 320:1-18.

Räsänen, L., M.L. Hattula, and A.U. Arstila. 1977. The mutagenicity of MCPA and its soil metabolites, chlorinated phenols, catechols and some widely used slimicides in Finland. Bull. Environ. Contam. Toxicol. 18:565–571.

Reddy, B.G., L.R. Pohl, and G. Krishna. 1976. The requirement of the gut flora in nitrobenzene-induced methemoglobinemia in rats. Biochem. Pharmacol. 25:1119-1122.

Redmond, C.K., A. Ciocco, J.W. Lloyd, and H.W. Rush. 1972. Long-term mortality study of steelworkers. VI. Mortality from malignant neoplasms among coke oven workers. J. Occup. Med. 14:621–629.

Redmond, C.K., B.R. Strobino, and R.H. Cypress. 1976. Cancer experience among coke by-product workers. Ann. N.Y. Acad. Sci. 271:102–115.

Reid, D.D., and C. Buck. 1956. Cancer in coking plant workers. Br. J. Ind. Med. 13:265–269.

Reuber, M.D. 1979. Carcinomas and other lesions of the liver in mice ingesting organochlorine pesticides. Toxicol. Annu. 3:231–256.

Reznik, Ya. B., and G.K. Sprinchan. 1975. [In Russian; English summary.] Gonadotoxic effect of Nemagon. Gig. Sanit. No. 6:101–102.

Rigdon, R.H., and J. Neal. 1965. Effects of feeding benzo[α]pyrene on fertility, embryos, and young mice. J. Natl. Cancer Inst. 34:297–305.

Rigdon, R.H., and E.G. Rennels. 1964. Effect of feeding benzpyrene on reproduction in the rat. Experientia 20:224–226.

Roberts, M.S., R.A. Anderson, and J. Swarbrick. 1977. Permeability of human epidermis to phenolic compounds. J. Pharm. Pharmacol. 29:677–683.

Robinson, D., J.N. Smith, and R.T. Williams. 1951b. Studies in detoxication. 40. The metabolism of nitrobenzene in the rabbit. o-, m- and p-nitrophenols, o-, m- and p-aminophenols and 4-nitrocatechol as metabolites of nitrobenzene. Biochem. J. 50:228–235. 50:221–227.

Robinson, D., J.N. Smith, and R.T. Williams. 1951b. Studies in detoxication. 40. The metabolism of nitrobenzene in the rabbit. o-, m- and p-nitrophenols, o-, m- and p-aminophenols and 4-nitrocatechol as metabolites of nitrobenzene. Biochem. J. 50:228–235.

Robinson, J.R., J.S. Felton, R.C. Levitt, S.S. Thorgeirsson, and D.W. Nebert. 1975. Relationship between "aromatic hydrocarbon responsiveness" and the survival times in mice treated with various drugs and environmental compounds. Mol. Pharmacol. 11:850–865.

Roe, F.J.C., A.K. Palmer, A.N. Worden, and N.J. Van Abbe. 1979. Safety evaluation of toothpaste containing chloroform. 1. Long-term studies in mice. J. Environ. Pathol. Toxicol. 2:799–819.

Rosenkranz, H.S. 1975. Genetic activity of 1,2-dibromo-3-chloropropane, a widely-used fumigant. Bull. Environ. Contam. Toxicol. 14:8–11.

Rusch, G.M., B.K.J. Leong, and S. Laskin. 1977. Benzene metabolism. J. Toxicol. Environ. Health Suppl. 2:23–36.

Salmowa, J., J. Piotrowski, and U. Neuborn. 1963. Evaluation of exposure to nitrobenzene. Absorption of nitrobenzene vapour through lungs and excretion of p-nitrophenol in urine. Br. J. Ind. Med. 20:41–46.

Sanotskii, I.V., S.I. Murav'eva, G.N. Zaeva, L.P. Anvaer, and N.N. Semiletkina. 1978. Metabolism of dimethylformamide in relationship to the intensity of its action. Gig. Tr. Prof. Zabol. (USSR No. 11:24-27.) [Chem. Absts. 90:17253r, 1979.]

Sax, N.I. 1968. Dangerous Properties of Industrial Materials. Third edition. Reinhold Book Corp., New York. 1,251 pp.

Schaumburg, H.H., and P.S. Spencer. 1976. Degeneration in central and peripheral nervous systems produced by pure n-hexane: An experimental study. Brain 99:183-192.

Scheufler, H. 1976. Testing of chemical agents for embryotoxicity, teratogenicity and mutagenicity, ontogenical reactions of the laboratory mouse: A critical analysis of the methods. Biol. Rundsch. 14:227-229. [EMIC 76:024418/Chem. Absts. 85:186581, 1976.]

Scheufler, H., and H.A. Freye. 1975. Embryotoxic and teratogenic effect of dimethylformamide. Dtsch. Gesundheitswes. 30:455-459. [ETIC 75:015105].

Schlede, E., R. Kuntzman, S. Haber, and A.H. Conney. 1970a. Effect of enzyme induction on the metabolism and tissue distribution of benzo(α)pyrene. Cancer Res. 30:2893-2897.

Schlede, E., R.Kuntzman, and A.H. Conney. 1970b. Stimulatory effect of benzo(α)pyrene and phenobarbital pretreatment on the biliary excretion of benzo(α)pyrene metabolites in the rat. Cancer Res. 30:2898-2904.

Selkirk, J.K., E. Huberman, and C. Heidelberger. 1971. An epoxide is an intermediate in the microsomal metabolism of the chemical carcinogen, dibenz(a,h)anthracene. Biochem. Biophys. Res. Commun. 43:1010-1016.

Selkirk, J.K., R.G. Croy, P.P. Roller, and H.V. Gelboin. 1974. High-pressure liquid chromatographic analysis of benzo(α)pyrene metabolism and covalent binding and the mechanism of action of 7,8-benzoflavone and 1,2-epoxy-3,3,3-trichloropropane. Cancer Res. 34:3474-3480.

Selkirk, J.K., R.G. Croy, and H.V. Gelboin. 1975. Isolation by high pressure liquid chromatography and characterization of benzo(a)pyrene-4,5-epoxide as a metabolite of benzo(a)pyrene. Arch. Biochem. Biophys. 168:322-326.

Senczuk, W., W. Baer, and W. Mlynarczyk. 1971. Excretion of 2,4-dinitrophenol and 2-amino-4-nitrophenol. Bromatol. Chem. Toksykol. 4:453-460.

Shabad, L.M., and A.P. Il'nitskii. 1970. Perspective on the problem of carcinogenic pollution in water bodies. Hyg. Sanit. 35:268-273.

Sharma, A.K., and S. Ghosh. 1965. Chemical basis of the action of cresols and nitrophenols on chromosomes. Nucleus 8:183-190.

Sheveleva, G.A., E.E. Strekalova, and E.M. Chirkova. 1979. Study of embryotropic, mutagenic, and gonadotropic effects of dimethylformamide during inhalation action. Toksikol. Nov. Prom. Khim. Veshchestv. 15:21-25, 145-150. [Chem. Absts. 91:169399b, 1979.]

Shimkin, M.B., and G.D. Stoner. 1975. Lung tumors in mice: Application to carcinogenesis bioassay. Adv. Cancer Res. 21:1-58.

Simmon, V.F. 1977. Structural correlations of carcinogenic and mutagenic alkyl halides. Pp. 163-171 in I.M. Asher and C. Zervos, eds. Symposium on Structural Correlates of Carcinogenesis and Mutagenesis. A Guide to Testing Priorities. Proceedings of the Second FDA Office of Science Summer Symposium held at the U.S. Naval Academy, August 31-September 2. [DHEW Publ. (FDA) No. 78-1046.] Department of Health, Education, and Welfare, Washington, D.C.

Simmon, V.F., K. Kauhanen, K. Mortelmans, and R. Tardiff. 1978. Mutagenic activity of chemicals identified in drinking water. Mut. Res. 53:262, Abst. No. 191.

Sims, P. 1970. Qualitative and quantitative studies on the metabolism of a series of aromatic hydrocarbons by rat-liver preparations. Biochem. Pharmacol. 19:795-818.

Sims, P., and P.L. Grover. 1974. Epoxides in polycyclic aromatic hydrocarbon metabolism and carcinogenesis. Adv. Cancer Res. 20:165-274.

Smith, R.P., A.A. Alkaitis, and P.R. Shafer. 1967. Chemically induced methemoglobinemias in the mouse. Biochem. Pharmacol. 16:317-328.

Smyth, H.F., Jr., and C.P. Carpenter. 1948. Further experience with the range finding test in the industrial toxicology laboratory. J. Ind. Hyg. Toxicol. 30:63-68.

Snyder, R., and J.J. Kocsis. 1975. Current concepts of chronic benzene toxicity. CRC Rev. Toxicol. 3:265-288.

Snyder, R., L.S. Andrews, E.W. Lee, C.M. Witmer, M. Reilly, and J.J. Kocsis. 1977. Benzene metabolism and toxicity. Pp. 286-301 in D.J. Jallow, J.J. Kocsis, R. Snyder, and H. Vaninio, eds. Biological Reactive Intermediates: Formation, Toxicity, and Inactivation. Plenum Press, New York.

Sorrell, R.K., H.J. Brass, and R. Reding. 1980. A review of occurrences and treatment of polynuclear aromatic hydrocarbons. Environ. Int. 4:245-254.

Spector, W.S., ed. 1956. Handbook of Toxicology: Acute Toxicities of Solids, Liquids and Gases to Laboratory Animals. Vol. 1. W.B. Saunders, Co., Philadelphia, Pa. 408 pp.

Spencer, H.C., V.K. Rowe, E.M. Adams, and D.D. Irish. 1948. Toxicological studies on laboratory animals of certain alkyldinitrophenols used in agriculture. J. Ind. Hyg. Toxicol. 30:10-25.

Spencer, P.S., M.C. Bischoff, and H.H. Schaumburg. 1978. On the specific molecular configuration of neurotoxic aliphatic hexacarbon compounds causing central-peripheral distal axonopathy. Toxicol. Appl. Pharmacol. 44:17-28.

Springer, E.L., M. Benjamin, W.C. Feist, L.L. Zoch, Jr., and G.J. Hajny. 1977a. Chemical treatment of chips for outdoor storage. Evaluation of sodium N-methyldithiocarbamate + sodium 2,4-dinitrophenol treatment. Tappi 60:88-91. [Chem.Absts. 86:108228v, 1977.]

Springer, E.L., W.C. Feist, L.L. Zoch, Jr., and G.J. Hajny. 1977b. Evaluation of chemical treatment to prevent deterioration of wood chips during storage. Tappi 60:93-97. [Chem. Absts. 86:141865y, 1977.]

Stamova, N., N. Gincheva, M. Spasovskii, A. Bainova, S. Ivanova, S. Kurkchiev, V. Khristeva, M. Mukhtarova, N. Karadzhova, et al. 1976. Labor hygiene during the production of Bulana synthetic fibers. Khig. Zdraveopaz. (Bulgarian) 19:134-140. [Chem. Absts. 86:175464u, 1977.]

Stein, K., J. Portig, and W. Koransky. 1977. Oxidative transformation of hexachlorocyclohexane in rats and with rat liver microsomes. Arch. Pharmacol. 298:115-128.

Stenback, F., and H. Garcia. 1975. Studies on the modifying effect of dimethyl sulfoxide and other chemicals on experimental skin tumor induction. Ann. N.Y. Acad. Sci. 243:209-227.

Stephen, H., and T. Stephen, eds. 1963. Solubilities of Inorganic and Organic Compounds. Vol. 1, Binary Systems, Part I. Pergamon, New York. 960 pp.

Stevenson, A., and R.P. Forbes. 1942. Nitrobenzene poisoning. Report of a case due to exterminator spray. J. Pediatr. 21:224-228.

Stjernsward, J. 1966. Effects of noncarcinogenic and carcinogenic hydrocarbons on antibody-forming cells measured at the cellular level in vitro. J. Natl. Cancer Inst. 36:1189-1195.

Stjernsward, J. 1969. Immunosuppression by carcinogens. Antibiot. Chemother. 15:213-233.

Stockdale, M., and M.J. Selwyn. 1971. Influence of ring substituents on the action of phenols on some dehydrogenases, phosphokinases and the soluble ATPase from mitochondria. Eur. J. Biochem. 21:416-423.

Stula, E.F., and W.C. Krauss. 1977. Embryotoxicity in rats and rabbits from cutaneous application of amide-type solvents and substituted ureas. Toxicol. Appl. Pharmacol. 41:35-55.

Sulzberger, M.B., and F. Wise. 1933. Drug eruptions. II. Dermatitis eczematosa due to drugs. Arch. Dermatol. Syphilol. 28:461-474.

Sunderman, F.W., and J.F. Kincaid. 1953. Toxicity studies of acetone cyanohydrin and ethylene cyanohydrin. AMA Arch. Ind. Hyg. Occup. Med. 8:371–376.

Swamy, S.A. 1953. Suicidal poisoning by dinitrophenol. J. Indian Med. Assoc. 22:504–505.

Swenberg, J.A., G.L. Petzold, and P.R. Harbach. 1976. In vitro damage/alkaline elution assay for predicting carcinogenic potential. Biochem. Biophys. Res. Commun. 72:732–738.

Szybalski, W. 1958. Special microbiological systems. II. Observations on chemical mutagenesis in microorganisms. Ann. N.Y. Acad. Sci. 76:475–489.

Tainter, M.L., A.B. Stockton, and W.C. Cutting. 1933. Use of dinitrophenol in obesity and related conditions. A progress report. J. Am. Med. Assoc. 101:1472–1475.

Tanaka, K., N. Kurihara, and M. Nakajima. 1977. Pathways of chlorophenol formation in oxidative biodegradation of BHC. Agr. Biol. Chem. 41:723–725.

Teranishi, K., K. Hamada, and H. Watanabe. 1975. Quantitative relationship between carcinogenicity and mutagenicity of polyaromatic hydrocarbons in Salmonella typhimurium mutants. Mutat. Res. 31:97–102.

Thakker, D.R., H. Yagi, A.Y.H. Lu, W. Levin, A.H. Conney, and D.M. Jerina. 1976. Metabolism of benzo[a]pyrene: Conversion of (±)-trans-7,8-dihydroxy-7,8-dihydrobenzo-[a]pyrene to highly mutagenic 7,8-diol-9,10-epoxides. Proc. Natl. Acad. Sci. USA 73:3381–3385.

Thakker, D.R., H. Yagi, H. Akagi, M. Koreeda, A.Y.H. Lu, W. Levin, A.W. Wood, A.H. Conney, and D.M. Jerina. 1977. Metabolism of benzo[a]pyrene. VI. Stereoselective metabolism of benzo[a]pyrene and benzo[a]pyrene 7,8-dihydrodiol to diol epoxides. Chem. Biol. Interact. 16:281–300.

Thakker, D.R., M. Nordqvist, H. Yagi, W. Levin, D. Ryan, P. Thomas, A.H. Conney, and D.M. Jerina. 1979. Comparative metabolism of a series of polycyclic aromatic hydrocarbons by rat liver microsomes and purified cytochrome P-450. Pp. 455–472 in P.W. Jones and P. Leber, eds. Polynuclear Aromatic Hydrocarbons: Third International Symposium on Chemistry and Biology—Carcinogenesis and Mutagenesis. Ann Arbor Science, Ann Arbor, Mich.

Torkelson, T.R., S.E. Sadek, V.K. Rowe, J.K. Kodama, H.H. Anderson, G.S. Loquvam, and C.H. Hine. 1961. Toxicologic investigations of 1,2-dibromo-3-chloropropane. Toxicol. Appl. Pharmacol. 3:545–559.

U.S. Bureau of Mines. 1976. International Petroleum Annual. U.S. Department of the Interior, Bureau of Mines, Division of International Petroleum and Natural Gas, Washington, D.C.

U.S. Environmental Protection Agency. 1977. Rebuttable Presumption Against Registration and Continued Registration of Pesticide Products Containing Dibromochloropropane (DBCP). Fed. Reg. 42(184):48026, Thursday, Sept. 22.

U.S. Environmental Protection Agency. 1978. Final Position Document for Dibromochloropropane (DBCP). Special Pesticide Review Division, Office of Pesticide Programs. U.S. Environmental Protection Agency, Washington, D.C.

U.S. Environmental Protection Agency. 1979a. Benzene: Ambient Water Quality Criteria. Criteria and Standards Division, Office of Water Planning and Standards. U.S. Environmental Protection Agency, Washington, D.C. 79 pp. (Available from National Technical Information Service, Springfield, Va., as PB-292-421.)

U.S. Environmental Protection Agency. 1979b. Chlorinated Phenols. Criteria and Standards Division, Office of Water Planning and Standards. U.S. Environmental Protection Agency, Washington, D.C. 109 pp. (Available from National Technical Information Service, Springfield, Va., as PB-296-790.)

U.S. Environmental Protection Agency. 1979c. Nitrobenzene. Criteria and Standards Division, Office of Water Planning and Standards. U.S. Environmental Protection Agency,

Washington, D.C. 61 pp. (Available from National Technical Information Service, Springfield, Va., as PB-296-801.)

U.S. Environmental Protection Agency. 1979d. Nitrophenols. Criteria and Standards Division, Office of Water Planning and Standards. U.S. Environmental Protection Agency, Washington, D.C. 134 pp. (Available from National Technical Information Service, Springfield, Va., as PB-296-802.)

U.S. Environmental Protection Agency. 1979e. Polynuclear Aromatic Hydrocarbons: Ambient Water Quality Criteria. Criteria and Standards Division, Office of Water Planning and Standards. U.S. Environmental Protection Agency, Washington, D.C. 83 pp. (Available from National Technical Information Service, Springfield, Va., as PB-297-926.)

U.S. Environmental Protection Agency. 1979f. Toluene: Ambient Water Quality Criteria. Criteria and Standards Division, Office of Water Planning and Standards. U.S. Environmental Protection Agency, Washington, D.C. 97 pp. (Available from National Technical Information Service, Springfield, Va., as PB-296-805.)

U.S. International Trade Commission. 1976. Imports of Benzenoid Chemicals and Products, 1974. USITC Publication No. 762. U.S. International Trade Commission, Washington, D.C. 99 pp.

U.S. Occupational Safety and Health Administration. 1978. Occupational exposure to 1,2-dibromo-3-chloropropane (DBCP), occupational safety and health standards. Fed. Reg. 43(53):11514-11533, Friday, March 17.

Van Duuren, B.L. 1977. Chemical structure, reactivity, and carcinogenicity of halohydrocarbons. Environ. Health Perspect. 21:17-23.

Vernot, E.H., J.D. MacEwen, C.C. Haun, and E.R. Kinkead. 1977. Acute toxicity and skin corrosion data for some organic and inorganic compounds and aqueous solutions. Toxicol. Appl. Pharmacol. 42:417-423.

Vogel, E., and J.L.R. Chandler. 1974. Mutagenicity testing of cyclamate and some pesticides in *Drosophila melanogaster*. Experientia 30:621-623.

von Oettingen, W.F. 1941. B. The aromatic nitro compounds. 1. Nitro-benzene and its derivatives. Pp. 76-92 in The Aromatic Amino and Nitro Compounds, Their Toxicity and Potential Dangers: A Review of the Literature. Federal Security Agency, U.S. Public Health Service, Washington, D.C. Public Health Bull. No. 271.

von Oettingen, W.F., ed. 1949. The nitrophenols. Pp. 232-285 in Phenol and Its Derivatives: The Relation Between Their Chemical Constitution and Their Effect on the Organism. Natl. Inst. Health Bull. No. 190. Washington,D.C.

Weast, R.C., and M.J. Astle, eds. 1978. Handbook of Chemistry and Physics. A Ready-Reference Book of Chemical and Physical Data. 59th edition. CRC Press, West Palm Beach, Fla. 2,488 pp.

Wedding, R.T., C. Hansch, and T.R. Fukuto. 1967. Inhibition of malate dehydrogenase by phenols and the influence of ring substituents on their inhibitory effectiveness. Arch. Biochem. Biophys. 121:9-21.

Weisburger, E.K. 1977. Carcinogenicity studies on halogenated hydrocarbons. Environ. Health Perspect. 21:7-16.

White, A.E., S. Takehisa, E.I. Eger, S. Wolff, and W.C. Stevens. 1979. Sister chromatid exchanges induced by inhaled anesthetics. Anesthesiology 50:426-430.

Whorton, D., R.M. Krauss, S. Marshall, and T.H. Milby. 1977. Infertility in male pesticide workers. Lancet 2:1259-1261

Whorton, M.D., and T.H. Milby. 1980. Recovery of testicular function among DBCP workers. J. Occup. Med. 22:177-179.

William, R.T., ed. 1959. Detoxication Mechanisms: The Metabolism and Detoxication of

Drugs, Toxic Substances and Other Organic Compounds. Second edition. John Wiley & Sons, New York.

Williams, G.M., and M.F. Laspia. 1979. The detection of various nitrosamines in the hepatocyte primary culture/DNA repair test. Cancer Lett. (Ireland) 6:199-206. [Chem. Absts. 91:50429w, 1979.]

Windholz, M., S. Budavari, L.Y. Stroumtsos, and M.N. Fertig, eds. 1976. The Merck Index. An Encyclopedia of Chemicals and Drugs. Ninth edition. Merck and Co., Inc., Rahway, N.J. 1,313 pp.

Wirtschafter, Z.T., and R. Wolpaw. 1944. A case of nitrobenzene poisoning. Ann. Intern. Med. 21:135-141.

Wislocki, P.G., A.W. Wood, R.L. Chang, W. Levin, H. Yagi, O. Hernandez, D.M. Jerina, and A.H. Conney. 1976a. High mutagenicity and toxicity of a diol epoxide derived from banzo[a]pyrene. Biochem. Biophys. Res. Commun. 68:1006-1012.

Wislocki, P.G., A.W. Wood, R.L. Chang, W. Levin, H.Yagi, O. Hernandez, P.M. Dansette, D.M. Jerina, and A.H. Conney. 1976b. Mutagenicity and cytotoxicity of benzo(a)pyrene arene oxides, phenols, quinones, and dihydrodiols in bacterial and mammalian cells. Cancer Res. 36:3350-3357.

Wisniewska-Knypl, J.M., J.K. Jabonska, and J.K. Piotrowski. 1975. Effect of repeated exposure to aniline, nitrobenzene, and benzene on liver microsomal metabolism in the rat. Br. J. Ind. Med. 32:42-48.

Wolfe, M.A., V.K. Rowe, D.D. McCollister, R.L. Hollingsworth, and F. Oyen. 1956. Toxicological studies of certain alkylated benzenes and benzene. Experiments on laboratory animals. AMA Arch. Ind. Health 14:387-398.

Wolfsie, J.H. 1960. Glycolonitrile toxicity. J. Occup. Med. 2:588-590.

Wood, A.W., P.G. Wislocki, R.L. Chang, W. Levin, A.Y.H. Lu, H. Yagi, O. Hernandez, D.M. Jerina, and A.H. Conney. 1976a. Mutagenicity and cytotoxicity of benzo(a)pyrene benzo-ring epoxides. Cancer Res. 36:3358-3366.

Wood, A.W., W. Levin, A.Y.H. Lu, H. Yagi, O. Hernandez, D.M. Jerina, and A.H. Conney. 1976b. Metabolism and benzo[α]pyrene and benzo[α]pyrene derivatives to mutagenic products by highly purified hepatic microsomal enzymes. J. Biol. Chem. 251:4882-4890.

Wood, A.W., W. Levin, R.L. Chang, H. Yagi, D.R. Thakker, R.E. Lehr, D.M. Jerina, and A.H. Conney. 1979. Bay-region activation of carcinogenic polycyclic hydrocarbons. Pp. 531-551 in P.W. Jones and P. Leber, eds. Polynuclear Aromatic Hydrocarbons: Third International Symposium on Chemistry and Biology—Carcinogenesis and Mutagenesis. Ann Arbor Science, Ann Arbor, Mich.

World Health Organization. 1970. European Standards for Drinking-Water. Second edition. World Health Organization, Geneva, Switzerland. 58 pp.

Wulff, L.M.R., L.A. Emge, and F. Bravo. 1935. Some effects of alpha dinitrophenol on pregnancy in the white rat. Proc. Soc. Exp. Biol. Med. 32:678-680.

Yamada, Y. 1958. Studies on experimental chronic poisoning with nitrobenzene. Kobe J. Med. Sci. 4:27-39.

Yang, S.K., J. Deutsch, and H.V. Gelboin. 1978a. Benzo[α]pyrene metabolism: Activation and detoxification. Pp. 205-231 in H.V. Gelboin and P.O.P. Ts'o, eds. Polycyclic Hydrocarbons and Cancer: Environment, Chemistry, and Metabolism. Vol. 1. Academic Press, New York.

Yang, S.K., P.P. Roller, and H.V. Gelboin. 1978b. Benzo[a]pyrene metabolism: Mechanism in the formation of epoxides, phenols, dihydrodiols, and the 7,8-diol-9,10-epoxides. Pp. 285-301 in P.W. Jones and R.I. Freudenthal, volume eds. Carcinogenesis— Comprehensive Survey. Volume 3. Polynuclear Aromatic Hydrocarbons: Second International Symposium on Analysis, Chemistry, and Biology. Raven Press, New York.

Yasuhira, K. 1964. Damage to the thymus and other lymphoid tissues from 3-methylcholanthrene, and subsequent thymoma production, in mice. Cancer Res. 24:558–569.

Yoshikawa, K., H. Uchino, and H. Kurata. 1976. [In Chinese; English summary.] Studies on the mutagenicity of hair dye. Bull. Natl. Inst. Hyg. Sci. No. 94:28–32.

Zaebst, D.. and C. Robinson. 1977. Walk-Through Survey Report, Dupont May Plant, Camden, South Carolina. National Institute for Occupatonal Safety and Health, Cincinnati, Ohio. 6 pp.

Zeitoun, M.M. 1959. Nitrobenzene poisoning in infants due to inunction with false bitter almond oil. J. Trop. Pediatr. 5:73–75.

Zeligs, M. 1929. Aniline and nitrobenzene poisoning in infants. Arch. Pediatr. 46:502–506.

Index

ABS (*see* acrylonitrile-butadiene-styrene)
absorption (*see* metabolism)
acetonitrile, 202–206
   health effects, 204–205
   metabolism, 203–204
   SNARL, 205–206
   TWA standard, 203
   see also nitriles
A/C pipe (*see* asbestos-cement pipe)
acrylonitrile-butadiene-styrene pipe, 4, 13
acute diseases, waterborne, 5
   bacteria, protozoa, and viruses implicated
      in, 137
   defined, 138
   outbreaks of, 140–149
Aerobacter, 29
Aggressiveness Index, 19
   A/C pipe and, 20–21, 49–57, 61
   A/C pipe degradation and, 44–45, 58
   adjustment, 58
   applications of, 20–23
algae
   growth in reservoirs, 98–99, 124, 141
   polysaccharides produced by, 113
alicyclics, 247, 251
alkanes, 247, 251
alkalinity, A/C pipe effect on, 51
aluminum, 95, 155–167
   conclusions and recommendations per-
      taining to, 166–167

daily intake, 156
   health effects, 158–166
   metabolism, 157–158
   SNARL, 166
   sources in human diet, 156
   uses, 156, 158
aluminum chloride, 164
aluminum nitrate, 164
aluminum salts, 156, 163
aluminum sulfate, 156, 164
Alzheimer's disease, 160, 167
amebiasis, 5, 138
American Water Works Association
   on chlorination, 130
   specifications for A/C pipe, 46
   study of asbestos in drinking water, 43
ammonia, chlorine interaction with, 96–97
anthracene, 4, 99
aromatic hydrocarbons in petroleum, 247,
      248, 249, 252
arsenic, 95, 167
asbestos, 6
   health effects, 3–4, 43, 150
asbestos-cement pipe, 2, 42–61
   advantages of, 45
   city water supplies with asbestos concen-
      tration from, 54
   composition, 45–46
   corrosion, 3, 22–23
   deterioration control, 58–60

289